Jean de Brébeuf

Jean de Brébeuf

1593-1649

JOSEPH P. DONNELLY, S.J.

LOYOLA UNIVERSITY PRESS

Chicago, Illinois 1975

© 1975 Loyola University Press
Printed in the United States of America
Cover and maps by Deborah Brown

LIBRARY OF CONGRESS
CATALOGING IN PUBLICATION DATA

Donnelly, Joseph Peter, 1905-
   Jean de Brébeuf, 1593-1649.

   Bibliography: p.
   1. Brébeuf, Jean de, Saint, 1593-1649.
2. Huron Indians—Missions.

E99.H9B743   282'.092'4 ₍B₎   75-5682

ISBN 0-8294-0233-0

for
JEAN and JACK LYNCH
whose generosity made this book possible

CONTENTS

viii   Contents

PREFACE

A tourist, driving eastward from Midland, Ontario, on Highway 12, is only a mile and a half from the city limits when he encounters an impressive collection of buildings constructed of stripped logs surrounded by a very high palisade. An attractive historical marker announces that this is Fort Sainte Marie of the Hurons which the Canadian Province of Ontario, in cooperation with the Society of Jesus, has reconstructed with meticulous historical accuracy. This seventeenth-century central residence of Jesuit missionaries was devoted to the Christianization of the Huron nation.

Begun in 1639, Sainte Marie became a bustling French village set in the Canadian wilderness more than eight hundred miles from Quebec. For almost exactly a decade, some twenty French Jesuit missionaries, with nearly an equal number of dedicated laymen, zealously labored at Sainte Marie, striving to Christianize the already sedentary Hurons.

Of those missionaries, the most noteworthy, physically as well as spiritually, was Father Jean de Brébeuf who was cruelly done to death on March 16, 1649, by the powerful Iroquois, implacable enemies of the Hurons. The basis of the Iroquois-Huron enmity was primarily economic. With the introduction of goods of European manufacture into the lives of the Indians of northern New York and southern Ontario, ancient trade relations were violently upset. Europeans offered iron axes, metal pots, woven cloth, and especially guns in exchange for peltries, particularly beaver. Once these fabulously European items were available, possession of them quickly became essential to every Indian nation. Northern New York, never very rich in fur-bearing animals, was rapidly trapped out by the Iroquois who traded, at first, with the Dutch at Albany. Searching for new sources of peltries, the Iroquois sought to gain control of the fur sources available to the Hurons.

Since 1600, the Hurons had acted as middlemen between the fur-rich northern Algonkins and the corn-tobacco growers south and west of the Huron country. Through their contacts with the French, especially Samuel de Champlain, the Hurons became allies of the subjects of Henri IV, who, in turn, strove to maintain the loyalty of the Hurons by promising to aid them against their most powerful enemy, the Iroquois.

When their own sources of peltries dried up, the Iroquois were obliged to invade the Huron economic monopoly or perish as a powerful nation. The Iroquois already nourished a cordial hatred for the French allies of the Hurons because, through their zealous missionaries, the French were seeking to Christianize the Indian nations. Once the Iroquois understood what Christianity meant, they perceived that what the missionaries preached would effect a cataclysmic revolution in the Iroquois ancient life-style. For that reason, the Iroquois hated the missionaries. In their plan to eliminate the Hurons as economic rivals, the Iroquois determined to wipe out the Jesuit apostles to the Hurons.

Of these missionaries, Father Jean de Brébeuf was by far the most outstanding. He had begun the mission among the Hurons, had been the longest among them, spoke the Huron language with the most fluency, and had the keenest insight into the Huron mentality. Physically, Jean de Brébeuf was a typical Norman, very tall, broad-shouldered, possessed of phenomenal physical strength, rugged in appearance with a full black beard and striking features. He bore the excruciating pain of a broken clavicle for two years without ever referring to the disability. His fellow Jesuits on the Huron mission considered him the kindest, most charitable man they ever knew. Now and then they teased him, trying to catch him off guard and annoy him into expressing impatience. But, ". . . his look was always benign, his words were in mildness and his heart calm."

In the midst of the wilderness of the Huron country, surrounded by a native population knowing little moral restraint, Jean de Brébeuf communed with God in an extraordinary manner. His interior life was replete with frequent celestial visitations in which Christ and his mother as well as the blessed in heaven appeared to him and conversed familiarly. But he ". . . kept those favors so secret and concealed, except from those from whom he could not in conscience conceal anything, that he never spoke of them, nor gave anyone at all the least indication of them."

Seized at the satellite mission of St. Louis, a bare three miles from Sainte Marie, Father Brébeuf, together with Father Gabriel Lalemant and a host of Huron neophytes, was dragged off to the mission of St. Ignace II, some three miles east of St. Louis. There he was forced to run the gauntlet between two rows of infuriated Iroquois braves. Informed by a renegade Huron that this was the great *Echon,* the most powerful "sorcerer" of the Christian French, the Iroquois determined to outdo themselves in the cruelty of their torture, making of him such a horrible example that every other Blackrobe would flee and every Indian convert to Christianity would gladly apostatize to avoid a similar fate.

Howling and cavorting around their victim, the Iroquois warriors burned him with torches, hung white-hot iron hatchets around his neck, pressed them under his armpits and into every other sensitive part of his body. They cut great strips of flesh from his arms and legs, broiled them, and ate them before him. When he suffered without flinching, they tore off his lips, thrust burning coals down his throat, and chopped off his feet. In mockery of baptism, his tormentors poured boiling water over him several times. They wrapped him in resinous bark and set it afire. Finally, they scalped him, broke his jaw with a hatchet, cut a great gaping hole in his chest, and tore out the still beating heart. Father Paul Ragueneau, who saw Jean de Brébeuf's horribly mutilated body, rightly declared that the Iroquois inflicted on the martyr ". . . as many cruelties as ever the rage of tyrants obliged the martyrs to endure . . ."

Perhaps because there is a kind of pious morbidity in the horrible manner of Father Brébeuf's martyrdom, related in such vivid details by his contemporaries, he has not been particularly fortunate in his biographers. Some few have dwelt unduly on the harrowing details of his martyrdom, neglecting the man himself. Others, taken perhaps too much with his exalted mystical life, have lost contact with Brébeuf, the missionary. Few have understood Father Brébeuf's profound impact on an aboriginal folk with whom he spent all but a very few years of his apostolic life. Above all, Jean de Brébeuf had a profound understanding of his Indian neophytes. He admired their good qualities and understood their life-style which he sought not to change, but to modify. Toward the Hurons he was father, brother, friend, and valiant defender. These are important facets of the saint which merit close attention.

Since, apparently, none of Jean de Brébeuf's surprisingly few biographers has striven to probe into the wealth of documentation existing regarding the man, it would appear that there is place for an accurately documented biography of that profoundly admirable saint and martyr. This effort seeks to present a carefully documented biography of Jean de Brébeuf. Beginning with the earliest available record of any of his ancestors, an effort is made to follow Jean de Brébeuf, step-by-step, adhering scrupulously to documentary sources. This biography is not, it is hoped, hagiography, but sound history.

The author is indebted to Reverend John Harland Williams, S.J., who encouraged the undertaking. He is particularly grateful to Jack and Jean Lynch and their family for subsidy which has enabled the author to search for documentation in many far places.

Chapter I

Jean de Brébeuf

That stretch of northwestern France opposite England, from the Gulf of St. Malo eastward to the mouth of the Somme, and extending inland a distance of some sixty-five miles, encompasses the approximate geographic extent of the old Duchy of Normandy. Upper Normandy, from the right bank of the Seine to the Somme, is open plains country lending itself profitably to the production of various grains. West of the Seine, Lower Normandy is a land of rolling hills much like northern Wisconsin and Upper Michigan. This is dairy country noted for its butter, cheese, and apples. Before the introduction of tractors, powerful draft horses bred in the area were highly prized throughout France. Traveling westward from Rouen, Normandy's ancient capital, one encounters frequent outcroppings of limestone and a great deal of dark schist. Rivers, such as the Orne and the Vire, have scoured out many deep valleys in this soft stone which time has darkened until the valleys present a dour and brooding atmosphere to the observer. Thanks to the bold Cotentin Peninsula, jutting far out into the English Channel, plus the influence of the warm Atlantic

1

current, Normandy's climate is much more temperate than its geographic position would lead one to expect.

In the ninth and tenth centuries Normandy was a prize which Scandinavian raiders wrested from earlier inhabitants, an amalgam of Romans, Celts, Franks, and Norsemen. The admixture produced a hardy race of tall, broad-shouldered, powerful men, devoted to their native soil, intrepid warriors loyal to their leaders, but fiercely jealous of their traditional privileges. Below the ranks of the great Norman lords was a host of lesser landowning nobles who, side by side with the peasants, tilled the rich Norman soil on fiefs granted them. In time of war these noblemen belted on their swords and, with a contingent of their peasants, joined the military force of the great lord to whom they owed fealty. From the middle of the eleventh century such occasions arose with frequency.

In the early summer of 1066, William, duke of Normandy, summoned his vassals, high and low, to assist him in gaining the throne of England which he claimed in virtue of an alleged promise made him by Edward the Confessor, a Norman by rearing, who died on January 5, 1066. With an army of twelve hundred Norman knights, William sailed from St. Valéry, at the mouth of the Somme, on Wednesday, September 27, and joined battle with Harold the Saxon at Hastings on October 14, 1066. Barely victorious, William marched on London, pillaging as he went, where he was crowned king of England at Westminster on Christmas day. Since to the victor belongs the spoils, William made generous grants of English soil to his companions in arms. To his half brother, Odo, bishop of Bayeux and a doughty warrior who wielded a mighty sword at Hastings, the Conqueror granted great stretches of Kent. Among Odo's vassals was Hugh de Brébeuf who received from his episcopal lord some five hundred acres of land.[1] With this Hugh, the Brébeufs emerged from the mists of early Norman history.

The native heath of the Brébeuf family was an extensive fief on the Vire River some ten miles south of St.-Lô. History records

---

[1] Frederick G. Marcham, *A History of England*, 80-81. Edward and William were cousins, having both descended from Richard, duke of Normandy. All of the Norman knights in William's invasion force were volunteers because he could not oblige them to serve beyond the seas.

nothing about the family for nearly a century after the Battle of Hastings. At that time Raoul de Brébeuf was residing in Lincolnshire during the reign of Henry II (1154-1189). In the Domesday Book, Raoul is recorded as owing military service of three knights to his liege, Wilhelm de Roumare.[2] Not all the Brébeufs abandoned their native Normandy for, in 1248, Nicolas de Brébeuf accompanied St. Louis IX of France on the Seventh Crusade. Nicolas is credited with leading the Norman knights in their attack on Damietta at the mouth of the Nile. The battle began on June 7, 1249, and Damietta capitulated on the same day.[3] The Brébeufs, however, were not always loyal to the crown of France. During the Hundred Years' War (1338-1453), a Jean de Brébeuf, on May 7, 1418, swore fealty to the English king, Henry V, who subdued Normandy after his great victory over the French at Agincourt on October 25, 1415.[4] A half century later, in 1468, another Jean de Brébeuf gave his allegiance to the French crown, serving in the military company of Jean d'Estouteville, for which he was paid ten *livres*.[5]

Following the close of the Hundred Years' War, Lower Normandy enjoyed a century of peace until the outbreak of the French religious wars, 1562-1598. Since the Huguenot strongholds were major seaports and popular trading centers, such as Dieppe, Eu, and Rouen, Normandy was the scene of many bloody conflicts. In Lower Normandy, the Huguenots were particularly vicious in pillaging churches, monasteries, and ancient shrines. Destruction was wrought not so much by German mercenaries, hired by Huguenot leaders, as by the French people themselves. The disgraceful cruelty of the shameful civil war reached close to the Brébeuf landholdings when St.-Lô was captured by the Huguenot forces in 1567 and again in 1574 when the Catholic forces recaptured the town and put its populace to the sword.[6] Perhaps our Jean de Brébeuf's grandfather had some part in driving the Huguenots out of St.-Lô. In 1574 he was surely a mature

[2] William Page, editor, *The Victoria History of the County of Kent*, III, 230.
[3] René Lanchantin, *Condé-sur-Vire*, 32.
[4] Ibid.
[5] Ibid.
[6] James W. Thompson, *The Wars of Religion in France, 1559-1576*, 187, 472.

man, while the saint's father, Gilles, could well have been only a stripling.

In 1599, when Henri IV was consolidating his control of France, he ordered a sort of census taken of all the nobility so that he could levy taxes and determine more accurately the validity of land titles. From the Condé-sur-Vire area, the commissioner in charge, one Roissy, reported the presence of: "Robert de Brébeuf, sieur of the area, living at Condé-sur-Vire, Georges, his son; a cousin Jean, residing at the same place, Jean's father; Gilles, Jean's brother, residing near Condé-sur-Vire, and his two sons, Jean and Robert."[7] It was further reported that the Brébeufs had been considered members of the nobility since at least 1463.

It should not be imagined that the Brébeuf family was a noble house of great wealth and political importance. Rather, the family pertained to the lesser nobility residing on small manor farms, working the land beside their peasants and carting their excess produce to market towns. Today the manor farm of Gilles de Brébeuf lies some four miles south of Condé-sur-Vire on an ancient fief known as Boissais. The lonely remains of the old manor still crown a rather steep hillside sweeping majestically southward to a lovely valley. Originally, the manor, built in the form of the letter E, must have been an imposing structure of at least two stories. As one faces the entrance, the right arm of the manor seems to have been a stable with a hayloft above it. The central section of the building is surprisingly shallow, giving the impression of being no more than a passage between the two arms of the building. In the left arm of the old manor there is just one undivided room on the ground floor with the remains of a large fireplace on the west wall.[8] Since nothing is left of the upper story, one can only surmise that it contained family sleeping quarters.

Not fifteen paces north of the old manor is a typical Norman farm dwelling constructed of the same dark schist as its neighbor. Possibly the old manor's walls were "quarried" to build the house which is presently occupied by a pleasant Norman farmer, his bustling wife, and a brood of chubby children. A flock of nervous

---

[7] Lanchantin, *Condé-sur-Vire*, 33.

[8] Ibid., 34-35. The large living room of the manor may once have contained a modest shrine to St. Jean. A small statue representing him was found in the ruins of the room.

chickens scurry about and a comfortable old farm dog reluctantly waddles out to greet you. Fat Norman cows browse on the hillside and an extensive apple orchard wafts the scent of ripening fruit. Fortunately, the ruins of the old manor and its more modern neighbor are removed about a mile from any modern highway so that the visitor views the setting much as it must have been over three centuries ago.

At some point in their long history the Brébeufs acquired a coat of arms depicting a black bull rampant, with golden horns and hooves, imposed on a silver shield. Once there must have been a family motto accompanying the coat of arms, but now no one knows what that might have been.[9]

Early biographers of Jean de Brébeuf declared that he was born and baptized at Bayeux in an old feudal manor on the Chemin de Bellefontaine in the parish of St. Exupère on March 14, 1592. Because his mother, Marie Le Dragon, was a cousin of the Bigne family of Bayeux, a tradition arose holding that the future martyr was born at Bayeux while his mother was on a visit there. Since no baptismal record at Condé-sur-Vire is older than the first years of the seventeenth century, it was not until records of the Society of Jesus became available that the place and date of Jean de Brébeuf's birth were accurately determined. When he became a Jesuit, Brébeuf, as was required, recorded that he was born on March 25, 1593, at Condé-sur-Vire in the diocese of Bayeux. He was the eldest child of his parents, Gilles de Brébeuf and Marie Le Dragon, who, as far as we know, had only one other child, Robert, who, as a grown man, fathered numerous progeny.[10]

Literally nothing is known about Jean de Brébeuf's childhood. As the son of a *habereau*, a country squire, the boy's early years must have been of a piece with that of any farmer's son. He probably herded sheep, fed the stock, and, when old enough, took on heavier chores. Perhaps on market days Jean's father took him into Condé-sur-Vire, riding atop the family cart piled high with

[9] Ibid., 31.
[10] General Archives of the Society of Jesus, Rome. Francia 22, Catologi, 1558-1639, 138. Subsequently this primary source is referred to as ARSJ. Brébeuf himself reported that he had been born at Condé-sur-Vire in the diocese of Bayeux on March 25, 1593.

produce from the manor farm. As the years advanced, Jean sprouted into a tall, rangy lad who developed into a powerful young giant.[11]

What sort of early education Jean de Brébeuf may have received is entirely unknown. Possibly he learned his letters at home or from the parish priest at Condé-sur-Vire. There may have been some sort of academy for boys at St.-Lô where sons of neighboring families were taught Latin, preparing them to enter institutions of higher learning at Caen, Rouen, or even Paris. No extant document indicates that young Brébeuf received such training. We know, for certain, only that when he was about seventeen he began an academic career lasting about six years. During that time he studied rhetoric for two years, philosophy for another two, and "cases" or moral theology for a final two. Brébeuf's biographers generally assume that those six years, from about 1608 to 1614, were spent at one of the many colleges affiliated with the University of Caen. That conclusion seems to be based chiefly on the proximity of Caen to Condé-sur-Vire, a distance of about thirty-five miles, a comfortable day's horseback ride away.

Brébeuf's first contact with the Jesuits probably occurred at Caen. In 1609, by order of Henri IV, the Jesuits were given the Collège du Mont, an affiliate of the University of Caen.[12] The college, now the Musée de Antiquaires, 83 rue Caumont, was just across the street from the church of St. Etienne which William the Conqueror built and in which he was buried.[13] No one now knows whether Jean de Brébeuf originally intended to join the

[11] Lanchantin, Condé-sur-Vire, 33. Brébeuf's nephew, Georges, described his uncle as ". . . very strong, able to carry the heaviest loads and do the hardest work, blessed with excellent common sense, neglecting no material means to insure success of an enterprise." Georges, Robert de Brébeuf's son, born 1617, became a priest and a noted minor poet.

[12] Pierre Delattre, editor, Les établissements des Jésuites en France depuis quatre siècles, I, 991. The Collège du Mont existed as part of the university for two hundred years before the Jesuits took charge of it. The institution had been established by Robert Jolivet, abbot of the famous Mont St. Michel, in 1431. The Jesuits assumed control on August 31, 1609. One of the most illustrious alumni of the school was St. John Eudes, probably one of Brébeuf's fellow students.

[13] In 1793, when revolutionaries desecrated the church, William's tomb was ransacked and his bones thrown out. Probably only a thighbone of the great Conqueror rests in the tomb today.

ranks of the clergy of the diocese of Bayeux but it is rather likely that for this reason he chose to take courses in theology.

In 1614, when Brébeuf was twenty-one and a man grown, he interrupted his studies to return to his home where he remained until the fall of 1617. Not a single documentary source helps us explain that hiatus in his academic life. It has been conjectured that perhaps his father required the aid of his elder son. Possibly Jean himself wished time to consider his future while separated from a predominately academic atmosphere. Conjecturally, in the fall of 1617 when his brother Robert was competent to manage the family's estates, Jean was free to pursue the vocation he had chosen.

In France the Society of Jesus, which Jean de Brébeuf wished to join, was not, in his day, the highly respected religious order which it came to be before the end of the seventeenth century. Though St. Ignatius, founder of the Jesuits and a former student at the University of Paris, was anxious to establish houses in France, especially at Paris, he was in his tomb ten years before the Parlement of Paris granted official permission, in 1565, for Jesuits to take up residence.[14] Thirty years later the Jesuits were expelled from France and all their property confiscated, when a nineteen-year-old youth, Jean Chastel, briefly an employee at the Jesuit college in Paris, attempted to assassinate Henri IV on December 24, 1594. Ten years later, in 1604, Henri IV himself rescinded the decree of banishment, but not all of their property was restored to the Jesuits.[15] As Jean de Brébeuf knew them, the Jesuits conducted a few small colleges of no great note. Their major work, especially in Normandy, was chiefly what we would call home missions, attempting to win the populace away from the Huguenots and back to their ancient faith. Though Jesuits in Spain and Portugal had already opened missionary activities in the Orient and Mexico, French Jesuits had made only one tentative mission effort in North America and that had ended disastrously. Jean de Brébeuf's motive, then, for seeking entrance to the Society of Jesus could hardly have been any other than his desire to work for the salvation of souls in France plus his wish to

[14] Martin P. Harney, *The Jesuits in History*, 132.
[15] Ibid., 184.

imitate Christ our Lord according to the ideal presented by St. Ignatius Loyola.

On Wednesday, November 8, 1617, tall, rugged Jean de Brébeuf entered the Jesuit novitiate at Rouen. The building then housing the novices was not the starkly unadorned dark granite building on the rue du Gril, some of which still survives. The novitiate was established at Rouen in 1604 through the generosity of Isabeau de Moncel, a twice-widowed wealthy matron who contributed 30,000 *livres* for a building and another 4,000 for a chapel. She expressed the hope that ". . . from the novitiate, a true and perfect school of piety, would emerge many devout religious who would cultivate our Lord's vineyard not only in France but throughout the whole world."[16] During Brébeuf's two years there, the novices dwelt in a row of jerry-built houses in anything but adequate conditions. The superior of the house, as well as master of novices, was Father Lancelot Marin, aged fifty, who had already held the same position in the Jesuit novitiate at Paris. Experience gave him the competence to lead his charges, prudently and patiently, to embrace the exalted ideals proposed to them.

Quite a few years older than most of his fellow novices and probably accustomed to responsibility, Brébeuf must have given himself with a greater fervor to the religious life. In the absence of any documentary evidence, it is assumed that the future martyr pursued the normal course of training undergone by hundreds before him and thousands after him. He spent thirty days alone, in silence, undergoing the complete Spiritual Exercises outlined by St. Ignatius over ninety years before. During the subsequent months, besides learning how to pray effectively, Brébeuf took his turn at helping the cook, doing the laundry, sweeping floors, nursing the sick in the local hospitals, and teaching catechism to the children of the poor of Rouen. At some point during his two years he was sent out with a companion on a month's pilgrimage, begging his food and lodging as he went. At the completion of his novitiate, when about to pronounce his vows, Brébeuf asked to join the ranks of the lay brothers rather than aspiring to the priesthood, ". . . considering himself unworthy of the priesthood

---

[16] Charles de Beaurepaire, "Notice sur le noviciat de Rouen," *Bulletin de la Commission des Antiquités de la Seine-Inferieure* VIII (1888), 58 sq.

but properly fitted for the most humble tasks for which he [felt himself] extremely well suited."[17] But, since he was ". . . far from unfit for more vital labors, . . ." he was directed to prepare for the priesthood.[18] It should be recalled here that Brébeuf was then twenty-six years old, by no means a wide-eyed, callow youth, carried away by a falsely pietistic notion. Brébeuf was honestly evaluating himself. God had not endowed him with a superior intellect, but he was physically strong and blessed with a fund of common sense. Since, objectively, these were his talents, would they not be put to more effective use as a lay brother? But his superiors judged otherwise.

His novitiate completed, Jean de Brébeuf was sent, for the fall term of 1619, to teach the *sixième*, or youngest group of boys, at the Collège de Bourbon at Rouen. The school received its name from Charles, cardinal de Bourbon, archbishop of Rouen, brother of Antoine, king of Navarre and uncle of Henri IV.[19] Today the vast college building, on the rue de la République, houses the Lycée Corneille, the local teachers' college. It is still an impressive structure in the flamboyant Norman style with great arched windows and intricate decorations carved in stone. The chapel of the old college, a separate structure, still survives, probably much as it was in Brébeuf's day. The newly appointed master must have been quite familiar with the college for it was only around the corner from the novitiate. He must have often heard the

[17] *Rapport de l'Archiviste de la Province de Québec, 1924-1925*, 64. The quotation is taken from a biographical sketch of Brébeuf written by his last Jesuit superior, Father Paul Ragueneau. Henceforth this primary source will be quoted as RAPQ.

[18] Ibid.

[19] Charles de Bourbon, though a cardinal and archbishop of Rouen, was never ordained a priest. He, of course, only held the title of archbishop and drew the revenues of the diocese. He gave the Jesuits his Rouen palace, the Manoir du Grand Maulévrier, with its courts, gardens, and outlying farms. The Parlement of Rouen so opposed the opening of a Jesuit school in their city that the cardinal was three years in his grave before it began, in 1593. When all Jesuit property was sequestered by the crown in 1595, the school was closed. Henri IV, himself, caused it to be reopened on February 28, 1604. In 1615 Marie de Medici, the rotund little Tuscan widow of Henri IV, laid the first stone of the chapel. The present name of the college is quite fitting. Pierre Corneille (1606-1684) was born at Rouen and attended the college while Brébeuf was there. Though a lawyer, Corneille became France's first true playwright. See Delattre, *Établissements*, IV, 521-24.

younger boys shouting at their games and seen the lordly elder classmen strolling by in adolescent dignity.

Anyone who has taught boys of twelve, especially in a boarding school, will readily admit that this is a task to try men's souls. At that age a boy's attention span is brief; his head is full of grandiose dreams or of fun-loving devilry. From break of dawn, boys of that age are a constant challenge. And Brébeuf, willy-nilly, had the responsibility of his mercurial charges for all of their classes, their periods of recreation, their prayers, and even bedding them down for the night. What those boys first thought of their teacher cannot now be ascertained. However, they must have, at first, been in awe of that great giant of a man towering over them. Later, perhaps, they understood that he was a gentle, understanding guardian who healed their cuts and bruises, held their aching heads when they were sick and defended them against all comers, though he probably was a strict, but just, disciplinarian. The boys must be coaxed, cajoled, or simply driven to study assiduously. Before the close of the academic year they must have a perfect command of Latin grammar, an ability to write a correct French sentence, possess facility in simple mathematics, and above all know their catechism. Without these skills, when the group passed on to the next class, the *cinquième*, it would be unable to master the more difficult work.

The following year, 1620, when school opened on the traditional day, the feast of St. Luke, October 18, Jean de Brébeuf faced the same group of students he had taught the year before. Customarily, a teacher stayed with the same students through the *cinquième, quatrième,* and so on, until he left for higher studies of his own. Jean de Brébeuf finished the academic year, 1620-1621, but that was the end of his teaching career. For the following year, 1621-1622, the catalog of the Province of France, listing each member and his occupation, reports: "Because of ill health, Brother de Brébeuf has no occupation."[20]

What could have so seriously damaged the health of that Norman giant that he was unable to work? Certainly it was a serious ailment for Brébeuf was no malingerer. Some have suggested that

---

[20] ARSJ, Franc. 22, 180. "Joannes de Brébeuf, ob infirmam valitudinem, nullo officio occupat."

the complete absence of outdoor exercise, to which he had been accustomed on his father's farm, was too severe an adjustment for him. That can hardly be correct since Brébeuf had already spent six confining years at Caen as well as two much more stringently regulated years of novitiate at Rouen, seemingly without ill effects. It has been suggested that he might have contracted a serious lung infection in the damp, chill halls of the college. Since, in Brébeuf's day, everyone dwelt in unheated buildings, that explanation seems to lack validity. Whatever the reason, Jean de Brébeuf, whose companions jokingly called him the *vrai boeuf*, a real ox, was withdrawn by his superiors from active work.[21]

Certain biographers of Jean de Brébeuf suggest that during his illness he was encouraged to continue theological studies so that he might soon receive ordination to the priesthood. Though he might well have dipped into various theological treatises while ill, this would not have been a necessary prerequisite for ordination. In 1563 the Council of Trent had decreed that candidates for ordination should have completed a course of theology lasting approximately four years, but no sanction was attached to the decree. Besides, in 1549, Paul III, in his *Licet debitum*, had granted major Jesuit superiors the privilege of presenting candidates for ordination to any bishop whenever they considered a subject ready. The same concession was granted the Jesuits by Gregory XIII in 1582, a full nineteen years after the decree of the Council of Trent.[22] Thus, Brébeuf could have been presented for ordination by his superiors even without any formal study of theology.

It was during the academic year, 1621-1622, that Jean de Brébeuf received sacerdotal ordination. On September 18, 1621, he received the subdiaconate in the ancient cathedral of St. Peter at Lisieux, fifty miles west and a little south of Rouen where the Torques River meets the Obriquet. Exactly three months later, on December 18, Brébeuf was at Bayeux, over a hundred miles west of Rouen, where he received the diaconate in the cathedral of Notre Dame, considered one of the most beautiful examples of

---

[21] One wonders whether the family name might not have arisen from the French *"bref boeuf,"* much in the manner that so many very large men acquire the sobriquet "Tiny." Thus, *bref boeuf* could be translated as little ox.

[22] For a complete explanation of this point, see Joseph P. Donnelly, *Jacques Marquette, 1637-1675,* 271-72.

early Gothic architecture in France. Five months and one day later, on Saturday, February 19, 1622, Brébeuf became a priest at Pontoise, a little city on a hill overlooking the Oise, twenty-five miles north of Paris where the Jesuits had a small residence. Tradition holds that Father Brébeuf celebrated his first Mass on the feast of the Annunciation. Though the date of the feast is normally March 25, Brébeuf's birthday, that year, 1622, Good Friday fell on March 25. The feast of the Annunciation was, therefore, postponed until April 4. On that morning Jean de Brébeuf ascended the altar, probably in the chapel reserved for the exclusive use of the Jesuits at the Collège de Bourbon, and offered the holy sacrifice of the Mass with the intense devotion felt in his soul.[23]

For purposes of effective governance, the provincial of each Jesuit province is required to send to the general at Rome a triennial list containing the names of every member of the province with an evaluation of each person's qualities and abilities. The lists are compiled on form sheets divided into several categories such as place of origin, health, experience, and the like. Such a list was forwarded to Rome in 1622 from the Province of France, of which Brébeuf was a member. In it he is listed as a Norman by origin, born on March 25, 1593, admitted to the Society on November 8, 1617, at Rouen. His health was judged to be "*satis firma*," that is, very sound. As to his academic status, the report declares that he had completed two years' study of philosophy and another two of "cases" before he became a Jesuit. As to active work, he had two years' experience teaching "grammar." He had no academic degrees and was, as yet, without final vows.[24] The information is scanty, but, at least, we know that by mid-1622 Jean de Brébeuf had regained his normal, robust health and was ready for active work. And an assignment was soon given him.

[23] ARSJ, Franc. 22, 189. See also RAPQ, 1924-1925, 71. Brébeuf's own report of the dates and places of his reception of the various orders. It is worth noting that between September 1621 and February 1622 Brébeuf traveled well over four hundred fifty miles. Considering the inherent difficulties, this was no mean accomplishment for a man pronounced too ill to work.

[24] ARSJ, Franc. 11, Catologi Trienniales, 1615-1633, f 139v-140. See also *The Constitutions of the Society of Jesus*, translated and edited by George E. Ganss, 325.

When the catalog for the Province of France was issued in the fall of 1622, Father Jean de Brébeuf was listed as being at Rouen and occupied as procurator, or treasurer of the Collège de Bourbon.[25] Managing the financial affairs of the college required Brébeuf's full attention. The enrollment numbered fifteen hundred students ranging in age from small boys of twelve or younger to young theological students in their twenties. Except for extracurricular courses such as lessons in dancing, fencing, painting, or horseback riding, students paid no tuition. The treasurer must meet expenses from annual revenues gained from various endowments. The college received an annual grant of 6,000 *livres* from the crown and another 2,000 from the city of Rouen. It also received revenues from the farmland pertaining to the estate of Charles, cardinal de Bourbon, as well as from lands of several suppressed monasteries such as the priories of Grandmont, Deux-Amants, and Basqueville.[26] Supervising these dispersed properties was probably employment enough in itself. But, of course, the treasurer necessarily dealt with the purveyors of supplies to the college, everything from butter to horses. Then there were servants to be hired and paid as well as teachers of the various extracurricular courses.

From the merchants of Rouen, if from no other source, Jean de Brébeuf must have garnered a great deal of information about France's young colony in North America. For many years wealthy merchants at Rouen had been investing heavily in various monopolistic trading companies organized to exploit the fur trade. Frequently, by royal decree, peltries collected in New France could be sold only at Rouen. Brébeuf must have heard innumerable tales about the poor, benighted aborigines of New France, who, some said, needed but dedicated missionaries to convert them rapidly to Christianity. Shortly, Brébeuf met the major Jesuit superior who would send him to New France. A serious crisis for the Jesuits in Normandy brought about that meeting.

In 1619, the Jesuits, through the generosity of Alexandre Bouchard, sieur de Caudecoste, opened a simple residence on the winding little rue de Boeuf close to the massive old Gothic cathedral at Dieppe. That city, at the mouth of the Arques River, some

[25] ARSJ, Franc. 22, 189. "P. Joannes de Brébeuf, Rouen, Procurator."
[26] Delattre, *Établissements*, IV, 521-24.

forty miles northwest of Rouen, was a major port for ships engaged in the fur trade. During the Wars of Religion the place had
been, and still was, a Huguenot stronghold. Bouchard and a co-
terie of militant Catholics hoped that Jesuits might convert their
Huguenot fellow townsmen. The Jesuits, happy to attempt that
apostolic effort, rejoiced to have a house at Dieppe where missionaries, hopefully in the future, bound for New France, might
lodge while awaiting passage.[27]

During the first days of 1625, one of the Jesuits at Dieppe,
Father Ambroise Guyot, a simple, credulous religious, was ac-
cused by one François Martel of plotting high treason against
Louis XIII. Though a priest, Martel, with the willing cooperation
of his servant, Nicolas Galeran, devoted himself to the most revolting immoral excesses. The scandalous priest was arrested
with his servant, tried and condemned, by the Parlement of
Rouen, to death by boiling in oil and his servant to be hanged.
Attempting to save himself, Martel declared that in his presence
Father Guyot concocted a plot with three Spanish sailors to overthrow the French king in favor of Philip IV of Spain.[28]

The charge was so ridiculous that it would have been laughed
out of court had not the Parlement's first president, Faucon de
Ris, nursed a grudge against the Jesuits, especially Father Gas-
pard de Ségurin, formerly the king's confessor. The first president
firmly believed that it was out of malice that Ségurin blocked his
appointment to the office of keeper of the royal seal. Here was a
ready-made opportunity for vengeance. Faucon de Ris ordered
the arrest not only of poor, timid Ambroise Guyot but also of
the other two Jesuits at Dieppe, Father Etienne Chapuis and
Brother Benoit.

[27] Henri Fouqueray, *Histoire de la Compagnie de Jésus en France des
origines à la suppression (1528-1762)*, IV, 62-63.

[28] Ibid., 63. The so-called plot was manufactured from an innocent incident.
While strolling along the docks at Dieppe, Father Guyot and Brother Benoit were
approached by three stranded Spanish sailors asking for alms. Penniless himself,
Guyot brought them to his supposed friend, Martel. In the course of the conversation there, the sailors boasted that their king, Philip IV, was a more vigorous
champion of Catholicism than Louis XIII. "Would to God," Guyot averred, "that
our king was as loyally served as these Spaniards support their king." Imprudently, Martel declared that Philip IV ought to be king of France.

The incident now became a serious matter. The rector of the Collège de Bourbon, with the help of friends at Rouen, soon discovered that De Ris was suborning witnesses in preparation for Guyot's trial. If the case got into the courts, it was quite likely that it would adversely affect not only the Jesuits at Rouen but the whole Society of Jesus in France. Prudently, the rector at Rouen, Honoré Nicquet, referred the case to his provincial, Father Pierre Coton, who resided at Paris. Since time was of the essence, Nicquet appointed perhaps the strongest man in his community and the best equestrian to ride by post horse to Paris, carrying with him proof of Guyot's innocence as well as of the first president's devious activity.[29] For that job, Jean de Brébeuf was the obvious man.

Galloping down the broad valley of the Seine, changing horses at post stations, Jean de Brébeuf clattered into Paris to the Jesuit residence on the rue Saint-Antoine where he presented his documents and related the story to the provincial. Pierre Coton was no stranger to either the ambitions of the nobility or of the devious means they would resort to in seeking revenge.[30] Advised by his consultants, Coton took two decisive steps. First, he sent Brébeuf back to Rouen in company with Father Jean Phelippeau who had only recently been relieved of the office of rector of the college at Rouen. Phelippeau had been very popular there and had many friends among the members of the Parlement of Rouen. Then Coton appealed to his former pupil, Louis XIII, requesting that the case be remanded to the king's council. A forthright, outspoken man, Phelippeau might have done more harm than good at Rouen. Reaching there on January 28, 1625, he boldly approached Faucon de Ris at a social gathering that very night and loudly accused the man of malice and underhanded dealing. Had not the king granted Coton's request, poor Guyot

[29] Ibid., 65. It is known that Brébeuf used post horses returning from Paris to Rouen. It would seem logical that he did so on the journey to Paris.

[30] Pierre Coton was born at Néronde in 1564 and entered the Society of Jesus at Turin on September 15, 1583. In 1608 he was appointed royal confessor and tutor to the future Louis XIII. After the murder of Henri IV, Coton continued at court until 1617, when the young king finished his education. In December 1624 Coton was appointed provincial of the Province of France. He was an ardent supporter of the effort to introduce Jesuit missionaries into New France. While holding the office of provincial, Coton died at Paris on March 19, 1626.

could have languished in prison for days and months. But, on February 21, a royal bailiff arrived with a *lettre de cachet* taking the case out of the hands of the Parlement of Rouen. At Paris, before the king's council, Father Guyot was declared innocent. Rather than adding insult to injury for Faucon de Ris, Father Coton did not allow Guyot to return to Dieppe, but sent him to Pontoise to help the Jesuits there.[31] For Jean de Brébeuf that brief, chance meeting with Father Pierre Coton was to determine the giant Norman's whole future.

Throughout the latter half of the sixteenth century and into the seventeenth, platoons of Jesuits from Spain and Portugal sailed off to the Far East or the New World, zealous for the conversion of India, China, Japan, or the aborigines of South and Central America. French Jesuits, equally anxious to spread the gospel, lacked opportunities beyond the seas because France enjoyed no stable foothold in either the Orient or the New World. Practical interest of the French in the North American continent quickened during the reign of Henri IV. He granted a series of monopolistic charters to various privately financed trading companies whose predominently Huguenot stockholders were not anxious to further the spread of Catholicism among the Indians with whom they traded for furs. Nonetheless, royal charters generally required recipients to draw the Indians ". . . to the knowledge of God and the light to the Christian religion."[32]

The first opportunity for French Jesuits to exercise their missionary zeal abroad arose when Fathers Pierre Biard and Enemond Massé arrived at Port Royal on May 11, 1611.[33] They

[31] Ibid., 67. Before his execution Martel confessed that the supposed plot existed only in his own mind. The revelation did not save him for he was put to death with his servant in the manner previously described.

[32] Camille de Rochemonteix, *Les Jésuites et la Nouvelle-France au XVIIe siècle*, I, 22. This authority is subsequently referred to as Rochemonteix.

[33] Port Royal was located on the north side of Annapolis Basin in the present Canadian Province of Nova Scotia and not far from Lower Granville. The original *habitation*, built from the plans drawn by Champlain, has been carefully reconstructed on the original site by the Canadian government.

Pierre Biard was born at Grenoble in 1567 or 1568. On June 3, 1583, he entered the Jesuit novitiate at Tournon. He studied philosophy and theology at Avignon and was ordained a priest there in 1599. As early as 1602, he asked the Jesuit general to be sent to the Indies. While teaching at Lyons in 1608 he was appointed to begin the mission in New France. He sailed from Dieppe with

promptly set about learning the local native language without which skill they would never be able to convey to the Indians the quite abstruse concepts of Christianity.[34] Maintaining cordial relations with Charles de Biencourt, young son of the colony's proprietor, Jean de Biencourt, sieur de Poutrincourt, soon proved quite as difficult as instructing the Indians. Expecting to extricate the missionaries from that complex situation, their generous benefactress, Antoinette de Pons, marquise de Guercheville, financed an independent expedition which she dispatched with orders to her agent, René Le Coq de La Saussaye, to pick up the two Jesuits and establish an independent colony set up solely to effect the conversion of the Indians. Reaching Port Royal in May 1613, aboard the *Jonas*, La Saussaye collected Biard and Massé with whom he sailed off across the Bay of Fundy, planning to begin a new colony.[35]

Coasting southward along the western shore of the Bay of Fundy, La Saussaye entered an inlet behind Mt. Deseret Island where he chose to locate the new colony.[36] There he landed his twenty-seven colonists, the two Jesuits from Port Royal, and two new recruits, Father Jacques Quentin and Brother Gilbert Du

---

Father Enemond Massé on January 26, 1611. After the expulsion of the Jesuits from Saint-Sauveur, Biard reached France in April 1614. In 1616 he published, at Lyons, his *Relation de la Nouvelle-France*, a complete account of his years in Acadia. He died at Avignon on November 17, 1622, while serving as an army chaplain.

Enemond Massé, son of a baker, was born at Lyons on August 3, 1575. He entered the Jesuit novitiate at Avignon on August 22, 1595. After his novitiate, he received a very truncated course in theology and was ordained at Dôle in 1602. In 1609 he was sent to assist Father Coton as royal confessor. In 1610 he was chosen to accompany Father Biard to New France. Returned to France in 1613, Massé was sent to La Flèche where he stayed until 1625, holding the office of spiritual director to young Jesuits. Then he returned to Quebec until the English expelled him in 1629. Four years later, in 1633, he was back in New France, again working at Quebec. He finally died at Sillery, aged seventy, on May 12, 1646.

[34] Biard called the Indians Souriquois. They really were members of the Micmac confederacy.

[35] Lucien Campeau, editor, *Monumenta Novae Franciae: La Première Mission d'Acadie (1602-1616)*, Introduction, 211-22. This is by far the most thorough and scholarly discussion of the whole situation. This source is subsequently cited as Campeau.

[36] Saint-Sauveur was located, most probably, not far from the present town of Lamoine, Maine.

Thet.[37] The site was called Saint-Sauveur. Most imprudently, La Saussaye set his colonists to planting before building any sort of fortifications against hostile Indians or possible European raiders. On July 2, 1613, Sir Samuel Argall, sailing out of Jamestown, Virginia, attacked the new colony, killing Brother Du Thet and capturing all the French. The Jesuits were returned to France, thus ending their first missionary effort.[38]

Though French efforts at colonization along the Atlantic met with no great initial success, they prospered in the St. Lawrence River valley. Samuel de Champlain, cooperating with Pierre Du Gua, sieur de Monts, French trader and explorer, established Quebec on July 2, 1608. Seven years later, when Champlain had already concluded an alliance with the Hurons, he imported four missionaries, Franciscans of the strictest observance, the Recollets. They were the first missionaries to dwell among the Hurons in their homeland where Father Jean de Brébeuf would spend nearly two decades of his apostolic life.

[37] Jacques Quentin was born at Abbeville in 1572. He was already a Master of Arts and a priest before he entered the Jesuit novitiate at Nancy in 1604. He was appointed to accompany the expedition of 1613 to replace Biard, if the latter had died. If not, Quentin was to return to France. On returning to France in 1614, Quentin was sent to Charleville where he died on March 18, 1647.

Brother Gilbert Du Thet was born at Chantelle in about 1575 and made his novitiate at Verdun from 1594 to 1596. In 1611 Du Thet was appointed a sort of business agent to look after the interests of the marquise de Guercheville at Port Royal. He went there in December 1611 and remained until June 1612 when he returned to France, reporting to the marquise that nothing was being done by the French laymen to aid Biard and Massé in their apostolic work. He returned to Port Royal with the expedition launched by the marquise to found a new colony. He was killed by Argall's guns at Saint-Sauveur on July 3, 1613.

[38] Reuben Gold Thwaites, editor, *The Jesuit Relations and Allied Documents*, III, 275-83; IV, 69-75. Subsequently, this source is referred to as *Relations*. Argall had already distinguished himself in the art of treachery in Virginia. It was he who kidnapped Pocahontas, holding her hostage to restrain her father, Powhatan, from attacking the English settlers at Jamestown.

Chapter II

The Huron Nation

Because Father Jean de Brébeuf's missionary life was directed, almost exclusively, to the Hurons, understanding the man requires an adequate perception of the character of the aboriginal nation to which he was so devoted. Who were these Indians; whence did they come; what were their traditional religious beliefs, their form of government, their manner of living? Why were the French so anxious to maintain the friendship of the Hurons to the exclusion, say, of an equally powerful aboriginal tribe, the Iroquois? What persuaded the missionaries that the Christianization of a primitive people some eight hundred miles removed from Quebec merited their earliest and most elaborate effort?

The origin of the Huron nation is lost in the mists of prehistory. Philologists, anthropologists, and archaeologists propose that once these aborigines were one nation with the Iroquois. Scholars surmise that the Huron-Iroquois migrated from the Mississippi Valley, moving north and east until they settled along the lower reaches of the St. Lawrence River. In 1535 Jacques Cartier encountered them occupying two strongly fortified centers, Stadacona, near the present Quebec, and Hochelaga, on the island of

Montreal. Sixty-eight years later, in 1603, when Samuel de Champlain arrived, only Algonkins were found from the mouth of the Saguenay as far westward as the Richelieu River, a good three hundred miles up the St. Lawrence. How the Algonkins accomplished a victory over the more advanced group remains a mystery. Through the history of New France, the Algonkins never once demonstrated any such ability.

It is assumed that in fleeing westward the Huron-Iroquois family separated at the eastern end of Lake Erie. The Iroquois elected to migrate along the southern shore, settling in the beautiful lake country of northern New York and along the valley of the Mohawk. The Hurons, choosing the northern shore of Lake Erie, continued westward until they came to rest along the southern shores of Georgian Bay. Crowding in behind the Hurons, to the south, resided the Petuns, or Tobacco Nation and the Neutrals, both speaking a dialect of the Huron language.

The Huron nation proper occupied an area almost exactly coextensive with the northern half of the present County Simcoe, Ontario, Canada. In extent, the territory, at its broadest east-west axis, is about forty miles wide. From north to south it measures somewhat under thirty miles. Almost completely surrounded by inlets of Georgian Bay, the Severn River, Lake Simcoe, and the Nottawasaga River, the land of the Hurons is practically an island. Probably for that reason, the Hurons called themselves the Wendat or "People of the Island." The title of Huron was an opprobrious sobriquet given them by French sailors who, on first meeting them, with hair roached down the middle of their heads and standing erect like bristles, exclaimed in amusement, "*Quelles Hures!*" or "What boar heads!"

Topographically, the Huron country is composed of gently rolling hills with few noticeable elevations. It is drained by four small, serpentine rivers, the Coldwater, the Sturgeon, the Hog, and the Wye. All flow northward, emptying into one or other inlet of Georgian Bay. The soil is adequately fertile for the cultivation of grains. But it requires a great deal of moisture, for the subsoil is so very sandy that water is not retained near the surface for long. Once the country was heavily wooded with evergreens, oak, maple, and birch. During the late nineteenth century lumber industries denuded the forests, leaving very little hardwood. Today there is hardly any area of the old Huron country even faintly resembling what it was like when Jean de Brébeuf first saw it.

If Jean Jacques Rousseau had met the Hurons, he might well have believed that these were, indeed, the noble savages portrayed in his *Discours*. Physically, the Hurons were much taller than seventeenth-century Europeans. They were well-formed, strong, with very few deformed persons among them.[1] Their bronzed skin, jet black hair, and flashing teeth gave them a very attractive appearance. Their vision, sense of smell, and hearing were all more acute than those of Europeans. Inured to hardship, the Hurons endured cold, heat, hunger, and fatigue with unwavering good humor.[2] Among themselves they were consistently gentle and affable, not easily annoyed and given to concealing wrongs afflicted.[3] To strangers coming among them, the Hurons were the soul of hospitality, never excluding them and sharing whatever they had.[4] Father Francesco Bressani, who lived with the Hurons from 1645 to 1648, declared them to have ". . . clever understanding . . . and matters, of which they possessed the fundamental elements, they handle just as well as the most sagacious European."[5]

While attesting to their virtues, Europeans who wrote about them pointed out the vices to which the Hurons were addicted. Father François Peron, Jesuit missionary to the Hurons, considered them ". . . importunate, visionary, childish, thievish, lying, deceitful, licentious, proud, lazy . . ."[6] Brébeuf, who certainly knew the Huron better than any other European, reported, in 1635: "As regards morals, the Hurons are lascivious . . . They are very lazy, are liars, thieves, pertinacious beggars."[7] In defense of the Hurons, one may fairly ask whether these were vices by the code of morality the Hurons themselves recognized. What, for example, is theft in a society wherein so much is held in common? In 1645 Father Jerome Lalemant, describing the Huron character, remarked: "In truth their customs are barbarous in a thousand

[1] *Relations*, XXXVIII, 257.
[2] Ibid., VIII, 127.
[3] Ibid., 125, 127.
[4] Ibid., 129.
[5] Ibid., XXXVIII, 261.
[6] Ibid., XV, 155.
[7] Ibid., 125, 127.

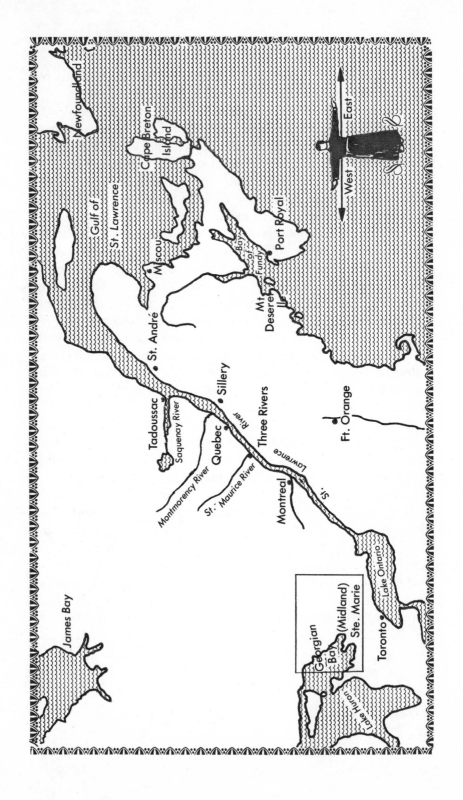

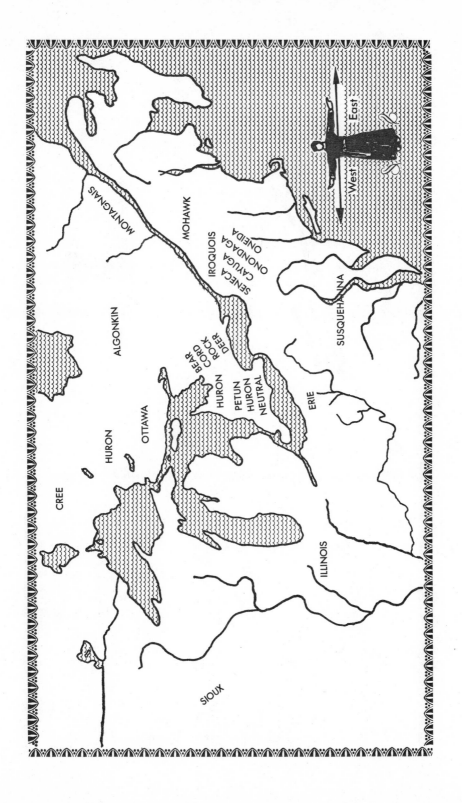

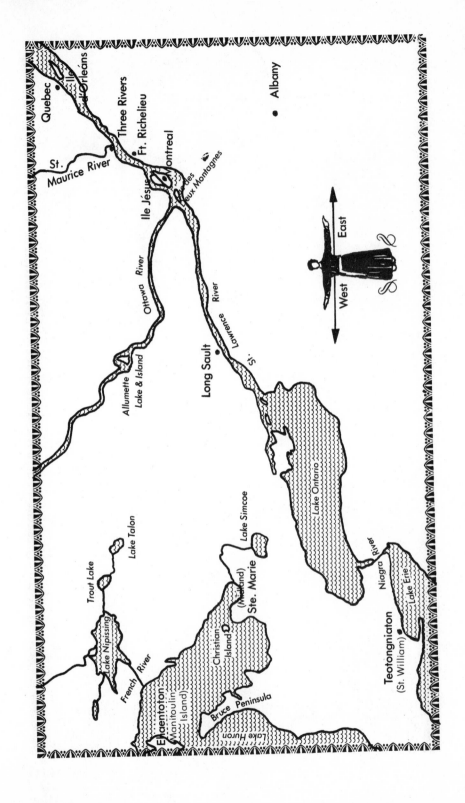

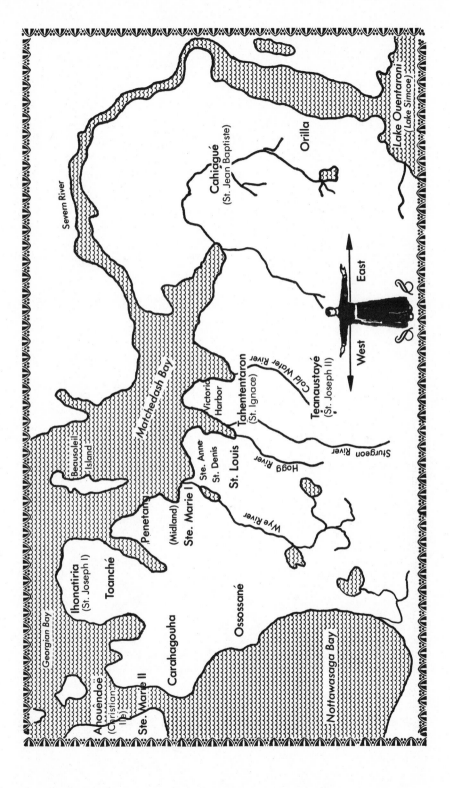

matters; but after all, in those practices which among them are regarded as evil acts and are condemned by the public, we find without comparison much less disorder than there is in France, though here the mere shame of having committed the crime is the offender's punishment."[8] It should be noted, parenthetically, that Lalemant was not a particularly sympathetic observer.[9]

The Huron nation was organized into four major tribes or phratries, the Bear, the Rock, the Cord, and the Deer clans. The territory of the Bears included all the area from the Wye River northwestward to Georgian Bay. Numerically, they were the largest group and proved the most inclined to embrace Christianity. South of the Bears, along the ridge of hills east of the present village of Hillsdale, dwelt the Cords. They were not as numerous as the Bears, but more populous than the remaining two groups. The

---

[8] Ibid., XXVIII, 163.

[9] Jerome Lalemant was born at Paris, April 27, 1593. He was, therefore, a month and two days younger than Jean de Brébeuf and six years younger than his brother Charles. Jerome entered the Jesuit novitiate at Paris on October 20, 1610. He studied philosophy at the University of Pont-à-Mousson (1612-1615) and theology at the most respected Jesuit college in France, Clermont at Paris (1619-1623). After his ordination he was stationed at Clermont from 1627 to 1632. Then he held the office of rector of the Jesuit college at Blois from 1632 to 1636. His interest in the missions of New France must have been quickened by his older brother, Charles, also a Jesuit, who was superior of that mission from 1625 until his return to France in 1627. Jerome reached Quebec on June 25, 1638, and was sent by the superior, Father Paul Le Jeune, to the Huron country where he succeeded Father Brébeuf as the superior of the Huron mission. Lalemant was utterly lacking in any knowledge or experience with Indians and knew not one word of the Huron tongue. He it was who conceived the idea of establishing the elaborate center at Sainte Marie which, in effect, created a French enclave. That policy was in direct opposition to Brébeuf's belief that the missionaries should, in as far as possible, become Indians among the Indians. In his first report from the Huron country Lalemant wrote: ". . . the customs and practices of these people . . . always appeared to us like stagnant, ill-smelling pools . . . it cannot be believed what a stench and what wretchedness we have found . . ." Ibid., XVII, 145. Lalemant's *Relation* of 1639. During his years as superior of the Huron mission he did not change that opinion. In 1645 Jerome Lalemant was appointed superior of the whole mission in New France, a position he held until 1650. During that time, Jerome's nephew, Father Gabriel Lalemant, was martyred with Father Brébeuf in the Huron country on March 17, 1649. In 1650 Jerome went back to France to plead the cause of the mission. From 1651 to 1656 he labored, chiefly at Quebec, until he was recalled to France. In 1659, at the pressing request of Bishop Laval, Lalemant was again appointed superior of the whole Jesuit mission of New France. Replaced in 1665 by Father François Le Mercier, Lalemant remained in Canada until his death at Quebec on January 26, 1673.

northern shore of Lake Orr was the homeland of the Deers, a very small group often known as "the one white lodge." The large stretch of country between the present cities of Coldwater and Orillia, on Lake Simcoe, was the territory of the Rock clan. These natives, the easternmost of all the Hurons, were those first contacted by the French. Therefore, by tribal custom, the Rocks had the right to regulate that trade.[10] The total population of the Huron nation, in 1615, was estimated by Champlain to be about thirty thousand, dwelling in eighteen villages, six of which were palisaded.[11] In 1640, Father Jerome Lalemant reported the results of an accurate census, just completed. The missionaries found ". . . thirty-two hamlets and straggling villages, which comprise in all about seven hundred cabins, about two thousand fires and about twelve thousand persons."[12]

As did the league of the Iroquois, the Huron nation developed a thoroughly democratic form of local and national government which functioned quite well without any sanctioning authority over the citizen other than the influence of public opinion. The basic institution, on both the village, the clan, and the national level, was an assembly of the ancients. These met regularly in the villages, frequently on the clan level but less often on a national scale. In these meetings all questions of import to the general welfare were discussed and decided by majority vote.[13] Implementation of decisions was the responsibility of the chiefs, or captains, who procured cooperation of the people mainly by means of the personal magnetism each captain was able to exercise.

The position of captain among the Hurons is not easy to define with clarity. Father Brébeuf, well informed concerning the organization of the Huron nation, declared: "Now there are as many sorts of captains as of affairs."[14] Normally, in each village there was a captain responsible for purely civic affairs, such as

[10] Ibid., X, 225. See also Elisabeth Tooker, *An Ethnography of the Huron Indians, 1615-1649*, 11.

[11] Samuel de Champlain, *The Works of Samuel de Champlain*, edited by H. P. Biggar, IV, 302. This work is henceforth quoted as Champlain.

[12] *Relations*, IX, 127. At approximately the same period, the population of the Iroquois was estimated to have been about seventeen thousand. See ibid., I, 11.

[13] Ibid., X, 251.

[14] Ibid., 231.

public order, another concerned with war, including, perhaps, defense of the village. There were captains, too, for regulating dances, games, and for some, but not all, religious ceremonies. The same system of authority applied on the higher levels of the clan and the whole nation.

Those who held these posts attained the office ". . . on account of their intellectual superiority, popularity, wealth, or other qualities which render them influential in the country."[15] The manner in which a man attained the office of captain was partly through election and partly through family relationships. However, succession was not from father to son but from father to nephew or grandson, ". . . but only insofar as they have suitable qualifications, . . . and are accepted by the whole country."[16] After securing office, the captain had no power to compel anyone to follow his directions. Success on the part of a captain depended solely on his ability in persuading others to follow him. Save for respect among his fellows, the captain gained nothing from the office except the onerous burden of being constantly involved in the public affairs of the village, the clan, or the nation.

Despite the apparent absence of any really effective internal authority, domestic tranquillity pertained. Mutual respect and ancient traditions supplied for the Hurons what civil codes furnished Europeans. It was unseemly for a Huron to manifest impatience or hostility, even when wronged.[17] Certain actions, especially theft and murder, were promptly visited with condign punishment. When apprehended, a thief could be despoiled not only of the stolen property but also of everything he possessed.[18] Punishment for murder was not visited on the perpetrator only but on his whole village. They were required to make reparation to the family of the victim in the form of many valuable presents.[19] In particularly vicious crimes, a whole village was pauperized to pay the debt incurred by a murderer. Such drastic punishment was a powerful deterrent against serious crime.

[15] Ibid.
[16] Ibid., 233.
[17] Ibid., XXXVIII, 267.
[18] Ibid., 269.
[19] Ibid., X, 215-33.

The Hurons located their villages, whenever possible, at the oxbow bend of a creek or river, especially if the banks were reasonably steep. Thus situated, the Indians built a high palisade of poles interwoven with brush at the narrow end of the oxbow. This system of defense gave the village the greatest natural protection against attack. In theory, at least, warriors attacking from the river could be repelled as they climbed the steep banks. Those assaulting the palisade would be driven off by braves mounted on scaffolds near the top of the wall. Within the village, dwellings were placed in an orderly pattern, much like streets. Ample room was allowed between the cabins to decrease the hazard of fire spreading easily from one structure to another.

The Huron lodge was an ingenious architectural product. The French, on first describing it, likened it to a long, high grape arbor covered with the bark of trees. In length, the lodges varied from twenty to as much as two hundred feet. Their width was approximately twenty feet and their height about the same. The lodges were constructed of thick poles buried upright in the ground and bent together at the top where they were bound with bark cordage. At intervals, from top to bottom, the Indians attached latitudinal cross poles for a framework. The whole was covered with the bark of ash, elm, spruce, or cedar. An opening, about two feet, was left along the length of the ridge to allow smoke to escape. The ends of each lodge were closed by woven mats which served as doors.[20]

The interior furnishings of a lodge goes far toward revealing the life-style of the Hurons. For the full length of the dwelling, on each side, was a raised platform, approximately a yard above the bare ground. At regular intervals along the center aisle was a series of fire pits, each serving two families occupying compartments opposite one another. Clothing, utensils, and the like, were stored under the platform or suspended from the roof. The communal style of living eliminated any possibility of privacy. But it probably went far toward engendering a common bond. Sheer necessity inevitably obliged the members of each lodge to bear and forbear. A given cabin was usually home to from eight to

[20] Ibid., VIII, 107-09; XXXVIII, 247.

twenty families with an average of four or six persons to a family unit.[21]

For food, Hurons depended principally on Indian corn grown in fields near the village. Each family was assigned as much land as required for its needs.[22] Several days before planting the women soaked carefully selected kernels in water after which they put nine or ten of them in holes set a pace apart. The fields received no other care save keeping them cleared of weeds. At harvesttime the women gathered the ears of corn and husked them, allowing the bracts to adhere to the stems of the ears. Tied in bundles, these were suspended in the lodges until dried. Then the ears were shucked and the kernels stored in bark vats until needed. Corn was prepared for consumption by pounding it into a coarse flour which, mixed with hot water, produced an unseasoned mush. Besides corn, the Huron women cultivated squash, beans, sunflowers for their seeds, and some tobacco. In season, they gathered wild fruit, strawberries, plums, apples, and blackberries.[23] Preserved by drying it in the sun, fruit furnished a sort of garnish for the cornmeal mush. The whole agricultural effort, from planting to harvesting devolved on the women, except, perhaps, the original operation of clearing fields of large trees.

Hunting and fishing, exclusive prerogatives of Huron men, were not neglected, though they could not be relied upon as a major source of daily food. Fish, so abundantly available in the waters surrounding the Huron country, were caught to supplement diet, but game, especially bear or deer, was scarce. Small game, rabbits, muskrats, beaver, could be trapped in snares, though even these seem not to have abounded. Large animals, whose hides were so useful for clothing, were hard to come by. Even beaver had already become scarce in the Huron country by the time the French reached it.[24]

The scarcity of hides and peltries in their homeland naturally led the Hurons to establish a quite effective trading empire. By

---

[21] Diamond Jenness, *The Indians of Canada*, 290.

[22] Gabriel-Theodat Sagard, *The Long Journey to the Country of the Huron*, edited by George M. Wrong, 103.

[23] W. Vernon Kinietz, *The Indians of the Western Great Lakes, 1615-1760*, 16-20.

[24] Ibid., 23-24.

the time Champlain visited them, in 1615, these clever aborigines had become middlemen between the Petun-Neutral complex and the Ottawa-Algonkin market. The Petuns and Neutrals produced an abundance of tobacco, corn, and hemp. The Ottawa and Algonkins grew none of these essential commodities, but they had ready access to peltries and dried fish. Astutely, the Huron confederacy provided an exchange emporium, profitable to themselves and to both sets of customers. Hurons brought tobacco and corn to a trading rendezvous at Cap de la Victoire where these were exchanged with the Ottawa and Algonkins for furs and smoked fish. The fish was, in turn, passed on to the Neutrals and the Petuns in exchange for tobacco and corn. The trading empire worked well so long as the Hurons could hold the tribes at each end of the operation in a sort of economic bondage. But, if a foreign power, Indian or European, invaded the area, capturing one or other economic dependent, the whole enterprise was bound to collapse.

Having ceased to be economically independent, the Hurons perceived the vital necessity of protecting their economic empire. For that reason they strove to prevent the French traders or missionaries from making any direct contact with the Neutrals or the Petuns. There was no possibility of excluding the French from trade relations with the Algonkins and Ottawa for, to reach the Hurons, the Europeans perforce passed through the country of each. The Iroquois remained a constant economic threat to the Hurons chiefly because that powerful nation might at any moment make economic captives of the Neutrals and Petuns. If that disaster occurred, the Hurons might well starve even if the Iroquois did not slaughter them. Hence the Hurons, because of the precarious nature of their economy, had dire need for as large a standing army as they could muster.[25]

Previous to the coming of the white man, with his highly desirable metal tools, woven cloth, durable utensils, and guns, intertribal conflict may have been more of a dangerous sport than true warfare. Among the Hurons, when a captain or a prominent warrior announced his intention of attacking another tribe he enlisted followers, all of whom were volunteers. For no one could

[25] George T. Hunt, *The Wars of the Iroquois, a Study in Intertribal Trade Relations*, 52-65.

be coerced into marching to war, even for the defense of his country. The Hurons apparently sought to avoid futile conflicts by maintaining paid spies in the countries of both their allies and their enemies so that secret plans made there might be known to the Hurons.[26]

When war was decided upon, several of the older, more daring captains were given command of the braves. The field generals visited the various villages seeking recruits. Volunteers obliged themselves to go to war as well as rendering unquestioned obedience to the plans of the leaders. After a great feast, including much boasting of former deeds of valor and promises of braver deeds to follow, the recruited army marched off to battle. Each brave armed himself with a bow, arrows, a war club, and sometimes a wicker shield used to fend off flights of enemy arrows. Every brave carried his own supply of food, enough parched corn to last the expected duration of the punitive expedition.[27] If the campaign succeeded, the prize was neither territory nor much booty, but prisoners. They were brought home to be tortured to death by their victors as well as all the inhabitants of the village where that gruesome ceremony took place in all its horrors.[28]

Though the refinements of cruelty visited by almost every Indian tribe on their war captives revolt the twentieth-century mind, it is only fair to remind the reader that torture remained a legal weapon in England, Spain, France, Italy, even the Papal States, the Netherlands, and the Scandinavian countries until nearly the end of the eighteenth century. Indians probably tortured captives to instill fear in the hearts of their enemies, a rather ineffective practice because all native tribes, at least in eastern North America, employed the same gruesome methods. However, not all captives were tortured to death. Many were incorporated into the victorious tribe as a means of maintaining fighting strength. The practice was apparently quite successful.

[26] *Relations*, X, 229.

[27] Sagard, *Long Journey*, 153.

[28] For an enlightening discussion of the aboriginal practice of torture, consult Nathaniel Knowles, "The Torture of Captives by the Indians of Eastern North America," *Proceedings of the American Philosophical Society* LXXXII (1940), sect. 2, 151-225.

There are innumerable instances of naturalized Hurons fighting valiantly against their former friends and relatives.

Life in the Huron nation had its lighter side. The people frequently held dances and participated in various games. Of the latter, straw, lacrosse, and dish were the most common. Little is known about the first, except that it was played with three or four hundred white rushes, each about a foot long. Lacrosse, perhaps the grandfather of modern hockey, was a strenuous, violent sport. Opposing teams strove to drive a ball through a goal which was not behind the defending team but at the right or left. Fields where contests took place were sometimes a mile in length. Teams numbered as many as a hundred players on each side. Rivalry must certainly have been intense, especially when villages competed against one another. Sometimes lacrosse took on a quasi-religious character when staged because a sick person dreamed that he would die unless a game was played. On occasion, sorcerers would declare that unless a contest was held some grave disaster would befall the country.[29] Whenever lacrosse was played, especially between villages, bets were placed, even expensive ones such as beaver robes and stacks of wampum, the money of the country.

Inveterate gamblers, the Hurons enjoyed most their game called dish. This consisted of employing a wooden bowl in which were placed five or six fruit pits painted white on one side and black on the other. A player shook the dish and then struck it sharply on the ground. One side won when all the pits came up the color previously chosen by the player. Just as gamblers do today, the Hurons employed lucky charms, incantations, and even the presence of certain persons thought to give luck to the player. Also, of course, each side selected a player with a good reputation for winning.

When a game of dish was in progress, people involved lost all sense of proportion. They wagered tobacco, valuable beaver pelts, the clothes off their backs, and even parts of their bodies. One Huron, having lost everything he owned, bet his hair and lost it. Others bet parts of their hands and, on losing, quite calmly allowed one or two fingers to be cut off.[30] In the *Relation* of 1636,

[29] *Relations*, X, 185, 187.
[30] Ibid., XVI, 201.

Father Brébeuf recounted an occasion when a whole village returned, during the winter, from gambling at a neighboring town. He wrote: "You might have seen this winter a great crowd returning from here to their villages, having lost their moccasins at a time when there was nearly three feet of snow, apparently as cheerful, nevertheless, as if they had won."[31] Probably the Hurons were no more addicted to gambling than any other aboriginal nation. We are told of a certain Mohawk, going to another Iroquois tribe to purchase peltries with a horde of wampum, ". . . began to gamble and lost all he had brought with him."[32]

The Hurons, in common with all aboriginal peoples of North America, performed many different sorts of dances, though the purpose of none seems to have been pure pleasure. The Indians danced to welcome visitors, to propitiate the spirits, to prepare for war, to celebrate victories, to prevent illness, or to cure disease of an individual or of the whole nation. For participants, the most essential quality was sheer endurance. For hours or even days, the master of the dance chanted monotonously while the dancers kept time with their feet and gyrated their bodies. Some dances required the participants to dress grotesquely and paint their faces. Others obliged the dancers to wear a minimum of clothing or, in certain cases, nothing at all.[33] Children were never permitted to join the dancers, but they were allowed to watch, sitting in a circle with the older folk.

In answer to the question, whence came man, the Hurons subscribed to a myth generally held by the Indian tribes of eastern North America. They believed that a pregnant woman, called Ataentsic, accidentally fell through a hole in the sky and landed gently on the back of a turtle. To provide living space for the lady, a beaver dove down below the turtle and brought up enough earth to establish an island on the turtle's back. The woman gave birth to two sons, Tawiscaron and Iouskeha. When the boys grew up they quarreled. Iouskeha, employing the horns of a stag as a weapon, wounded his brother so badly that poor Tawiscaron ran through the land dripping blood as he fled. Showing no mercy, the cruel brother overtook Tawiscaron and slew

[31] Ibid., X, 187, 189.
[32] Ibid., XVII, 77.
[33] Ibid., XIII, 263.

him. So, naturally, every person alive was a descendant of Ious-keha, the victor.[34]

Religious beliefs of the Hurons were a subject of paramount interest to the missionaries. Jean de Brébeuf, an astute student of that phase of Huron life, felt that these aborigines retained at least a rudimentary knowledge of a supreme being, but they rarely paid him any noteworthy honor or service.[35] For the Huron, everything visible, sky, earth, water, trees, plants, rocks, and animals, was inhabited by a spirit which could be offended and must, therefore, be constantly propitiated.[36] Every Huron owned a personal amulet, the dwelling place of his own individual guiding spirit. These spirits manifested themselves to their owners in dreams, directing the lives of individuals. Each one was obligated to obey these supposed instructions, no matter how preposterous they might seem to be.[37]

Superstitions of this character were fostered by the shamans whom the missionaries called sorcerers or jugglers. Those functionaries claimed the ability to cast spells, predict the future, control the weather, and determine the cause of illnesses as well as cures for them. Though whatever efficacy these charlatans exercised may be attributed to the credulity of the Indians, sorcerers did, at times, produce effects or accurately predict the future in a manner unexplained by purely natural causes.[38] In spite of these adumbrations, the Hurons, in times of grave danger, invoked a superior being.[39]

The Huron life cycle manifested a striking nexus to the tribal religious practices. Children were the most prized possession of the nation since, potentially, they were the support of the elderly in their declining years and the defenders of the country in time of war. More rejoicing met the birth of a girl than a boy because on the women depended the ". . . multiplication of the country's inhabitants."[40] During infancy, babies were wrapped in skins

---

[34] Ibid., X, 127-31.
[35] Ibid., VII, 117.
[36] Ibid., VIII, 117.
[37] Ibid., X, 169-73.
[38] Ibid., XXXIII, 193.
[39] Ibid., 225, 227.
[40] Ibid., XVI, 183.

filled with reed down or powder scraped from rotting wood. Strapped to a cradleboard, the infant was carried on the mother's back or kept by, propped against a convenient post or tree. When able to walk, the child played, completely unclothed, in the cabin or out-of-doors, no matter what the weather. In time, little girls began emulating their mothers in the household tasks. Small boys played with miniature bows and arrows. When older, boys were gradually trained in the essential skills of hunting, handling a canoe, stalking the enemy, and the elements of aboriginal warfare.

On attaining marriageable age, both young men and young women were free to select a mate of their own choice. However, it was observed that people never married ". . . anyone related in any degree whatever, either direct or collateral, but always made new alliances, which is not a little helpful in maintaining friendship."[41] Theoretically, Hurons practiced monogamy, but divorce was frequent, indulged in by both husbands and wives, and for the most capricious of reasons.[42] Sexual promiscuity among the young, as well as those already married, carried no stigma for either participant. For that reason, perhaps, the captain's nephew, child of his sister, ordinarily succeeded him rather than his recognized son. Inferentially, every Indian child knew for certain which woman was his own mother, but there appeared to be some question as to which man was his father. Once a couple became parents, the marriage seemed to assume greater stability, though the presence of children was no guarantee that one spouse might not divorce the other. A major stumbling block to the Christianization of the Hurons was the ideal of monogamy. As one of the Hurons put it: "If we take a wife, at the first whim that seizes her, she will at once leave us; and then we are reduced to a wretched life, seeing that it is the women in our country who sow, plant, and cultivate the land and prepare food for their husbands."[43] If the opinions of the Huron women had been recorded also, they would, undoubtedly, have complained as bitterly about the fickle character of the Huron braves.

Together with most aborigines, the Hurons measured time, years, months, and days by observing the phases of the moon.

[41] Ibid., X, 213.
[42] Ibid., VIII, 119, 121.
[43] Ibid., XIV, 235.

Undoubtedly they adopted that system because the moon waxes and wanes visibly while the sun does not.[44] In actual practice, the lives of the Hurons could be said to have been governed by ". . . wild beasts, the fish, the birds, and the vegetation."[45] In spring and summer large numbers of the braves were off on trading expeditions. The women, during that time, busied themselves planting and cultivating the crops. Toward the fall, fishing and hunting kept everyone occupied. Only during the late fall and winter were the Hurons generally all gathered into their villages. Confined to their cabins by cold weather, the Indians were free to listen to missionaries explaining the tenets of Christianity. At their leisure, the Hurons loved carrying on long discussions and the missionaries offered them a subject for endless debate both with the French priests and among themselves.

Though a sedentary folk, the Hurons had long since perceived the hygienic necessity of moving the location of their villages approximately every twelve years. In the absence of any system of sewage disposal, the soil in and immediately surrounding Indian dwellings eventually became so contaminated that it provided an excellent breeding ground for pernicious germs. With passing years, refuse heaps spilled over into adjacent streams, polluting the drinking water. Supplies of wood at convenient distances slowly disappeared, obliging the women to go farther and farther afield for firewood. Also, Indians, completely ignorant of the necessity of enriching the soil of their fields, found that about every decade or so crop yields became less and less bountiful. Eventually, villagers vacated old sites for new and cleaner areas. Moving was not the monumental task one might expect. The Huron cabin was, in a true sense, a prefabricated home. Once the bark walls were removed, the framework was easily taken apart and just as easily assembled at a new location. The major labor consisted of clearing new fields of underbrush and preparing them for cultivation. If the transfer occurred before the great Feast of the Dead, probably the most painful task was the dismantling of the village cemetery and its reestablishment.

---

[44] Ibid., XV, 157. The Hurons believed that an eclipse was caused by the great turtle who upheld the earth. When he changed his position he brought his shell before the sun. See ibid., XII, 73.

[45] Ibid.

At the approach of death, the Huron was expected to face his demise bravely and with equanimity. Frequently the dying made farewell feasts, inviting all their friends. At the celebration the moribund sang his farewell song, recounting the deeds of bravery performed during his lifetime, without manifesting any fear of death.[46] As soon as the dying man expired, the body was placed ". . . in a crouching position, almost the same that a child has in its mother's womb."[47] Then the corpse was bound snugly in the finest robes available and placed on a mat where it remained, constantly attended, until the time of burial. Friends from neighboring villages were invited to a mourning feast at which the women continually wailed, groaned, and sighed.[48] After three days of mourning and feasting, the body was carried to the cemetery and placed on a scaffold, eight to ten feet high. Placing the corpse on this tomb, the whole was covered with a bark roof, protecting it from birds and marauding beasts. There it remained until the whole clan, including all of its villages, celebrated the great Feast of the Dead.

In his *Relation* of 1636, Jean de Brébeuf remarked: "Our savages are not savages as regard the duties that Nature itself constrains us to render to the dead; they do not yield in this respect to many nations much more civilized."[49] Besides the respect offered the dead immediately at the demise, the Hurons, at intervals of approximately twelve years, celebrated their most renowned Feast of the Dead which the Hurons themselves called "the Kettle." In preparation for the feast, all the old men and notables of the country assembled to decide when and where the feast would be held as well as what "foreign nations" should be extended an invitation. Then a great captain of the feast, really a master of ceremonies, was chosen. In turn, each village within the nation appointed a captain responsible for preparing the dead of the village for interment in the nation's common grave.

In good time, the members of each village repaired to their cemetery whence they removed their dead. The remains of the

---

[46] Ibid., X, 61; XV, 67.

[47] Ibid., X, 227.

[48] Ibid. The audible mourning of the women could be turned off and on by command.

[49] Ibid., 265.

dead buried longest were nothing but skeletons. Those recently buried remained fairly intact or only partially corrupted. All of the bodies, no matter what the condition of each, were brought to the village where each family stripped the flesh off the bones and wrapped them in new, rich, animal skins.[50] Of course, weeping and mourning by the women accompanied that operation. When all was properly prepared, the whole village marched in solemn, lugubrious procession to the place where all the dead were to be buried in a common grave. Along with them the villagers brought the richest gifts they could manage, valuable beaver robes, porcelain collars, kettles, bows, arrows, and other weapons.[51] Since the presents constituted a sign of respect for the dead, no village wanted to be outdone by another. Arrived at the site of the common burial, people opened the parcels containing the remains of their dead to pay them final homage.

The common grave, a large circular pit surrounded by high scaffolding, had already been lined with animal peltry overlapping some distance beyond the edge of the pit. Each village brought its dead so that the packages could be suspended from the scaffold. The more recently deceased were deposited on the floor of the pit. In the very middle of the floor of the pit were placed three large kettles, supposedly containing food for the souls on their journey to the distant village in the west where they rested and found constant enjoyment.[52] During the rest of that afternoon and evening all the Indians remained at the pit mourning their dead. Early the next morning, all the bones attached to the scaffolding were hurled, helter-skelter, into the pit while several agile young men within it kept leveling off the piles of bones poured down upon them.[53] That operation signaled the

[50] Bodies of the most recently dead were left intact.

[51] Ibid., 289.

[52] Ibid., 297.

[53] The most complete description of the Feast of the Dead comes from the pen of Father Brébeuf who attended one in May 1636. His account may be consulted in *Relations*, X, 279-317. In 1947, Kenneth E. Kidd evacuated the very ossuary Brébeuf saw filled three hundred eleven years before. See Kidd's most enlightening article about the evacuation, "The Evacuation and Historical Identification of a Huron Ossuary," in *American Antiquity* XVIII (1953), 359-79. Kidd located the site of the ossuary as on lot 7, concession XIV, Tiny township, Simcoe county, Ontario. The site is just a little west of the western edge of Penetanguishene, Ontario.

closing of the period of mourning and the inception of universal feasting.

As for the presents brought by each group of villagers, only a
few of them were consigned to the common grave and, of those,
the least valuable ended under the dirt covering the great ossuary. The rest, gathered in a great heap before the master of the
feast, were parceled out to the living in a manner wholly incon-
sonant with the somber atmosphere of the crowd moments before.
All scrambled for a part of the loot, squabbling over beaver pelts,
axes, and the like.[54] Brébeuf, who witnessed the Feast of the
Dead in 1636, relates how one shrewd Indian, instead of scram-
bling with everyone for a share in the prizes, stood aside with a
supply of tobacco available. With this precious commodity, he
bartered with those who scrambled with the rest of the mob
for prizes.[55]

The whole elaborate ceremony was far from absurd, as it
might seem to us. The occasion presented the Huron leaders an
excellent opportunity to recall to their people the brave deeds of
now departed great men. The feast also offered occasion for heal-
ing old wounds between villages, contending families, and even
individuals. One could not well continue a grudge when the bones
of his family, his leaders, and his rivals lay in a common grave.
Besides, foreign nations, who came by invitation, were not only
allowed, but encouraged to mingle the bones of their dead with
those of the Hurons. Indians considered the invitation a great
mark of respect as well as an effective means of welding alliances
for the always precarious future.

By and large then, the Hurons were an orderly, reasonably
prosperous people. Constant in their loyalties, even to the French,
they were implacable foes of traditional enemies. Daring and bru-
tal in war, they were as much a scourge of other nations as the
Iroquois became for the Hurons.[56] Receptive in the beginning to
Christianity, they soon saw that what the missionaries preached
was a revolution, upsetting their traditional life-style. One can
hardly blame them for finding it difficult to accept such a violent

[54] *Relations*, X, 301.

[55] Ibid.

[56] Hunt, *Wars of the Iroquois*, 73. Previous to about 1640, the Hurons not
only had no fear of the Iroquois but they were actually contemptuous of them.

change with equanimity. Had not natural disaster intervened in the early years of Brébeuf's apostolate, large numbers of at least some of the four Huron clans would have accepted the teachings of the missionaries. But epidemics, bad example of French traders, greed of the European layman, and the highly organized Five Nations ended the missionary effort just when there seemed to exist sound hope of phenomenal success for Jean de Brébeuf and his dedicated cohorts.

Chapter III

New France

The malicious banishment of the French Jesuits from their nascent mission in the New World by the Virginia freebooters grieved the heart of many a Gallic follower of St. Ignatius. Late in the sixteenth century, at the conclusion of the disruptive Wars of Religion, hosts of zealous clerics dedicated themselves to the conversion of the Huguenots, the revitalizing of the faith among French Catholics, and to an interest in spreading the gospel to pagans sitting in darkness beyond the seas. In the forefront of the campaign in France, French Jesuits found no occasion to labor abroad chiefly because France could lay claim to only a part of North America, one which as yet remained barely exploited by subjects of the French crown. While platoons of Spanish and Portuguese Jesuits sent home glowing accounts of innumerable conversions in India and the New World, French Jesuits, piously jealous, were told by their general, on applying for permission to join the missionaries overseas, that France was their India.[1] Just

[1] Campeau, 4. Aquaviva to Biard, July 15, 1602.

as the mission-minded French Jesuit looked on the foundation at Port Royal as a heaven-sent opportunity, so its untimely closing was, they hoped, only a temporary delay. Surely, the returned "exiles" would find a way to go back, taking with them troops of eager followers.

Reaching France, the expelled Jesuits enthusiastically broadcast the story of their experiences. Pierre Biard wrote his lengthy *Relation de la Nouvelle-France* recounting, in depth, the rich apostolic opportunity offered for converting the aborigines.[2] Jacques Quentin, assigned to the Jesuit college at Charleville, acquainted the Jesuits of central France about the marvelous mission which needed only sufficient laborers to reap an untold harvest. The "exiled" missionary destined to wield the most telling influence with his brethren was Enemond Massé. Reaching Paris in October 1613, Massé was sent, in 1614, to the Jesuit college at La Flèche, where large numbers of young Jesuits pursued their ecclesiastical studies. Undoubtedly, those students listened enthralled to Father Massé's account of his experiences much as people today did to the first man who walked on the surface of the moon. Some of the young men were so enamored of the prospect of a missionary career in New France that they began a crusade of prayer storming heaven for the favor of allowing the Jesuits to return to Canada.[3] Though opening another mission on the shores of the Atlantic seemed unwise, considering the danger from piratical Englishmen, Samuel de Champlain had founded a little settlement far inland, hundreds of miles up the St. Lawrence. As early as 1608 he had besought the French Jesuits to send missionaries to his infant colony.[4] That invitation was declined, with regrets, because Jesuits had already been committed

[2] Biard's *Relation* was published at Lyons by Louis Muguet in 1616 while its author was at Embrun filling the office of preacher. The little book was replete with typographical errors as well as omissions. Thwaites reproduced the text in *Relations*, III, 27-283; IV, 9-165. A much more scholarly edition of the work appears in Campeau, 456-637.

[3] Some of these were Paul Le Jeune, Charles Lalemant, Barthélemy Vimont, Jacques Buteux, Paul Ragueneau, and Anne de Noüe. All were missionaries in New France. Buteux and De Noüe both died there.

[4] Morris Bishop, *Champlain: The Life of Fortitude*, 183. In 1610 Champlain set aside 3,600 *livres* for the support of Jesuit missionaries, but they had already agreed, in 1608, to go to Port Royal.

to the settlement at Port Royal. Now it was rumored that Champlain was again seeking evangelical laborers. Perhaps God would hear the fervent prayers of those zealous young men at La Flèche and enlighten superiors to accept the new post if it should be again offered.

The pious hopes of those young zealots were dashed when it was learned that Champlain had offered the mission field to the Recollets, Franciscans of the Province of St. Denis. Even more disappointing was the fact that the Recollets received exclusive responsibility for all missionary endeavor in the whole of New France.[5] Pierre du Gua, sieur de Monts, whose Company of Merchants enjoyed a monopoly of the fur trade in New France, contracted to support the Recollets and the clergy of France, attending the Estates General in 1614, subscribed 1,500 *livres* toward furthering the work of the Recollets at Quebec.[6] On April 24, 1615, four zealous Recollets, Fathers Denis Jamet, Jean Dolbeau, and Joseph Le Caron, with Brother Pacifique du Plessis, sailed from Honfleur aboard the *Saint Etienne* with Samuel de Champlain. Arriving at Tadoussac on May 25, the little apostolic band reached Quebec on June 2, ready and eager to launch their work of evangelization.[7]

At Quebec, the Recollets realized the immensity of the apostolic field they had before them. The country of Canada was vast beyond imagining and the numbers of aboriginal tribes, each, apparently, speaking its own language, unlike another, compelled the missionaries to outline a plan of campaign. Father Jamet, the superior, with Brother du Plessis, would reside at Quebec, ministering to the French and such Indians as dwelt in the neighborhood. Father Dolbeau chose to evangelize the Montagnais, a tribe of nomads whose language he hoped to learn. On December 2, 1615, Dolbeau accompanied some Montagnais on their wandering winter hunt. But, after two months, the acrid smoke abounding in their rude shelters so affected his eyesight that he was

---

[5] Gabriel-Theodat Sagard, *Histoire du Canada*, I, 32-35. Sagard's *Long Journey* was published at Paris in 1632. Four years later, in 1636, he issued his *Histoire du Canada*, a four-volume work. The second work is an elaboration of the first. Subsequently, Sagard's second book is referred to as *Histoire.*

[6] Christian Le Clercq, *First Establishment of the Faith in New France*, I, 63.

[7] Sagard, *Histoire*, I, 36-37.

forced to return to Quebec. Excusing Dolbeau, Brother Gabriel-Theodat Sagard wrote: ". . . our Lord did not require him to go blind, but to exercise a prudent care of his health, which is vital in such a vast field of labor."[8]

More impetuous than the others, Father Joseph Le Caron hardly paused at Quebec before he was on his way with Father Jamet to meet the Indians coming to the trade fair held at Cap de la Victoire at the mouth of the Richelieu River. After celebrating Mass on Thursday, June 25, Le Caron met the Hurons present and was so taken with them that he hastened back to Quebec to procure requisite supplies so that he could return with the Hurons to their own country.[9] Though Champlain considered Le Caron's desire imprudent and ill-considered, the Recollet was allowed to have his way, perhaps mainly because Champlain himself planned to visit the Huron country that year, fulfilling a promise made in 1613 that he would come with a powerful force to help the Hurons defeat their enemies, the Iroquois. Shortly before July 9, 1615, Le Caron was off with the departing Hurons, accompanied by twelve well-armed Frenchmen. The troops were not so much a bodyguard for the priest as they were simply the advanced contingent of men composing Champlain's military force, the rest of whom would come up with Champlain himself.

Arriving among the Hurons, his hosts brought Father Le Caron to their village of Carhagouha on the western shore of Lake Simcoe, where he was made exceedingly welcome.[10] When the Hurons offered him space in whatever cabin he might choose, the priest ". . . represented to them that he had to negotiate with God affairs so important, involving the salvation of their whole nation, that they deserved to be treated with more respect, in solitude and retreat, far from the tumult and trouble of their families. They hearkened to his remonstrance, [and] with poles and bark built him a cabin apart from the village. Here he raised an altar to offer God the holy sacrifice of the Mass and perform his spiritual exercises. In these places the Indians went to visit

---

[8] Ibid., 39-40.

[9] Le Clercq, *First Establishment*, I, 87.

[10] Arthur E. Jones, *8endake Ehen; or Old Huronia*, 45. He locates the site of this village as lot 20, concession XVII, Tiny township, Simcoe county, Ontario. This work is henceforth cited as Jones.

him to be instructed in the mysteries of Christianity and learn of him how to pray to God."[11] When Champlain arrived, on about August 1, he found the Recollet happily ensconced in his own cabin and hard at work striving to master the intricacies of the Huron tongue.[12]

For all his apparent impetuosity, Father Joseph Le Caron was not deluded by false hopes of what he might accomplish on this first visit which was, after all, a preliminary survey of the situation. During his stay of nearly a year in the interior he went on to the Petuns, but they received him coldly. When the time came for the Hurons to go down for their annual bartering, Le Caron accompanied them, reporting to his superior that ". . . all he was able to accomplish in this first voyage was merely to acquire a knowledge of the ways and doings of this people, to learn their language passably well, and dispose them to accept a more decent and civilized mode of living."[13] To have effected even that much required no small labor. The missionary brought back with him the beginnings of a Huron dictionary which became the cornerstone of all future efforts to acquire that tongue. After Le Caron's return to Quebec, paucity of personnel compelled the Recollets to confine their activities to Quebec and Tadoussac until 1623 when additional man power enabled them to resume the effort among the Hurons.

Though the devoted Recollet missionaries could not immediately continue their effort among the Hurons in their home country, these sons of St. Francis laid long-ranged plans for the evangelization of the aborigines of New France. Several times one or other of them risked the long, dangerous sea voyage to France in order to petition the crown, as well as the king's viceroy of New France and merchants holding the monopoly of trade, for practical aid in their work. At Quebec the Recollets set about, with the assistance of imported craftsmen, building a substantial convent on the St. Charles River in which they hoped to house an adequate number of fellow missionaries together with a novitiate

[11] Le Clercq, *First Establishment*, I, 97-98.

[12] Bishop, *Champlain*, 189. Instead of the expected large, well-armed force, Champlain arrived in the company of ten Huron Indians and only two Frenchmen, Etienne Brûlé and Thomas Godefroy.

[13] Sagard, *Histoire*, I, 42.

and a school for Indian children. Describing the sturdy convent, Father Jamet wrote: ". . . it is thirty-four feet long and twenty-two wide. It has two floors. We divided the lower floor into two rooms. One is our chapel . . . the other . . . serves for our kitchen and the quarters for our workmen. On the second floor we made one large room and four small ones . . . the walls are stone . . . beneath is a basement twenty feet square and seven feet deep."[14] Clearing the land adjacent to their convent, the priests planted crops which they hoped would eventually furnish foodstuffs. They also imported geese, ducks, chickens, pigs, and, in 1623, a pair of donkeys. When the Indians first heard the donkeys bray, they fled in terror, ". . . without anyone looking back to defend himself from these demons."[15]

When the ships from France arrived at Quebec, on June 28, 1623, there were on board two new Recollet apostles to swell the missionary ranks. These were Father Nicolas Viel and Brother Gabriel-Theodat Sagard, the first true historian of New France. Only eighteen days after their arrival they, together with the experienced Father Joseph Le Caron, went up to Cap de la Victoire, at the mouth of the Richelieu River, fully prepared to accompany the Hurons back to Huronia. Arranging passage with the Hurons, each missionary in a separate canoe, they departed on August 2, 1623, and reached the Huron country on August 20.[16]

Of that harrowing journey, made by so many Jesuits after him, Sagard wrote:

In order to practice patience in good earnest and to endure hardship beyond the limit of human strength, it is only necessary to make a journey with the Indians, and long ones especially, such as we did; because besides the danger of death on the way, one must make up one's mind to endure suffering more than could be imagined from hunger, from the stench that these dirty, disagreeable fellows emit almost constantly in their canoe, which is enough to disgust one utterly with such unpleasant companions, from sleeping always on the bare ground in open country, from walking with

---

[14] Odoric-Marie Jouve, *Les Franciscains et le Canada: l'établissement de la foi, 1615-1629*, 157. The convent was called Notre Dame des Anges in honor of the first little chapel St. Francis had at Assisi. That chapel was called Our Lady of the Angels.

[15] Sagard, *Histoire*, III, 676.

[16] Thirteen French laymen were in the party, but not as a bodyguard for the missionaries. They had come to trade with the Hurons in their homeland.

great labor in water and bogs and in some places over rocks, and through dark, thick woods, from rain on one's back and all the evils that the season and weather can inflict, and from being bitten by a countless swarm of mosquitoes and midges, together with difficulties of language in explaining clearly and showing one's needs, and having no Christian beside one for communication and consolation in the midst of one's toil.[17]

Reaching Huronia, the three missionaries, after a brief period of separation, settled at Carhagouha among the Hurons of the Bear clan who built them a cabin.[18] Besides attempting to teach the truths of Christianity to the Hurons, Father Le Caron profited by the friendliness of the Indians to perfect his dictionary and make something of a start at a Huron grammar. In May 1624, when the trading season came, Le Caron and Brother Sagard accompanied the Huron trading fleet, expecting to obtain needed supplies and return when the trading was completed.[19] Father Viel, however, remained in the Huron country to continue the mission, believing that, come fall, his companions would return.

At their convent of Notre Dame des Anges near Quebec, the Recollets were facing an impasse. The vast extent of the apostolic field, for which they alone had responsibility, was, quite clearly, beyond their physical capacity. They were so few in number, even in France, that they could not hope to staff adequately such an extensive mission, certainly not within the foreseeable future. Further, despite generous promises of financial support by the company holding the monopoly of trade, only the barest necessities were supplied to the missionaries. Even worse, except perhaps for Champlain himself, employees of the company in New France resented the presence of missionaries. Interpreters having a smattering of the native languages flatly refused to teach the Recollets what they knew. Traders threatened reprisals if the missionaries made efforts to render the Indians sedentary, fearing that such a change in the Indian manner of life would reduce the fur harvests.[20] Frustrated from nearly every side, the Recollets determined, in the summer of 1624, to seek the cooperation of some other religious order with resources, man power, and influ-

---

[17] Sagard, *Long Journey*, 57-58.
[18] Ibid., 76-78.
[19] Ibid., 244.
[20] Sagard, *Histoire*, I, 165.

ence sufficiently powerful to offer effective help in the conversion of the Indians of New France. Father Irénée Piat, in New France since May 15, 1622, received orders to return home to petition aid from the crown as well as authority to invite, officially, the Jesuits to send missionaries.[21]

Irénée Piat reached Paris at a propitious moment. Henri, duc de Montmorency, admiral of France and viceroy of New France since 1619, was only too ready to be relieved of a responsibility which, he said, ". . . proved more troublesome than [the duties] of admiral of old France."[22] In January 1625 Henri de Levis, duc de Ventadour, purchased the viceregal office from his uncle for 100,000 *livres*. A solidly pious young man of twenty-nine, Ventadour sincerely desired the conversion of the aborigines. He was urged by his spiritual director, Father Philibert Noyrot, a Jesuit, to obtain the position in which much could be done to further missionary work.[23] If we accept a contemporary account, Noyrot, by mere chance, called on the Duc de Ventadour at the very moment Piat was petitioning the viceroy's permission to invite the Jesuits to cooperate with the Recollets in New France.[24] Informed of the request, Noyrot, with characteristic impetuosity, accepted in the name of Father Pierre Coton, provincial of the Jesuit Province of France, to which Noyrot did not even belong.

Fortunately, Pierre Coton had enthusiastically supported the mission effort of the Jesuits in the New World ever since Biard and Massé went to Port Royal in 1611. From an ample list of volunteers, the provincial chose five Jesuits who were directed to depart for Quebec at the first opportunity. Father Enemond Massé, despite his fifty years of age, received permission to go because of

[21] Le Clercq, *First Establishment,* I, 226.

[22] Henry P. Biggar, *The Early Trading Companies of New France,* 125.

[23] Philibert Noyrot was born near Autun in October 1592. He entered the Jesuit novitiate at Paris on October 16, 1617, and was very nearly dismissed soon thereafter because of a very hampering speech defect which he never overcame. He came to Quebec in July 1626 with twenty workmen hired to build a residence for the Jesuits. He was sent back to France that same summer so that he could use his influence there for the good of the mission and the colony. In 1629, Noyrot sailed for Quebec aboard a ship he had chartered and provisioned with funds he collected. The ship sank in a violent storm off Cape Breton Island. Noyrot and fourteen members of the crew were drowned, including two of his nephews.

[24] Sagard, *Histoire,* III, 784.

his previous experience. Father Charles Lalemant, aged thirty-eight, a Parisian born and bred, was named superior. His interest in the missions of New France reached back to his days as a student of theology at La Flèche, 1615-1619, where he and a group of like-minded students launched a crusade of prayer begging God for the grace of spending their days converting the aborigines of New France. Of the two brothers accompanying the priests, François Charton and Gilbert Burel, nothing is known. The youngest of the priests, certainly physically the strongest but least experienced, was Jean de Brébeuf. Then thirty-two, Brébeuf had been a Jesuit a bare eight years. Perhaps the only quality recommending him at that time was his great strength of body and docility of manner. Only later would his companions come to realize his value.

The departing missionaries were given little time to collect the requisite equipment for the new mission, including food supplies in sufficient quantity to last for at least a year. Forgathering at Dieppe, the five Jesuits took up residence at the order's small house on the rue Buffalo where they waited to take ship with Guillaume de Caën, stockholder and "general of the ships" of the monopolistic Company of De Caën, which controlled the fur trade in Canada. After packing their numerous supplies as securely as possible in boxes and bales, the Jesuits delivered their mountain of baggage to the dock and then waited with what patience they could muster until De Caën's ship was ready for sea. At last, on Thursday, April 24, the feast of St. Fidelis, a martyr, De Caën's ship upped sail, leaving the chalk cliffs of Dieppe behind. No precise account of that crossing survives, except that Charles Lalemant, writing a note of thanks to Samuel de Champlain, who remained in France that particular year, said: ". . . we arrived after having one of the most successful voyages ever yet experienced."[25]

The almost eight weeks aboard ship was surely used profitably because of the presence on board of a young Montagnais, Pastedechouan by name, whom the Recollets had brought to France in 1620. Petted and pampered by his godfather, the Prince de Guemenée, a relative of the powerful De Rohan family, the youngster

[25] *Relations*, IV, 171.

had been baptized and named Pierre Antoine. A bright lad, he had adapted to European ways so well, even to speaking French, that he had forgotten his native tongue.[26] During the long weeks of the ocean crossing, the young Indian must have wearied of answering the thousands of questions put to him by the eager Jesuits who had yet to meet a group of Indians. Also aboard was the Recollet, Father Joseph de la Roche Daillon, son of a nobleman from Anjou, who, like the Jesuits, was going to the New World for the first time. With such interesting company and excellent sailing weather, no wonder time passed quickly.

After weeks of breasting Atlantic rollers, the ship bearing the Jesuits rounded the great island of Newfoundland and began coasting along the northern shore of the Gulf of St. Lawrence. At their first sight of the Canadian mainland with its stark, rocky coast and its dark, brooding forests, they might well have agreed with Jacques Cartier, who found the country so forbidding that he called it the land God bequeathed to Cain as a punishment for killing his brother Abel. Then it was that the band of Jesuits first really understood the vastness of New France. They sailed over a thousand miles up the St. Lawrence before reaching the first French outpost, Tadoussac, where traders had long since established business relations with the Indians of eastern Canada.

Certainly Tadoussac was the most picturesque location for the arriving Jesuits to make their first contact with the aborigines whom they hoped to civilize and Christianize. The torrential Saguenay roars out of a towering, brooding chasm gouged out of nearly jet-black granite, meeting the St. Lawrence at the foot of a steep precipice at whose base there is a bare shingle of shore, hardly wide enough to furnish space for a ship landing. On that barren, narrow beach, or perhaps on the uneven plain high above it, the Recollets had, in 1617, erected a rude little chapel where they cared for the religious needs of the visiting French traders

---

[26] Sagard, *Histoire*, III, 785-86. Pastedechouan came to a sad end. Returning to New France in the summer of 1625, the boy was sent back, much against his will, to live with his tribe so that he would relearn Montagnais and influence his people to accept Christianity. The boy begged Father Le Caron, the Recollet superior, not to require him to return to ". . . those beasts who did not even know God." Ibid., 786. By 1632, the Indian had so reverted to his native customs that he rejected any vestige of Christianity. In 1636 he died of starvation alone in the woods.

and sought to evangelize the Indians who were attending the annual trade fair.[27]

Pushing another three hundred miles up the St. Lawrence in a small barque, the Jesuits gratefully watched the mountains recede in favor of wide, fertile, rolling alluvial plains, thickly forested with hardwoods, reminding them, or at least Brébeuf, surely, of French Normandy. Finally their craft skirted the lovely Ile d'Orléans, swept past the impressive Montmorency Falls and came to rest, on June 19, 1625, in the roadstead under the massive granite promontory brooding protectively over the minute settlement at Quebec.[28] There the Jesuits were welcomed ". . . by the winterers (the name by which the *habitans* of Quebec are known) with joy and courtesy . . ."[29]

But where were the new arrivals to live? Since the whole matter of their coming had been hastily arranged in the early months of 1625 and news of it could not possibly have reached Quebec ahead of their arrival, no quarters had been prepared. Emery de Caën, left in charge of Quebec since Champlain's departure in August 1624, had no authority from the company officials permitting the Jesuits to enter the colony. Besides, where could these missionaries be housed? Most of the fifty-two people at Quebec were crowded into the building erected by Champlain in 1608. That structure was in such bad condition that, before leaving for France in 1624, Champlain had ordered it torn down and a new one erected. But nothing had been done about that. Fort St. Louis, built by Champlain on the brow of the majestic promontory overlooking the St. Lawrence at Quebec, was in such bad repair that it was hardly even a hovel.

Since the summer months were entirely dedicated to trading, on which the very life of the settlement depended, men could not be spared to throw up any sort of shelter for the Jesuits. There-

---

[27] Ibid., I, 27.

[28] The exact date of Brébeuf's arrival at Quebec does not seem to have been recorded in any contemporary document. Félix Martin, in his *Hurons et Iroquois: le P. Jean de Brébeuf: sa vie, ses travaux, son martyre*, 24, gives the date as June 19. Francis X. Talbot, in his *Saint among the Hurons*, 35, gives the date as Sunday, June 15. He apparently accepted the date given by Rochemonteix, I, 153, who gives the date as June 15. René Latourelle, in his *Etude sur les écrits de Saint Jean de Brébeuf*, I, 23, dates Brébeuf's arrival as June 19.

[29] Sagard, *Histoire*, III, 787.

fore, the commandant, De Caën, advised that unless the Recollets would house the Jesuits, at least temporarily, the newly arrived missionaries must return to France.[30] Learning of the difficulty, the Recollets generously offered the Jesuits hospitality, assigning them a full half of their small convent which was hardly large enough to house their own few people. With true gratitude, the Jesuits accepted.

Settling in with the Recollets, Father Lalemant and his four companions were anxious to begin active apostolic work. But, since they were invited guests, not only in the Recollet convent but also in New France itself, the Jesuits sought the advice of their hosts. How should this vast mission field be divided between the two groups and what had the Recollets learned regarding methods of converting Indians? From their years of experience, the sons of St. Francis had devised a simple program. They established permanent mission stations at Tadoussac and Cap de la Victoire, the centers frequented in large numbers by the Indians each summer. During the trade fairs the missionaries sought to make friends, imparting to the aborigines at least some vague notion of the purpose the strange Frenchmen in the gray habits and sandaled feet had in coming among them. When Indian bands drifted off, at the conclusion of the trading, a Recollet missionary accompanied one or other group, hoping thus to learn a native tongue and acquire a more intimate knowledge of that band. At various times the Hurons had been visited for periods of a year or more.

Scarcely two weeks after the landing of the Jesuits an opportunity to venture to the homeland of the Hurons was presented. Father Joseph de la Roche Daillon, though only a newcomer, expected to go forthwith to Huronia to reside with Father Nicolas

[30] Emery de Caën's reputation has suffered greatly at the hands of nineteenth-century historians who assumed that he was a bigoted Calvinist. See Joseph Le Ber, editor, "Documents inédits," *Revue d'Histoire de l'Amerique française* III (1949-1950), 587-94. Emery de Caën was a lifelong Catholic. Lalemant and his companions, far from criticizing De Caën, spoke kindly of him. In his note of thanks to Champlain, written soon after his arrival at Quebec, Lalemant said: "Monsieur the General [Emery de Caën] after telling us that it was impossible to give us lodging either in the settlement or in the fort, and that we must either return to France or withdraw to the Recollet Fathers constrained us to accept the latter offer." *Relations,* IV, 171.

Viel. It was expected that when the Hurons came down for the summer trading Viel would accompany them to obtain supplies and Daillon could go back with him. Since, in the opinion of the Recollets, the Hurons appeared most receptive to Christianity, Father Charles Lalemant appointed Jean de Brébeuf to begin his apostolic work with that nation, accompanying the Recollets when they went off with the returning Huron fur brigade.[31]

Preparing for an extended stay with an Indian nation involved, for a missionary, far more than taking along an adequate supply of Mass wine and altar breads. The Indians were hospitable enough to passing guests, but rightly expected permanent residents among them to supply their own needs through personal effort or by purchase. Thus, besides a Mass kit containing vestments and sacred utensils, Father Brébeuf laid in a supply of hatchets, knives, iron kettles, needles, gaudy beads, ribbons, and other trinkets to use in trade for food or as a reward for services rendered him by the Indians. Laden with that unwieldy baggage, acquired mostly at Cap de la Victoire, Brébeuf and his Recollet companion were prepared to undertake the long journey to Huronia.[32]

When the colorful flotilla swept up to the beach at Cap de la Victoire, Father Viel was not in any of the canoes. Hesitantly, the Hurons revealed that the Recollet, together with a young Huron Christian, had drowned when their canoe overturned at the last rapid above Montreal, ". . . the deep and rapid waters of which engulfed them in a moment."[33] Searching questions put to the Indians by the French gave them reason to suspect that the disaster was no accident. Not only had everyone else in the canoe escaped drowning, but the Indians in it saved Viel's equipment, dividing it among themselves.[34] If it was true, as rumored, that ". . . three wicked and impious Indians . . . hurled him [Viel] into the water with his little disciple,"[35] the missionary's death required severe

[31] Ibid., 177, 179. Lalemant to the Jesuit general, Vitelleschi, August 1, [1626]. No year is given, but from the letter's contents it was written in 1626.

[32] Sagard, *Histoire*, III, 794.

[33] Le Clercq, *First Establishment*, I, 245.

[34] Pierre François Xavier de Charlevoix, *The History and General Description of New France*, translated and edited by John Gilmary Shea, II, 37. Hereafter, Charlevoix's work is cited as Charlevoix.

[35] Le Clercq, *First Establishment*, II, 245.

treatment by the French. But, with Champlain absent in Europe, it seemed best to defer action for the moment. However, ". . . there was not a soul [among the French] . . . who was not of a mind that Fathers Daillon and De Brébeuf should put off for a time their journey [to the Huron country]."[36] There was nothing for it but to return to Quebec and wait for a more auspicious occasion, perhaps next year, when the Huron trading fleet returned.

At Quebec, the most pressing problem for the Jesuits was housing. The gracious Recollets must not be inconvenienced a moment longer than necessary. After consulting with the French, Father Lalemant selected a stretch of level ground on the north side of the St. Charles River, roughly opposite the Recollet convent, on which to erect a home for the Jesuits. On September 1, 1625, Lalemant invited all the French to attend a ceremony marking the beginning of the Jesuit effort at Quebec. On that day, as Lalemant later wrote to his brother, Jerome,

. . . we planted the holy cross . . . with all possible solemnity upon the place we had chosen. The Reverend Recollet Fathers took part in the ceremony with the most prominent of the French, and after dinner all of them went to work. We have continued this work ever since, we five, uprooting trees and breaking the ground whenever we had time. The snow intervened and we were compelled to give up our work until spring.[37]

It can be readily conjectured that Jean de Brébeuf's patience and charity were sorely tried during the weeks of that fall. A farmer's son, certainly handy with an axe, he must have often clamped his teeth over his tongue as Charles Lalemant, city bred, a lawyer's son, and Enemond Massé, son of a Lyons baker, wrestled ineptly at grubbing out stumps, felling trees, and hacking away at age-old underbrush. When the hard winter came and the traders had nothing to do, Emery de Caën generously lent the Jesuits every able-bodied man who was willing to help build their home. With their aid, at the end of Lent in 1626, the cabin was

[36] Charlevoix, II, 37.

[37] *Relations*, IV, 209. The St. Charles River appears to have received its name from Charles des Boues, a benefactor of the Recollets. Locating the first residence of the Jesuits on Canadian soil, Morris Bishop, in his excellent biography of Champlain, says: "It stood just to the east of the St. Charles, between the small streams of Lairet and St. Michel. The motorist crossing the Dorchester Street Bridge faintly troubles its shades." Bishop, *Champlain*, 259.

finished by the Monday of Holy Week.[38] It must have been with a sigh of relief that the charitable Recollets accepted the thanks of the Jesuits and saw them settle, bag and baggage, into their own small quarters. If it is true that no kitchen is big enough for two women, it is much more true that no building is spacious enough to house two religious communities, each with its own spirit and customs.

Though procuring their own living quarters was useful to the Jesuits, overcoming the language barrier between themselves and the various Indian nations constituted the major problem in evangelizing the aborigines. Thus far, French traders who, perforce, had picked up a working knowledge of several native tongues, flatly refused to assist the Recollets in their efforts to acquire any Indian language. Sagard angrily reported: "Such is their lack of zeal that a man of importance (by profession a Catholic) told us, Father Nicolas and I, that if we sought to render the Indians sedentary, as we planned to do . . . he would drive us off."[39] Contrary to his expectation, when Lalemant approached a Frenchman versed in Montagnais, the trader ". . . promised me that, during the winter, he would give me all the help that I could ask of him."[40] Assent did not necessarily indicate a change of heart or a charming personality on Lalemant's part. The trader, whose name is unknown, was in trouble and about to be expelled from the colony. A second trader, fluent in another language, also agreed to assist. The Jesuits did not ask of that one ". . . all that we would have wished; as we noticed in him a mind somewhat coarse, it would not have been to our advantage to have urged him beyond his depth."[41]

At length, by late fall, Lalemant concluded that the only sure way of acquiring the native tongues was to attach one's self to a given group and, dwelling with them, acquire their language as a child learns. After consultation, it was agreed that one of the Jesuit priests would spend the winter with a group of Indians. "So the good fortune," Lalemant reported, "fell to the lot of Father Brébeuf. He left on the 20th of October and returned on the 27th

---

[38] *Relations*, IV, 217.
[39] Sagard, *Histoire*, I, 165.
[40] *Relations*, IV, 211.
[41] Ibid., 213.

of March [1626], having been distant from us 20 or 25 leagues all the time."[42] The method was not a new departure. The Recollets had experimented with it and Father Massé had tried it at Port Royal. In the summer of 1612, Massé accompanied a hunting expedition led by Louis Membertou, the son of a Micmac chief called Membertou. On that occasion, Massé ". . . fell seriously ill from long fasting and the continual annoyances of a wandering life; and, although he did not die, he was reduced to the utmost weakness."[43]

As yet, no missionary had wintered with a nomad group. Brébeuf left no account of his five-month sojourn in dead of winter with a group of wandering natives dependent on chance encounters with wild game for their sustenance. Eight years later, Father Paul Le Jeune underwent the same experience with a small group of wandering Montagnais from October 18, 1633, to April 9, 1634. The appalling physical suffering from bitter cold, continued hunger, exhausting marches through deep snow over rugged mountainous terrain was enough to sap the energy of the strongest European. Even more trying was the constant effort at acquiring a language foreign in structure to any European tongue. Added to those burdens was the revolting experience of having intimate contact with a gross, sensuous people who knew no restraints in any direction.[44]

In one respect, at least, Jean de Brébeuf was blessed. As Samuel de Champlain testified, ". . . he had such a striking gift for learning languages that . . . he grasped in two or three years what others would not learn in twenty."[45] Certainly, after five months Brébeuf must have acquired sufficient mastery of the Montagnais dialect of Algonkin that others, building on that knowledge, could grasp the language with greater ease.

Returning from the long, bitter winter with the Montagnais, Brébeuf was delighted to discover how well his brethren had adapted themselves to the new country. Father Lalemant, with the cooperation of his French interpreter, had made some progress toward a command of the Montagnais language. The cabin

---

[42] Ibid.
[43] Ibid., II, 239.
[44] Ibid., VII, 67-209.
[45] Champlain, VI, 47.

for the Jesuits was completed and beside it was stacked a good supply of sawn lumber ready for expanding the small home.[46] During the winter Father Daillon, with the aid of some Hurons wintering nearby, acquired some facility with the Huron language in preparation for his expected work among them. Perhaps, when the Hurons came down in the summer, Daillon would be able to return with them. And Jean de Brébeuf sincerely hoped that he would find place to accompany the zealous Recollet. But these plans must wait until the coming of summer in that cold land where, even in August, a raw wind can sweep the mighty St. Lawrence as though it was blowing down the valley of that great river through a giant funnel straight from the North Pole.

Finally, when the frost loosened its hold on the ground, the Jesuits planted a vegetable garden and waited, with everyone at Quebec, for the arrival of the fleet from France. At last, on July 5, 1626, Samuel de Champlain arrived aboard the *Catherine* and with him Father Joseph Le Caron, the Recollet, whose experience with the Hurons and facility in their language outstripped that of everyone else. On July 14 Father Philibert Noyrot landed, bringing with him Father Anne de Nouë, Brother Jean Gaufestre, and twenty craftsmen, all of whom had promised to stay in New France for at least a year while they built suitable housing for the Jesuits.

The stuttering, enthusiastic Noyrot had quite a story to tell his confreres. He wheedled and begged funds from everyone he could approach in France until he procured sufficient *livres* to buy everything the Jesuits would require for a year. When he reached Dieppe with his mountain of bales and boxes, the unfeeling Guillaume de Caën, chief of the monopolistic company controlling New France, obstinately refused to ship the supplies or grant passage to Noyrot, his two Jesuit companions, and the twenty laborers he had hired, though Champlain and Father Le Caron were welcomed aboard De Caën's ship, the *Catherine*. Undaunted, the determined little Noyrot went begging again until he had sufficient funds to charter his own ship, the *Allouette*, a craft of eighty tons.[47] It must have been with pardonable pride

---

46 *Relations*, IV, 217.
47 Champlain, VI, 83.

that Philibert Noyrot paraded his twenty workmen through the settlement at Quebec, under the very nose of Emery de Caën. Emery's cousin, Guillaume, was bested. The Jesuits would have their expanded house, their large kitchen garden, and all their supplies after all. Champlain was particularly pleased at the arrival of the craftsmen. "Father Noyrot," he noted,

brought 20 workmen whom Father Lalemant employed to build a residence and plant crops, losing no time, like a wise and industrious group acting in concert without discord. In a short time they have accomplished more towards raising their own food . . . than the company has in twenty-three or twenty-four years.[48]

And it would be years before the colony was not wholly dependent for its staple foods on what the ships brought from France.

With so many missionaries available the superiors of the Recollets and the Jesuits could jointly plan an apostolic campaign. Since the Recollets had already established quasi-permanent residences at Tadoussac and Cap de la Victoire, it seemed practical for the Jesuits to direct their efforts toward the Montagnais in the neighborhood of Quebec as well as to help the Recollets care for the spiritual needs of the French. The Hurons, however, were deemed a race apart, a nation whom the Recollets confidently believed could be quickly induced to accept Christianity with sincerity and understanding. Not only were they long accustomed to a sedentary life in well-ordered villages, but they were already friends and allies of the French, a relationship they were anxious to continue. Besides, the Hurons were traditionally merchant traders, maintaining valuable economic contacts with nations to the north, the west, and the south of their country.[49] Perhaps, through the conversion of the Hurons, the many nations beyond them could be won to salvation.

Father Joseph de la Roche Daillon, the Recollet already assigned to laboring among the Hurons in their homeland, spent the winter of 1625-1626 learning the Huron language, aided by the dictionary compiled by Father Le Caron and by practicing with a few Hurons who wintered at Quebec. As for the Jesuits, Father Charles Lalemant appointed Jean de Brébeuf and a new

[48] Ibid., V, 206.
[49] Hunt, *Wars of the Iroquois*, 53-65.

recruit, Father Anne de Noüe, to accompany the Recollet. Reaching Quebec on July 14, 1626, the thirty-seven-year-old De Noüe had barely become accustomed to solid ground under him when he was sent with Brébeuf up to Cap de la Victoire where, it was hoped, the Hurons would grant them space in the canoes of the fur brigade returning to Huronia.[50] Writing to his brother, Jerome, Charles Lalemant stated:

I am sending his companion with Father Brébeuf, 300 leagues from here to one of those tribes which has a permanent location[51] . . . Your Reverence will be surprised, perhaps, at my sending Father Brébeuf, who already has some knowledge of this tribe [i.e. the Montagnais]; but the talents that God has given him influenced me, the fruits which are expected from those tribes being very different from those hoped for here.[52]

Already Brébeuf's outstanding ability to learn a native language was appreciated. If the Hurons were to have an apostle capable of understanding them, Jean de Brébeuf was clearly that man.

Leaving Quebec a day or two after July 15, 1626, the three hopeful missionaries, Daillon, De Noüe, and Brébeuf, went up the St. Lawrence to ". . . Cap de la Victoire where the bartering was going on with the divers nations gathered there."[53] They were enthusiastically welcomed by the French traders who

---

[50] Anne de Noüe, scion of a noble family, was born near Reims on August 7, 1587. In his youth he served first as a page and later as an officer of the privy chamber in the court of Henri IV. On September 20, 1612, he entered the Society of Jesus at Paris. He arrived at Quebec together with Father Philibert Noyrot on July 14, 1626. A few days later, he went to the Huron trading fair and left there on July 25. After only a year among the Hurons Noüe returned to Quebec. Though he possessed keen intelligence and profound good will, he was unable to learn a native language or adapt himself to life among the Indians. Returning to Quebec, he assumed responsibility for the practical details of the house. In 1646, while stationed at Three Rivers, he set out alone in dead of winter to walk to Fort Richelieu (the present Sorel) in order to minister spiritually to the soldiers who were stationed there. Losing his way in a blizzard, he froze to death on February 1 or 2, 1646.

[51] The "his companion" refers to Noüe. Just previous to the passage quoted, Lalemant explained that he had directed Noyrot to return to France to act as a fund raiser and advocate for the mission. Continuing, Lalemant remarked that he had sent Noyrot's companion, Noüe, to the Hurons with Brébeuf. Relations, IV, 219, 221.

[52] Ibid., 221.

[53] Sagard, Histoire, III, 793-94.

. . . offered to supply them with whatever they stood in need of for the journey. They supplied them with strings of colored beads, knives, kettles, and other domestic utensils. These were accepted either to be made use of by themselves when they arrived in the country, or to be bestowed on their Indians and whoever might supply them with food or render them any service.[54]

The next important step was persuading the Hurons to grant the missionaries passage in their canoes bound for the homeland. Father Daillon, already on friendly terms with some Hurons who wintered near the Recollet convent at Quebec, was quickly granted space. The two Jesuits were less fortunate. The Recollet in his gray habit represented a figure with whom the Hurons were already familiar. But who were these two new, strange Frenchmen whom their fellow countrymen obviously respected? Dressed in dead black from head to toe, they might well be harbingers of evil. Besides, one of them, Brébeuf, a great hulk of a man, couldn't possibly fit in any but the very largest canoe. Most of the Hurons declined accepting the great giant.

This was a civil refusal and not devoid of reason; for if a large person leans ever so little on one side more than the other, or if in getting in he does not set his foot down gently and in the very middle of the canoe, over it goes, and everything is spilled into the river. Then comes the question are you able to swim in your heavy clothes? It is a difficult feat, for accidents may happen in places where the Indians themselves cannot escape drowning.[55]

What could be done? Was this first major foray of the Jesuits to be thwarted simply because God blessed Jean de Brébeuf with a splendid physique? Not if he could help it! Hastily opening his store of goods, the great Norman Jesuit heaped valuable gifts beside him, offering what was to the Indians a king's ransom for the privilege of going with them. Avarice overcoming prudence, one Huron captain agreed to accept Brébeuf as a passenger and another received Father Anne de Nouë. Thus, Jean de Brébeuf ". . . at last found place in a canoe and started off with the others under the protection of our Lord and his good Angel."[56] On Sunday, July 26, 1626, the feast of the Apostle St. James, Jean de Brébeuf, barefooted, his shoes tied together and slung around his neck,

[54] Ibid., 795.
[55] Ibid., 794-95.
[56] Ibid., 795.

the skirts of his cassock tucked up around his waist, gingerly eased his great bulk into a canoe, knelt cautiously, easing his weight onto his calves, and began an excruciatingly painful eight-hundred-mile journey to the country of the Hurons.[57]

During his first days voyaging with the Hurons, Jean de Brébeuf learned much about them. On a journey the Indians spoke little, saving their energy for paddling their average of ten leagues, about thirty miles, a day. Squatted on their haunches, immobile for hours on end, except for the swing of their arms and shoulders wielding the paddle, they generally had no small talk. Rising at dawn, the Hurons heated water into which they dropped a portion of coarsely pounded corn which usually contained bits of bark, small pebbles, ashes, or whatever extraneous material happened to fall into the corn as it was being beaten into flour. When the mixture became a watery gruel, the mess was poured into bark bowls which each man carried with him. Slurping down their scanty meal, the Hurons launched the canoe and began another day's silent travel. When continued exercise brought out the perspiration, Indians emitted an odor that Europeans found to be most disagreeable.[58] In the evening when the light began to fail the Indians, making camp for the night, ate their *sagamité*, as their corn mush was called, and stretched out on the bare ground to sleep. The swarms of mosquitoes, deer flies, and other insect pests seemed not to bother the Indians, though Europeans, who were not yet immunized to American insect poisons, suffered agonies. Then, at dawn, the whole painful process began all over again.

Leaving Cap de la Victoire, Brébeuf's Hurons paddled their frail craft along the northern shore of the St. Lawrence into the

[57] *Relations*, XII, 117-23. About a decade after Brébeuf made his first journey to Huronia, he wrote a set of instructions for Jesuit missionaries about to make the trip for their first time. In these he specifically directs that one must enter a canoe with bare feet and the cassock tucked up out of the way. The fragile birchbark skin of a canoe was so easily punctured that every effort was made to prevent sand or gravel being even inadvertently introduced into it.

[58] Sagard, *Long Journey*, 56-57. It might be remarked that there does seem to be a difference and mutual repulsion in racial sweats. Perhaps the Hurons reacted to Sagard, in this matter, as he did to them, but no Huron reported what he thought of the odor wafted to him from Sagard in his heavy gray habit which, rain or shine, he never had off his back.

roistering little Rivière des Prairies to the beautifully placid Lac des Deux Montagnes, an elbow-shaped body of water which receives the tawny floods of that broad, beautiful, capricious river, the Ottawa. In truth the Ottawa is not so much a river as it is a series of lovely, placid lakes joined together by a series of treacherous rapids deliberately designed, it would almost appear, to prevent the human race from using it as a highway into the heart of the north. Between Lac des Deux Montagnes and the mouth of the Mattawa River there were about eighteen portages, some as long as six miles and others only a few feet. At each, all the baggage in the canoe had to be removed and carried to the spot where the craft could again be loaded. On occasions the canoe itself must be carried overland until it could be launched again in safe water.[59]

Perhaps Father Brébeuf paid scant attention to the majestic beauty of the Ottawa Valley, expanding widely between two ranges of rugged granite walls. Did he wonder what lay behind the dark curtains of evergreens hiding the flanks of those hills? At night the two-toned rattle of tree toads and the wild, screaming laughter of the loons probably interrupted the tired missionary's rest. By day, on the river, with the sun beating down relentlessly, he might well have hungered for the fat fish leaping out of the water or watched the large blue herons struggle to become airborne. A farmer's son, it might have been that Brébeuf's reaction was much the same as Champlain's who considered it ". . . an ill-favored region full of pines, birches, and a few oaks, very rocky and in many places rather hilly."[60]

Some two weeks and five hundred miles from Cap de la Victoire, Brébeuf's Hurons turned their canoe sharply westward and entered the Mattawa River as it rushed into the Ottawa between two massive granite guardians. Seemingly a placid stream in its lower reaches, it flows over a series of low granite ridges requiring eight or nine portages before one wets a paddle in Lake Talon, Trout Lake, and the slimy little creek which the French so

[59] Most of the traditional portages on the Ottawa have fallen victim to industrial sites, canal building, or hydroelectric developments. Now the only identifiable portages remaining are Chaudière and Des Chats, both of which are near the city of Ottawa.

[60] Champlain, III, 37.

properly called La Vase. On that westwardly flowing stream the travelers crossed a continental divide and emerged onto the broad, shallow Lake Nipissing whose surface a mild summer storm can whip into mountainous waves. Prudently the Indians hugged the southern shore until they reached the French River. That wild, angry, black stream boils with white water and requires many a portage before one finally emerges onto Georgian Bay.[61]

To the Hurons, Georgian Bay was *Mare Nostrum*. At the head of the bay, where they entered it, they were still a good hundred miles from home. But they knew the eastern shore of the great bay, with its estimated thirty thousand islands of which modern tourist maps now boast. Threading their way through the maze of islands, large and small, the Hurons unerringly pushed on toward home. In the oppressive heat of late August 1626, the Huron canoe bearing Father Brébeuf was paddled down the western shore of Beausoleil Island and pushed across a mile of open water at the head of Penetang Harbor where the Indians beached their canoe at the mouth of a small creek.[62] Unloading the small craft, the Hurons walked inland to the Bear clan village of Toanché. At that village, among the people of the Huron Bear clan, Jean de Brébeuf began his life's work.[63]

[61] Most of the portages along the Mattawa and the French River are still much as they were when Brébeuf first saw them.

[62] *Relations*, VIII, 79. Brébeuf says of his journey to the Huron country in 1626: "I did not then ply the paddles nor carry burdens; nor did the other religious who made the trip." On each of the other four occasions on which he made the same journey, up and down, he "plied the paddle." It might be added that Brébeuf could not swim. See ibid., 83.

[63] The exact location of Toanché is thought by Jones to have been lot A, concession XVI, Tiny township, Simcoe county, Ontario. That location places it about a half mile east of Lake Farlane. See Jones, 47. Others, for example, Parkman and Laverdière, following a map of the Jesuit missions within Simcoe county drawn by J. C. Taché, place the village on the shore of Thunder Bay. See *Relations*, V, 293. Jones, 46, states the Huron word "Toanché" means "landing place."

Chapter IV

Huronia and France

Striding along toward the village of Toanché behind his Huron companions, happily burdened with their purchases obtained at the fur fair, Jean de Brébeuf must have prayed earnestly for divine assistance. Knowing but a few faltering words of the Huron tongue and practically ignorant of their habits and customs, how easily he could irreparably offend the Indians by inadvertently violating some hallowed tradition of which he was completely unaware! Accepting hospitality from some Indians who invited him into their cabin, Brébeuf at once began what could have seemed an impossible accomplishment. In the midst of curious, undisciplined children, prattling women, clouds of acrid smoke, endless comings and goings,[1] how could one concentrate sufficiently to acquire a language totally foreign, in structure and

[1] *Relations*, XVII, 13, 15. In his *Relation* of 1639 Father Jerome Lalemant, who had just reached Huronia, gave the following description of a Huron cabin: "If you go to visit them in their cabins, and you must go there oftener than once a day, if you would perform your duty as you ought, you will find there a miniature picture of Hell, seeing nothing, ordinarily, but fire and smoke, and on every side naked bodies, black and half roasted, mingled pell-mell with the dogs, which are held as dear as the children of the house, and share the beds, plates, and food of their masters. Everything is in a cloud of dust, and, if you go within, you will not reach the end of the cabin before you are completely befouled with soot, filth, and dirt."

usage, to anything approaching the orderly languages of Europe with their roots nicely buried in their ancestral Latin? But learn the language he must for how otherwise could he communicate with the Hurons? And so perfect must his command of their language be that he could explain to them the abstruse concepts of Christianity so that the Hurons would understand. There was nothing else to do but to acquire the language as a child might, stammering over the unfamiliar sounds, pointing to various objects, and asking questions.

In due time, with the arrival of the rest of the fur brigade, Brébeuf's fellow missionaries, De Noüe, the Jesuit, and Daillon, the Recollet, joined him.[2] At their request the Hurons assigned them a cabin of their own where they could celebrate daily Mass and enjoy a modicum of privacy, that most civilized of luxuries.[3] During the day they could go about the village becoming acquainted with their neighbors. And in the evenings they could retire to their cabin to say their prayers in comparative peace and concentrate on learning to speak the Huron tongue.

This little language school lasted until October 18, 1626, when Father Daillon received a letter from his superior at Quebec, Father Joseph Le Caron, directing him to transfer his apostolic efforts to the Neutral nation which had, as yet, never been contacted by a missionary.[4] The Recollet departed for the country of the Neutrals on October 18 accompanied by two Frenchmen, Gronelle and La Vallée, and a few Hurons. The incursion was an apostolic failure chiefly because the Hurons convinced their neighbors that the missionary was an evil magician who came to them only to cause serious illness among the Neutrals. In their own country the Hurons broadcast a rumor that the missionary

[2] The order in which the three missionaries arrived among the Hurons is nowhere recorded. It is certain that each made the trip in a different canoe.

[3] Le Clercq, *First Establishment*, I, 263. The author, himself a Recollet, speaks of the cabin as "our house." Possibly, therefore, the two Jesuits were guests. The Hurons were probably not surprised at the request of the missionaries for a cabin of their own. Father Le Caron had done so at Carhagouha in 1615. See ibid., 97. Viel, Sagard, and Le Caron followed the same practice at Ossossané. See Sagard, *Histoire*, I, 43. The inhabitants of those towns were members of the Huron Bear clan as were those at Toanché. Hence, it could be assumed that the custom would be readily accepted.

[4] Le Clercq, *First Establishment*, I, 264. The author is quoting a quite lengthy letter Daillon wrote to a friend at Paris on July 18, 1627.

and his two French companions had been brutally slain by the Neutrals. Greatly concerned, Father Brébeuf induced a few Frenchmen to investigate. Luckily, the rumor was false and in March 1627 Father Daillon returned to Toanché safe and sound.[5] He was very content, he said, among the Neutrals until the Hurons heard that he was urging his newfound friends to establish direct trade relations with the French. Then the Hurons started rumors to discredit him.[6]

When spring stole over the rolling hills of Huronia, Father Brébeuf, as the superior, was faced with a most unpleasant decision. Anne de Noüe, the highly intelligent, quondam gentleman of the French court, a man consumed with zeal for the conversion of the Hurons, was obviously a square peg in a round hole. No matter how diligently he applied himself, he could not learn the Huron language. What he grasped today was gone tomorrow. His orderly mind simply could not twist itself around the seemingly formless native language.[7] The hard fact, however, was that boundless zeal was not enough; a mute missionary was, after all, only an extra mouth to feed from the slender resources at Brébeuf's command. When, therefore, the Hurons set off in the early summer of 1627, poor, dedicated De Noüe departed with them, leaving Brébeuf and Father Daillon to continue their apostolate.[8]

Totally unknown to Jean de Brébeuf, in his forest fastness some three hundred leagues northwest of Quebec, not only his own missionary effort but New France itself was tottering on the brink of disaster. When a supply ship expected by the Jesuits in the summer of 1627 failed to appear, Father Charles Lalemant, the

[5] Ibid., 265. Daillon noted in his letter that he came back because both the Jesuits and the French ". . . feared more misfortune than profit by my death . . ."

[6] Sagard, *Histoire*, III, 803. If the Neutrals began trading directly with the French, the Huron economic control over them would have ended.

[7] De Noüe was far from unique in this. In 1636 Father Brébeuf wrote a little disquisition for the benefit of ". . . those whom it shall please God to call to New France . . ." Regarding learning Huron, he wrote "You will have accomplished much if, at the end of a considerable time, you begin to stammer a little." See *Relations*, X, 91.

[8] Champlain, V, 233. De Noüe was back at Quebec before September 2, 1627. Father Charles Lalemant left for France on that day, taking with him all but four or five of the laborers previously shipped out. The Jesuits left at Quebec were Enemond Massé (acting superior), De Noüe, and a brother, probably Gilbert Burel.

superior, was obliged to send back to France most of the twenty workmen imported the year before. All through the spring and summer of 1627 Charles Lalemant waited anxiously for Philibert Noyrot to arrive, bringing the supplies essential to the continuation of the Jesuit effort. Unlike the Recollets, supported by those enjoying the fur monopoly, the Jesuits depended entirely on their own resources, chiefly gifts of money or goods begged from a generous public.[9] On October 2, 1627, by which time it was evident that no more ships could be expected from France before the next spring, Father Lalemant secured passage for his workmen and himself aboard the *Catherine*, commanded by Raymond de la Ralde, vice-admiral of the fleet dispatched by the sieur Guillaume de Caën for the trade in peltries.[10] Assuming that Fa-

[9] In 1625, when the Recollets invited the Jesuits to cooperate with them in New France, opponents of the Jesuits warned the Recollets that the sons of St. Ignatius would, by devious means, have them excluded from New France. When that ploy failed, a rumor was spread that though the company holding the fur monopoly was obliged to support six Recollets, the Jesuits were arranging to have two of their own men receive part of that stipend. The Jesuits scotched the rumor by announcing that they would wholly depend on their own resources. See Rochemonteix, I, 150-51. Providing as best he could for the three Jesuits he was leaving at Quebec, Lalemant ". . . got some ten casks of [sea] biscuits from the Company's storehouse at the same price that was charged the Indians, namely: seven beaver-skins a cask, which skins the said Father had picked up from one and another, paying a crown in cash for each skin; he thus bought dearly things of absolute necessity, and received no courtesy in the transaction." See Champlain, V, 233-34. Wholeheartedly devoted to the mission in New France, Lalemant had, perhaps, sound reason to believe that unless someone went home to plead the cause, even the Jesuits in France might well give up the effort. An inkling of such a feeling crept into Lalemant's first letter from New France to the Jesuit general. Near the end of his epistle, he remarked: "With the consent of his superiors, Father Noyrot returns [in 1626] to France to promote as hitherto the interest of our enterprise. He stands in need of the influence of Your Paternity in order to negotiate freely with those who have charge of our affairs. Our own Fathers at Paris, for some reason, put difficulties in our way, and seem rather unfriendly to our mission; so that but for the favor of Father Coton, of blessed memory, our affairs would have fallen to the ground." See *Relations*, IV, 181. As provincial of the Jesuits at Paris, Coton had approved the opening of the mission in New France. He died soon after, on March 19, 1626.

[10] Champlain, V, 232-34. Guillaume de Caën, a native of Dieppe and a Huguenot, was from 1621 until 1627 the actual head of the company holding the monopoly of the fur trade in Canada. La Ralde, a relative by marriage of the De Caëns, a Catholic, obtained his position because, in 1626, the crown insisted that the De Caëns must have a Catholic at the head of their trading fleet. La Ralde's religious persuasion aroused in him little sympathy for the missionary effort regarding the Indians. See ibid., 234.

ther Noyrot had either been lost at sea or captured by the English, someone must go home to seek aid. And Charles Lalemant, possessing ". . . in truth the courtesy, the good-breeding, the pleasant bearing and conversation . . . ,"[11] was the obvious man to go for few could resist him.

When winter set in at Quebec matters went from bad to worse. Bitter cold gripped the land, but the snow was so light that large game easily fled over the frozen ground, escaping the arrows of the hunters, and small game just disappeared. Soon the neighboring Indians came begging for food which the French could not spare since their own stores were dwindling daily.[12]

It was hoped by the fifty-odd French at Quebec that when the Hurons came down to trade they would bring ample supplies of corn to tide the French over until the supply ships arrived from France. But the fleet of twenty Huron canoes contained very little corn because Huronia itself, as well as her neighbors, was suffering the effects of a drought which struck the country the previous summer. For that reason, perhaps, the Indians had brought with them Father Daillon and most of the French traders living among the Hurons.[13] Father Brébeuf and a small band of French laymen stayed on. Hungry people might not be inclined to listen to Brébeuf's explanation of Christianity, but at least he could continue improving his command of the Huron tongue and, by going hungry with them, he could clearly demonstrate his devotion to the Hurons.

On July 9, 1628, when Champlain's tiny colony was in desperate straits, a cruelly false hope arose. An Indian, arriving from Tadoussac, announced that some great ships lay at anchor in the roadstead there.[14] Everyone confidently expected that, in a day or two, small sloops would come up the river bringing the desperately needed supplies. Instead, Champlain learned that the ships were manned by hostile Englishmen whose country had been at war with France for a year and more.

The basis of that futile conflict, lasting from 1627 to 1629, arose from the imprudent ambition of George Villiers, duke of

[11] Ibid., 235.
[12] Ibid., 248.
[13] Sagard, *Histoire*, IV, 847, 943.
[14] Champlain, V, 273-75.

Buckingham, who sought to present the England of Charles I as the champion of the Protestant cause. When the forces of Louis XIII besieged La Rochelle, a Huguenot stronghold, Buckingham induced his king to send a fleet as well as ground forces to the aid of the Huguenots. Since the English navy, still recovering from a disgraceful defeat off Cadiz, in October 1625,[15] was no match for French sea power, Charles I authorized letters of marque and reprisal, allowing English sea captains to capture any French ship encountered.[16] The futile little war dragged on, with no noteworthy victories by either side, until a truce was arranged at Chêf-de-Boys on March 29, 1629. By that document it was agreed that any ship or territory captured within two months after that date would revert to the original owner.[17]

The opening of hostilities between France and England offered Jarvis Kirke, an English merchant residing at Dieppe, an opportunity to attempt exploitation of the fur resources available in the St. Lawrence River valley. He and a group of London merchants formed a trading company with that objective. In March 1628 the company placed three ships at the disposal of Kirke's son, David, who, with his four brothers, sailed to New France determined to capture it for his father's company and England. Reaching Tadoussac, David Kirke easily subdued it and promptly prepared to capture Quebec. On July 10, 1628, Champlain received a polite note from Kirke calling on him to surrender. Equally courteously, Champlain replied that he and his followers ". . . should not be worthy of the name of men in the presence of our King, but rather be reprehensible and merit chastisement in the sight of God and men, honor demands that we fight to the

---

[15] William E. Lunt, *History of England*, 409. As part of the marriage contract between Charles I of England and Henrietta Maria, sister of Louis XIII, England agreed to give France four warships. Shortly after the marriage took place, on May 11, 1625, France demanded the ships. They were, indeed, dispatched, but, instead of sailing to France, they were ordered by Buckingham to attack Spanish ports seeking to plunder treasure ships. The fleet attacked Cadiz and landed troops. But the men were so poorly disciplined that they got drunk. Twenty-five hours later the English were forced to withdraw and return home in disgrace. England's navy was, at the moment, riddled with inept commanders and poorly conditioned ships.

[16] Biggar, *Trading Companies*, 139.

[17] Gustave Lanctôt, *A History of Canada*, I, 135.

death."[18] Champlain's courageous reply fell on deaf ears. Since Kirke already controlled the St. Lawrence he could easily prevent aid reaching Quebec and, in due time, it would fall to him without his firing a shot.

Only a week later, on July 19, 1628, near Miscou, David Kirke encountered four French ships, commanded by Claude de Roquemont, bringing ample supplies to the colony as well as four hundred settlers sent out by the recently founded Company of New France. A day-long battle ensued in which the English forced the French to strike their colors. Kirke packed all the French into two ships and sent them home, but retained two others as prizes of war. Gambling on the unlikelihood of France forwarding further help that season, Kirke sailed for England where he made preparations to subdue Quebec the following summer.[19]

At Quebec, Champlain and the French tightened their belts in preparation for a long, hungry winter. After twenty years of existence the colony still had not broken enough ground to the plow so that it could feed itself, depending almost entirely on imports from France.[20] If the war did not end so that the English blockade could be lifted, New France was bound to fall. Hopefully, some food might come down with the Huron fur brigade during the summer of 1629 but, when it arrived, there was hardly enough spare corn in the canoes to feed the Indians themselves. One great prize the Hurons did bring with them. On July 17, 1629, Jean de Brébeuf and all the remaining French traders residing in the Huron country returned, adding more mouths to feed at Quebec.[21] Brébeuf's departure from Huronia was not his decision. Rather it was Father Enemond Massé, acting superior of the Jesuits in the absence of Father Charles Lalemant, who directed his valuable subject to come down to Quebec lest, perhaps, he be stranded should the French lose the colony.

How well Father Brébeuf had won the hearts of his dusky friends is somewhat touchingly demonstrated by their sadness at his departure.

[18] Champlain, V, 284.
[19] Lanctôt, *History of Canada*, I, 133.
[20] Champlain, V, 206.
[21] Ibid., VI, 45.

What is this? They said to him. Are you deserting us? Three years ago you came here to learn our language, in order that you might teach us to know your God, and to worship and serve him, having come for that special object, as you testified to us. And now that you know our language more perfectly than anyone else who ever came among us you are abandoning us; and if we do not know the God whom you adore, we shall call him to witness that it is not our fault but yours for leaving us in this fashion. He explained to them that the obedience that he owed to his superiors made it impossible for him to remain with them for the present . . . but he assured them that, by the grace of God, he would come to them again, and bring whatever was necessary for teaching them to know God and serve him; and so he took his departure.[22]

While the gaunt colonists of New France barely kept themselves alive through the winter of 1628-1629 on a scant ration of peas and roots, the Kirkes, in association with Sir William Alexander prepared to take Canada by force. In March 1629 the Kirkes sailed from Gravesend with a fleet of six ships in which they infested the Gulf of St. Lawrence. They had hardly reached there before France and England finally concluded the treaty of Susa on April 24, 1629. By it, the high contracting parties agreed that any ship or territory seized by either side for a period of two months after the treaty must be returned. Thereafter, of course, all belligerent acts by subjects of either side were forbidden, being nothing more than simple piracy.[23] But the international development of April 1629 which would protect New France from seizure by the English was not known to the Kirkes. They had left England at least a month before the treaty was concluded, and were unaware that their letters of marque were no longer valid.

Learning of Champlain's desperate situation, David Kirke sent his two brothers, Lewis and Thomas, in small sloops to demand the surrender of Quebec. Champlain, only too well aware of the hopelessness of his situation, procured the best terms he could arrange and capitulated on July 19, 1629. The victors agreed to grant safe passage to all the French who wished to return to France, allowing the officers to retain their weapons, clothing, and the peltries each owned. But the missionaries, both Jesuit

---

[22] Ibid., 46-47.
[23] Biggar, *Trading Companies*, 146.

and Recollet, were permitted to take only the clothes on their backs and their breviaries.[24]

During the negotiations, the English agreed to post soldiers at the convent of the Recollets and the Jesuit residence as well as at homes of the few French not residing at Champlain's *habitation*. But when the British troops landed on July 20, they promptly looted the quarters of the Jesuits.[25] The Kirkes justified that flagrant violation of their pledged word by maintaining that not only were the Jesuits Judaizers, that is, false Christians, but much richer than the Kirkes themselves. Thomas Kirke declared: "I expect on visiting them to unearth a great supply of beaver."[26] Much to his disappointment Kirke found no peltries but only some pictures, books, and sacred vessels. Some of these he confiscated and allowed the Protestant chaplain of his fleet to take some of the books that the minister coveted.[27] Kirke showed great kindness to the Recollets because he said he knew them to be poorer than church mice.[28]

On Saturday, July 28, 1629, eight days after the English took command at Quebec, all the remaining Jesuits were shipped off to Tadoussac to await repatriation. Before allowing them to embark, Lewis Kirke insisted on searching their meager baggage. Discovering a chalice, Kirke demanded it, but the Jesuits begged him to let them keep it because it was sacred and should not be put to profane use. Though Kirke sneered at the request, declaring that such things bred superstition, he nonetheless allowed the priests to retain the chalice.[29] This was not the last uncomfortable encounter between the Jesuits and the English.

At Tadoussac the missionaries were forbidden by David Kirke to celebrate Mass or hold any other public religious service,

---

[24] Champlain, VI, 60, 67-68. Sagard, *Histoire*, IV, 896-97, says that Daillon acted as interpreter in the negotiations, speaking Latin since the English deputy, sent by Kirke, could not speak French. This is quite probably an exaggeration. The negotiations, according to Champlain, were carried on by letter. All the Kirkes were born and reared at Dieppe so they certainly were fluent in French.

[25] Sagard, *Histoire*, IV, 904.

[26] Ibid., 901.

[27] Champlain, VI, 67-68.

[28] Sagard, *Histoire*, IV, 904.

[29] Champlain, VI, 69. Thus, Kirke relaxed his original, harsh order given the clergy.

though the French Huguenots present were allowed to do so.[30] And, of course, the English chaplain held services. Apart from their personal disappointment at Kirke's restrictions, the Jesuits and Recollets alike were gravely concerned at the effect such action might have on the Indians who were present. Even more, the missionaries were in despair at the scandalous conduct of the English as well as some of the French in their dealings with the Indian women.

In this regard, none were worse than Etienne Brûlé, Nicolas Marsolet, and a couple of other young Frenchmen whom Champlain himself had nurtured from boyhood. These ungrateful wretches had gone over to the English, lock, stock, and barrel. By far the worst offender of this sort was Jacques Michel, an experienced pilot on the St. Lawrence, a native of Dieppe, and a renegade.[31] His intimate knowledge of the river went quite far toward making it possible for the Kirkes to capture Quebec. Champlain called him a ". . . downright traitor and rebel . . . who had conducted the English [to Quebec] not only on the first but on the second occasion."[32]

During the six weeks the Jesuits were detained at Tadoussac, while the Kirkes careened their ships in preparation for the Atlantic crossing, they were frequently subject to abuse. On one occasion David Kirke taunted the Jesuits:

"Gentlemen, you have pretty much your own way in Canada and derive the benefit of what belonged to the Sieur de Caën, whom you have dispossessed." "Pardon me, Sir," said the Father [Brébeuf],[33] "it is nothing but a pure desire to promote the glory of God and effect the conversion of the savages in these parts, that has brought us here to brave all the perils and dangers." Then Michel spoke insistently and said, "Yes, yes, to convert the savages! Say rather, to convert the beavers." The Father replied somewhat quickly and without thinking: "That is false." Michel raised his hand and answered: "It is only out of respect for the General that I don't slap your face for giving me the lie." The Father said, "You will excuse me, I do not mean to give you the lie, I should be very sorry to do so. The term I employed is one we use in our schools when a doubtful statement is advanced,

---

[30] Ibid., 142.
[31] Ibid., 136.
[32] Ibid., 81.
[33] Ibid., 137. Brébeuf's name was inserted into the margin of the text.

and we do not regard it as offensive. I beg, therefore, that you will pardon me, and believe that I do not say it with any intention of offending you."[34]

Thenceforth, quite likely, Jacques Michel gave Father Brébeuf a wide berth. The significance of the incident lies in the insight it allows into the character of Jean de Brébeuf. In this first recorded direct statement from the man, the future martyr would rather suffer fools gladly than offend them.

If the irreligious Jacques Michel thought he had bested Brébeuf in their brief encounter, the renegade did not enjoy his triumph for long. A few days later he was stricken with apoplexy and died without regaining consciousness. David Kirke honored Michel with an impressive military funeral, attended by two hundred soldiers and saluted by the big guns of every English ship. But scarcely had the ships sailed away when ". . . the Indians exhumed his body, and showed it every imaginable indignity, tore it to pieces and gave it to their dogs; but such are the wages of traitors."[35]

Through August and early September 1629, waiting patiently on that rugged, barren Tadoussac, the French, especially the Jesuits, could not help wondering why no French fleet came to expel the English and rescue them, particularly since they knew that the war between France and England was already at an end.

They had learned from Emery de Caën that on April 24, 1629, a treaty had been signed restoring peace between the two nations. On his way up the river to Quebec, De Caën fell afoul of the very ship on which the English were bringing Samuel de Champlain to Tadoussac. The poor, distraught founder of Canada, confined below the deck of Thomas Kirke's ship, heard ". . . Emery de Caën, who in a craven spirit cried out quite loudly, 'Quarter! Quarter!' "[36] Informed that France and England were no longer at war, David Kirke simply ignored the report because

---

[34] Ibid., 137-38.

[35] *Relations*, V, 41. The treatment given Michel's body by the Indians was reported by Father Paul Le Jeune, in his *Brief Relation of a Journey to New France* which he wrote at Quebec. The account of the journey is dated August 28, 1632. Le Jeune says he learned the story not from the Indians themselves, but from the French at Quebec.

[36] Champlain, VI, 77. Champlain left Quebec on July 24. De Caën's ship was captured the next day.

De Caën could produce no official document proving the fact.[37] Then Kirke was told that a French supply fleet, convoyed by warships under command of Admiral Isaac de Razilly, France's most brilliant naval commander, had already sailed for New France and could be expected any day. David Kirke replied that even if he encountered the French fleet he would attack it just as successfully as he had done in the summer of 1628.

Finally, on September 14, 1629, a Friday, David Kirke set sail for England. Sad at heart, Jean de Brébeuf watched the rocky headland of Tadoussac fade into the distance. Would he ever see this wild land and his cherished Hurons again? If Emery de Caën's story was true, New France would certainly be restored to her mother country. But when? How long might it be before Jesuit missionaries could return? Diplomatic negotiations could drag on for years and years. And even if those tiresome bureaucratic details were concluded in favor of France, would Brébeuf have the good fortune to be sent back, supposing that the Jesuits were again called to return? He had a whole month on the high seas to ponder the problem.

At long last, on October 20, 1629, the English ships reached Plymouth.[38] There David Kirke learned that indeed France and England had been at peace for a few days over six months. His capture of Quebec had been illegal. Instead of a returning hero, Kirke feared he might well be severely punished for having seriously endangered diplomatic relations between France and England. But, fulfilling his promise to repatriate the French, Kirke sailed to Dover where he arranged passage to France for all his captives. So Jean de Brébeuf, after an absence of four years, found himself, to his way of thinking, an exile in his homeland for he had left his heart among the Hurons.

Only on their return did the missionaries learn why France had failed to defend her colony as well as why the Jesuits apparently did nothing to assist their brethren abroad. The Jesuits in France, they quickly found, had made heroic efforts in favor of

---

[37] Ibid., 87. Thomas Kirke probably did not know of the peace treaty. However, his brother, David, had been informed several days previously. With a certain amount of justification, David Kirke refused to believe what he was told because Emery de Caën had no documentary proof.

[38] Ibid., 145.

their mission in New France. Philibert Noyrot, that astonishingly influential stammerer, lost no time once he reached Paris in the fall of 1627. Conferring with his spiritual child, the duc de Ventadour, viceroy of New France, Noyrot convinced him that conversion of the Indians would never be furthered by stockholders óf a monopolistic company interested only in exploiting the fur trade. Company officials opposed converting the Indians lest they cease collecting peltries and settle into orderly agricultural pursuits. They equally opposed the immigration of colonists whose presence would only denude the land of forests and thus drive fur-bearing animals out. Encouraged by influential friends at court, Noyrot, surely in fear and trembling approached the august presence of Armand, cardinal, duc de Richelieu, the most powerful man in France. At that meeting, Noyrot the stutterer became Noyrot the golden-tongued orator, explaining eloquently the dire spiritual and material state of New France. The stammerer must have really been struck speechless when he soon learned that the cardinal had dissolved the monopolistic company in favor of a newly chartered Company of New France whose declared purpose was the Christianization of the Indians and the colonization of Canada.[39]

Bubbling over with enthusiasm, Philibert begged sufficient funds to procure supplies for the mission and a ship to convoy them to Quebec. But while the craft lay at anchor in the harbor at Honfleur Guillaume de Caën seized the ship and its cargo on the score that, though his company no longer enjoyed a monopoly in New France, he personally still exercised authority over shipping bound for Canada.[40] That arbitrary, and thoroughly illegal, exercise of authority caused much suffering to the Jesuits left at Quebec. If that was De Caën's purpose, he certainly succeeded.

[39] Lanctôt, *History of Canada*, I, 129. Noyrot cannot be said to have done more than give Richelieu a useful occasion for reorganizing colonization policy. Some historians credit Charles Lalemant and Samuel de Champlain for urging the cardinal to establish the company. However, neither was in France at the time. The company was chartered on April 29, 1627. Lalemant did not reach France until the fall of 1627 and Champlain did not get to France until late in 1629.

[40] Technically, De Caën was within his rights. His company retained rights in Canada for a year after the charter was dissolved. De Caën is usually accused of acting out of pique to punish the Jesuits for Noyrot's influence with Richelieu.

Without the supplies Noyrot so lovingly gathered for shipment in 1627, bitter hardship visited the Jesuits in New France during that long, cold winter of 1627-1628. When the shipping season opened in 1628, Noyrot was at it again. This time he must have believed he would surely succeed for he sailed, again in a ship chartered by himself, but in convoy under the protection of Admiral Claude de Roquemont, but commanding no ships of the line. Besides, Father Charles Lalemant and Father François Ragueneau were aboard Roquemont's flagship.[41] At the mouth of the St. Lawrence, Roquemont's passage was disputed by five English ships commanded by David Kirke. On July 19, 1628, after a ten-hour battle, Roquemont gave quarter ". . . because all his ammunition was gone, even to the lead on his fishing-lines."[42] Lagging behind the French fleet, Noyrot avoided capture, but prudently fled back to France.[43] Still undaunted, little Philibert Noyrot, begging funds from long-suffering benefactors, packed still a third chartered vessel with the needs of the desperate missionaries at Quebec and sailed, on June 16, 1629, in convoy with Captain Charles Daniel, brother of Father Antoine Daniel, the future Jesuit martyr. On board with Noyrot were two Jesuit priests, Charles Lalemant and Alexandre de Vieuxpont as well as Brother Louis Malot.[44] On August 24, 1629, in a violent storm off Cape Breton Island, the ship floundered, drowning the brave little Noyrot, Brother Malot, and twelve others, including two of Father Noyrot's nephews.[45] Certainly after hearing all of this, the

[41] François Ragueneau, older brother of Father Paul Ragueneau, was born at Blois on June 14, 1597. He entered the Jesuit novitiate at Paris on April 16, 1614. After his ecclesiastical studies, he was teaching at Moulins when he was directed to accompany Father Charles Lalemant to Quebec in 1628. Returned to Europe by the Kirkes, François never came back to New France.

[42] Ibid., 133.

[43] Euclide Gervais, "Le Père Philibert Noyrot," *Lettres du Bas-Canada* XIII (1959), 37. Noyrot turned back on July 31, 1628.

[44] Alexandre de Vieuxpont was born at Auxeville in Normandy on December 25, 1599. He entered the Society of Jesus at Rouen on September 13, 1620. In June 1629 he sailed with Noyrot.

[45] *Relations*, IV, 237, 239. Lalemant's vivid account of the disaster. Lalemant was taken back to France by some Basque fishermen who landed him at San Sebastien whence he made his way to Paris. Vieuxpont was taken to Cape Breton Island where Captain Charles Daniel established a fort at Bras d'Or Bay. Vieuxpont worked there with Father Barthélemy Vimont who had come out from France aboard Captain Daniel's ship.

returned missionaries knew only too well that their brethren in France had bent every effort to help them in their need.

As far as the royal government of France was concerned, the small outpost at Quebec might well have been allowed to vanish were it not for the ambitions of Cardinal Richelieu. For him, ". . . a France overseas would be a France more glorious and influential."[46] In 1626 Isaac de Razilly, knight of Malta, France's ablest seaman and Richelieu's cousin, had pointed out to the cardinal, in a long memorandum, that ". . . whoever is master of the sea has great power over the land."[47] And colonies certainly encouraged a nation to build up her sea power. New France offered just such an opportunity. Besides, Père Joseph, that shadowy Gray Eminence whom Richelieu had appointed Apostolic Commissary in 1625, was urging the cardinal to take some effective action concerning the conversion of the aborigines.[48] Richelieu, Louis XIII's Minister of the Army, the Marine, Finance, Interior, and Foreign Affairs, all rolled into one, revoked all previous trading charters and established the Company of New France, imposing on it the specific obligation of colonizing Canada and Christianizing the aborigines. The great cardinal, himself, assumed the office of viceroy of New France and invested his personal funds in the project.[49] Quite in character, the flamboyant Richelieu signed the official documents in the military camp before La Rochelle, on April 29, 1627, while he was actively engaged in the siege of that

[46] Daniel Patrick O'Connell, *Richelieu*, 150.

[47] Ibid., 146.

[48] Père Joseph's proper name was François Leclerc du Tremblay. Born at Paris in 1577, he entered the Capuchin order at the turn of the century. The name Joseph became his on joining the Capuchins. Officially, he was the cardinal's secretary, but he was given many important assignments of a diplomatic, and often secret, nature. Richelieu apparently had faith in the man's judgment, especially in religious matters.

[49] Richelieu delegated the actual management of the company to Jean de Lauzon, scion of an old Breton family dedicated to the law. He was governor of New France from 1651 to 1656. In his position as Richelieu's deputy, Lauzon did right well for himself and his son. He got possession of the whole island of Montreal, Ile d'Orléans, a great part of the seigneury of Beaupré, and all of the seigneury which bore his name. For his son, François, Lauzon procured all of the land on the south bank of the St. Lawrence from the present city of Sorel southward to Châteauguay opposite the western end of the island of Montreal, a stretch of land about sixty miles long.

Huguenot town.[50] One wonders if, when he signed the documents, the cardinal was dressed for battle in a

. . . weird half-ecclesiastical, half-military costume . . . Over black clothes he wore a metal cuirass of natural steel color, and over this in turn a prelate's starched collar. There was a feather in his hat and he carried a rapier beneath his cloak of cardinal red.[51]

In theory, at least, the constitution of the Company of New France, known familiarly as the Hundred Associates, was a kind of Bill of Rights for French colonists and their descendants as well as for the Indians. The company's charter piously declared that its avowed objective was

. . . to establish a colony for the purpose of trying, with divine assistance, to bring the [native] people living there to the knowledge of the true God, to civilize them and instruct them in the Roman, Catholic and Apostolic faith.[52]

To furnish proper spiritual support to the French colonists and the Indians, the company obligated itself to supply three priests for each French settlement and to furnish the clergy with everything needed for fifteen years. For the conversion of the Indians, the company promised to supply, if need be, a

. . . great number of ecclesiastics . . . for the missions, all at the expense of the said Society, for a term of fifteen years. Even after fifteen years, neither the Society nor his Majesty will neglect the ecclesiastics . . . or any others going to New France for the salvation of souls.[53]

The newly minted Company of New France presented highly attractive offers to possible stockholders and to those who might wish to migrate. Though only native-born French Catholics were eligible, their children born in New France would be considered as natives of France with all the rights of Frenchmen. Craftsmen

---

[50] Lanctôt, *History of Canada*, I, 129-30. Each share in the new company cost 3,000 *livres* with a requisite immediate payment of 1,000. The company acquired its sobriquet from the fact that there were thought to be one hundred subscribers. In actual fact there were one hundred six, one of whom was Champlain. One of the subscribers was a widow, Nicholle Langlois, relict of Nicolas Blondel. See *Collection de manuscrits . . . relatifs à l'histoire de la nouvelle-France*, I, 82.

[51] O'Connell, *Richelieu*, 166.

[52] *Collection de manuscrits*, I, 62.

[53] Ibid., 65.

migrating to Canada would, if they returned, receive the status of masters in their craft. Twelve titles of nobility were available to be conferred by the directors of the company. Even the Indians, if Christianized, were to be considered in Canada and France itself as native-born Frenchmen.[54]

The only thing the company did not have was New France itself which, soon after the inception of the Hundred Associates, fell into the hands of the Englishman, David Kirke. If the company wanted the country, it was up to that body to get it back. The first effort in that direction made, as noted above, by Claude de Roquemont in the summer of 1628, ended in disaster and cost the company 164,720 *livres*.[55] Captain Charles Daniel's attempt to subdue Kirke, in 1629, came to naught, chiefly due to the lateness of the season. By the time Daniel returned home, late in 1629, the French, already aware that Kirke had illegally seized Quebec, had dispatched Admiral Isaac de Razilly to England in an effort to obtain the restoration of New France from Charles I. For those vitally interested, negotiations dragged on interminably. Had it not been that Charles I desperately needed money, which a hostile parliament refused, New France might never have been restored. But Louis XIII still owed Charles 400,000 crowns of the 800,000 promised as a dowry when the French Henrietta Maria married Charles.[56] Therefore, the treaty of Saint Germain-en-Laye, concluded on March 23, 1632, restored New France to Louis XIII, who, in turn, paid Charles I the remainder of the long overdue dowry.

In the waning weeks of 1629, Father Jean Filleau, provincial of the Jesuit Province of France, considered how best to employ his repatriated subjects. Father Enemond Massé, aged fifty-four, went back to the Collège Henri IV at La Flèche where he had waited patiently for eleven years, 1614 to 1625, before returning to New France in 1625. He would be content there, again awaiting the summons to his adopted homeland. In the meantime, he could inflame the young Jesuits studying their philosophy and theology at La Flèche with a desire to devote themselves to the aborigines. Father Anne de Noüe, a middle-aged forty-two, was

---

[54] Ibid., 70.
[55] Ibid., 79. Daniel's effort in 1629 cost 103,976 *livres*.
[56] John Lingard, *The History of England*, VII, 274.

posted to Amiens and later to Orléans, charged with managing the practical details of colleges in each city. Father Charles Lalemant, also forty-two, after a brief stay at Paris, was sent to assume administration of the Collège de Bourbon at Rouen, a post he held until 1633 when he was directed to become superior of the Jesuit college at Eu.[57]

The tall, gaunt Jean de Brébeuf was sent back to Rouen and the college he knew so well, where he had begun his teaching a decade before. If he could not have New France and the Hurons, the giant Norman should be happy in Normandy's capital. Since the academic year was already two months old when Brébeuf arrived, late in December 1629, instead of a teaching task, the missionary was assigned purely spiritual duties, hearing confessions and preaching to the students.[58] One can readily imagine with what interest the students listened to this man who had gone to a world so far removed from everyday France. Not the least intrigued of his hearers were two young Jesuits, both destined to die in New France. The future martyr, Isaac Jogues, at twenty-two, was just beginning his years of teaching. A mite of a man, he looked so young and fresh that he could easily pass as one of the students.[59] Simon Le Moyne, three years senior to Jogues, had been teaching at Rouen since 1627. The life of every gathering, Le Moyne had a keen wit and was a clever mimic. As a priest in New France he would spend eleven years, 1638 to 1649, among the Hurons.[60]

At the opening of the new year, 1630, Jean de Brébeuf committed to paper some of his intimate reflections:

March 25. This year, 1630, I will complete my thirty-seventh year. I was born on the feast of the Annunciation in 1593. January, 1630. I sense within myself a consuming desire to suffer something for Christ's sake. I fear my rejection because up to now He has dealt so kindly with me, especially since I might have gravely offended his divine majesty. Only when opportunities for suffering are given me will I be hopeful of my salvation.[61]

[57] Delattre, *Établissements*, I, 191; II, 907; III, 1011; IV, 541.
[58] ARSJ, Franc. 22, Catologi Prov. Franc., 243.
[59] Francis X. Talbot, *Saint among Savages*, 34.
[60] Rochemonteix, II, 140.
[61] Latourelle, *Etude sur . . . Brébeuf*, II, 202. The original manuscripts of Brébeuf's spiritual notes no longer exist. Copies of them were made, apparently by Father Paul Ragueneau, Brébeuf's last superior. Ragueneau's manuscript,

These few lines, the earliest preserved from Brébeuf's pen, reveal the spiritual heights to which he had already attained. But there was more to come.

Having been a Jesuit for twelve years, Jean de Brébeuf was directed by his provincial to begin a spiritual retreat in preparation for the pronouncement of his final religious vows.[62] On January 11, 1630, while meditating on the heinousness of offending God, he wrote:

Reflecting on the gravity of my sins, I seem aware that the Divine Mercy, extending his arms, embraces me lovingly, indulgently condoning all my sins, revitalizing the merits of my good deeds, performed out of charity but destroyed by my sinfulness; inviting me to intimate friendship, repeating [his] invitation to St. Paul: He will be to me a vessel of election to carry my name to the nations. Accordingly, I give thanks, offering myself, saying: Lord, fashion me into a man according to your heart; teach me what you wish me to do. In future, nothing will separate me from the love of you, neither nakedness, nor the sword, nor death, etc. If I, a member of the most holy Society, cooperate, I shall become an apostle of Canada. Though not blessed with the gift of tongues, I have been granted noteworthy facility in them. Alas, the wickedness, the foulness, the disorder of my life.[63]

To the uninitiated, Father Brébeuf's remark regarding his own sinfulness might be interpreted as the repentant declaration of

---

dated 1652, has been preserved. This manuscript is found in the archives of the Gallo-Canadian Jesuit province at Notre-Dame de Montserrat, Saint Jérôme, P. Q., Canada. Ragueneau's complete manuscript is entitled: "Mémoires touchant la mort et les vertus des pères Isaac Jogues, Anne de Noüe, Antonie Daniel, Jean de Brébeuf, Gabriel Lallement, Charles Garnier, Noël Chabanel & un seculier René Goupil, 1652." Brébeuf's spiritual notes are found on pp. 224-40. Spiritual notes of Brébeuf, not found in that manuscript, were included by Father Ragueneau in his *Relation* of 1649. These may be examined in *Relations*, XXXIV, 158-94. In his excellent work on the writings of Brébeuf, Father Latourelle had presented a critically annotated text of most of Brébeuf's writings, including his spiritual notes. For the purposes of this book, when quoting Brébeuf, reference will be made to Father Latourelle's study. For those who might prefer to study Brébeuf's writings in their original French dress, they may be found in *Rapport de l'Archiviste de la Province de Québec*, 1924-1925.

[62] Before St. Ignatius founded the Society of Jesus, those entering religious orders spent one year of noviceship and, at its completion, pronounced solemn, perpetual vows. St. Ignatius introduced a system whereby those entering his order made two years of noviceship after which they pronounced simple vows which perpetually bound the subject to the order, but not the order to the subject. After a number of years in the Society, subjects pronounced their "final" vows. At that time the Jesuit order committed itself irrevocably to the subject.

[63] Latourelle, *Etude sur . . . Brébeuf*, II, 302.

one who had, in his past, led a dissolute life. On the contrary, this is the self-judgment of one who clearly perceives that even the least hesitancy in serving God constitutes a disloyalty unworthy of the good and faithful servant who is profoundly aware of the majesty and benignity of our heavenly Father. It is of the spirit animating St. Peter who fell on his knees before the divine Master, exclaiming: "Depart from me, for I am a sinful man."[64] Brébeuf himself confirmed this by a final sentence.

I never perceived within myself any attraction towards venial sin in such wise that I would take pleasure in committing one. Lest God cut me down as an unfruitful tree, I prayed that he still pass me by this year so that I might bring forth better fruit.[65]

At the completion of his retreat, Father Brébeuf recorded in his private notes:

On January 20, 1630, I pronounced the vows of a formed coadjutor in the chapel of the college at Rouen before Father Jacques Bertrix, the rector.[66] In 1621, in September, I received the sub-diaconate at Lisieux. In the same year I received the diaconate at Bayeux. At the beginning of Lent, 1622, I was ordained a priest at Pontoise. I offered the Holy Sacrifice to God for the first time on the feast of the Annunciation.[67]

The terse little note to himself seems to smack of a spiritual bookkeeper totaling up his company's profits. It is as though Brébeuf were reviewing his assets so that he might invest them profitably for the apostolic work he longed to perform.

Three weeks after completing his retreat, Jean de Brébeuf reported an incident, in his notes, which foreshadowed a vital factor in his whole future life. On February 9, 1630, he wrote: "Suddenly I seemed to be lifted above my senses and united to God. This devout experience lasted but a moment. In it there remained some awareness of the body."[68] This was not, perhaps, a true mystical experience, but subsequently Brébeuf attained to an

[64] The biblical quotation is found in Luke 5:8.

[65] Latourelle, *Etude sur . . . Brébeuf*, II, 202-03.

[66] St. Ignatius originally intended his order to be composed of priests only, all of whom would pronounce solemn vows. When it was discovered that apostolic work was being seriously hampered for lack of helpers, Ignatius, with papal approval, accepted candidates who would not pronounce solemn vows. These were technically known as spiritual coadjutors.

[67] Ibid., 203.

[68] Ibid.

exalted level of mysticism. An effort to explain mysticism and its effects on those so fortunate as to experience it, leads one to fall back on the introductory remark to the cinema version of Franz Werfel's *Song of Bernadette*: "To those who believe, no explanation is necessary; to those who do not, no explanation is possible." Mysticism has been defined as an incommunicable and inexpressible knowledge and love of God or religious truth without previous effort or reasoning.[69]

The exalted spiritual state of the mystic is attained, almost invariably, only after a long apprenticeship of physical and mental suffering, a purification by spiritual darkness and trial. When a soul, thus tried, is rendered completely free of the least inordinate attachment to things material and seeks, with its whole being, union with God alone, mystical experiences may be enjoyed. These rare souls, always profoundly humble and unswervingly obedient to their spiritual directors, normally suffer persecution, often from their closest associates. They are imbued with an overpowering love of the suffering Christ, a love which compels them to imitate him as closely as is humanly possible. Eventually, their union with God is so intimate that they acquire intuitive understanding of the divine which surpasses explanation. Ecstasies, visions, foretelling the future are divine graces frequently granted by God to these chosen souls. And, into this rare band Jean de Brébeuf was welcomed. In due time, after rigorous trial by spiritual fire, he would rise to the rarefied atmosphere of the mystics.

In the course of his annual retreat, in 1631, Father Brébeuf progressed further on the road to complete mystical union with God. In his tersely phrased spiritual diary, he wrote:

During the exercises in 1631, begun on May 12: Lord Jesus Christ, my Redeemer, who, by your blood and precious death redeemed me, I promise to devote my whole life to your service, a promise which I sign in my blood with my own hand, ready to pour out my life as freely as I do this drop of blood.[70]

It may well be asked why the apparently melodramatic gesture by one already bound to God by perpetual vows to accomplish what Brébeuf's solemn promise appears but to repeat. The

[69] David Knowles, *The Nature of Mysticism*, 13.
[70] Latourelle, *Etude sur . . . Brébeuf*, II, 203.

commitment, so solemnly entered, contains a significance peculiar to the mystical state. Progressing toward intimate union with the divine majesty, the developing mystic reaches a spiritual cross-road, a point at which, as Father Louis Lalemant, a highly prized director of chosen souls and a contemporary of Brébeuf, says that the eager soul crosses the threshold entering a rare atmosphere in which he is drawn to give himself entirely to God. Shakespeare expressed a similar commitment on the purely natural level when he had one of his characters declare: "Lead on Macduff, and I shall follow to the last gasp of love and loyalty."

Jean de Brébeuf's exalted spiritual life detracted no whit from his active ministry in France. During 1630, while still at Rouen, he wrote and published his little Huron-French catechism, *The Christian Doctrine of Rev. Father Ledesma, S.J., Translated into the Canadian Language, other than Montagnais, for the Conversion of the People of that Country.* The little duodecimo volume of twenty-six pages was published at Rouen in 1630 by Richard L'Allemant. It was the first effort of any European to bring to public notice the language of the Hurons.

After something over a year and a half at Rouen when, possibly, it seemed that years would pass before New France would again fly the flag of France, Jean de Brébeuf was, as it were, absorbed back into the normal routines of the Province of France. St. Luke's day, 1631, found him at Eu, along the west coast of France, not many miles north of Dieppe. There, Father Noël Etienne, the rector, put Brébeuf to work as bursar of the college as well as managing all the material details and keeping a sympathetic eye on the sick in the community. The quondam missionary kept the accounts, paid the bills, and saw to the housekeeping. During his first year there the Princess de Conti, daughter of the founder of the college, Henri de Lorraine, duke of Guise, died and was buried with elaborate ceremonies in the impressive college chapel which her mother, Catherine of Cleves, erected at great expense as a monument to her husband whom Henri III, king of France, had treacherously murdered on December 25, 1588. What Jean de Brébeuf thought of all this vain, expensive ostentation is nowhere recorded. Gazing out across the Manche, which the British call the English Channel, would he not sigh for his Hurons, reflecting how much could be accomplished among them with the funds dispensed to bury one girl because her mother happened to be of the nobility?[71]

While Jean de Brébeuf was kept occupied with his innumerable duties at Eu, Charles Lalemant stormed the convents of Paris begging for a crusade of prayers beseeching God to allow the Jesuits to go back to their mission. Enlisting the nuns in the convents of contemplatives at Paris, heaven was deluged by their incessant pleas. The nuns at the Carmelite convent in Paris were particularly cooperative because the prioress, Anne du Saint Sacrament, and two of her subjects were Lalemant's nieces, sisters of his nephew, Gabriel Lalemant, the future martyr.[72] Soon Charles Lalemant was hopeful. On December 31, 1631, he wrote to Father Etienne Charlet, adviser to the Jesuit general on French affairs:

There is promise of happy results in the matter of Canada. The English are putting out feelers regarding the restoration of Canada . . . It would be good if Father General would write to the provincial telling him that there would be no objection to our returning if we were asked.[73]

The longed for happy result came to pass on March 29, 1632, with the signing of the treaty of Saint Germain-en-Laye whereby Canada was finally and officially restored to France.

Restoration of New France did not automatically assure the Jesuits that they could promptly sail for Quebec. Given the intimate relationship between church and state in seventeenth-century France, the decision as to what group would be selected for continuing the evangelization of the Indians of Canada rested with the crown's bureau of missions whose director was the Capuchin, Père Joseph. Somewhat understandably, he offered the field to his own religious brethren. The decision amazed the Recollets, surprised the Jesuits, and disconcerted the Capuchins. These courteous religious politely declined, pointing out that a mission field opened by others ought to be at least offered to

[71] Delattre, *Établissements*, II, 416. Henri de Lorraine, duke of Guise, acquired the title of Count of Eu by his marriage to Catherine, daughter of Francis of Cleves, duke of Nevers. Though Catherine was the widow of a staunch Huguenot, she apparently had no objection when her second husband, the duke of Guise, founded the Jesuit college at Eu. Henri, his wife, and some of their fourteen children were buried in the college chapel at Eu.

[72] Rochemonteix, II, 87.

[73] Ibid., 186.

them. Since the Recollets were the proto-evangelists of New France and the Jesuits were, after all, only invited guests, in all fairness, the Recollets ought to be given the right to return to their field. But, their admirable poverty and their small numbers weighed against them. After lengthy negotiations, Cardinal Richelieu declared for the Jesuits, putting the Recollets off with vague promises. Naturally the Recollets felt slighted, convinced that the Jesuits had underhandedly gained a field to which they had no right.[74] The Jesuits, grateful to the depths of their souls, sent clouds of thankful prayers heavenward.

When Emery de Caën, at Richelieu's command, sailed from Honfleur for Quebec on Sunday, April 18, 1632, he had aboard ship Father Paul Le Jeune, Father Anne de Nouë, and Brother Gilbert Burel chosen by the Jesuit provincial to reopen missionary work in Canada. The party landed at Quebec on July 5, 1632, and a week later, on July 13, Thomas Kirke formally surrendered the place to the French. That very day Thomas Kirke weighed anchor and sailed for England, taking with him all of his followers and a fortune in furs.

If Jean de Brébeuf was disappointed at not accompanying Father Le Jeune, the latter's first report to the Jesuit provincial, Barthélemy Jacquinot, rejoiced his heart. Le Jeune recounted that several Indians had asked for Brébeuf by name, inquiring whether that missionary would ". . . return next year."[75] Finally, Brébeuf's orders came, freeing him from his humdrum tasks, allowing him to return to the land of his heart's desire. On the Wednesday of Holy Week, March 23, 1633, just two days before his fortieth birthday, Jean de Brébeuf with Enemond Massé sailed from Dieppe on the *Saint Pierre*. Also aboard was Samuel de Champlain, newly appointed governor of New France, an old and cherished friend. Just two months later, on Monday, May 23, Jean de Brébeuf set foot once more on the soil of New France.

---

[74] For a quite thorough discussion of the controversy, consult Etiénne M. Faillon, *Histoire de la colonie Française en Canada*, I, 279 ff. There is no doubt that both the Recollets and the Jesuits employed what influence they could. Perhaps the deciding factor was the preference of the Company of New France for the Jesuits who could be expected to be less of a financial burden than the Recollets.

[75] *Relations*, V, 55, 57.

Chapter V

Permanent Opening
of the Huron Mission

On Friday, May 19, 1633, the French at Quebec learned that a few days before an English ship had put in at Tadoussac.[1] Did this portend a new attack, another loss of the colony with the attendant banishment of the missionaries only one short year after their return? Emery de Caën, interim commander until the arrival of Samuel de Champlain, issued instructions to be followed in case the settlement suffered an attack. If the people heard two cannon shots fired in quick succession, everyone was to take refuge at the fort.[2] On Monday, May 22, early in the morning the brooding quiet of Quebec was rudely shattered by the booming report of a cannon fired twice without interval. Promptly, Father Anne de Noüe dashed off to the fort with a friendly Indian companion to discover the meaning of the signal. Just as quickly, and far more excitedly, he rushed back to Notre Dame des Anges bringing the most wonderful news. The signal was a welcoming

[1] *Relations*, V, 199.
[2] Ibid.

shot fired in honor of the sieur de Champlain who had just arrived. And with him was Father Jean de Brébeuf. Hardly were the words out of the messenger's mouth when the giant Norman was at the door. "God [alone] knows," wrote Le Jeune,[3] "with what joyous hearts we received and embraced him." And Brébeuf himself, brought great news. Father Enemond Massé was already at Tadoussac and would soon reach Quebec. Besides, Father Antoine Daniel and Father Ambroise Davost, who had been working with the Indians at Captain Daniel's Fort St. Anne on Cape Breton Island, were coming to Quebec.[4]

Jean de Brébeuf earnestly hoped that his stay at Quebec would be brief. As soon as the Huron fur brigade came down and completed the trading, he expected to go back to Huronia and

[3] Paul Le Jeune was born in 1591 at Vitry-le-François of Calvinist parents. As quite a young man he abjured Calvinism and became a Catholic, much against the wishes of his parents. At twenty-two he entered the Jesuit novitiate at Paris and, two years later, was sent to La Flèche for his studies. There he met Father Enemond Massé, back from Acadia only two years. Le Jeune was one of the pious band anxious for the Jesuits to regain Canada. In 1631, while at Dieppe, Le Jeune was appointed superior of the mission of New France. He sailed from Honfleur on April 18, 1632. He held the office of superior until 1639 and continued in Canada as a simple missionary, except for visits to France in 1641 and 1642 seeking help, both civil and ecclesiastical, for the colony. In 1649 he was recalled to France to act as agent for the Jesuit mission in Canada, an office he exercised with great success for many years. It was he who began the *Jesuit Relations*. The founding of Montreal was in no small measure made possible by his influence. He died at Paris on August 7, 1664.

[4] Antoine Daniel was born at Dieppe on May 27, 1601, of a seafaring family. Three of his brothers, Charles, André, and François were sea captains. Antoine was apparently destined for the law and had begun those studies when he entered the Jesuit novitiate at Rouen on October 1, 1621. Before his ordination, while teaching at Rouen, he may have had charge of a young Huron, Amantacha, whom Father Charles Lalemant had sent to Rouen to be educated by the Jesuits. Certainly Brébeuf had something to do with instilling an interest in New France in Daniel for the two were together at Eu. Daniel first worked at his brother's fort during 1632. Then he went to Quebec where he arrived on June 24, 1633. He went to Huronia in 1634 where he spent the greater part of his subsequent life. He was martyred on July 4, 1648.

Ambroise Davost was born at Laval in France on November 13, 1586, and entered the Jesuit novitiate at Rouen on October 14, 1611. He was already forty-six when he came to New France in 1632. After a year with Daniel at Cape Breton, he came to Quebec whence he went to Huronia in 1634. In 1636 he returned to Quebec for the purpose of helping found a seminary for Huron boys, an experiment which proved a dismal failure. After he came back to Quebec the man was constantly unwell. In 1643 he was sent back to France for treatment. He died before arriving and was buried at sea.

take Daniel and Davost with him. But a whole month passed before any group of Indians put in an appearance. A day or two after June 23, a group of twelve or fourteen canoes beached at Quebec. These were not Hurons but Iroquets, a small band of Ottawa who derived their name from their captain. Yet their arrival was a welcome sign that the Ottawa River route to the West was not infested by hostile Iroquois bands.

While awaiting the arrival of the Hurons, Jean de Brébeuf, the only missionary versed in Montagnais, was called upon to persuade an Indian family to allow a dying child to be baptized. Hurrying off to the Indian cabin late at night, Brébeuf procured the consent of the child's mother to baptize it, but, fearing that her husband might not agree, she insisted on notifying him. Regretfully, the father ". . . was drunk and asleep in another cabin."[5] Informed by a companion of the matter, the father announced: "Though I am drunk, I understand very well . . . go and bid these Fathers baptize my son . . . if he recovers I shall give him to them to be educated."[6] With all the palavering, it was very late at night before Brébeuf got back to his bed. Then Father Le Jeune asked if he was not pleased to have ended the day so well. "Ah!" replied the true apostle, "I would come expressly from France and cross the great Ocean, to reclaim one little soul for Our Lord."[7] Coming from Father Brébeuf, the remark enunciated a simple truth.

Not all of his contacts with the Indians at Quebec resulted so happily. On July 2, a Frenchman, while washing some clothes in a brook near the fort, was wantonly attacked. Brébeuf, who happened to be nearby, ran to the poor victim. He was so severely wounded that he was speechless and two days later he died. This was a serious business. When questioned, the Montagnais at first declared that a skulking Iroquois had murdered the Frenchman. But, shortly, it emerged that an Ottawa, long frustrated in his effort to kill another Indian, struck down the Frenchman in a moment of senseless wrath.[8] Not daring to ignore the incident,

[5] Ibid., 229.
[6] Ibid.
[7] Ibid., 231.
[8] Ibid., 225. The murderer was a member of the Petite Nation, a small Algonkin band of Ottawa living along the lower reaches of the Ottawa River.

Champlain apprehended the culprit and clapped him in irons, determined to inflict capital punishment. But among the Indians punitive justice was satisfied by presenting valuable gifts to the offended party, whom, in this case, the Indians considered to be Champlain himself. They offered him two young children to ". . . replace the morsel . . . cut from your heart," asking him to ". . . deliver up the prisoner so that we may all rejoice together."[9]

The unhappy incident would have serious repercussions affecting Brébeuf's immediate future. Unable to grasp the reason why these strange white men failed to be satisfied with their offer, the Ottawa warned the French that if the murderer was held prisoner, or, what would be worse, put to death, all of the members of his tribe would consider the act a hostile gesture to their whole people. They told the French that the prisoner's relatives would begin a vendetta against any and all of them passing up the Ottawa River, the only practical route to the Huron country.[10]

Both the French and the Ottawa were uneasy over the murder when, on July 28, 1633, the Huron flotilla, numbering nearly one hundred fifty canoes, bearing some seven hundred braves and a rich harvest of furs, finally arrived at Quebec.[11] The Ottawa had gone far up the St. Lawrence to meet the Hurons in an effort to dissuade them from direct contact with the French, some of whom, they knew, expected to go back to their homeland with the Hurons. Relating the punishment meted out to the murderer, the Ottawa warned that his relatives would certainly try to kill any Frenchmen caught on the Ottawa River. If and when that happened, the French would surely blame the Hurons.[12] While the Hurons were shrewd enough to realize that the Ottawa were

[9] Bishop, *Champlain*, 294.

[10] A much less difficult route to the Huron country would have been to paddle up the St. Lawrence to Lake Ontario and into the Bay of Quinte. From there one could reach Huronia by means of a series of lakes and rivers and one long portage from Balsam Lake to Lake Simcoe. The Hurons were certainly familiar with this route for they took Champlain over it in 1615. In his *Relation* of 1635 Brébeuf explained why the route was avoided. ". . . the fear of enemies and the few conveniences to be met with, caused that route to be unfrequented." *Relations*, VIII, 75. In his *Champlain*, 201, Bishop details the route, using the present names of the lakes and streams traversed.

[11] *Relations*, V, 239.

[12] Ibid., 239, 241.

really using the incident of the murder chiefly to give themselves control of the Ottawa trade route, they, themselves, bore a guilty secret causing them to approach the French with some trepidation. Not long before the flotilla left Huronia, Etienne Brûlé had been vindictively slaughtered and his body devoured in one of their villages.[13]

The diplomatic complications of the situation were very grave, especially because none of the French as yet understood the native languages well enough to be certain of all the ramifications present. Fortunately for the French, Amantacha, who understood French, could help. Reaching Quebec on July 4, 1633, well ahead of the Huron flotilla, Amantacha, whom the French called Louis de Sainte-Foy, was dispatched back up the St. Lawrence by Champlain to allay the fears of the Hurons. The French, the emissary assured his countrymen, held no grudge against them over the death of Brûlé. Because he defected to the English in 1629, the French considered him as a traitor whom they, themselves, would have punished severely had he fallen into their hands. Amantacha declared to his people that he would willingly allow them to kill him if the French did not give them a warm welcome.[14] Thus assured, the great Huron flotilla, sweeping into Quebec on July 28, 1633, set up camp around Champlain's *habitation* on the plain below the fort and began trading.[15]

Protocol required that the Hurons meet with Champlain in solemn council to exchange presents and discuss mutual interests. The conclave met on July 29, the Indians ". . . grave and serious in their rather long speeches."[16] Attesting that they came to assure the French of their friendship, the Hurons presented Champlain with three large bundles of rich beaver skins. In turn, Champlain informed the Hurons that he considered them to be brothers and would extend the protection of his powerful king to them. As proof of the truth of what he said, Champlain gave his visitors valuable presents. Further, he announced that he was sending Jesuit missionaries back with the Hurons to dwell among them.

---

13 Ibid., 239.
14 Ibid., 241.
15 Ibid., 239.
16 Ibid., 249.

These are our Fathers . . . [he said] we love them more than our children
or ourselves; they are held in very high esteem in France; it is neither hunger nor want that brings them to this country; they do not come to see you
for your property or your furs . . . If you love the French people, as you say
you do, then love these Fathers; honor them, and they will teach you the
way to heaven. This is what makes them leave their country, their friends,
and their comforts, to teach you, and especially to teach your children a
knowledge so great and so necessary.[17]

At that announcement,

. . . all the Indians, according to their custom, evinced their satisfaction by
their profound aspiration: ho! ho! ho! Then they surrounded Father Brébeuf, each one wanting to carry him away in his canoe.[18]

If the Hurons had been prepared to depart that very day, they
would have gladly welcomed the missionaries assigned to go with
them. But, during the week of trading, the Ottawa labored mightily to thwart the departure of the Jesuits or, for that matter, any
other Frenchman seeking to accompany the Hurons to their country. Finally, on the night before the Hurons planned to leave,
they and the Ottawa captains held council at which the wishes of
the Ottawa prevailed. The Hurons announced that they could not
agree to take any French, even missionaries, with them because
the Ottawa opposed their coming and, after all, the river was not
theirs, but belonged to the Ottawa.[19] Despite every effort by
Champlain and the missionaries, the Hurons held fast to that decision. Peace between the Ottawa and the Hurons was an economic necessity for without it trade would be at an end for the
Hurons. If the Hurons ignored the wishes of the Ottawa, braves
of that nation were bound to waylay and murder one or other
Frenchman traveling under the protection of the Hurons. Such a
catastrophe inevitably meant a disastrous war between the two
nations and all the allies of each. Since Champlain would not release the Ottawa prisoner, the Hurons could not risk inviting any
Frenchmen to come with them.

And that was the end of it. Again, as in 1625, Brébeuf's longing to go to the Hurons was thwarted. Gravely disappointed, he
and his two companions retrieved their baggage from each of the

[17] Ibid., 253.
[18] Ibid.
[19] Ibid., VI, 11.

Huron groups who had already agreed to embark them. Down-hearted, they made their sorry way back to the Jesuit residence, fervently hoping for better luck next year. Through the summer and fall of 1633 Father Brébeuf devoted himself to perfecting his own command of the Huron tongue while teaching it to Antoine Daniel and Ambroise Davost.[20] On October 18, 1633, Father Paul Le Jeune left Quebec with a band of Montagnais, determined to spend the winter with them so that he might learn, at first hand, their language and their customs.[21] During his absence Father Brébeuf acted as superior for the group. When Le Jeune returned, on April 9, 1634, he found a contented community, all anxious for the Hurons to return for the trading so that Brébeuf and his companions might be off to the land of their desire.[22]

When the annual fleet from France arrived in the early summer of 1634, the little outpost of Quebec bustled with activity. On June 2, Father Charles Lalemant arrived bringing with him Brother Jean Liégeois.[23] Two days later Robert Giffard de Moncel came, accompanied by his family and ". . . many persons whom he brought to settle this country."[24] With so many new recruits, both Champlain and Father Le Jeune could lay plans for expanding their activities. A major concern for Champlain was the establishment of a satisfactory site at which to hold the annual rendezvous with the various tribes coming to trade with the French. Quebec would not do because it was too great a distance for the Indians to come and also because a fur fair with its roistering Frenchmen and celebrating Indians was hardly conducive to the dignity and respect with which Champlain wished his capital city to be endowed. As early as 1604, Champlain, on seeing the site where the triple-mouthed St. Maurice River enters the St. Lawrence, remarked that

20 Ibid., 21.

21 Ibid., VII, 71.

22 Ibid., VI, 37.

23 Jean Liégeois was born in 1599 or 1600 and entered the Society of Jesus at Paris in 1623. He reached Quebec on June 2, 1634. He must have been at least a journeyman carpenter, considering his skill as a builder. In about 1640 he built a residence and a chapel at Three Rivers. He erected a mill at La Vacherie in 1646 and the first college building at Quebec in 1648. He was sent to France four different times between 1644 and 1652. While erecting a fort at Sillery he was slain by a band of Mohawks on May 29, 1655.

24 Ibid., VII, 211, 213.

. . . a settlement at Three Rivers would be a boon for the freedom of some tribes who dare not come that way [that is, to Tadoussac] for fear of their enemies, the said Iroquois, who infest the banks all along the said river of Canada [that is, the St. Lawrence] . . .[25]

Settling on Three Rivers as the permanent meeting place between trading Indians and the French, Champlain, on July 1, 1634, dispatched a competent fur trader, Laviolette, upriver with a few soldiers and laborers to build a stockade enclosing a warehouse and dwellings. Landing on July 4, Laviolette and his crew promptly began establishing their quarters.[26]

Now, at last, arose the proper occasion to launch an adequately staffed and properly equipped apostolic offensive. On the sloop carrying Laviolette and his contingent to Three Rivers, Jean de Brébeuf was aboard with Antoine Daniel, six laymen pledged to serve them on the mission, and all the supplies, material and ecclesiastical, the missionaries might need.[27] The hopeful apostles were hardly ashore before all but insurmountable difficulties confronted them. Instead of a great fleet of canoes manned by Hurons, only eleven arrived at Three Rivers. The Hurons explained that in the spring they had launched a disastrous attack

[25] Champlain, I, 137.

[26] *Relations*, VII, 213. Historians have been unable to discover anything about Laviolette, even his Christian name, except that he was a fur trader and commanded at Three Rivers from 1634 to 1636. The French were not newcomers to the site. The Recollets maintained a mission there from 1615 to 1628. The fort at Three Rivers is said to have been built near the location of an Algonkin village. See ibid., IV, 201.

[27] Ibid., VII, 213. En route to Three Rivers, Brébeuf wrote a note of thanks to one of his Jesuit friends at Rouen who had evidently sent him some small gifts. Brébeuf wrote: "I am very grateful to your Reverence for remembering me and the trouble you took to write as well as for the excellent Agnus Dei and the holy pictures. We here cannot repay you in kind but if God deigns to send you to the Hurons, where we hope to go this year, we shall then repay our obligations to you. I do not include any news because you will get it from the *Relation* where you will learn of the conversion and happy death of two adult Indians and the baptism of three little infants of whom one has already gone to heaven. I beg the continuation of your prayers and Holy Sacrifices of which we are in dire need during the trip to the Hurons which we are now attempting. Be assured of our prayers for and remembrance of you. Please remember us to all the Fathers and Brothers of the college at Rouen." The letter is dated July 3, 1634, "From New France on the way to Three Rivers." See Latourelle, *Etude sur . . . Brébeuf*, II, 42-43.

against the Iroquois who roundly defeated them, killing some two hundred and capturing another hundred.[28] Besides, the Hurons who came to the rendezvous were sick, suffering from an epidemic afflicting all the nations along the Ottawa River and in Huronia.[29] At first, while Father Brébeuf bargained for places in their canoes, the Hurons showed no enthusiasm, understandably arguing that, sick as they were, it would be hard enough to get home themselves without being burdened with a large group of Frenchmen and their baggage. Encouraging the reluctance, the Partridge, an Algonkin captain, through whose country the Hurons must pass on their return, ". . . made a speech recommending them not to take any Frenchmen on board."[30] Even though the Algonkin captain's motive was purely economic, the Hurons, grasping at the straw, ". . . became very cold . . ."[31] to the efforts of Brébeuf.

How frustrating it must have been! After five long years of waiting, the door to the promised land was about to be slammed in Brébeuf's face. Proffered presents were rejected. The Hurons would take some Frenchmen, but only such as were well armed, not ". . . these long robes who carried no guns."[32] Thwarted by men, Jean de Brébeuf sought the intercession of St. Joseph, who had been chosen as the heavenly patron of Canada. He wrote to Le Jeune,

It was by a providential chance that we were taken and through the power of the glorious Saint Joseph, to whom God inspired me to offer, in my despair of all things, the promise of 20 masses in his honor.[33]

Then the unyielding attitude of the Hurons began to weaken. Perhaps they did so because, on July 5, Charles Du Plessis-Bochart, chief clerk of the Company of New France, arrived

---

[28] *Relations*, VII, 213, 215.

[29] The illness, which later precipitated a major crisis for the Jesuits among the Hurons, was described by Le Jeune as ". . . a sort of measles and an oppression of the stomach." Ibid., 221.

[30] Ibid., 215.

[31] Ibid.

[32] Ibid., 217.

[33] Ibid.

bringing Father Ambroise Davost with him.[34] Mayhap only for the sake of maintaining that official's goodwill, the Hurons yielded a little at a time. They would take a few missionaries, but not all, and certainly not the mountain of baggage the Jesuits wished to transport. And, the missionaries must work, paddling and carrying at the portages along with the Indians.[35] At that, the Hurons agreed to take only Brébeuf, Daniel, and one lay helper, Simon Baron, an amateur surgeon. As to Father Davost and the other lay assistants, Du Plessis-Bochart promised that he would gain places for them and the baggage as other Hurons came to Three Rivers. At last, on July 7, with a deep sigh of relief, Jean de Brébeuf pushed off from Three Rivers for the land of his heart's desire. His departure was honored ". . . with several volleys, to recommend us still more to our Indians."[36]

Jean de Brébeuf's experiences on his journey to the Huron country in 1634 differed greatly from those he encountered eight years before, in 1626. Then he had been accepted as a paying passenger, expected to extend no effort paddling or transporting his own baggage at the thirty-five or more portages or the fifty stretches of shallow water where a canoe, empty of everything, was dragged by someone struggling barefoot over the sharp stones of a lake or river bottom.[37] But, in 1634, Brébeuf agreed to ". . . paddling continually, just as much as the Indians."[38] Besides, he contracted with the Hurons that he and his companions would ". . . carry our [own] baggage at the portages, which was as laborious for us as it was new, and still more for others than for me, who already knew a little what it is to be fatigued."[39]

Embarking, probably about midday on July 7, 1634, Brébeuf and his Huron companions pushed against the strong current of the St. Lawrence around Pointe du Lac and into the slack water

[34] Charles Du Plessis-Bochart was by profession a naval officer. As chief clerk of the Company of New France, he was probably empowered to dispense goods and funds. He is thought to have been a rather close relative of Cardinal Richelieu. He was an intelligent and zealous officer who served well and faithfully for the few years he was in New France.

[35] Ibid., 221.

[36] Ibid., VIII, 75.

[37] Ibid., 77. This was Brébeuf's estimate.

[38] Ibid., 79.

[39] Ibid.

of Lac Saint Pierre. Threading through the islands at the western end of the lake, the great river again challenged them. Fifty miles of strenuous paddling brought them to the Rivière des Prairies dividing the island of Montreal from the Ile Jésus, allowing them to avoid the fearful Lachine Rapids near the western end of the island of Montreal. Conquering the Rivière des Prairies, the weary paddlers pushed gratefully into the placid waters of the Lac des Deux Montagnes, twenty-five miles of quiet water. But then they encountered the rough, capricious Ottawa where it narrows between Pointe Fortune and Saint André. Only a short distance onward, some fifty miles from the island of Montreal, the travelers entered the Long Sault, a six-mile stretch of water so impeded by rapids that three separate portages were required to negotiate it.[40]

At the Long Sault, Brébeuf found an opportunity for sending a brief report back to Father Le Jeune in care of some Hurons going down to Three Rivers to trade. "We are going on," he wrote, "by short stages, quite well, as far as we are concerned; but our Indians are all sick . . . All our Indians are very much pleased with us . . . ; they speak well of us to those whom they meet, persuading them not to embark any others."[41] It was important to Father Brébeuf for him to gain the respect and good-will of Hurons bound for Three Rivers so that they would be willing to bring back with them the other missionaries as well as the lay helpers and the baggage.

Slowly, day by day, Brébeuf and his fever-ridden Hurons worked their tedious way up the Ottawa until they reached the backbreaking portage around boiling Chaudière Falls at the site of Canada's present national capital, Ottawa. Then they could paddle through placid Lake Deschene, so gentle and idyllic that

[40] Hugh MacLennan, *Seven Rivers of Canada*, 92.

[41] *Relations*, VII, 219, 221. Latourelle, in *Etude sur . . . Brébeuf*, I, 10, thinks that Brébeuf was at the Long Sault on about July 10, three days after departing from Three Rivers. Under ideal conditions, Indians could travel by canoe in fresh water about thirty miles a day. See Donnelly, *Jacques Marquette*, 239. Brébeuf's note to Le Jeune is not dated. Though the site of the Long Sault is not much over one hundred miles from Three Rivers, it would seem that Brébeuf and his party advanced more slowly than thirty miles a day, since he says that they were going on by short stages, which would indicate many stops. The meaning of Brébeuf's remark, ". . . persuading them not to embark any others . . ." would seem to mean French traders rather than missionaries.

one could barely believe it to be part of the Ottawa River. Yet, beyond was Lac des Chats, aptly named for barely submerged under water were myriads of jagged rocks, sharp as angry cat's paws ready to rip the paper-thin bark canoes to shreds. Escaping that hazard, the party must needs negotiate the difficult Portage du Fort. And a little less than fourteen miles above it was the mile-long Grand Calumet portage, giving entrance to Allumette Lake where the Ottawa bifurcates, forming Allumette Island, an Ottawa nation stronghold. And there Brébeuf and his still ailing Indians rested for a day, as well they might, before attacking the nearly seventy miles of the Rapides des Joachims with its constant obstructions of the river.[42]

Finally, at the end of that wearisome toil, they met the mouth of the Mattawa River, swirling out between its two rocky guardians. Having made this journey in 1626, Jean de Brébeuf knew what lay ahead. The Mattawa, a swift, narrow stream, opposed the paddlers every inch of its thirty miles and several portages, one of which, Paresseux Talon, was considered by Alexander Mackenzie, the eighteenth-century explorer, to be the most difficult portage between Montreal and the Rocky Mountains. Gliding out of the Mattawa, into its source, Lake Talon and its neighbor, Trout Lake, the party found placid water surrounded by low, rolling hills. At the western end of Trout Lake they paddled to the bottom of Dugas Bay and portaged three times around shallow beaver ponds to reach the little La Vase River, so appropriately named because of the slime deposited on its bottom. That unattractive stream drains westward into the eastern end of Lake Nipissing near the present North Bay.

Edging along the southern shore of Lake Nipissing, they reached the outlet to the black, angry French River, rushing down a granite channel which barely contains it. Beyond Eighteen Mile Island, the French River is squeezed into a millrace until it opens into Allen Lake which subdues the river to a pleas-

[42] *Relations*, VIII, 89. Brébeuf was nearly drowned just above Allumette Island. In his report on the state of the Huron mission dated May 27, 1635, he wrote: "For myself, not knowing how to swim, I once had a very narrow escape from drowning. As we were leaving the Bissiriniens [the Ottawa dwelling at Allumette Island], while descending a rapid we would have gone over a precipice had not my Indians promptly and skillfully leaped into the water, to turn aside the canoe which the current was sweeping on." Ibid., 83.

ant placidity, leading gently into Georgian Bay, just above Bustard Island.

Now the ailing Indians must have taken heart for home was only ninety miles to the south. Making their way down the eastern shore of Georgian Bay, paddling from island to island, the Hurons hastened toward home. At last, on August 5, 1634, the feast of Our Lady of the Snows, thirty long, exhausting days out of Three Rivers, Brébeuf and his companions lifted their battered and patched canoe out of the water onto a sandy beach on the western bank of Penetang Harbor.[43] Much to his surprise and disappointment, Brébeuf saw his Indian companions shoulder their baggage and stalk off with hardly a backward glance. They had agreed to give the missionary a place in their canoe if he worked his passage. Well, they had fulfilled their part of the bargain; let him now fend for himself. Recounting his arrival, Brébeuf wrote:

My Indians, forgetting the kindness I had lavished upon them and the help I had afforded them in their sickness, and notwithstanding all the fair words and promises they had given me, after having landed me with some Church equipment and some other little necessities, left me there quite alone, without any provisions and without shelter, and resumed their route towards their villages, some seven leagues distant.[44]

Here was a pretty kettle of fish. Eight years ago the little cove where Brébeuf landed had been frequented by many people. But now the once adjacent village had been removed but to where, Brébeuf knew not. After a month of grueling travel, during which much of the physical work fell on his broad shoulders, Jean de Brébeuf was so exhausted that he was unable to carry his small bundles nor could he risk leaving them unguarded to be carried off by the first Indian who stumbled upon them.[45] He asked the Indians to help him carry his baggage to the village, which could not be far off, or at least to stay with his equipment until he made inquiries and returned with help. "But their ears were deaf to my prayers and my remonstrances. The only consolation they gave me was to tell me that some one would find me there."[46]

---

[43] Ibid., 91. Jones, 57-58, holds that the exact location of Brébeuf's landing is at a creek flowing into Penetang Harbor at Picotte's Beach.

[44] Relations, VIII, 91.

[45] Ibid.

[46] Ibid.

During the three years Brébeuf had dwelt among the Hurons, 1626 to 1629, he had lived at a village called Toanché which had then been located not far from where he landed on his return. Having acquired many friends there, Brébeuf was anxious to make this the starting point of the crusade for the conversion of the Hurons. He knew the village had been removed, in part because Etienne Brûlé had been killed there and partly because it was simply time to move the village to a more sanitary location. But where had it been located? Left alone, Jean de Brébeuf resorted to prayer.

. . . I prostrated myself at once upon my knees to thank God, our Lady and Saint Joseph, for the favors and mercies I had received during the voyage. I saluted the Guardian Angel of the Country, and offered myself to our Lord with all our little labors for the salvation of these poor Peoples, taking hope that God would not abandon me there . . . Then, . . . I hid my packages in the woods; and taking with me what was most precious, I set out to find the village, which fortunately I came upon at about three-quarters of a league, having seen with tenderness and emotion, as I passed along, the place where we had lived, and had celebrated the Holy sacrifice of the Mass during three years . . . likewise the spot where Etienne Brûlé was barbarously and traitorously murdered . . .[47]

The welcome Jean de Brébeuf received from his old friends and neighbors must have warmed his heart. When the people noticed him, someone shouted: "Why, there is Echon come back again."[48] Delightedly they gathered around him, calling to him: "Well, well, my nephew, my brother, my cousin, you have finally come back to us!"[49] Greeting them all warmly, Brébeuf first found a place to stay for the night and, after a brief rest, explained his predicament to them. Would anyone be willing to go back with him and bring his baggage? Though it was getting dark, a whole host of young people gladly volunteered to return with Echon to collect his packages. Jabbering away to him, the young people

[47] Ibid., 93.
[48] Ibid. Brébeuf's Huron name, Echon, has been variously translated as The Great One, The Strong One, and so forth. Father Chaumonot, who bore the name after Brébeuf's martyrdom, said that it really was the name of a certain tree which the Hurons believed had some medicinal properties. See ibid., V, 287.
[49] Ibid., VIII, 93.

walked the two miles, gathered the hidden bundles and paraded back, reaching the village an hour after sunset.[50]

Once arrived in the Huron country practical problems confronted Father Brébeuf. If all went well, there would soon be two more Jesuits and several lay helpers dependent upon him for food and shelter. Assuming that all the supplies, so carefully selected and packaged, came through the long, hazardous journey without mishap, Brébeuf would be able to purchase food, such as it was, from the Indians and pay them for erecting a cabin in which the little band of apostles and their assistants could live and even, at times, have the luxury of a little privacy. But, if disaster struck, causing the loss of everything, then what? The Hurons were ". . . exceedingly hospitable towards all sorts of persons, even towards strangers . . . who were welcome to stay as long as they wished, . . . being always well treated . . ."[51] But from Frenchmen, the Hurons expected some recompense, at the guest's discretion. And well the Hurons might, for in their eyes the French were wealthy beyond imagining.

Knowing the financial resources of many families, Brébeuf considerately chose to ". . . lodge with a man named Aouandoié, who is, or at least was, one of the richest of the Hurons. I did this on purpose," Brébeuf explained, "because another with smaller means might have been inconvenienced with the large number of Frenchmen whom I was expecting, and who had to be provided with food and shelter until we had all gathered together, and our own cabin was ready."[52] Truly grateful, Brébeuf took time in his report to explain that Aouandoié was a naturally good, charitable man who generously gave of his bounty when a disastrous fire twice burned his village to the ground while his cabin was spared. Father Brébeuf and, in due time, others ate Aouandoié's food and shared his cabin ". . . for the space of more than a month and a half until we took possession of our new cabin."[53]

[50] Ibid. The Hurons called the village Taendeuiata. Jones, 57-58, locates it at lot 3, concession XIX, Tiny township, Simcoe county, Ontario. This would place it within an area which is now a Provincial Park Reserve.

[51] *Relations*, VIII, 91, 93.

[52] Ibid., 93.

[53] Ibid., 97.

For the first couple of days after his arrival Brébeuf was busy receiving his old friends who thronged his host's cabin to greet him and welcome him back with a heartening demonstration of gladness. Once the news of Echon's return spread to neighboring villages they too sent delegations to welcome him. They revealed their gladness on learning that he had reached Quebec and was preparing to return to them. His very presence, they avowed, would assure them of abundant crops. Since he had left they had experienced nothing but famine. They were not above admitting, however, that with Echon in Huronia the French would surely continue to trade with them. Until now they feared that, because Brûlé had been killed among them, the French would exclude them from trading. And cutting them off from the European market would have been a great disaster, so much had they come to depend on goods of European manufacture.[54]

As time passed during the next couple of weeks, Father Brébeuf heard of the arrival of various members of the missionary contingent at widely separated villages. Collecting the scattered party obliged him to spend himself gathering them together. Unable to communicate with the Indians, each of the party would have experienced endless time and undergone great trouble just to join, finally, with their superior, Father Brébeuf. One ingenious layman found his way by endlessly repeating *Echon, Ihonatiria* which, Father Brébeuf explained, ". . . are my name and that of our village."[55]

Each arriving Jesuit and layman had his own tale of hardships, frustrations, and for some, ill-treatment by the Indians.

Father Davost . . . was very badly treated. They stole from him much of his little outfit. They compelled him to throw away a little steel mill, and almost all our books, some linen, and a good part of the paper that we were taking, and of which we have great need. They deserted him at the Island [Allumette] among the Algonkins, where he suffered in good earnest. When he reached the Hurons, he was so worn out and dejected that for a long time he could not get over it.[56]

[54] Ibid., 99.
[55] Ibid.
[56] Ibid., 81. When Davost made this journey he was three months short of his forty-ninth birthday.

Father Daniel and Simon Baron left Three Rivers in a wretched canoe manned by three ailing Indians. By the time they reached Allumette Island both Indians and Europeans longed to be shut of one another. The Indians wanted to abandon Father Daniel there, but a captain of the Huron village of Ossossané, who met Daniel in 1633, gave the priest place in his own large canoe which was manned by ". . . six powerful savages, quite healthy and good natured."[57]

The faithful Simon Baron had more than his share of difficulties. Responsible for most of the equipment forwarded to the Huron country, he was an object of envy on the part of his Indian traveling companions. What was this one Frenchman doing with all those attractive goods? At Allumette Island, his original Indian companions had enough of Baron and his mountain of baggage. They would have abandoned him there were it not for the captain of the island who demanded that Simon and his boxes and bales be taken aboard by another group. Even so, he was forty days on the road, far longer than any of the others. And, besides, he received no help at the portages and often he and only one Indian were left to manage the heavily laden canoe. Summing up Baron's experiences, Brébeuf wrote: "He had to carry all his packages himself; he had narrow escapes three or four times in the torrents; and, to crown his difficulties, much of his property was stolen."[58]

Poor little Eustache Martin, only thirteen years old, suffered more than any of the others. The Hurons with whom he traveled left him behind at Allumette Island ". . . where he remained so long that he was about two months on the road, and only arrived among the Hurons on the nineteenth of September."[59] Like so many young boys after him, Eustache was sent out to learn the language and ways of the Indians so that he could become a fur trader. After all, thirteen was not so young, if it is recalled that a

[57] Ibid., 85.

[58] Ibid., 85, 99.

[59] See Paul Desjardins, "Le frère coajuteur Dominique Scot et Eustache Martin," *Lettres du Bas-Canada* X (1956), 208-31. The author holds that Eustache Martin was the son of Abraham Martin and his second wife, Marguerite Langlois, whom he married before coming to New France. Eustache was born at Quebec and baptized there on October 24, 1621. Desjardins thinks that Eustache died in Huronia during a smallpox epidemic in the summer of 1635.

boy of fourteen was considered by the French in New France old enough to bear arms in the defense of the colony, as many did.

While waiting for his small contingent to assemble, Father Brébeuf surveyed the country of the Huron Bear clan where he would have the Indians build him a cabin to house his people. Once again, as at Quebec in the summer of 1633, captains of various villages competed for the distinction of having the Jesuits settle in their village to the exclusion of others.[60] These captains, not necessarily interested in what the missionaries wished to teach the people, were sufficiently astute to realize that wherever the Jesuits settled was bound to become a rendezvous for French traders coming into their country. Hence, the place the Jesuits chose was sure to become an emporium for European goods, and an important one.

Now in the summer of 1634, the captain of the village of Ossossané, named by the French, La Rochelle, made a strong case, urging Brébeuf to settle there. He pointed out that in his village the Jesuits would be ". . . as it were in the center of the nation."[61] If Brébeuf felt that Ossossané was too far inland from Georgian Bay, the captain promised that his braves would gladly act as porters, carrying anything back and forth to open water. The generous offer tempted Father Brébeuf so much that he left all the baggage brought there by Father Daniel for quite some time, ". . . intending to carry the rest [of their equipment] thither and abide there."[62] However, this was a touchy business. Whatever location Father Brébeuf chose was bound to offend someone. The choice involved diplomatic implications as well.

Le Borgne, captain of the [Allumette] Island Ottawa, striving to prevent the French from trading directly with the Hurons, launched a rumor that Champlain had forbidden the missionaries to settle among any of the former residents of the abandoned village of Toanché where Etienne Brûlé had been murdered. The people residing in the small villages near the old Toanché had all

---

[60] *Relations*, V, 255, 259.

[61] Ibid., VIII, 101. Jones, 134, locates Ossossané at lot 18, concession VIII, Tiny township, Simcoe county, Ontario. At present the site of the village is obscured by scrub timber. Below the bluff on which the village stood is a group of none too attractive summer cottages. On the sand beach where Huron canoes clustered are the usual roadside stands dispensing soft drinks and picnic food.

[62] *Relations*, VIII, 101.

belonged to that now accursed place. If Brébeuf chose some other location, Le Borgne would certainly claim a victory which might, perhaps, so influence the Bear clan, at least, that they might well cease going down to the French trade fair.[63] Then, how would the Jesuits obtain supplies and recruits for the mission among the Hurons?

Jean de Brébeuf's choice of a location was a master stroke of diplomacy. He would settle among the former residents of Toanché, but somewhat removed from any of the satellite villages sprung from that now abandoned center. Hurons from the villages of Oenrio and Taendeuiata were induced ". . . by means of presents given them . . ." to build a Huron cabin for the Jesuits.[64] The structure was ". . . only six *brasses* long, and about three and a half *brasses* wide."[65] Instead of the single, long open space of the native cabins, the missionaries installed two partitions, dividing their poor shelter into three rooms. The first, nearest the door, was used for storing supplies. The second served as living quarters, workshop, refectory, and dormitory, all rolled into one. The third small room was divided lengthwise, forming two compartments. One of these was a chapel ". . . in which we celebrate holy Mass every day and retire there daily to pray to God . . . In the other part we put our utensils."[66]

[63] Ibid., 103.

[64] Ibid., 107. For the location of Taendeuiata, see note 50 above. Jones locates Oenrio at lot 5, concession XVII, Tiny township, Simcoe county, Ontario, which places it only a few yards from Farlane Lake.

[65] *Relations*, VIII, 109. A French *brasse* was about six feet or the span of a man's two outstretched arms. The cabin measured, roughly, twenty by thirty-six feet.

[66] Ibid. The internal arrangement of the cabin was really not a Jesuit invention. Sagard, in his *Histoire*, I, 214-15, describes the cabin the Recollets caused to be erected at Carhagouha. He writes: "Our poor cabin was about twenty feet long and ten or twelve feet wide, shaped like an arbor and covered with bark . . . we divided our cabin into thirds with that [portion] nearest the door for eating and sleeping . . . the second, less large, was [used] for storing our equipment . . . in the third we built a wooden altar . . . this was our chapel . . . Close to our cabin we planted a small garden, enclosing it with a fence to keep the children out. The peas, herbs and other things we planted flourished very well." The site of Carhagouha is thought to have been on lot 21, concession XVII, Tiny township, Simcoe county, Ontario. A modest historical marker indicates the location which is about two miles northwest of the present village of Lafontaine.

The French laymen were of very little help in erecting this crude home for they had no experience in handling the materials involved. Thus, the Indians themselves did most of the work, but slowly and reluctantly, partly because the site chosen by Father Brébeuf was in the neighborhood of, but not within any existing Huron village. It was located near the village of Taendeuiata where the wealthy Aouandoié had so generously fed and housed the Jesuits for many weeks. The cabin was built on a bluff overlooking Georgian Bay, directly above a snug little harbor, protected from wind and wave, where canoes coming from Quebec could take refuge and be unloaded with ease. The Jesuits dedicated their little mission center to St. Joseph, but the Hurons called the place Ihonatiria, which, in their language, meant "the little hamlet above the loaded canoe."

At long last, very late in September, six hard, trying weeks after Jean de Brébeuf reached the Huron country, all of the missionaries and their lay helpers were gathered together under one roof, such as it was.[67] And with that tiny band of three priests and five laymen, Jean de Brébeuf, the only one who even knew the language, unhesitatingly expected to convert a nation of some twenty thousand people.

[67] *Relations*, VIII, 107.

Chapter VI

Superior
of the Huron Mission

At last, on a crisp day in early October 1634, with the maple trees a riot of color behind it and the sparkling blue waters of Georgian Bay smiling before it, Jean de Brébeuf could gaze fondly at the permanent residence of the Jesuits among the Hurons. This was his apostolic Rachel for whom he served one more year than did Jacob to be eligible for her hand.[1] Now Brébeuf and his two fellow apostles could take the first tentative steps toward the conversion of the Hurons, if they could be attracted to listen and understand the word of God.

After settling in and unpacking their scant possessions, the missionaries were continually visited by an unending stream of callers. The interior arrangement of the Jesuit cabin, with its several partitions, was something most of those Indians had never seen. They thought the French were extremely clever for having

[1] In Genesis 29:20, it is related that Jacob served Laban, Rachel's father, seven years for Rachel. Brébeuf waited eight years, 1626 to 1634, before he saw the establishment of a permanent mission among the Hurons. Of course, the analogy limps. By trickery, Jacob was given Leah at the end of seven years. He served another seven before he was given Rachel.

devised it.[2] The Hurons were also constantly surprised at the astonishing things they saw within the cabin. A small hand mill for grinding wheat, which the Jesuits brought, was a continued source of delight. They were forever using it, always surprised to witness the results. As for the small striking clock, they were so sure it was a living being that they called it the captain of the day. Whenever the clock struck the hour, the Indians quickly counted all of the French to see if one of them had not stolen away to cause the effect. Sometimes, for a joke, one of the French laymen, at the last stroke of the hour, would call out: "That's enough." And, of course, the clock would fall silent.[3] When the Indians asked what the clock said, they were told that when it struck four it said: " 'Go out, go away that we may close the door' . . . The other, that at midday it said . . . 'Come put on the kettle'; and this speech is better remembered than the other, for some of these spongers never fail to come at that hour, to get a share of our Sagamité."[4]

The Hurons were equally astonished at a magnet's power to attract iron, a prism with eleven facets, craftsmen's tools and a small phial ". . . in which a flea appears as large as a beetle."[5] But, most of all, they were intrigued by the simple skill of writing. They could not understand how squiggles committed to a sheet of bark by one missionary could be understood by another who was at a great distance from the original writer. They tried hundreds of times themselves without any success. "All of this," remarked Father Brébeuf, "serves to gain their affection, and to render them more docile when we introduce the admirable and incomprehensible mysteries of our Faith; for the belief they have in our intelligence and capacity causes them to accept without question what we say to them."[6]

But, as Hamlet said in his lengthy soliloquy, ". . . ay, there's the rub . . ."[7] How would Jean de Brébeuf find a point of common

---

[2] It is possible that some of the Hurons from the Bear clan saw the cabin erected by the Recollets at Carhagouha, also a Bear clan village located about five miles west and a little south of the cabin built for Brébeuf.

[3] *Relations*, VIII, 111.

[4] Ibid., 113.

[5] Ibid.

[6] Ibid.

[7] *Hamlet*, Act III, scene 1.

contact with these literal-minded Hurons on which he could build to lead them over the bridge from their purely materialistic concepts of man and his nature to the knowledge, understanding, and acceptance of the revealed truths of Christianity? One small, weak flame shone forth in the darkness of their superstition. "They believe," reported Brébeuf, "in the immortality of the soul, which they believed to be corporeal."[8] Even so, at least the Hurons believed in a life after death, one free from care, in a place far to the west where everyone is happy. If the missionaries could just learn the Huron language sufficiently well, in time they would be able to lead these people to a true knowledge of man's nature and his relationship to God. To that end, Brébeuf, in his first *Relation* of 1635, remarked:

In the first place, we have been employed in the study of the language, which, on account of the diversity of its compound words, is almost infinite . . . Fathers Davost and Daniel have worked at it beyond all; . . . As for me, who give lessons therein to our French, if God does not assist me extraordinarily, I shall yet have to go a long time to the school of the Indians, so prolific is their language.[9]

During the fall and early winter little could be done evangelizing the Indians on a wholesale scale for they were too busy fishing, hunting, or trading with the neighboring tribes. In early January 1635, when cold weather and heavy snow gathered the Hurons into their cabins with time on their hands, Brébeuf and his two missionary companions began their apostolate in good earnest. With the cooperation of the captain of the village, the people were regularly gathered together in the cabin of the Jesuits. There, vested in surplice and biretta, Father Brébeuf taught the Indians the Our Father in their own language and had them chant it antiphonally. Then he gave them an instruction on one or other Christian truth, chiefly laying emphasis on the immortality of the soul and the obligation of every man, by his good life on earth, to gain heaven and avoid hell. At subsequent meetings he repeated his instruction by catechizing the children or by having two little French boys catechize each other. The Indian children who answered correctly were rewarded with a glass bead, much to the delight of their parents. "Finally, the whole was concluded

8 *Relations*, VIII, 121.
9 Ibid., 133.

by the talk of the old men who propounded their difficulties, and sometimes made me listen to the statement of their beliefs."[10]

These early efforts were not crowned with any noteworthy success. In fact, from the time of his arrival, in August 1634 until April 1635, Brébeuf baptized only twelve people. Four of these were dying infants and eight were adults who soon passed away. Far from disappointed, Brébeuf wrote: "These, then, are the first fruits that we have gathered from our visits and private instructions . . . May our Lord be pleased to accept these few first fruits, and give us strength and opportunities to gather more of them."[11]

In the spring of 1635, when planting time rolled around, the women cleared the brush from their fields and, with their planting sticks, put the usual nine or ten carefully selected kernels of corn in each hole, spaced a pace from its neighbor. All during the previous summer and fall the country had been so dry that forest fires broke out. In the early spring of 1635 three villages had burned to the ground.[12] Because the soil in the territory of the Bear clan was particularly sandy and the Indians had no tools enabling them to plant their corn very deeply, a successful corn crop vitally depended on abundant rain. But day after day cloudless skies domed the country of the Bears. Tender shoots of the new corn pushed up through the baked earth only to languish for lack of moisture. Soon the whole Bear clan was in a panic for the gaunt specter of famine stalked the land. Shortly, the people of the Bear clan were ". . . imploring, according to their custom, the help of the Sorcerers or Arendiowane who are here held in reverence, because they promise to turn aside the misfortunes with which Heaven threatens them."[13]

Then arose the first test of wills between the missionaries and the sorcerers. They demanded presents, ordered the celebration of feasts, and performed their most powerful incantations, all to no avail. Tehorenhaegnon, most famous of all the sorcerers, declared that his incantations failed because of the presence of the great cross standing before the cabin of the Jesuits. Besides, he

[10] Ibid., 143, 145.
[11] Ibid., 141.
[12] Ibid., X, 35. Brébeuf's *Relation* of 1636 which was published as Part II of Father Paul Le Jeune's *Relation* of the same year.
[13] Ibid., 35, 37.

said, ". . . the house of the French was a house of demons or of ill-disposed people who came into the country to make them [the Hurons] die."[14] Promptly, the Indians ordered the priests to throw down the cross, threatening that, if the crops failed, the missionaries would be beaten to death. When Brébeuf refused to comply, some angry young men, fashioning a cross, mounted it on the ridge of the Jesuit cabin and shot at it with arrows. ". . . but our Lord did not permit them to hit it even once."[15] Others blasphemed God so horribly that ". . . one would have had to be [made] of bronze not to be irritated by such insolence."[16]

At Ihonatiria the immediate neighbors of the small Jesuit community did not resort to the sorcerers, but begged the Fathers to make it rain, firmly believing that nothing was impossible for their French neighbors. Father Brébeuf gently explained that only God could cause it to rain. If they, here and now, repented their sins, resolving henceforth to serve God, the Jesuits would hold a daily procession, imploring the divine majesty to grant them rain. Doing their part, the priests offered Masses for nine successive days in honor of the Blessed Virgin and offered other prayers of petition, imploring the blessing of rain. On the last day of the novena, June 13, 1635, which happened to be the feast of Corpus Christi, the heavens opened and for a whole month there was plentiful rain.[17] In mid-July a second dry spell, lasting about ten days, again threatened the crops. But after the missionaries offered another nine days of Masses in honor of St. Ignatius, whose feast occurs on July 31, rain fell in such abundance that ". . . there was as much corn this year as there had been for a long time."[18]

When the rains saved the crops, insuring an ample food supply for the coming winter, the grateful Hurons came in droves to thank the missionaries, loudly proclaiming that ". . . God was in truth good and that we were also good; and that in the future they would serve God, adding a thousand abusive words in reference to all their Arendiowane or soothsayers."[19] Making the most

14 Ibid., 37.
15 Ibid., 39.
16 Ibid.
17 Ibid., 41.
18 Ibid., 43.
19 Ibid.

of the newly engendered goodwill, Brébeuf and his fellows traveled about, imparting spiritual instruction and, also, what material aid they could offer. Because hostile incursions were always a threat, the Hurons were given iron arrowheads, a great improvement in weaponry, and also shown the value of building their palisades in the form of a square, with strong bastions at the corners, allowing fewer men to defend them.[20]

Striking as the providential rainfall was to the simple minds of the Hurons, Jean de Brébeuf perceived clearly that this volatile people would soon forget the matter. Remarking on the incident, he wrote:

> . . . if there were anyone here endowed with the gift of miracles, as were those who first announced the Gospel to the world, he would, in my opinion, convert all these Barbarians without difficulty. But God dispenses such favors when, how, and to whom he pleases; and perhaps he wishes us to wait for the harvest of souls with patience and perseverance. Besides, certainly, they are inclined as yet to their duty only by temporal considerations, so that we may well apply to them the approach of the Gospel: Amen, amen I say to you, you seek me, not because you have seen miracles, but because you did eat of the loaves and were filled.[21]

Even so, if the way to a man's heart is through his stomach, at least the missionaries had gained esteem.

As summer waned the men went off trading while the women were busy reaping the harvest. With their village thus mostly depopulated, the Jesuits employed the time of quiet to make their annual eight-day retreat and to work at perfecting their knowledge of the Huron language, particularly in striving to compile a grammar. Father Brébeuf explained that their grasp of the language was, as yet, too incomplete to set down anything worth printing. It was ". . . indeed an exceedingly laborious task to understand in all points a foreign tongue . . . as different from our European language as heaven is from earth."[22]

In mid-June, perhaps after the threat of drought was averted for the first time, the Huron trading fleet departed for Three Rivers. Father Paul Le Jeune had been very concerned about the fate of his apostles among the Hurons since early April. On the fifth of

---

[20] Ibid., 53.
[21] Ibid., 49. The scriptural quotation is found in John 6:26.
[22] Ibid., 55.

that month a Montagnais reached Three Rivers bearing tragic news which he swore the Ottawa, near neighbors of the Hurons, gave him. All of the French who went to the Huron country the previous summer, he declared, had been tied securely to trees in the forest and left to starve. The Hurons had done this because all the Indians conveying them fell ill from a malady inflicted on them by the French. And now the illness had spread throughout the whole Huron country.[23] Not until July 10, 1635, when two French laymen arrived from Huronia, bearing letters from Brébeuf and the others, did Le Jeune learn that all of the Jesuits were well and anxiously awaiting the return of the fur flotilla bringing them supplies and, it was hoped, new recruits.[24]

The Hurons, finished with their trading at Three Rivers on July 22, 1635, held solemn council with Samuel de Champlain before taking their departure. Now a benign old patriarch of almost seventy, Champlain harangued his "children" of the forest, as it happened for the last time.[25] Speaking through an interpreter, never having mastered an Indian language, he

. . . very affectionately recommended our Fathers and the French who accompanied them to these Tribes; . . . if they wished to preserve and strengthen their friendship with the French, they must receive our belief and worship the God that we worshipped . . . they must next year bring many of their little boys, whom we will lodge comfortably, and will feed, instruct and cherish as if they were our own little brothers.[26]

Both Father Paul Le Jeune and Samuel de Champlain expected great things from the school for Huron boys which they yearned to establish. Le Jeune, of course, looked forward to the time when the products of the school would return to their clans and become dedicated lay apostles, helping in the conversion of the people. Perhaps Champlain hoped that the Indian graduates of the school would augment the corps of young Frenchmen whom he had originally placed among various bands of Indians

---

[23] Ibid., VIII, 43.

[24] Ibid., 45.

[25] Champlain died on Christmas day, 1635. Despite his many years living among the Indians, he never mastered any of the native tongues, always requiring an interpreter when he addressed them. The Montagnais once chided him because in all his years among them he never learned their language. See Bishop, *Champlain*, 298.

[26] *Relations*, VIII, 49.

to become proficient in the native languages. In his address to the
Hurons, Champlain instructed them

. . . that, inasmuch as all the captains could not come there [that is, Three
Rivers], they should hold a council upon this matter in their country to
which they should summon *Echon*, it is thus they call Father Brébeuf; and
then, giving them a letter to bear to him, he added, "Herè I inform the
Father of all these points. He will be in your assembly and will make you a
present that his Brothers send him; There you will show whether you truly
love the French." . . . To that discourse a chief replied that they would not
fail to deliver this letter and to hold a council upon the Matters proposed.[27]

Attending the council between Champlain and the Hurons
were two new Jesuit recruits most anxious to join the returning
flotilla bound for Huronia. These were Father Pierre Pijart, who
arrived at Quebec from France on July 10, 1635, and Father
François Joseph Le Mercier, barely disembarked since he landed
at Quebec only three days previously, on July 20, 1635.[28] With his
new apostles in tow, Father Le Jeune went to visit those Hurons
who had agreed to take the two Fathers with them. Uncon-

[27] Ibid.

[28] Ibid., 45. Pierre Pijart was born at Paris on May 17, 1608, and entered the
Jesuit novitiate there on September 16, 1629. Endowed with practical common
sense, but not much academic ability, he was given only one year of theological
studies before he was sent to New France where he arrived on July 10, 1635. He
spent nine years on the Huron mission, returning to Quebec in 1644 because of ill
health. On August 23, 1650, he sailed for France, still plagued by ill health. He
never returned to New France, dying at Dieppe on May 26, 1676. He is sometimes confused with his elder brother, Claude, who was also a missionary among
the Hurons.

François Joseph Le Mercier, son of a goldsmith and valet to the king of
France, was born at Paris on October 3, 1604. He entered the Society of Jesus at
Paris on October 22, 1622. He made all of his ecclesiastical studies at the College
of Clermont, later called Louis le Grand, in Paris and taught there for four years.
He was ordained in 1633 and went to New France in 1635, where he arrived on
July 20 and left Three Rivers for Huronia three days later. He acquired outstanding ability in the Huron tongue. After his arrival among the Hurons,
Brébeuf assigned him the task of compiling the *Relations* for the Huron mission,
a duty he fulfilled until the arrival of Father Jerome Lalemant in 1638. Le Mercier continued as a missionary among the Hurons until the demise of the mission.
In 1653 he was appointed superior of the whole Jesuit mission in New France
and held that office until 1656. He was appointed to the same post in 1665, this
time for six years. In 1673 he was sent to govern the French Jesuit missions in
the West Indies. He held the office of superior there until 1681. He died in Martinique on June 12, 1690, at the age of eighty-six.

sciously revealing Jean de Brébeuf's thoughtfulness, Le Jeune remarked:

. . . Father Brébeuf had designated certain ones [that is, Hurons] to me in his letter. They gazed attentively at the Fathers, measured them with their eyes, asked if they were ill-natured, if they paddled well; then took them by the hands and made signs to them that it would be necessary to handle the paddle well.[29]

The next day, July 23, the Indians, pleased with the trading, embarked with their two Jesuit working passengers and one young French boy who had already spent a year among the Hurons. In his *Relation* of 1636 Father Brébeuf reported that Father Le Mercier arrived on August 13 and Father Pijart on August 17, both having been ". . . well treated on the way."[30]

Perhaps because Father Antoine Daniel had attained passable facility in the Huron tongue by the fall of 1635, Jean de Brébeuf could begin traveling about the country, visiting distant villages. On October 15, he and a companion went to the village of Oenrio, about three miles southeast of the Jesuit cabin. With the aid of a quite well-instructed Huron girl, Brébeuf ". . . dispelled the fear of a poor sick woman that baptism would shorten her life, . . . she at last gave way and another with her."[31] The opposition to baptism, expressed by the dying Huron woman would continue to plague the missionaries. Adults in good health could not be baptized unless they were sufficiently instructed to accept the sacrament willingly as well as agreeing to live as Christians. To act otherwise would have made a mockery of the sacrament. But those evidently dying could be baptized if they but expressed a desire to receive the sacrament. Over the years many adults, already moribund, died soon after the administration of baptism. Inevitably, the Hurons concluded that baptism was the kiss of death. Not for years would the dedicated missionaries dispel that false notion and only after a goodly number of healthy adults freely accepted baptism.

Soon after his brief foray to Oenrio, Father Brébeuf went off, on November 4, to visit Louis de Sainte-Foy whose father had

[29] Ibid., 51.

[30] Ibid., X, 57.

[31] Ibid., 67. Jones, 262, locates Oenrio at lot 5, concession XVII, Tiny township, Simcoe county, Ontario.

come to the Jesuit residence at Ihonatiria, on September 20, 1635, asking that his whole family be baptized.[32] Louis and his people were members of the Cord clan, living in a village called Teanaustayé located seven or eight leagues to the south of the Jesuit cabin.[33] During the week Brébeuf spent instructing Louis and his family, the major obstacles to the conversion of the Hurons clearly emerged. The people readily agreed that the Ten Commandments were reasonable, even admirable, but most difficult to observe. While Louis informed his family that in France thieves were frequently executed, they replied that if such a practice were introduced in Huronia the ". . . country would very soon be depopulated . . . a Huron and a thief being almost the same."[34] Conjugal fidelity seemed to them not only an impossible ideal, but one the French traders living among the Hurons also disregarded. Louis de Sainte-Foy's shrewd old father pointed out that ". . . the French who had been here had never spoken to them of God, but had been as much addicted as they to run after and dally with the women."[35]

In midwinter when the Hurons usually kept to their cabins, avoiding the snow and biting cold, the Jesuits concentrated on instructing the Hurons dwelling nearby. Father Brébeuf was gratified to report that during the month of December twenty-eight Hurons were baptized, though many soon died. On February 2, 1636, the feast of the Purification, the few Christians available were introduced to the charming Catholic custom of blessing the children. Vested, holding a crucifix aloft, Father Brébeuf solemnly pronounced the following prayer in Huron:

Hear me, You who created the earth, You the Father, You his Son, and You, Holy Spirit; listen to a matter of profound importance. Look upon these children who have been baptized. With the consent of these assembled women, we present them to You. Protect and defend them from sickness and sin. Shield them from all evil. If plague, famine, or war threaten them, turn it from them. If the demon provokes us or the wicked, who cause death

---

[32] *Relations*, X, 61.

[33] Ibid., VIII, 139. Jones, 22, locates Teanaustayé at lot 7, concession IV, Medonte township, Simcoe county, Ontario. Today, Canada's Highway 400 passes quite close to the site.

[34] *Relations*, X, 67.

[35] Ibid., 63.

by poison, turn them from us. Lord Jesus Christ, we implore this from your Father who refuses You nothing. Mary, virgin mother of Jesus, implore this for us. Amen.[36]

If Jean de Brébeuf harbored any dream of gaining the Hurons to Christ without the interference of political influence from beyond Huronia's borders or from within them, the early spring of 1636 quickly banished that notion. On March 28, 1636, four Ottawa, accompanied by a young Frenchman, François Marguérie, arrived with rich presents, requesting the Hurons to join them in an attack on the Iroquois, who, after agreeing to peace, had massacred twenty-three Ottawa. When the Hurons declined the presents, thereby indicating their unwillingness to join in the war, Le Borgne, leader of the Ottawa, threatened to cut the Hurons off from access to the French trading center at Three Rivers. Since the Hurons still refused, Le Borgne strove to induce the Jesuits to abandon the Hurons in favor of his own people, promising to make Brébeuf a great captain among the Ottawa. With consummate tact the missionary informed Le Borgne that the Jesuits had not left France in the hope of becoming captains among the Indians, much less of gaining riches, but solely to teach ". . . the way of salvation at the peril of our lives; for the rest we . . . would try to comport ourselves that other nations would have more reason to love us than to hate us."[37] To confirm his declaration, Brébeuf gave the Ottawa a canoe and other small gifts with which they were so well satisfied that they promised to treat the priests passing through their country with the utmost consideration. Such adroit diplomacy won for Brébeuf the respect of the Hurons as well as the friendship of the Ottawa.

After the Jesuits had resided in their obscure little village for about eighteen months, captains of larger towns in the country of

[36] Ibid., 69-73. Brébeuf's report of his instruction to the Hurons on the feast of the Purification most charmingly explains the meaning of the occasion. He wrote: "On the day of the Purification, having assembled all the Christian children, adorned as best they could, along with their parents, we performed in their presence the blessing of the candles; then we explained to the adults how on such a day our Lady had offered her Son in the temple to the Eternal Father, and how, in imitation of her, they ought also to present their children to the service of God, and if they did so God would take a more particular care of them; they were very well pleased with these statements."

[37] Ibid., 79.

the Huron Bear clan began to importune the missionaries to move their residence to a more populous center, chiefly, it would appear, because of the prestige the presence of the Jesuits gave to a village. Economic advantages also resulted since the Jesuits paid the Indians for food and services with gifts such as metal fishhooks, needles, awls, glass beads, small knives, and sometimes even porcelain.[38] Also, French traders coming into the area visited the Jesuits and tended to trade with the Indians in that neighborhood. Leaders of Ossossané, recognized capital of the Bear clan, earnestly pressed Father Brébeuf to remove there, pointing out the obvious advantage of a larger population and that it was there the Bears held all their important council meetings.[39]

But Aenons, captain of the village of Oenrio, nearest neighbor of the Jesuits, had other plans. When Etienne Brûlé had been barbarously, if justly, killed at Toanché, the numerous residents dispersed, fearing French reprisals. Now Aenons, hoping to outshine Ossossané, strove mightily to reassemble the former residents of Toanché. Perceiving that success depended on inducing the missionaries to join his plan, Aenons pestered Father Brébeuf for more than six months, giving him no rest. Finally, Brébeuf agreed to move to the new town, provided ". . . the captains . . . would promise us . . . in the name of all their subjects, that they would be content to receive the Faith, to believe all that we believe and to live as we do."[40] Assembling his council, Aenons announced Brébeuf's conditions, to which the grave elders replied: "That is well, we are satisfied. He will teach us, and we will do all he desires."[41] It was decided, however, to delay moving until after the celebration of the Huron Feast of the Dead, to be held in the spring of 1636. In the meantime, to manifest serious intent, Aenons called on his people to repair the missionary cabin.

[38] Long before the arrival of Europeans the Indians had established as a medium of exchange the shells of small mollusks. These were individually pierced and strung on animal tendons to form necklaces. The English and the Dutch called this arbitrary medium of exchange wampum and assigned various lengths of it a value in English or Dutch money. The French spoke of it as *porcelaine*, apparently because an individual shell somewhat resembled the porcelain bead the French manufactured, actually using porcelain, for trade on the African coast. See Charlevoix, II, 254, note 1.

[39] *Relations*, X, 235.

[40] Ibid., 245.

[41] Ibid., 247.

The zealous captain and his braves attacked the task with great industry, but so early in the morning that four Jesuits could not say Mass because the Hurons literally tore their cabin down around them.[42]

During the spring of 1636, the captains of all the villages of the Huron Bear clan met to arrange for the celebration of the great Feast of the Dead which was described in detail in Chapter II.

For Father Brébeuf and his missionary companions the solemn feast served a useful purpose. Since the Hurons obviously placed so much importance in the spirits of their dead gaining the village of the souls in their afterlife, by modifying that belief the Hurons could, perhaps, more easily be led to accept Christianity. Henceforth the missionaries constantly laid stress on the obligation of obeying God's law in this life in order to gain heaven. *E converso*, they emphasized the eternal punishment to be meted out to those who unrepentently offended God.

As the Hurons began preparing for their annual trading expedition to Three Rivers, Jean de Brébeuf sought to recruit some young boys for the school which both Champlain and Le Jeune were anxious to inaugurate. Lest the children be without an interpreter, Brébeuf directed Ambroise Davost and Antoine Daniel to accompany them. At first the Hurons agreed enthusiastically, but, in June, with the departure date at hand, the mothers, and even more the grandmothers, weeping and wailing, refused to allow any but a few boys to depart.[43] At Three Rivers, when the moment came to hand over their young sons, all the fathers, save one, ". . . drew back and sought a thousand excuses."[44] In the end, the Hurons agreed to leave Satouta, son of a noted captain of the Bear clan. Satouta's steadfastness in determining to stay with the French shamed the Hurons into allowing two other boys to remain with him. Shortly after August 19, 1636, Father Daniel took his three charges aboard a sloop and brought them to Quebec.

Parenthetically, it is worth recording Father Le Jeune's description of Antoine Daniel on his arrival at Three Rivers after his

[42] Ibid., 249.
[43] Ibid., IX, 283, 285.
[44] Ibid., 285.

two-year sojourn among the Hurons. In his *Relation* of 1636, Le Jeune, who witnessed Daniel's arrival, wrote:

On the nineteenth of the month of August a part of the main body of the Hurons arrived. As soon as we saw their Canoes appear upon the great River, we descended from the Fort to receive Father Daniel and Father Davost, and few of our French whom we were expecting; Monsieur the Commandant himself was there. Father Daniel was in this first company, Father Davost in the rear guard, which did not yet appear; and we even began to doubt whether the Island savages had not made them return. At the sight of Father Daniel, our hearts melted; his face was gay and happy, but greatly emaciated; he was barefooted, had a paddle in his hand, and was clad in a wretched cassock, his Breviary suspended [by a cord] around his neck, his shirt rotting on his back.[45]

Carefully tucked away in his small baggage Father Antoine carried with him two documents from his superior, Father Jean de Brébeuf. The more lengthy was Brébeuf's *Relation* of 1636, the last such report he would write himself.[46] The second, and, perhaps for Brébeuf, the more important document was a letter addressed to the Jesuit general at Rome, Mutius Vitelleschi. Brébeuf's communication to his major superior was penned to fulfill an obligation, incumbent on every Jesuit superior, to write at least annually, reporting the conditions, progress, and hopes for the future of the charge for which the superior was responsible. The Hurons, he recounted, were a sedentary folk, endowed with excellent sense and judgment, who do not scorn the truths of Christianity without readily accepting them. "Among other things that move them," he wrote, "they are frightened by the torments of hell; and, enticed by the joys of heaven, they open their eyes to the light of truth."[47] Pleading for more missionaries, he described the type of priest required. "Among other jewels with which the laborer in this mission ought to shine, gentleness and patience must hold the first rank; and never will this field produce fruit except through mildness and patience; for one should never expect to force it by violence and arbitrary action."[48]

---

[45] Ibid., 279.
[46] The *Relation* from the Huron country for the following two years was written by Le Mercier.
[47] Ibid., XI, 9.
[48] Ibid., 11.

If Jean de Brébeuf had been able to choose the recruits who joined him in the summer of 1636, he could hardly have found three more suitable volunteers. All were imbued with the gentleness and patience which he prized as essential requisites for those seeking to evangelize the Hurons. Father Pierre Chastellain landed at Quebec just fourteen days before he reached the age of thirty. A saintly man, he would spend forty-eight years in New France before his pious demise at Quebec in 1684. He arrived at the Jesuit cabin in Huronia on August 12, 1636.[49] Charles Garnier, also just over thirty, the most humble of men, endowed with striking talents, friend of the outcasts, reached Quebec on June 11 and arrived among the Hurons on August 13.[50] In an astonishingly short time he mastered the Huron tongue so well that even the Hurons themselves marveled at his command of their language. Of all the Jesuits laboring on the Huron mission, only Garnier's charming letters to his relatives survived in quantity. Isaac Jogues, a small, gentle person, seeming more boy than man at twenty-nine, reached New France on July 2, 1636, and promptly went on to Three Rivers. There he saw the Hurons at their worst as they cruelly tortured an Iroquois prisoner. Ten years and a few months later the Iroquois would torture him. If Brébeuf hoped for kind, gentle, generous, zealous missionaries, his wish could

---

[49] Ibid., XIII, 21. Pierre Chastellain was born at Senlis on June 25, 1606. Son of a prominent family, Pierre's father bitterly opposed his entrance into the Society of Jesus. Becoming a Jesuit on September 3, 1624, he did all of his ecclesiastical studies at Paris. He sailed from Dieppe on April 8, 1636, aboard the ship bringing Champlain's successor, Charles Huault de Montmagny. Reaching Quebec on June 11, he went up to Three Rivers on July 1. Leaving that trading center on July 21, he arrived in Huronia on August 12. He returned to Quebec only after the Huron mission was destroyed. The remainder of his long life was spent ministering to the French, more particularly to the nuns stationed at Quebec. He died at Quebec on August 15, 1684.

[50] Ibid. Charles Garnier, the second son of Jean Garnier, undersecretary to Henri III's household, was born at Paris in 1606. Entering the Jesuit novitiate at Paris in 1624, he was ordained in 1635 and sailed for New France in 1636 with Pierre Chastellain. Among the Hurons, where he arrived on August 13, 1636, he quickly became a great favorite of the Indians whose language he soon spoke so well that he could tell jokes in it. As a missionary he spent his short few years working with the forgotten Tobacco Nation without much success. He was martyred on December 7, 1649, by a band of Iroquois.

have been no better fulfilled when Isaac Jogues stepped out of the canoe in Huronia on September 11, 1636.[51]

Not long before Isaac Jogues reached Huronia, Father Brébeuf withdrew from active missionary work to make his annual eight-day retreat. During those days of prayer, Brébeuf wrote in his private notes, on September 4:

In His goodness God has granted me a spirit of mildness and gentleness and love for all, an indifference towards all things and patience to bear adversity. It is the wish of the Divine Majesty that through these means I attain perfection and eternal glory. Hence, I shall use this as the object of my particular examination of conscience to determine whether I properly use these gifts which God has given me.[52]

After Brébeuf's martyrdom, Father Paul Ragueneau wrote: "The oil of his mildness did not extinguish the ardor of his zeal, but rather inflamed it, and was one of the most powerful means which God had given him for winning hearts to the Faith."[53] Slowly but clearly, a portrait of Jean de Brébeuf begins to emerge. This great mountain of a man, with his striking black beard, brawny shoulders, and muscular arms, was, at heart, the gentlest of men, inflamed with a boundless love for everyone, but especially the Hurons who were both his charges and his children. Fractious and fickle they might be, but, with gentle patience and forbearance, he would lead them out of their pagan darkness into the saving light of Christianity.

---

[51] Ibid., 87. Born on January 10, 1607, at Orléans, Isaac Jogues was the fifth of nine children born to a prosperous merchant. He entered the Jesuit novitiate at Rouen in October 1624. He was ordained in January 1636 and left for New France on April 8, 1636. After a brief stay at Quebec and Three Rivers, Jogues reached the Huron country on September 11, 1636. In September 1641 he and Father Charles Raymbault accompanied the Chippewa to Sault Sainte Marie and were the first Europeans to see Lake Superior. In 1642, while returning to Huronia from Quebec, Jogues was captured by Iroquois and brought to Ossernenon (Auriesville, New York) where he was cruelly tortured and his companion, René Goupil, was martyred. In November 1643, aided by the Dutch, Jogues escaped and returned to France whence he came back to Quebec in 1644. Returning to the Iroquois in the fall of 1646, he was martyred on October 18. His companion, Jean de La Lande, was martyred the following day. Isaac Jogues, like Brébeuf, was a true mystic. Despite a frail constitution and an air of timidity, Jogues was fearless in his apostolate. Undeceived by his diffident exterior, the Hurons called him Ondessonk which in their language meant "bird of prey."

[52] Latourelle, *Etude sur . . . Brébeuf*, II, 203.

[53] *Relations*, XXXIV, 187.

It was this same spirit which imbued his lengthy chapter, in his *Relation* of 1636, entitled "Important Advice for Those Whom It Shall Please God to Call to New France, and Especially to the Country of the Hurons." Brébeuf devotes twenty pages in the Cramoisy edition of his *Relation* of 1636 listing in all their stark reality the overwhelming difficulties confronting those who might volunteer for the Huron mission. No obstacle was omitted, neither bitter cold, nor cruel hunger, nor revolting crudity of the Indians, nor ever present danger of painful death. Revealing his own consummate dedication, he ended his discourse thus:

If, at the sight of the difficulties and Crosses that are here prepared for us, someone feels himself so fortified from above that he can say it is too little or like St. Francis Xavier, More, More, I hope that our Lord will also draw from his lips this other confession, in the midst of consolations he will give him, that it will be too much for him, that he cannot endure more. It is enough, O Lord, it is enough.[54]

As though verifying Jean de Brébeuf's warning to prospective missionaries of hardships and sufferings awaiting them among the Hurons, a new affliction suddenly struck the small Jesuit community at Ihonatiria. Since the early summer of 1634 the Hurons, and the Ottawa as well, had been suffering from an epidemic the like of which the Indians had never experienced before. Brébeuf described the illness as ". . . a sort of measles or smallpox different, however, from that common in France, accompanied in several cases by blindness for some days, or by dimness of sight, and terminated at length by diarrhea which carries off many . . ."[55] Though the Hurons, with whom Father Brébeuf came up to Huronia in 1634, were suffering from the disease, neither he nor any of his companions, Jesuit or lay, contracted the ailment. Not until the fall of 1636 did any of the French living among the Hurons fall victim. The first to be infected was Isaac Jogues who certainly contracted the illness from a little French boy whom he brought to Huronia with him. Jogues left Three Rivers with the boy on August 24 and, after seven days on the road, the child fell ill. After a few days the little boy ". . . had not the strength to get

[54] Ibid., X, 113, 115.
[55] Ibid., VIII, 89.

out of the canoe, much less to walk the length of the rapids."[56] Exactly twelve days after the child fell ill, Isaac Jogues came down with the disease. We may note parenthetically that the incubation period for smallpox is exactly twelve days. Five days after Jogues was forced to take to his bed, Mathurin, a lay assistant, was stricken. On September 23, Dominique Scot, also a layman, fell ill. Before long the Jesuit cabin was ". . . changed into an infirmary, or rather a hospital, there being as many nurses as there were well persons, and these were few for the number of patients."[57]

Through the rest of September and the first half of October 1636, the missionaries and their devoted lay assistants fell victim, one after another, to the disease. Only Father Brébeuf and the capable Father Pierre Pijart escaped as did the layman, François Petit-Pré. Nursing the sick fell to the gentle hands of Jean de Brébeuf while Father Pijart continued visiting the Hurons, striving to keep alive in their minds the few simple religious truths already imparted to them. François Petit-Pré escaped, but his whole time was occupied roaming the countryside, hunting game to feed the sick.[58] Lacking any sort of medicine to treat the sufferers, Father Brébeuf gave them ". . . some broth of wild purslane stewed in water, with a dash of native verjuice."[59] One great delicacy was sometimes available. Having brought up a rooster and one lone hen, the group waited anxiously for the hen to lay an egg so that the sickest may have it.[60]

Sickness among the French was a great novelty to the Hurons who had never seen a European fall ill.[61] They crowded into the cabin, offered suggestions, talked loudly, and generally made the

[56] The boy is thought to have been Jean Amyot who was then about eleven years old. He spent about nine years on the mission as a lay helper. He grew to be quite a strapping young athlete who could best the Indians in any contest. On May 23, 1648, he was drowned near Three Rivers just before he was to have been married.

[57] Ibid., XIII, 91.

[58] Ibid., 97. Petit-Pré bagged at least something every day but one. That day, Father Brébeuf offered to buy a pet turkey from a Huron, proffering a whole deerskin for the bird. But the Huron refused.

[59] Ibid., 93. Purslane is a herb which can be used in salads. Verjuice was probably employed as an emetic since it is the juice of green fruit.

[60] Ibid.

[61] Ibid., 101.

poor sick people very uncomfortable. When Father Le Mercier pleaded with the Indians to lower their voices out of consideration for the sick, they suggested he quiet the rooster's crowing since he made more noise than they and he was never asked to be still.[62]

The physicians of the country, the medicine men, were quick to offer their assistance to the ailing missionaries. Tonneraouanont, ". . . one of the most famous sorcerers of the country . . . ," stopped by, at the request of one of his Huron patients.[63] He maintained that he was really a demon who lived under the ground until the fancy seized him to assume the form of a man.[64] For a price, ten glass beads and one extra for each patient, the sorcerer offered to show Father Brébeuf a root which would infallibly cure all the sick within three days. With exquisite courtesy Brébeuf replied that while he would gratefully employ any natural remedies the sorcerer might suggest, spells and incantations could not be permitted. Despite the absence of any effective remedies, European or Huron, all the members of the small Jesuit community recovered by October 15, 1636.

It turned out that the affliction was really a blessing in disguise. In his account of the Huron mission for that period Father Le Mercier noted:

. . . perhaps we would be dead by now if we had not been sick. It was oftentimes said, during the evil reports that were current about us throughout the country, that if we had not been afflicted as well as the others, they would not have doubted that we were the cause of the disease. Your Reverence knows how they treat poisoners here; we informed you of it last year and we have lately seen an example of it with our own eyes, the danger going so far as to enable us to say that we might not have come out of it very cheaply.[65]

As soon as the Jesuits recovered they began caring, as best they could, for the numerous victims of the epidemic, not only in their village of Ihonatiria but in the hamlets round about. The remedies consisted of water sweetened with sugar, which the Hurons called French snow, dried prunes, raisins, senna, and broth made from the flesh of wild game. While these harmless potions gave some slight relief, proffering them furnished the missionaries

[62] Ibid.   [64] Ibid., 105.
[63] Ibid.   [65] Ibid., 111.

ready access to the cabins wherein they were able to baptize many of the dying and, at the same time, explain the teachings of Christianity to the bystanders. As the epidemic continued unabated, even into the winter, the Hurons, losing faith in their sorcerers, begged the missionaries to avert what was becoming a national disaster. Disclaiming any magic power, Father Brébeuf ". . . represented to them that the true and only means of turning away this scourge of heaven, was to believe in God and to make a firm determination to serve him and keep his Commandments."[66] At a meeting of the village council, on November 29, 1636, the ". . . chief men of the village resolved to do all that we considered proper to incline God to mercy and to obtain from his goodness some relief from this public calamity."[67] In a burst of enthusiasm, the Indians at Ihonatiria, as well as those at Ossossané, capital of the Bear clan, promised to erect a small chapel in each village and openly to profess Christianity.[68]

But, when the epidemic continued to rage with unabated fury, the Hurons soon forgot their promises and turned on the Jesuits, just as they had on their sorcerers. Because so many of the afflicted died after receiving baptism, the people started pernicious rumors asserting that the Jesuits not only caused the epidemic, but, when an Indian began to recover, the missionaries administered a potion which caused him to die.[69] Wherefore, the Hurons began to shun the missionaries, forbidding them access to the sick. A captain of one village openly threatened to split the head of the first Frenchman he saw if anyone living in his cabin died.[70] The lives of the Jesuits were spared, for the moment, by Aenons, captain of Ihonatiria, who reminded the Hurons that slaughtering the Jesuits would certainly mean the end of trading with the French. That, in itself, would bring about ". . . the destruction and ruin of the country . . ."[71] Fortunately, with the coming of spring, the virulence of the affliction abated somewhat. But this was not the last of the trouble.

By the spring of 1637 Father Jean de Brébeuf planned on launching a wider campaign for the conversion of the Hurons. Until his fellow workers became accustomed to life in a Huron

[66] Ibid., 159.
[67] Ibid.
[68] Ibid.

[69] Ibid., 213.
[70] Ibid.
[71] Ibid., 215.

village and could converse with some fluency in the native tongue, Brébeuf designedly confined his small group to the village of Ihonatiria. Now, he decided, the time had come to launch a broader attack. So, on March 29, 1637, he assembled the chief men of the village to inquire into their plans. Did they intend gathering the nearby hamlets into one large village before winter and, if so, were they willing to accept the teachings of Christianity?[72] As to the first point, the Indians announced that they intended to stay where they were. As for accepting Christianity, some believed what the Jesuits taught, but others did not. That response sufficed to convince Brébeuf that it was time ". . . to establish other residences elsewhere."[73] And the logical location for opening the first was Ossossané.

Jean de Brébeuf was no stranger to Ossossané, having visited it often since 1634 when he was considering settling there. On May 17, 1637, he approached the captain of that village, announcing his intention of establishing mission headquarters at Ossossané. When the proposal was revealed to the assembled council, the people offered to build the Jesuits a

. . . cabin of about twelve brasses, begging us, if they did not make it larger, to consider that the malady had carried off a part of the young men, and that the rest were nearly all gone trading or fishing; . . . giving us their word to make it as long and as wide as we should wish, the following year. The council over, each took his hatchet and they all went away in a crowd to prepare the site.[74]

Just a little over three weeks later on June 9, when the cabin was completed, ". . . forty or fifty Indians came . . . to Ihonatiria to get part of our corn and a few little articles of furniture, the captain being in the crowd."[75] Brébeuf dedicated the new center to the Immaculate Conception. Leaving Chastellain and Jogues to continue the mission of St. Joseph, Jean de Brébeuf moved to Ossossané, taking Le Mercier and Garnier with him.

For about a month after the missionaries settled at Ossossané, Hurons from miles around flocked to visit them and admire the new cabin and its extraordinary contents.[76] The Indians never

---

[72] Ibid., XIV, 23, 25.
[73] Ibid., 25.
[74] Ibid., 57.

[75] Ibid., 105.
[76] Ibid., XV, 17.

wearied of examining two life-sized paintings of Christ and his Blessed Mother which they believed to be living beings, not mere flat representations. But, as the epidemic failed to subside totally, people began to think that the affliction was, somehow, caused by the pictures. Presently the Hurons believed that the French priests were prolonging the epidemic. Henceforth, when the missionaries appeared, ". . . they wrapped themselves in their robes and covered their faces, for fear of speaking to us; others, upon seeing us, hastened to close the doors of their cabins . . ."[77]

Superstitious fear of the missionaries was particularly intense at Angoutenc, a village only three-quarters of a mile south and east of Ossossané, where most of the people were afflicted.[78] On July 8, 1637, the elders proposed a village council and invited the Jesuits to attend. At the meeting everyone listened while the missionaries explained ". . . what had brought us into their country, and especially what our purpose was in visiting their sick."[79] One spokesman for the Hurons responded that the very presence of the Jesuits proved their affection for the Indians. Another of the elders warned that the young men of the village ". . . should be very careful not to strike a blow for which the whole country might groan."[80] But, for all the apparent friendship of the Hurons, the missionaries sensed that they were a hair's breadth away from martyrdom. Understanding the temperament of the Indians, Brébeuf directed his subjects ". . . to remain at anchor during the tempest."[81] He had been privately informed that after the missionaries left the meeting the council had ". . . resolved to kill some Frenchman, whoever he might be."[82]

Thereafter, rumors of evil intent on the part of the missionaries came to them from every side. Some Hurons declared that the Jesuits had brought a corpse from France for

. . . there was, without doubt, something in our tabernacle that made them die . . . Our crime was, they said, that we had established ourselves in the heart of the country that we might more easily procure its total ruin; to ac-

[77] Ibid., 23.
[78] Jones, 132, locates the site of this village at lot 11, concession X, Tiny township, Simcoe county, Ontario.
[79] *Relations*, XV, 27.
[80] Ibid., 29.
[81] Ibid., 31.
[82] Ibid.

complish this, we had killed a little child in the woods by stabbing it with a bodkin, which had caused the death of a great many children.[83]

Listening at night outside the fragile walls of the missionary cabin, the people of Ossossané heard the missionaries reciting the litany of the Blessed Virgin Mary and of the saints, a form of community evening prayers, customarily recited in every Jesuit house. Hearing the repetition of phrases, the Hurons concluded that the Jesuits were performing some sort of very powerful incantation. A weather vane mounted on a pole outside the Jesuit cabin became a sinister object for the Indians. The striking clock, once so fascinating, became the demon of death and paintings depicting the sufferings of the souls of the damned ". . . represented to them nothing more than what was happening to their sick people."[84]

Though the hand of nearly every Huron was raised against the missionaries, Jean de Brébeuf continued touring the country, visiting the sick, while his fellow missionaries daily expected to hear that some frenzied Indian had split his skull. Shortly, a terrified Huron, accompanied by two respected captains, reported Father Brébeuf's murder, relating the details and even naming the perpetrator of the deed. ". . . from that time on everyone deserted us and we were regarded only with dread."[85] When the rumor reached Brébeuf, he hurried home to relieve everyone's anxiety.

In the burning heat of July the virulent illness continued decimating the poor confused Indians who had suffered from plagues before, but none lasting well over a year. Frantically, on August 4, 1637, three of the four Huron clans met in council at Ossossané, ostensively to decide whether to wage a war, but actually to consider what remedies were required to end the widespread illness. Formally invited to the assembly, the missionaries took their places among the delegates of the Bear clan with whom they resided. In the presence of the council, the master of the solemn Feast of the Dead, chief of the assembly for the whole nation, openly accused the Jesuits of causing this national disaster. Each orator agreed and many of the speakers urged Brébeuf to produce the charm with which he had bewitched the whole people. Hour

83 Ibid., 33.
84 Ibid., 33, 35.
85 Ibid., 35.

after hour, harangue after harangue, grave ancients of the nation reiterated the same theme. Each assured Father Brébeuf that if he would only surrender the charm, his life would be spared. Long after midnight the meeting finally disbanded with little accomplished, except that they ". . . postponed the conclusion of the whole matter to the return of the Hurons who had gone down to Quebec."[86]

A few days after attending the council, while performing his evening devotions, Father Brébeuf again was visited by a mystical experience, which he described thus:

1637. On August 21 or 22 or 23, in the evening, during the [period devoted to the] examination of conscience and the [recitation of the] litanies of the [Blessed] Virgin, I seemed to perceive, by my intellect or my imagination, a vast horde of demons approaching to devour or at least wound me. But not one of them was able to hurt me. These creatures attacking me appeared to resemble horses of monsterous size, covered with long curly hair like that on a goat. I don't recall much else about their configuration. But I know that their shapes were so diverse and so terrifying that I never saw the like. The vision lasted about the space of a *Miserere*. I do not recall being afraid but, with confidence in God, I said: Do whatever God permits, you cannot harm a hair of my head without his permission.[87]

Recording the vision after Brébeuf's martyrdom, Father Paul Ragueneau interpreted its meaning thus: "Our Lord often gave him to understand that he held us in his protection, and that the powers of hell might indeed become furious against us, but that they were not unchained."[88]

Understandably, the missionaries among the Hurons anxiously awaited the return of the fur brigade which had gone down to Three Rivers in the summer of 1637. Because of the widespread illness among the various clans, the number of Indians composing the brigade was not nearly so large as usual. Father Pierre Pijart went along to deliver letters from the missionaries and to gather the mountain of supplies required for the coming year.[89] On Au-

---

[86] Ibid., 47.

[87] Latourelle, *Etude sur . . . Brébeuf*, II, 203-04. The *Miserere* mentioned by Brébeuf is Psalm 50. It can be recited in the space of about one minute.

[88] *Relations*, XXXIV, 171.

[89] Ibid., XII, 197. Father Paul Le Jeune, who was at Three Rivers when Pijart reached there, describes the arriving missionary thus: "The poor father was

gust 6, 1637, two Huron canoes, finished trading, started homeward only to have one return hastily, reporting that the other had
been ambushed and the Hurons in it captured. The governor,
Charles Huault de Montmagny, who was attending the rendezvous at Three Rivers, dispatched Jean Nicolet to attack the marauding Iroquois, but without success.[90] During the next days a
few more Huron canoes straggled in, their occupants sadly announcing that at least ten canoes had been ambushed.

No matter the danger from Iroquois raiding parties, supplies
for the mission were readied at Three Rivers for shipment to the
Huron country. There were a sufficient number of canoes available, but the Hurons themselves were so ill that ". . . they did not
wish to burden themselves with clothes or packages of other people."[91] Nor were they willing to accept new missionaries as passengers, though the Jesuits were very anxious to send more
helpers to Father Brébeuf. The only new Jesuit recruit to go with
the Hurons was Father Paul Ragueneau who left Three Rivers in
early August 1637.[92] Father Pierre Pijart followed on August 16.

---

all wasted away, having suffered greatly from fatigue and sickness on the journey.
He was barefooted, and wore upon his head a hat and upon his body a cassock
not worth two doubles; yet the house could not furnish him a change of clothes."

Charles Huault de Montmagny, Champlain's successor, was from a very distinguished family. Charles entered the Knights of Malta in 1622 after being educated by the Jesuits. He served for years aboard ships of war belonging to the
Order of Malta. He reached New France on June 11, 1636, and continued to
govern the colony until 1648.

90 Ibid., 199-203.

91 Ibid., 231.

92 Paul Ragueneau, one of the true giant missionaries of New France, was
born at Paris on March 18, 1608. On August 21, 1626, he entered the Jesuit
novitiate at Paris, following in the footsteps of his elder brother François, eleven
years his senior. He reached Quebec on June 28, 1636, and spent a year there
before being sent to the Huron mission where he arrived on September 1, 1637.
He was made superior of that mission in 1645 and was in charge when it was
abandoned. On his return to Quebec from Huronia he held the office of superior
of all the Jesuits on the mission of New France. In 1662 he returned to France
where for many years he served as French agent for the mission of New France.
He died at Paris, aged seventy-two, on September 3, 1680. He was so convinced
that Brébeuf and his martyred companions would one day be canonized, that he
drew up a document containing sworn testimony of all who knew the details of
the martyrdom. It is from that document that we learn many details concerning
Jean de Brébeuf. For the account of Ragueneau's arrival at Ossossané and his
near capture by the Iroquois on his way there, see ibid., XV, 135.

With the return of the fur brigade the Hurons, who believed the missionaries to be evil sorcerers, intensified the campaign against them. On October 3, 1637, when the flimsy bark residence of the Jesuits at Ossossané caught fire, the missionaries had reason to believe that some evil-minded Indian had caused the damage ". . . as for a long time they had threatened to burn us all when we least expected it."[93] A short time later at Ihonatiria, an Indian drew his bow, threatening to bury the arrow in the heart of a missionary.[94] At Ossossané a contingent from the Cord clan arrived fully determined to kill all of the missionaries. This threat was so serious that, in the absence of Father Brébeuf, who was at Ihonatiria, the missionaries at Ossossané proceeded to prepare their lay helpers to meet their end. That dauntless group of French laymen ". . . prepared themselves reverently, but with determination, nevertheless, they said, not to die with their arms folded, unwilling to let themselves be murdered without making some defense."[95]

If there was to be a council concerning the fate of the Jesuits, Father François Le Mercier wanted Brébeuf present since the great Echon spoke the language best of all the French and had the most penetrating perception of the Huron mind. Le Mercier hurried off to Ihonatiria and brought Brébeuf back. Arriving at Ossossané on October 28, 1637, the giant apostle learned that at their council the Hurons had determined on the death of all the missionaries. The evening before, Charles Garnier and Pierre Chastellain had been peremptorily summoned to a council meeting and told that the contagion afflicting the Hurons was all caused by the Blackrobes, especially Echon. When that wicked sorcerer, they said,

. . . came up to the country again, fully four years ago, he had said that this visit would be only for five years and, lo, the appointed time had almost expired; that this wicked man had already profited too much by their ruin, and that therefore a general council was demanded, in order to hear him thereupon, and to end the matter.[96]

[93] Ibid., 53.
[94] Ibid., 57.
[95] Ibid., 59.
[96] Ibid.

Jean de Brébeuf seriously expected that the general council of the nation would decree the death of the Jesuits. If so, the missionaries would, in all likelihood, meet their deaths unexpectedly at the hands of young braves attacking each one suddenly. It behooved Father Brébeuf, therefore, to make practical arrangements to avoid the desecration of sacred vessels as well as to leave some record for his superior at Quebec as to the motivation for the deaths of these beleaguered subjects. He, therefore, directed his fellow Jesuits and their lay assistants that if any survived the expected slaughter they take refuge in the cabins of Hurons at Ossossané who were friendly and might protect them. As for the sacred vessels, vestments, and the like, he instructed his companions to take them to the cabin of Pierre Tsiouenda-entaha, aged about fifty, ". . . a man of intelligence and one of the most discreet and influential persons in the country . . . ,"[97] the first adult Huron to be baptized while in health. He could be trusted to guard them until some missionary returned. Above all, Brébeuf charged his people to ". . . be especially careful to put our dictionary, and all that we have of the language, in a place of safety." If missionaries ever returned, the key to beginning again the conversion of the Hurons lay in the precious knowledge of their native tongue which was contained in the manuscript notes collected with so much difficulty.

With these mundane details attended to, Jean de Brébeuf composed a sort of last will and testament for his superior at Quebec, planning to put it into the hands of some trustworthy Huron who would bring it to Three Rivers to be forwarded to Father Paul Le Jeune. Brébeuf wrote:

We are, perhaps, on the point of shedding our blood and sacrificing our lives in the service of our Good Master, Jesus Christ. It seems that His Goodness is willing to accept this sacrifice from me, for the expiation of my great and innumerable sins, and to crown, from this hour forward, the past services and the great and ardent desires of all our priests who are here.

What makes me think that this will not happen is, on the one side, the excess of past wickedness, which renders me utterly unworthy of so wonderful a favor; and on the other side, because I do not believe that His Goodness will permit his workmen to be put to death, since, through His grace, there are already some good souls who eagerly receive the seed of the Gospel, despite the evil speech and the persecution of all men against

[97] Ibid., XIV, 77.

us. But yet, I fear that the Divine Justice, seeing the obstinacy of the majority of these barbarians in their follies, may very justly permit that they come and destroy the bodily life of those who, with all their hearts, desire and procure the life of the souls of these barbarians.

Be that as it may, I assure you that all our priests await the outcome of this matter with great calmness and serenity of soul. As for myself, I can say to your Reverence, with all sincerity, that I have not yet had the slightest dread of death for such a cause. But we all are grieved over this, that these poor barbarians, through their own malice, are closing the door to the Gospel and to Grace.

Whatever conclusion they reach, and whatever treatment they accord us, we will try, by the Grace of Our Lord, to endure it patiently for His service. It is a singular favor that His Goodness gives us, to allow us to endure something for love of Him. Now it is that we consider ourselves as belonging truly to the Society [of Jesus]. May He be forever blessed for having chosen us from among so many others better than we and destined for this country, to aid Him in bearing His cross.

In all things, may His Holy Will be done! If He wills that at this hour we die, oh! fortunate is the hour for us! If He wills to reserve us for other labors, may He be blessed! If you hear that God has crowned our insignificant labors, or rather our desires, bless Him. For it is for Him that we desire to live and to die; and it is He who gives us the grace to do so.

As for the rest, if any survive I have given orders as to all they are to do. I have deemed it advisable that our priests and domestics should withdraw to the houses of those whom they regard as their best friends. I have charged them to carry to the cabin of Peter, our first Christian, all that belongs to the chapel; and above all, to be especially careful to put our dictionary and all that we have on the language in a place of safety.

As for myself, if God grants me the grace to go to Heaven, I will pray to God for our people and for the poor Hurons; and I will not forget your Reverence. Finally, we beg your Reverence and all our Fathers not to forget us in your Holy Sacrifices and prayers, to the end that, in life and after death, God may grant us mercy. We are all, in life and in eternity,

> Your Reverence's
> Very humble and very affectionate
> servants in Our Lord.
> Jean de Brébeuf
> François Joseph Le Mercier

At the residence of
la Conception, at
Ossossané, this
28th of October

Charles Garnier
Paul Ragueneau

I have left Fathers Pierre Pijart and Isaac Jogues in the residence of St. Joseph, with the same sentiments.[98]

[98] Ibid., XV, 61-65.

Resignation to martyrdom, if it be the will of God, or even an eagerness to embrace it, was, under the circumstances, a luxury which Jean de Brébeuf felt could not be afforded, considering the consequences for the Hurons' spiritual future. If Brébeuf and his companions won the martyr's palm now, hope for the conversion of this aboriginal folk would die with them, and just at the moment when several of the missionaries were becoming sufficiently fluent in the Huron tongue to begin effective instruction of the people in their own language. The Jesuits would, therefore, storm heaven to avert such a disaster, not so much to themselves as to the nation they yearned to lead to the throne of God. Hence, Le Mercier wrote in his *Relation* of 1637: ". . . in this desperate state of affairs, we had recourse to the great saint Joseph, all making a vow to God to say holy Mass in his honor for nine consecutive days; we began this on the feast of Saints Simon and Jude."[99]

Besides the earnest petitioning of heaven, Jean de Brébeuf had one more arrow in his quiver. Above all, the Hurons must not think that the missionaries cowered before the threat of death. No Indian worthy of the name allowed himself to manifest fear of death whether it was met violently in battle or peacefully in his own cabin from natural causes. If opportunity offered, a dying man gave an *atsataion*, a farewell feast for his friends at which he partook of the best and sang, recounting his own great deeds, without manifesting any dread of his forthcoming demise. Well understanding how the Hurons interpreted such a feast, Jean de Brébeuf held his *atsataion*, publicly announcing, hereby, his expected demise. When the cabin overflowed with guests, Brébeuf seized the occasion to speak to them of life after death. As to the reaction of the Hurons present, Le Mercier reported: "The mournful silence of these good people saddened us more than our own danger."[100] Perhaps Father Brébeuf's bold gesture startled the Huron enemies of the Jesuits into reflecting on the economic consequences of wholesale murder of the missionaries. Perhaps St. Joseph intervened. From whatever cause, the Jesuits were amazed to discover that within a few days all threats of death

---

[99] Ibid., 67. St. Joseph had been chosen as heavenly patron of Canada by the Recollets. The feast of Sts. Simon and Jude is celebrated on October 28.

[100] Ibid.

faded away. The novena in honor of St. Joseph was not completed before ". . . all these storms were allayed . . . since the 6th of November, when we finished our votive Masses . . . we have enjoyed an incredible peace at which we ourselves wonder from day to day when we consider what condition our affairs were only one week ago."[101]

Relieved and encouraged, the missionaries again began visiting the cabins at Ossossané, ministering to the sick, offering each invalid a little sweetened warm water, a sliver of lemon peel, and a few raisins. When the supply of dried fruit was exhausted, the missionaries steeped the paper wrappings of the fruit in water so they would have something to offer the poor, sick Indians. Though the resulting potion ". . . tasted more of paper and ink than of sugar . . ." the sufferers found it refreshing.[102] More often than not, however, the ailing Hurons rejected any spiritual aid. One suffering Huron typified the majority. He readily welcomed ministration for his body, but coldly rebuffed the missionary when spiritual things were introduced. His reason, as he explained, was that he did not want to become a Christian for then he would be separated in eternity from all his relatives who had gone before him.[103]

Over a year before, Jean de Brébeuf, with his keen insight into the Indian mind, put his finger on the problem when he wrote from Ihonatiria, on July 16, 1636: "You might say that they are only waiting to see one of their number take the first dreaded step, and venture to run counter to the customs of the country."[104] Brébeuf, himself, unknowingly inspired one Huron to take that step while the great missionary was attending the Feast of the Dead in the spring of 1636.

Chihwatenhwa, a resident of Ossossané, a mature man of about thirty-five in 1637, was highly respected among the Hurons of the Bear clan. The nephew of the captain of that clan, Chihwatenhwa, though not wealthy, was a striking example of what Christian philosophers call the *homo naturaliter bonus*, a naturally good man. Endowed with a keen intellect and a phenomenal memory, he had never taken part in the practice of sorcery, though his brother was a noted medicine man. Contrary to com-

---

[101] Ibid.
[102] Ibid., 77.

[103] Ibid., 71.
[104] Ibid., X, 313.

monly accepted practice, he remained constantly faithful to the wife of his youth. He neither gambled nor used tobacco and never indulged in immodest feasts.[105] In the spring of 1636, at the Feast of the Dead, he listened to Father Brébeuf discoursing on the truths of Christianity. Thenceforward, Chihwatenhwa was ". . . deeply interested in us and our Holy Mysteries so that not long afterwards he presented us one of his little sons to be baptized and consequently, as he said, to go to Heaven."[106] When he fell victim to the epidemic and was thought to be dying, he was asked if he wished to be baptized. Joyfully consenting, he received the sacrament on August 16, 1637, and was given the name of Joseph. On his recovery, Joseph, according to custom on such occasions, gave a feast at which all the guests ". . . wondered to see him resolved to live as a Christian."[107]

Hardly had Joseph been baptized before he was tried by afflictions as a latter-day Job. The epidemic afflicted his family with particular violence. Promptly, his relatives accused him of causing their illness because he had become a Christian. Surmounting their reproaches, Joseph converted many of them. When death took his youngest son, the pride of his heart, Joseph accepted the blow with true Christian fortitude. Joseph's exemplary life offered Brébeuf the opportunity of performing the first Christian marriage witnessed by the Hurons. On March 19, 1638, Joseph's wife, Marie, was baptized and, fittingly, on that solemn feast of his patron, Joseph and Marie were married before a great concourse of Hurons.

Joseph's constancy, and that of his whole family, was particularly valuable to Brébeuf and his companions for no longer could the Hurons maintain that they were unable to observe the laws of the God of the Christians. As Father Le Mercier put it:

They no longer dared to tell us that our countries are different, and that, as their land cannot furnish them the fruits that grow in France, they are not (they say) as capable as we are of the virtues of Christianity. There is nothing more to hold them back, then, but their own weakness and want of courage, which is lacking to many European Christians as well as to the barbarians of this new world, from renouncing their own evil propensities.[108]

[105] Ibid., XV, 79.
[106] Ibid., 81.
[107] Ibid., 85.
[108] Ibid., 107, 109.

When the winter of 1637 closed in, drawing the Hurons away from outdoor activities, the time was ripe for attracting large numbers of them to hear the word of God. Inviting the captain of each cabin at Ossossané to a feast on December 8, Brébeuf proposed instituting regular meetings. All one hundred fifty captains approving, the first gathering was held on January 9, 1638, at the cabin of the foremost captain who ostensibly called the captains together to attend a feast. At the end of normal activities, the captain announced that the assembled captains were now holding a council whose members should listen attentively to what Echon had to say. Aided by Joseph Chihwatenhwa, Jean de Brébeuf discoursed eloquently on the subjects of hell and paradise, and so effectively that at the end an old brave declared ". . . that he earnestly wished we would oftener call them together thus."[109] A little less than a month later, on February 1, an audience larger than the first listened attentively to Brébeuf explaining the Christian doctrine concerning hell. There followed a lengthy debate resulting in the captains summoning a formal council. At that solemn meeting the members of the council declared that ". . . they must, after all, believe us and believe in God! Finally, they added, by common consent, that thenceforth they would recognize the Father Superior [Brébeuf] as one of the captains of the village, and that consequently he could assemble the council in our cabin at any and all times he might choose."[110]

Shortly, the meetings developed into a lively debating society, an activity which delighted the Hurons. Customarily, Father Brébeuf began the meetings with a prayer in the Huron language, employing the tone generally reserved by the Indians for their most solemn conclaves. Then all the Fathers, in concert, sang the Apostles' Creed in native rhymes. The catechism lesson itself was couched in the form of a dialogue between Joseph and one of the missionaries. Joseph accomplished wonders ". . . acting sometimes as objector, sometimes as ignoramus, and anon the Doctor, he gives opportunity to our Catechist to explain by Dialogue, and with more clearness, what otherwise would be only half understood."[111] The Jesuits were particularly pleased and hopeful of

[109] Ibid., 117.
[110] Ibid., 119.
[111] Ibid., 123.

success when, as a result of these meetings, some young men began to receive regular instructions, offering themselves with "... many evidences of good will."[112]

While Ossossané seemed, thus, well on the way to possessing a solid nucleus of Christians, the mission of St. Joseph at Ihonatiria was not far behind. Astan, foremost war chief of the whole country, asked for baptism and Pierre Tsiouendaentaha, the earliest of Brébeuf's converts continued, by his excellent example, to attract others. But St. Joseph's was already doomed to abandonment. The great captain of the area, Aenons, had died while at Three Rivers on a trading expedition and many were slowly abandoning the area, "... the majority of them having been carried off or scattered by the disease ..."[113] Foreseeing the eventual necessity of closing St. Joseph, Father Brébeuf paid a visit to the Cord clan dwelling quite a distance south and east of the Bears. The Cords were not only numerous, but, having been the first Hurons to contact the French, had by traditional right the monopoly of trade with them. However, the Cords, especially those living at their clan's capital, Teanaustayé, had been "... one of the principal shops in which were forged the blackest calumnies and most pernicious plots against us, to such an extent that the captains had publicly exhorted the young men to come and massacre us at this village of Ossossané, where we then were."[114]

But since the mission effort must be expanded to reach, at least, every Huron clan, Brébeuf's visit presented a heaven-sent opportunity.

Accordingly, sustained by God alone, Father Jean de Brébeuf repaired to this village [Teanaustayé], spoke to individuals and then to the Council, and did so well that he won them both over, so that in a little while they decided to receive us in their village and give us a cabin there. This was accomplished, and the first Mass was said there on the 25th of June [1638], to the great satisfaction of our Fathers, who could hardly believe what they saw, so greatly had this village abominated us a little while before.[115]

112 Ibid., 125.
113 Ibid., XVII, 59.
114 Ibid. Jones, 22, located Teanaustayé at lot 7, concession IV, Medonte township, Simcoe county, Ontario. Later archaeological investigation seems to indicate that the more likely site is lot 12 of concession IV. The village was where Antoine Daniel was martyred. Louis de Sainte-Foy resided at that Cord town.
115 Relations, XVII, 61.

The new center was given St. Joseph as its patron, the same heavenly advocate whom the Jesuits believed had obtained so many celestial blessings for them at Ihonatiria and Ossossané.

That summer of 1638, when the Huron fur brigade went down to Three Rivers, Father Pierre Pijart again went along to report conditions and assemble supplies for the coming year. To his delight, he discovered numerous new recruits arriving from France, some of whom were destined for the Huron mission. Perhaps best of all, Father Antoine Daniel, after two discouraging years at Quebec in charge of the ill-fated seminary for Huron boys, was going back. Of the newly arrived Jesuits, those assigned to Huronia were François Du Peron, Simon Le Moyne, and Jerome Lalemant.[116] None could speak the Huron tongue for each had been dispatched to the distant mission with hardly a pause at Quebec.

When Father Jerome Lalemant reached Ossossané on August 26, 1638, he informed Father Jean de Brébeuf that his responsibility as superior of the mission was ended.[117] No gift could have been more welcome to Echon and none more regretted by his associates. Father Brébeuf happily stepped back into the ranks, glad to be one who obeyed rather than one who commanded.

[116] François Du Peron was born at Lyons on January 26, 1610. He entered the Jesuit novitiate at Avignon on February 23, 1627. After his ecclesiastical studies he came to Canada where he arrived on June 30, 1638, and went directly to Huronia. When the mission was destroyed, he returned to Quebec in 1649 and returned to France the following year. He returned to New France five years later. After another period in France, he spent his last few years at Chambly as chaplain of the fort there. He died at Quebec on November 10, 1665.

Simon Le Moyne was born at Beauvais on October 22, 1604. He entered the Jesuit novitiate at Rouen on December 10, 1622. He reached Quebec on June 30, 1639, and was sent immediately to the Huron mission where he labored until the Jesuits returned to Quebec in 1650. He had a flair for languages and was an accomplished mimic. On several occasions he was employed as an ambassador to the Iroquois. He died at Cap de Madeleine on November 24, 1665.

[117] Lalemant reached Ossossané on August 26, 1638. He quite likely assumed his office as superior at once. Brébeuf may have already removed to Teanaustayé before Lalemant arrived. The first Mass celebrated at the new location was held on June 25, 1638. See ibid., XVI, 239; XVII, 61.

Chapter VII

St. Joseph's at Teanaustayé

Relieved of responsibility for the whole Huron mission effort, Jean de Brébeuf was assigned by his successor, Jerome Lalemant, to assume charge of the newly established post among the Cords at Teanaustayé. Taking Isaac Jogues, Simon Le Moyne, and Paul Ragueneau with him, the great Echon settled into a Cord cabin ". . . so poor and so mean that if the Savior of the world had not himself once, in time of need, taken lodging in the stable at Bethlehem, we would have been ashamed to give him a sort of new birth each day in this place, which is covered only with wretched bark, through which the wind enters from every side."[1] In the actual work of evangelizing the Cords Isaac Jogues was a valuable assistant. After a little over two full years among the Hurons, Jogues had mastered their language, at least well enough to converse easily, and was habituated to the customs of the people, even to their ruthless cruelty to prisoners taken captive in their raids.[2] Paul Ragueneau, after only a year among the Hurons had

[1] *Relations*, XVII, 61.
[2] Talbot, *Saint among Savages*, 139.

not, as yet, acquired the lingual fluency he would later manifest, but he was accustomed to Indian ways which had, months since, ceased to shock him. Simon Le Moyne, only just arrived in Huronia, was about to witness Indians at their worst.

Brébeuf and his companions were barely settled at the new mission of St. Joseph when a triumphant band of Hurons returning from a raid against the Iroquois brought back a hundred captives. A dozen or so of these were presented to the village of Teanaustayé. While the people with diabolical delight fell on their hapless victims, inflicting the most exquisite tortures, the missionaries stood by, awaiting an opportunity to instruct and baptize the unfortunate prisoners. Unbelievably, during periods of rest granted the captives, lest they expire too quickly, the Jesuits managed to instruct the Iroquois sufficiently in the basic truths of Christianity and baptize nearly all of them.

Among the captive Iroquois, Ononelwaia, named Pierre at baptism, astonished his captors by his bravery under torture. Cruelly burned, Pierre comforted and encouraged his fellow captives ". . . representing the blessedness they had found in their misfortune, and that which was prepared for them after this life."[3] Outlasting all the other prisoners, Pierre received the most refined cruelties the Cords could devise. Burned until his flesh hung in strips, his tormentors scalped him, but Pierre, summoning superhuman strength, snatched up firebrands and vigorously attacked his foe. Even after they rolled him over fires, Pierre charged his enemies with burning branches in his hands. When they cut off his hands and feet, he advanced against them on his knees and elbows. Finally, a Huron brave slashed off his head. Awed by such a manifestation of indomitable courage, the Cords attributed it to the saving waters of baptism. Therefore, they ". . . resolved no longer to allow us to baptize these poor unfortunates, reckoning it a misfortune to their country when those whom they torment shriek not at all, or very little."[4]

Nonetheless, Pierre's obvious belief in Christianity seemed to have so effectively sustained him that his tormentors confessed that the truths the missionaries preached must have some validity. The obstinate among the Cords, however, to show their disdain

[3] *Relations*, XVII, 65.
[4] Ibid.

of the Jesuits and their Christian message, defiantly hurled the severed hand of a slaughtered Iroquois into the missionary cabin, as if to offer the Jesuits their share of the cannibalistic feast which followed the roasting of the bodies of the dead captives. As the severed member pertained to a baptized Christian named Francis Xavier, the missionaries buried it within the confines of their cabin ". . . and prayed to God for the repose of his soul."[5]

Considering the long-standing opposition of the Cords to the missionaries, it surprised and delighted Father Brébeuf when, after only a six-month stay in Teanaustayé, Aochiati, an aged and highly respected captain of seventy summers, earnestly requested baptism. Because Aochiati was master of the dance of the naked, a particularly lascivious ceremony from the performance of which the master received rich rewards, Brébeuf, doubting his true intention, put him off, striving to test the man's sincerity. In the late fall, Aochiati reluctantly went off hunting, expressing deep regret that, in his unbaptized condition, a fatal accident might befall him and plunge him ". . . into fires which were never extinguished."[6] Two days later severe weather, plus a well-founded rumor of an enemy ambush, brought Aochiati back home.[7]

Fortunately, Joseph Chihwatenhwa, that valiant lay apostle from Ossossané, happened by to pay the Jesuits a visit. With Joseph's help Aochiati convinced Brébeuf of his unwavering determination to renounce paganism. So, on December 20, 1638, Aochiati was solemnly baptized along with two small granddaughters whom he dearly cherished. The neophyte was named Matthias in honor of the disciple chosen after Christ's resurrection to replace the traitorous Judas. The newly baptized captain proved so fervent a Christian that he willingly renounced every pagan practice, even offering to abandon the use of tobacco if that habit were forbidden. For an Indian such a deprivation, though not required, was ". . . one of the most heroic acts of which an Indian is capable, who, it seems, would as soon dispense with eating as with smoking."[8] Aochiati's example was followed a few days later by eleven other adults. On January 1, 1639, Jean

---

[5] Ibid., 77.
[6] Ibid., 79.
[7] Ibid., 79, 81.
[8] Ibid., 81, 83.

de Brébeuf announced that New Year's day would always be observed as the birthday of the new church located in the village of Teanaustayé.

Encouraged by such a propitious beginning among the Cords, Father Brébeuf cast about for another center for a mission. A little over two miles almost due north of the new St. Joseph's lay the village of Scanonaenrot, ". . . one of the most important of the country, itself alone forming one entire nation of the four that compose the Hurons . . ."[9] The Tohontaenrats, or Nation of the One White House, familiarly known as the Deer clan, were late-comers to Huronia. These people are thought to have been Laurentian Iroquois who migrated to the Huron country some time between 1590 and 1610.[10] Among the other Huron clans, the Deer, as we shall call them, were considered ". . . the demons of the country . . ."[11] because their clan rites and the practices of their sorcerers were far more depraved than those of the other clans. Going back and forth between Ossossané and Teanaustayé, Brébeuf often passed through Scanonaenrot and observed their depraved practices. Obviously, great effort must be expended to convert those pagans lest they corrupt the Christians living at Teanaustayé.

In the dead of winter, 1639, Jean de Brébeuf and a companion set out to breach the stronghold of Scanonaenrot. Caught in a severe snowstorm, the two soldiers of Christ lost their way and wandered in the cold aimlessly all night until by pure luck they stumbled onto their destination at four in the morning. By chance, they took refuge in a cabin occupied by only one family. Welcomed with true Huron hospitality, they remained with that family for the whole month of their stay.[12] As was proper protocol, Brébeuf first addressed an assembly of the dozen village captains, explaining the purpose of his visit. He came, he said, to bring to them knowledge of the ". . . one and only true God and of Jesus Christ, our Lord and Redeemer."[13] The hopeful apostle

---

[9] Ibid., 87.

[10] Tooker, *Ethnography of the Huron Indians*, 3. Jones, 263, places the village of Scanonaenrot at lot 17, concession III, Medonte township, Simcoe county, Ontario. If correct, this places it within what is now a reforestation area.

[11] *Relations*, XVII, 89.

[12] Ibid., 91.

[13] Ibid.

named the place St. Michael ". . . in honor of the holy angels, like to whom we did not despair that these poor people would one day become . . ."[14]

At first the novelty of the presence of the two Jesuits attracted droves of listeners. But quickly enough most of the Indians either lost interest or took to heckling the missionaries as they addressed the gatherings. Changing tactics, the missionaries began visiting individual cabins, searching out the few willing to listen to them.[15] Giving full attention to that small group, at the end of a month the missionaries were able to baptize their host and two other captains of the village. For the most part, though, people at St. Michael's firmly rejected Christianity, convinced that ". . . baptism causes death, or renders those who receive it liable to a thousand evils and miseries."[16] Though the three neophytes themselves were none too sure that these dire predictions might not be true, they bravely requested baptism, thinking ". . . I will receive it even if I must die for it."[17]

Roaming the countryside in search of other likely sites, Jean de Brébeuf found the tiny, isolated village of Tahententaron, six miles almost due north of the new mission of St. Joseph.[18] On St. Andrew's day, November 30, 1638, by accident Father Brébeuf happened upon a dying child. Also, he came upon a very old man ". . . who had no other ailment except that of his old age . . ."[19] Echon instructed the old patriarch who listened very willingly. When about to depart, the great apostle of the Hurons felt inspired to baptize the old warrior at once. Two days later, on the feast of St. Francis Xavier, when Brébeuf heard that a young Iroquois captive had been given to the villagers for torture, he hastily returned to Tahententaron, hoping to baptize the poor victim. There he found people preparing for a burial. On inquiry, Brébeuf learned that his aged neophyte had died the previous

[14] Ibid., 89.
[15] Ibid., 95.
[16] Ibid., 97.
[17] Ibid.
[18] Jones, 263, places Tahententaron at lot 22, concession VIII, Medonte township, Simcoe county, Ontario. The village, then, would have been quite close to the Sturgeon River, about a half mile south of Highway 23 and a bit north of a reforestation area.
[19] *Relations*, XVII, 101.

day, only a short time after he had received baptism. As for the
Iroquois, ". . . a young man of 22, as graceful and well made an
Indian as one could meet . . . ,"[20] his tormentors had already mutilated his hands and were gleefully preparing to continue torturing him that evening. Father Brébeuf instructed the suffering
youth who, instead of chanting defiance thereafter, loudly
chanted an act of contrition.[21] And that angered his tormentors
who felt that the missionary had cast a spell on their victim. Jean
de Brébeuf placed Tahententaron under the patronage of St.
Ignatius, evangelizing the village with the help of his companions at Teanaustayé.

As the numbers of Huron converts grew, the vast majority of
the people became increasingly concerned because the Christian
missionaries inveighed against nearly every social institution accepted by the Hurons from time immemorial. Sexual promiscuity,
unhesitating belief in dreams, faith in the activities of the sorcerers, cruel torturing of captive enemies, all of these were so much
a part of the warp and woof of Huron life that any change in
them presaged a social revolution. Sorcerers opposed the missionaries on economic as well as religious grounds. If these Frenchmen with their much more powerful spells were unopposed, they
would eventually discredit the Huron sorcerers. Then, how would
the native medicine men make a living? No longer would anyone
pay them to cast their spells and invoke their incantations.

Various important captains and respected elders among the
Hurons reflected long and earnestly as to what the Blackrobes
really sought in Huronia. Since the priests were clearly not traders nor were they interested in the Huron women, only one other
motive seemed to remain. The missionaries wanted to decimate
the Huron nation so that French laymen could possess the land.
The rite of baptism was the chief weapon, as anyone could see,
because nearly all the sick who received it died shortly thereafter.
Hence, sorcerers and Huron leaders constantly warned the people against the priests, who, they said, had no other purpose than
to undo and utterly ruin the Hurons.[22] Taking their cue from the

[20] Ibid.
[21] Ibid., 103.
[22] Ibid., 117.

leaders, the common people, especially the children and adoles-
cents, began openly abusing the missionaries.

Snowballs, clubs, cornstalks, and other rubbish, for lack of stones (which
are not always to be found in this country when they are wanted) have been
seen flying over the Fathers' heads, even during the Catechisms, and, in the
course of the day, through the holes of the cabin which serve as window and
chimney, to say nothing of many other indignities that occur every day,
living among a barbarous people, against whom we have, and can have
no defense.[23]

A less heroic soul might well have concluded that attempting
to convert these crude, haughty savages was a hopeless task. It
was frustrating, indeed, to realize that the Hurons, far from listening humbly to missionaries who had sacrificed all to aid them,
looked upon their visitors much as a nineteenth-century native
New Englander viewed the eastern European immigrant who
spoke no English and clung to his European customs. Not so Jean
de Brébeuf, however. In the spring of 1639 it was his duty, as superior of the mission of St. Joseph, to give an account of his stew-
ardship. On May 13, 1639, he wrote to the Jesuit general, Mutius
Vitelleschi:

Last year, I received the letter which your Paternity sent me, dated at
Rome, January 1, 1638. All of us here are profoundly grateful for the singular blessings bestowed on us since the beginning of the year. It has been a
holy, fruitful and happy one, as you hoped for us, and it continues so, day
by day. Since we began this new church the number of converts continues
to increase, especially since the arrival among us of Father Jerome Lalemant, presently superior of this mission. We have every reason to expect
that he will indeed become the veritable apostle of the Hurons. His zeal is
so great that he neglects nothing which would advance our own religious
perfection or the conversion of the Indians. His profound charity and gentle
spirit has conquered the hearts of each of us. His solid virtue encourages us
all to strive for religious perfection. He has told your Paternity the state of
religion [among the Indians] here or he has referred you to this year's *Relation* which he composed. Hence, I need not expand, except to note that this
year we baptized about 300 people, of whom about 100 practice their faith,
frequenting the sacraments. Most of the rest, baptized when gravely ill or
dying, have gone to heaven or, once they recovered, failed to practice their
religion. However, we have a great number of catechumens who, we hope,
will join the flock of Christ, after their constancy has been sufficiently tested.
At the moment we are enjoying a period of peace. As the virulence of the

[23] Ibid.

epidemic abated, so, too, the rumors of violence to us died away. However, there is no lack of sources for suffering. If there is a famine this year, as many fear, everyone will blame us for it. But, if God is with us, who can be against us?

Your Paternity remarked that you would be pleased to hear of anything you might do to assist us. We are grateful for your thoughtfulness. We beseech you to consider favorably the petitions which Father Jerome Lalemant, our superior, is presenting this year. These requests, if granted, will greatly advance Christianity here. We are grateful that you remember us in your prayers and holy Sacrifices and ask that you continue and recommend us, likewise, to the prayers and sacrifices of the whole Society.

Your Paternity's most humble
and obedient servant in Christ,
Jean de Brébeuf[24]

From the residence of
St. Joseph
at the village of Teanaustayé
among the Hurons
May 13, 1639.

Jean de Brébeuf's unstinting admiration of Jerome Lalemant was not shared universally by all the Jesuits in Huronia. Father Charles Garnier, a most gentle, pious man and a future martyr, also reporting to Vitelleschi, wrote: "For superior, we have a man of singular virtue and noteworthy prudence, devoted to his subjects. However, there is this lacking in him, he is unable to win their hearts."[25] Father Paul Ragueneau, who was one of the most able Jesuits to work in New France, reported to the Jesuit general concerning Lalemant: "He would govern much more kindly if he had a less irascible nature; he ought to control his first inclinations."[26]

Jerome Lalemant initiated his term of office by introducing a program of "regularizing" the Huron mission. Henceforth, the missionaries would follow, as closely as possible, the daily order prevailing in established Jesuit communities at home in France. All arose at four in the morning and spent an hour in prayerful meditation. Then the priests each in turn said Mass. At eight the cabin door was opened to admit the Hurons. Some of the missionaries remained in the cabin to receive and instruct those Indians who came. Others made regular visits to each cabin in the vil-

---

[24] Latourelle, *Etude sur . . . Brébeuf*, II, 76-77. In the Jesuit archives at Rome, the original of this letter is identified as Gal. II, ff. 353, 353v, 354v.

[25] *Relations*, XXV, 83.

[26] Rochemonteix, I, 383. Ragueneau to Vitelleschi, May 29, 1642.

lage, baptizing the very ill and instructing those willing to listen. At two, all the missionaries gathered in their cabin where each spent fifteen minutes examining his conscience. Dinner followed at which one of the priests read aloud from the bible and one or other pious book. Then, until four in the afternoon the Indians were allowed to visit the cabin. Promptly at that hour the Hurons were dismissed and the priests recited the major portion of the day's Roman breviary in common. Afterwards they conferred together until 6:30 P.M. when they ate their frugal evening meal. At eight in the evening all recited night prayers in common and then retired.[27] The schedule undoubtedly effected a semimonastic manner of life for the Jesuits, but it also emphasized the wide cultural differences between the French missionaries and the Hurons whom the Jesuits had come so far and suffered so much to convert.

Just as he insisted on rigid observance in the community life of the Jesuits, so Lalemant determined to organize regular parochial life among the Huron Christians. At Ossossané, the sixty or so Hurons who became practicing Christians were treated as though they were members of the average Catholic parish at Paris. Every Sunday and major holy day there was a solemn parochial Mass, including all the accidentals attending the ceremony in France. The congregation was sprinkled with holy water at the beginning of the Mass. At the offertory a few Christian Hurons presented the celebrant with loaves of bread which were blessed and returned to the Indians. In the early afternoon on such days the missionaries, in the presence of the Huron Christians, chanted solemn vespers. At about five in the evening the Jesuits sang compline together while the Indians listened.[28] Pious as these practices may have been for the French, one cannot help wondering what Huron converts could possibly have thought of them. Perhaps they thought of the antiphonal singing and the like as some new form of incantation such as their own native sorcerers practiced. All in all, Jerome Lalemant simply did not understand Indians, nor even like them very much. He assuredly did not subscribe to Jean de Brébeuf's major principal regarding the proper approach to the Indians. A second St. Paul, the great Echon

[27] *Relations*, XVI, 241-45.
[28] Ibid., XVII, 169.

believed that to convert them he should, in as far as possible, become a Huron with the Hurons.

For all that, Jerome Lalemant's first major activity as superior of the Huron mission was a highly praiseworthy one. A competent administrator, he set about discovering the proportions of the problem of converting the Huron nation. How many people were there; how many villages and where was each located? Early in the spring of 1639 he and his fellow Jesuits set out determined to visit ". . . the villages of the country, large and small, intending not to leave a cabin of the Indians in which we did not present ourselves, and say and do whatever was necessary to carry out God's plan for his elect."[29] The Jesuits tramped through the slush and rain of the spring of 1639 taking an accurate census. When the task was completed the missionaries reported that Huronia consisted of thirty-two villages or hamlets, which comprised, in all, about seven hundred cabins, about two thousand fires, and approximately twelve thousand persons. The missionaries also drew a map locating all of the villages. On the occasion of the census each Huron village received the name of a saint and thenceforth each was referred to by that title.[30]

Having completed the survey of the Huron nation, Jerome Lalemant announced a major policy change, an innovation in the manner of evangelization. Jean de Brébeuf firmly believed that the key to converting the Hurons was the adoption of Huron culture, as far as possible. He sought, and encouraged his companions, to accept the Huron life-style following their diet, living in their villages, sharing their joys and their sorrows. Apparently, he hoped that, given the man power, every Huron village would possess its own mission "family," dwelling in a typical Huron cabin, participating in the life of the village. What matter if the village changed its location every ten or twelve years? Huron cabins were easily disassembled and reassembled at a new site. To Brébeuf, visiting an Indian village briefly and preaching to them occasionally was hardly enough. If the Hurons were to be led to embrace Christianity, the constant living example of the missionary in their midst seemed to him by far the most efficacious means

[29] Ibid., 105.

[30] Ibid., XIX, 125-27. The map drawn by the Jesuits in the spring of 1639 did not survive.

of accomplishing the purpose. The system might not be the most efficient or productive of the most rapid results, but, during his eight years of experience, it seemed to be slowly effecting the desired results among the Hurons.

To Jerome Lalemant the system favored by Father Brébeuf appeared to be inefficient and wasteful of man power. One central residence for all the missionaries seemed to him a much better approach. Explaining his decision to establish such a center, he wrote:

. . . having ascertained that the multiplicity of . . . residences [in various villages] was subject to many inconveniences, and that the conversion of these peoples could be further advanced through the channel of missions [that is, regular visits to villages], we resolved to combine our two houses into one. And so that in the course of years we should not be obliged to change places, as the Indians do, who transfer their village from one place to another after eight or nine years, we chose a place where we judged we could settle permanently; whence we might, according as we should have a supply at hand, detach a goodly number of missionaries who would have been trained for the purpose, to go with much more liberty, and convey to the villages and surrounding nations the holy Name of Our Lord.[31]

Something could be said in favor of Lalemant's plan. He proposed to establish a central mission, in part at least, as a means of partially alleviating the great economic burden the presence of missionaries so far from Quebec imposed on the whole Jesuit mission effort in New France. At his central mission station Lalemant planned to establish a farm for growing much of the food required. Also, craftsmen could be brought out, blacksmiths, cobblers, tailors, herdsmen, vintagers, and the like, whose skills would permit the erection of solidly constructed buildings. Hopefully, in time, the French would pass on their skills to the Hurons. Lalemant spoke longingly of the reductions in Paraguay where Iberian Jesuits had so very successfully transformed the Indians into skilled craftsmen, as Father Eusebio Kino would do with the Indians of the southwestern United States in the early eighteenth century. In the process, of course, the ancient Huron culture would inevitably disappear. But, that had already begun three decades before on the very day the Hurons first met Samuel de Champlain. A primitive culture cannot avoid rapid modification

---

[31] Ibid., 133.

once it encounters a much more advanced people. Goods of European manufacture, far superior to native products, were so eminently desirable to the Hurons that in a very brief time they simply ceased to produce articles which they could purchase from the French.

The site selected by Jerome Lalemant for his permanent mission center was within the area pertaining to the Ataronchronon whose villages were few in number and occupied by a group of no importance in Huron national affairs.[32] Traveling eastward from Ossossané for a little over two miles, one encounters the meandering Wye River which empties into a broad marshland overgrown with bulrushes so tall that a loaded canoe could easily glide through them unseen. The marshland gives way to a fairly respectable, though very muddy, lake which the Indians called Isaragui but on modern maps bears the name of Wye Lake. Pouring out of the northern end of the lake, the water forms a lovely continuation of the Wye River, emptying into Midland Bay, a small, attractive indentation of Georgian Bay. The fertile land near the lake and along the river would surely yield corn, wheat, vegetables, and, hopefully, a vineyard as well as grazing for domestic animals which the Jesuits expected to import. Besides, the lower reaches of the Wye River gave water access to Georgian Bay so that freight and arriving passengers could be deposited at the very door of the mission residence.[33]

In the early summer of 1639, when the new location had been selected, Jerome Lalemant and Jean de Brébeuf called on the Ataronchronon leaders, requesting permission to settle permanently among them. "There was reason to be apprehensive," Lalemant wrote, "at suggesting the proposal to this clan, the masters of the place. But it pleased God to assist us, for the proposition was immediately accepted. We promptly executed our part [of the proposal], delivering, at once, the presents we offered [to bind the contract]. If we had delayed two hours, I know not

[32] The Ataronchronon were known as the people dwelling beyond the fen or the intervening mud lake. Jones, 447, describes them as ". . . a congeries of the other clans." Until 1639 they had kept to themselves, avoiding contact with the French.

[33] In modern terms, the site selected is identified as lot 16, concession III, Tay township, Simcoe county, Ontario.

whether the affair could have ever succeeded."[34] Certainly, except for Jean de Brébeuf's consummate command of the Huron language and his understanding of the Indians, the request would have been peremptorily denied.

During the summer of 1639 the French laymen, assisting the Jesuits among the Hurons, shouldered their axes and went overland the eight miles to the newly purchased location and began erecting the mission center.[35] About thirty feet from the right bank of the Wye River and, perhaps, fifty yards south of the present Highway 12, they cleared the land and built a small cabin. Interiorly, the little structure, measuring only twenty by forty feet, included permanent divisions separating the area used as a chapel from the living quarters. But for that lone exception, any Huron entering the cabin felt at home. Down the center of the living area were four small fire pits and along the walls were the usual raised benches. Viewed from the outside, the cabin probably differed greatly from the dwellings built by the Hurons. Instead of the normal Huron rounded roof, the Jesuit cabin had a gabled roof surmounted by a small bell tower crowned by a cross. That innovation allowed space for sleeping quarters, at least over the living area.[36]

By dint of vigorous toil through the heat of summer, the devoted laymen completed the new residence by the middle of autumn. Then the mission at Ossossané was closed, leaving the chapel there in charge of Joseph Chihwatenhwa. All of the missionaries removed to the new mission except Jean de Brébeuf and Pierre Chastellain who remained at St. Joseph. In his *Relation* of 1640 Lalemant remarked:

We have given to this new house the name of sainte Marie, or Notre Dame de la Conception. The general and special obligations we are under to that

[34] *Relations*, XIX, 135.

[35] The laymen then present with the Jesuits on the Huron mission were: Simon Baron, called a surgeon; Dominique Scot, a general handyman; François Petit-Pré, a hunter; Mathurin, a domestic; Jean Amyot, a young boy; and Robert Le Coq, a carpenter by trade, but chiefly employed as the mission's business agent. See Jones, 310-11.

[36] Latourelle, *Etude sur . . . Brébeuf*, II, 223. That the cabin's roof was not rounded, but had a gable is known from a vision Brébeuf experienced on March 9, 1640, at Sainte Marie. Reporting it, he said that he saw ". . . behind the gable of the cabin at Sainte Marie four gigantic dogs with hanging ears, sitting on their haunches, staring at the cabin."

great Princess of heaven and earth make it one of our keenest disappointments that we are not able to show her sufficient gratitude. At least we claim henceforth this consolation, that as often as people shall speak of the principal abode of this mission of the Hurons, calling it by the name of sainte Marie, it will be so many homages which will be rendered to her for what we are to her and hold from her, and of what we wish to be to her forever.[37]

Though wrong in many things, Jerome Lalemant was right in this instance. Now, over three hundred years later, thousands of people visit the site annually and all of them know it as Fort Sainte Marie of the Hurons.

Misfortune shadowed Sainte Marie from its very inception. The Jesuits were barely settled there when a Huron, returning with the fur brigade in the fall of 1639, was deposited on the mission's threshold. He had contracted smallpox from a group of Algonkins encountered en route to Huronia. Unmindful of warnings about the highly contagious nature of the disease, the ailing Indian was carried off by his companions to his home village where he shortly expired. Commenting, Father Lalemant remarked: "Without being a great prophet, one could assure one's self that the evil would soon be spread abroad through all these regions . . ."[38] And spread abroad it surely was.

The next noteworthy victim of the dread disease to be brought to Sainte Marie was the business agent of the Huron mission, Robert Le Coq.[39] On a routine journey to Quebec, during the trading season of 1639, he fell victim to the disease and was cruelly abandoned by a flotilla whose members robbed him. Le Coq was particularly saddened by the loss of a package containing some relics of saints he was bringing back to the mission. Stripped naked and barely alive, he was heartlessly dumped on a

[37] *Relations*, XIX, 135, 137.

[38] Ibid., 89. Smallpox was introduced to New France by the French.

[39] Nothing is known about Robert Le Coq's early life, not even the part of France from which he came. He was, almost certainly, in New France in 1629 and was probably kept there by the British while they held the area. After the French returned, it seems that Le Coq promptly gave his services to the Jesuits, whom he served faithfully until his death at the hands of the Iroquois in July 1650. See Paul Desjardins, "Auxiliaires laïques des missions de la Nouvelle-France au XVIIe siècle. Le donné Robert Le Coq," *Lettres du Bas-Canada* XI (1957), 69-89.

rocky island along the shore of Georgian Bay when only two days paddling separated him from Sainte Marie. There he was discovered by a Huron whom Le Coq had rescued from a similar fate the year before. Though that Huron manifested no previous signs of gratitude, he and a companion brought the Frenchman to Sainte Marie, more dead than alive. His condition was so pitiable that he ". . . caused as much horror as compassion to all those who had courage enough to examine the ulcers with which all his limbs were covered."[40] Though no one expected him to live, within forty days after reaching Sainte Marie Le Coq was again in perfect health.

Meanwhile, the Huron sorcerers and the opponents of the missionaries spread a story throughout the country that the Jesuits had caused Le Coq's painful death. Besides, they maintained ". . . the Jesuits alone were the authors and the cause of the diseases which from year to year kept depopulating the country."[41] Such tales were particularly effective because many Hurons actually saw Le Coq in his horrible condition, from which none of them expected him to recover. Moreover, that Frenchman was very well known to many Hurons whom he had accompanied on their annual trading expeditions. When Le Coq recovered the stiff-necked Hurons announced that the Frenchman had agreed to be afflicted with the disease by the Jesuits, who promised him recovery, only to ". . . throw dust in their [the Hurons] eyes."[42] That explanation perhaps partially exonerated those Indians from the obligation of restoring the goods they had stolen. At least, they unabashedly returned the relics on November 1, 1639, the feast of All Saints.[43]

At the mission of St. Joseph among the Cords, where Jean de Brébeuf labored with Pierre Chastellain, the villagers, a particularly vicious and intensely superstitious lot, grew wildly incensed at the two missionaries when the smallpox epidemic invaded their cabins. Young braves hurled rocks at the Jesuit cabin, tore down the crosses mounted over it, and constantly threatened to kill the

---

[40] *Relations*, XIX, 111.
[41] Ibid., 97.
[42] Ibid., 115.
[43] Ibid., 113.

two priests. Some of the more respected elders, far from restraining the young hotheads, encouraged them to more violent deeds, openly condemning the missionaries ". . . as malefactors and the worst sorcerers in their lands," decreeing that the cabin housing the Jesuits ". . . must be demolished . . . adding that even though we should be massacred, we would receive our just deserts."[44]

In constant danger of martyrdom, Jean de Brébeuf, and his equally heroic companion, moved about the village manifesting no trepidation, as though they were two stoic captives about to be tortured. They bravely visited the Huron cabins, seeking to minister to the sick and baptize the dying. Brébeuf was the object of the villagers particular venom because there, and soon throughout Huronia, he was the one ". . . who in the minds of the poor Indians passes for the greatest sorcerer of the French and the cause of all the miseries which ruin the country . . ."[45] At last Father Brébeuf was ". . . unworthily treated and outrageously beaten in the village of St. Joseph."[46] It was not the physical suffering which distressed Brébeuf so much as the effect the attack had on the few adult converts he had won. He wrote to Lalemant:

The public belief that we were the cause of their misery then possessing their minds, and the fear of being included in the general massacre with which we were continually threatened, all these things have brought it about that many who had professed the faith in the preceding years, have not only returned to the practice of their former superstitions, but have also publicly declared that they renounced what they had embraced.[47]

The most distressing apostasy at St. Joseph's was that of Aochiati, the highly respected captain whom Father Brébeuf had characterized as having ". . . one of the best minds in the country, whose temperament and good qualities had always caused us to desire his conversion . . ."[48] Though Aochiati had enthusiastically accepted baptism hardly a year before, when the epidemic swept over his village bringing death to members of his own family, the new convert angrily ". . . made every sort of public

[44] Ibid., 183.
[45] Ibid., 195.
[46] Ibid.
[47] Ibid., 197, 199.
[48] Ibid., 199.

and private protestation of his renouncing Christianity."[49] The sadness which that important defection brought to Jean de Bré-beuf was, in some measure, lessened by the fidelity of a few, such as the aged Anne, a woman of seventy, who bore all sorts of abuse because of her steadfast adherence to the teachings of the missionaries.[50] And, as if to replace Aochiati, his son-in-law, who previously expressed only a passing interest in Christianity, quite suddenly insisted on receiving baptism. When long testing proved the young man's serious intent he was solemnly baptized and named Joseph.[51]

Let it not be thought that the opposition of the Hurons to Jean de Brébeuf was, at least in their minds, wholly without foundation. The great Echon was, after all, in every way, the most striking of the Jesuits. He was the first Blackrobe to dwell among them and had been with them the longest. He spoke their language perfectly and understood them better than any of the other missionaries. It was incontrovertibly true that ever since the Jesuits had entered the country, in 1635, the Hurons had suffered one disaster after another. The frightening decimation of the population was a terrible calamity. The loss of so many young children eliminated the basic source of support in their declining years for the elders of one family after another. Besides, if the ranks of the young braves were not constantly filled with adolescent males, who would be left to protect the nation from hostile invasions? Right or wrong, for generations this primitive folk sincerely believed that grave illness or natural disaster was the result of some mysterious force which, once aroused, could only be removed by placating it. Since the Hurons saw some sort of relationship between the presence of the missionaries and the long years of disastrous epidemics sweeping the land, these powerful French sorcerers, dressed so strangely in long black gowns, must be inflicting the Hurons. Obviously, so the Indians reasoned, if they only would, the missionaries could call a halt to the calamities afflicting them. If they did not, it was simply because they would not. Therefore, one way or another, the Blackrobes must go. Killing them out of hand would probably put an end to trade

[49] Ibid.
[50] Ibid., 201.
[51] Ibid., 205.

with the French. That solution ought to be avoided since the foreign goods supplied by the French had become a national necessity. But harassing the Jesuits, threatening them, driving them
out of one village after another might so discourage the missionaries that they would go away of their own accord. But Jean de
Brébeuf and his fellows were made of sterner stuff. As Jerome
Lalemant remarked in the introduction to his *Relation* of 1640,

. . . the more that they resist the plans that we have for their salvation, and
appear to plot our destruction, the more they have heightened the sound
and resonance of the tone of the Gospel; and will serve, at least some day,
to justify the merciful providence of God with respect to them.[52]

In midwinter when the bitter north wind off Georgian Bay
froze the streams and brought heavy snow to blanket the land the
smallpox epidemic abated. Now the Hurons at St. Joseph, huddled around the small fires in their cabins, lost interest in heckling the two Jesuits dwelling in their village. Jean de Brébeuf
seized that period of relative peace to retire to Sainte Marie for
his annual retreat which began on the eve of February 11, 1640.[53]
During those eight days of quiet retirement Brébeuf, the mystic,
was blessed with a series of striking spiritual experiences. On the
evening before his exercises began he recorded, as directed by
his superior:

On the day before I began my retreat, during the time of examination of
conscience, and confession and the saying of my penance, there appeared
two suns, shining with the utmost brilliance, in the midst of which was a
cross. The arms of the cross seemed to be of the same height and width, but
I did not see of what material the cross was made. On each of the ends
there was visible a lily or the face of a cherubim. On that part which
was uppermost, there appeared a likeness of Our Lord Jesus Christ, if
I am not mistaken. I was in doubt afterwards if it were not a likeness of
the Blessed Virgin. Then it was that I felt called interiorly to the cross
and mortification.[54]

Early the following morning, February 12, while occupied
with his first meditation, Brébeuf recalled:

On the following day . . . which was the first day of the exercises [that is,
of his annual retreat], when I was trying to employ myself only in loving

[52] Ibid., 79.
[53] Latourelle, *Etude sur . . . Brébeuf*, II, 204.
[54] Ibid., 219-20.

notions of God, and while I was rejecting from my mind all created things, and when I was disturbed by various distractions and bothered with annoyances, it seemed to me I heard inwardly: "Turn towards Jesus Christ crucified, and let him be both the basis and source of your contemplation." Thereupon I felt myself drawn to Christ.[55]

On that same day Father Brébeuf recounted:

Contemplating the enormity of my sins and their countless number, I saw Our Lord Who, in infinite mercy, was holding out His loving arms to embrace me. He pardoned me the past and forgot my sins. He restored in my soul both His gifts and His graces. He called me to his love and said to me what formerly he said to Saint Paul: "This man is to me a vessel of election to carry my name before the gentiles; I shall show him what great things he must suffer for my name's sake." Hearing these words, I thanked Him for them, and offered myself for all things, and said to Him: "What dost Thou wish me to do? Do strongly unto me according to Thy heart; nothing in the future will separate me from Thy love, not nakedness, not the sword, not death, etc."[56]

Two days later Jean de Brébeuf recorded a profound mystical experience which he did not fully comprehend.

On the 14th, during the time of meditation it seemed to me I saw Christ, Our Lord, hanging on the cross and coming toward me, as if He would remove the burden from Himself and would place it upon my shoulders. I willingly placed it on my own shoulders, but I do not know what happened. I know only that I perceived a body, separated from the cross, not as it appeared before, but as covered with leprosy, in no wise attractive. I considered it to be the body of Christ, Our Lord, because there were wounds in the hands. I reflected that the crucified Christ should not be contemplated as He is usually depicted, but as a leper, lacking any attractiveness.[57]

Toward evening of the same day, the retreatant was consoled. He recounted:

. . . when I was preparing to meditate on Christ's perfections, and on the many different relations that were between Him and me, and between miserable me and Him, I thought how all these designations ought to be referred to His extraordinary love for us, as to a central point. All at once, I seemed to see a huge rose, or some rounded flower, extraordinary at one time for its size, at another for its variety, all the varieties of which were proceeding from the center.[58]

[55] Ibid., 220-21.
[56] Ibid.
[57] Ibid., 205.
[58] Ibid.

On February 18 the day before he finished his retreat, Father Brébeuf was again enraptured. He wrote,

. . . I seemed to see the Blessed Virgin as if in a blue cloud, carrying the Child Jesus, while through different parts of the cloud there burst forth golden rays of remarkable beauty. I was expecting that the Blessed Virgin might present me to Christ, but she did not do so.[59]

As with all mystics, Brébeuf's spiritual experiences were, now and then, the work of the evil spirit. On February 23, 1640, probably before leaving Sainte Marie, while examining his conscience in the evening, there appeared to him the face of a man, looking like a Spaniard wearing a ruff around his neck and with a Spanish hat on his head. "It occurred to me at once," he reported, "that the devil was hiding behind the figure, trying to distract me from my prayers. I at once turned my mind to other things."[60]

What, one wonders, was the purpose and meaning of these profound mystical experiences? René Latourelle, the most penetrating student of the writings of Jean de Brébeuf, makes a sincere effort to answer. By means of these personal revelations, Brébeuf was drawn to concentrate his vibrant spiritual life on Jesus Christ. Further, by a most extraordinary influx of divine grace, Brébeuf was impelled to an overpowering desire to imitate, as literally as possible, the crucified Christ, longing with St. Paul, ". . . not . . . to know anything among you but Jesus Christ and him crucified."[61] These experiences were, in Latourelle's valuable opinion, a further advancement in the school of mysticism. St. Teresa of Avila, most respected pedagogue in that school, teaches that the less advanced soul does well to center attention on God, the pure divinity; but, as the soul progresses, he should be drawn to reflect on the humanity of Christ, our Lord, and how to imitate him ever more perfectly. Jean de Brébeuf, then, was far advanced on the steep road to personal sanctity.[62]

Physically refreshed and spiritually rejuvenated, Father Brébeuf returned gladly to his difficult post at Teanaustayé. Changes in personnel deprived him of the comforting Pierre Chastellain, but gave him a new, young, enthusiastic assistant, Father Pierre

---

[59] Ibid., 222.
[60] Ibid.
[61] 1 Corinthians 2:2.
[62] Latourelle, *Etude sur . . . Brébeuf*, II, 220-22.

Joseph Marie Chaumonot, a lovable, impetuous character, who had reached Huronia in the fall of 1639.[63] The hostility of the people had not lessened one whit. Having been strengthened for adversities during his retreat, Jean de Brébeuf now received a whole series of divine visitations. On the evening of February 26 while quietly saying his rosary Brébeuf saw ". . . the tabernacle in the cabin at Sainte Marie on which has been painted seven angels, whereat I was impelled to pray. Thereafter, I seemed to be in the chapel of the cabin, observing the relics kept there. I was drawn to invoke [the intercession of] all those saints."[64] Afterwards he saw in a vision the mission of Sainte Marie set upon by four great, slavering, vicious dogs.

[63] Pierre Joseph Marie Chaumonot was born March 9, 1611, at Châtillon-sur-Seine, the son of a poor vintager and his wife, the daughter of a poor schoolteacher. An uncle, a priest, offered to educate him for the priesthood. Soon the boy robbed his strict uncle and ran away. When he spent all the money he became a vagabond, wandering through Italy until he came to Loreto where he was so impressed with the Holy House that his wandering life was changed. He decided to be a hermit, but he was turned from that romantic notion by a Jesuit at Turni. He went to Rome and entered the Jesuit novitiate on May 18, 1632. While doing his ecclesiastical studies at Rome, he met Father Poncet de La Rivière who gave him a copy of Brébeuf's *Relation* of 1636. With characteristic impetuosity, Chaumonot promptly volunteered for the missions in New France. He sailed from Dieppe on May 4, 1639, and reached Tadoussac on July 31. On August 3 he was on his way to Huronia where he labored until the destruction of that mission. When the Hurons who survived the Iroquois massacre of 1649-1650 were brought down to Quebec, Chaumonot remained with them at Quebec, on Ile d'Orléans and later at Lorette where he established a village and a mission for them. The Hurons were his chosen apostolate, though not all his life was devoted to them. At Lorette he built a replica of the Holy House at Loreto in Italy and this became a place of pilgrimage for both the French and the Indians. He gave up active work at the age of eighty-one and retired to the Jesuit college at Quebec where he died on February 21, 1693, at the ripe old age of eighty-two. Fortunately, in 1688, Father Claude Dablon, major superior of the Jesuits in New France, asked Father Chaumonot to write the story of his life. Two hundred three years later, Father Félix Martin published that autobiography at Paris, in 1885. Perhaps the best indication of how much the Hurons respected Chaumonot is to recall that after Brébeuf's death they gave him that martyr's Huron name, Echon. At Lorette today the only indications of this really great man are a small marker, briefly relating his history and a none too impressive street named after him. One searches in vain in the very impressive parish church to find any indication that Pierre Joseph Marie Chaumonot was the founder of the parish and the city of Ancienne Lorette.

[64] Ibid., 223.

Some apparitions consoled and encouraged Father Brébeuf. On March 21, 1640, while saying his evening prayers, the missionary saw a winged being rising above the altar, beating its wings, striving unaccountably to ascend higher. "I thought," Brébeuf reported, "the vision signified that I, or someone else, strove to rise to heavenly contemplation, but was restrained by earthly things."[65] On March 30, while making his thanksgiving after celebrating Mass, Brébeuf saw a hand, whose he knew not, ". . . anointing my heart and my whole interior with an oil . . . This filled me with divine peace and tranquillity."[66]

Just when profound peace flooded Jean de Brébeuf's soul, he was most beset by opposition from the Hurons. During March 1640 the whole nation held a general council at the village of St. Louis, situated about a league southeast of Sainte Marie.[67] The purpose of the meeting was to arrive at a national decision about the missionaries. There it was resolved to kill them. "And the more promptly . . . the better it will be."[68] Only one Huron clan, probably the Bears, opposed the decision. Even they refrained only because they did not wish to end economic relations with the French, which, they felt, would surely result from slaughtering the Jesuits. Only one old captain raised his voice in defense of the missionaries. "As for me," he said,

I am of the opinion that we begin with ourselves; we are assured that there are a great many sorcerers among us, those would continue to cause us to die, even though we should have massacred all the black robes. Let us make a strict investigation of those wretches who bewitch us; then, when they shall have been put to death, if at that time the course of the disease does not cease, we will have reason to kill the French, and to prove whether their massacre will stop the trouble.[69]

Shortly after the close of the important national council Father Brébeuf became violently ill. Father Pierre Pijart went on a visit to the village of St. Jean,[70] where he fell into a discussion

[65] Ibid., 224.

[66] Ibid., 225.

[67] Jones, 263, locates the village of St. Louis as about three miles southeast of Sainte Marie at lot 11, concession VI, Tay township, Simcoe county, Ontario.

[68] *Relations*, XIX, 177.

[69] Ibid., 179.

[70] Jones, 263, places St. Jean at lot 6, concession X, Tay township, Simcoe county, Ontario.

with an aged sorcerer who became very angry and threatened him, warning that the missionaries must surely die. As proof, he informed Pijart that Echon was stricken with disease. Since Pijart, only three hours before, had left Father Brébeuf at St. Joseph in splendid health, he laughed at the old man, who responded, "You will see whether I am a liar; I have told you enough."[71] Returning to St. Joseph's mission the same day, Pijart found Father Brébeuf suffering from ". . . a heavy fever, a pain in the stomach, and headache, and in all the symptoms of a severe illness . . ."[72] At the moment the old sorcerer made his surprising revelation, he was a good six miles from St. Joseph and no Indian had come recently to St. Jean. Whatever the explanation, Jerome Lalemant, the author of the *Relation* of 1640, soberly recorded the fact, adding ". . . if the devil and his ministers are devising our death, the Father's prompt cure, he was not sick more than 24 hours, plainly showed us that there are spirits a thousand times more powerful, who watch for our defense and preservation."[73]

When the representatives to the national council returned to Teanaustayé, they, in effect, declared that it was open season on the missionaries. The prime mover of the attack was Ondihorrea, ". . . one of the principal and oldest captains . . ."[74] In 1638 when Ondihorrea fell victim to the epidemic, he tried the country's usual remedies, sorcerer's incantation and the like to no avail. He spurned all offers of aid tendered by Father Brébeuf. But, when he thought he was dying, the captain humbly accepted the missionary's ministrations for his body as well as his soul. He ". . . was instructed and baptized; and behold him immediately on his feet, to the astonishment of all those who had, a little while before, despaired of his life . . ."[75] But Ondihorrea was only a fair-weather Christian. He attended Mass only once but never again. A full-blown apostate by 1640, the captain urged his people, especially the young braves, to massacre the missionaries. Finally on April 11, 1640, Father Brébeuf reported, ". . . a quarrel broke out

[71] *Relations*, XIX, 179.
[72] Ibid.
[73] Ibid., 181.
[74] Ibid., XVII, 137.
[75] Ibid.

. . . in which Pierre Boucher[76] was wounded on the arm and Father Chaumonot and I were beaten."[77]

Recording his reaction to that violent, but unsuccessful, attack, Jean de Brébeuf wrote: "Suffering from injuries, we were all much afraid because we had been ordered by Ondihorrea and other leaders to leave the village. Later, when I was thanking God for all these things and, though mentally disturbed and in distress, I was striving to conform my will to the will of God, I seemed to perceive the Blessed Virgin portrayed as in sorrow with three swords piercing her heart. I felt interiorly as though the Blessed Mother of God were telling me that, though sorely afflicted, she, the Mother of God, was, nevertheless, always conformed to the divine will and ought to be an example to me in every adversity."[78] The interpretation which Father Brébeuf made of his vision was, no doubt, most important to him. It was an inspiration drawing him to accept and embrace the will of God. To us, perhaps, the far more important truth for understanding this gentle giant was his admission that he trembled and was sore afraid when confronted with a violent attack by the Hurons.

However willing Jean de Brébeuf and Pierre Chaumonot were to suffer reproaches for Christ's sake, Jerome Lalemant, their superior, judged it far from prudent to allow them to continue residing at Teanaustayé. In his *Relation* of 1640 Lalemant wrote: ". . . at the beginning to the spring [1640], the insolence of the Indians [at St. Joseph's] obliged us to do so [that is, permanently recall the Jesuits from St. Joseph's to Sainte Marie] much sooner than on other accounts we had decided to do so."[79] Regretfully, one may be certain, Jean de Brébeuf shook the dust of Teanau-

[76] Pierre Boucher was born at Mortagne in France and baptized there on August 1, 1622. He was brought to New France in 1634. In 1637 he was taken to Huronia under the care of the Jesuits, to learn the Huron tongue and accustom himself to the ways of Indians. In 1641 he returned to Quebec and became a soldier and interpreter. By 1645 he was settled at Three Rivers where he became that post captain and, eventually, principal citizen. Eventually he became a man of stature and importance not only in Canada but in France as well. He died in 1717. He was the founder of Boucherville where some of his descendants still live. He was the author of the *Histoire véritable,* a most important source of information regarding seventeenth-century New France.

[77] Latourelle, *Etude sur . . . Brébeuf,* II, 225-26.

[78] Ibid.

[79] *Relations,* XIX, 135.

stayé from his shoes and took up residence at Sainte Marie. The abandonment of St. Joseph's must have been a source of real sorrow to Father Brébeuf for he clearly understood that he, himself, was the object of the hatred of the Hurons there. That giant Norman, with the soul of a mystic, needs must surrender the struggle to the powers of darkness. Yet his last word regarding the mission of St. Joseph was: "During the time I was at Teanaustayé, I was frequently lifted up to God in raptures of love."[80]

Shortly before his recall to Sainte Marie, Jean de Brébeuf was vouchsafed a vision, which, as it were, foretold his immediate future. "On May 17 [1640]," he recorded,

while praying during the day, I felt elevated in spirit to contemplate a cross. It was similar to the one at Sainte Marie in which relics are enclosed or earth from the Holy Land or like some crosses made in the form of stars. The vision endured for a long time. While it lasted, I could only wonder whether God wished to send me some new cross.[81]

Not one but a series of crosses awaited him, ending with his virtual exile from his Hurons.

[80] Latourelle, *Etude sur . . . Brébeuf*, II, 227.
[81] Ibid.

Chapter VIII

Apostolic Assault
on the Neutral Nation

The first of the new crosses burdening Father Jean de Brébeuf
was the sad loss of his devoted friend, Joseph Chihwatenhwa, the
rock and foundation of the Christian community at Ossossané.
Since his baptism by Father Brébeuf on August 16, 1637, Joseph
had become a tireless lay apostle, preaching to his fellow townsmen by word and example. In the autumn of 1639 when the Jesuits closed their cabin at Ossossané, Joseph was placed in charge
of the rather pretentious chapel erected there. They felt that he
would care for it, guarding it with his life if necessary. The
Hurons at Ossossané, who opposed the missionaries, resented Joseph partly because of his Christian zeal but, perhaps also, out of
jealousy, concluding that his friendship with the Jesuits would
redound to his economic advantage. Seeking to discredit him, his
enemies spread a rumor that Joseph was in league with the Jesuits
in their supposed effort to destroy the whole Huron nation. The
French, they maintained, had taught Joseph all their secrets and

had made him a past master in casting their powerful spells.[1] If the pagan Hurons at Ossossané actually resorted to physical violence, Joseph Chihwatenhwa would surely be their first victim.

To strengthen his faith and prepare him for possible grave persecution, the Jesuits deemed it prudent to ask Joseph to come to Sainte Marie for a while to ". . . inform him with some more particular instruction, so as to strengthen his courage, as one who was to serve as an example to all the others."[2] At Sainte Marie the Jesuits ". . . gave him some acquaintance with the Spiritual Exercises [of St. Ignatius]." To their astonishment Joseph was delighted, saying that he had often seen missionaries dwelling in his cabin praying without moving their lips. Much as he desired to imitate them, he refrained from inquiring about that manner of prayer ". . . believing that if you had judged me capable, you would have taught me and consequently I must wait to be found worthy thereof."[3] Edified and astonished, Father Lalemant deputed François Le Mercier to direct this chosen soul in a retreat of eight days. The incident, unique in the whole history of the Jesuit missionary effort in New France, cannot possibly be explained, except by conceding divine inspiration. How could this unlettered Huron, a Christian of barely two years standing, possibly grasp, as he certainly did, the abstruse truths proposed to him during the eight days he was closeted with François Le Mercier? Tangentially, that Joseph was able to be so instructed speaks volumes for Jean de Brébeuf's grasp of the Huron tongue, which he taught to Father Le Mercier so well that the latter could adequately explain to his retreatant the truths proposed for his consideration.

On completing the eight days, Chihwatenhwa went forth from Sainte Marie with a spirit ". . . something like that of the Apostles, when they went forth from the place where they had received the Holy Spirit."[4] Visiting his brother who lived at a village not far from Sainte Marie, Joseph made an earnest, but fruitless, effort to convert him. As if foreseeing his own cruel death, Joseph warned his brother that he would probably soon

[1] *Relations*, XIX, 153.
[2] Ibid., 137.
[3] Ibid., 139.
[4] Ibid., 151.

hear that ". . . the resolution to kill me is adopted, or even that they have already split my head."[5] It was a whole year later when the blow fell. Toward noon, on August 2, 1640, Joseph, accompanied by three young nieces, went off to his field where the children at their uncle's direction gathered some ripe squashes. Then Joseph dismissed them, admonishing them to go directly home because ". . . they were not in a secure place."[6] Joseph, however, tarried to cut some lengths of cedar needed to finish a canoe he was making to carry him down to Quebec. When he failed to return members of his family went searching and found his mutilated body. The village elders, having examined the scene of the crime, decided that two Iroquois issuing from a nearby woods ran him through with a long javelin, felled him with two blows of a hatchet, scalped him, and promptly fled.[7] That judgment which many, the Jesuits among them, considered false, averted open attack on the small band of Christians at Ossossané, at least for the moment. But not a few believed that Joseph Chihwatenhwa was Huronia's protomartyr, gaining his crown at the hands of the Hurons themselves.

It was Jean de Brébeuf's sad privilege to celebrate the solemn obsequies for his treasured spiritual child. Trudging across the country from Sainte Marie, Brébeuf said the funeral Mass in the chapel at Ossossané and buried his friend's body in consecrated ground. That evening Brébeuf's sorrow at the loss of Joseph must have been translated into profound joy because of a consoling spiritual visitation granted him. He wrote:

On the fourth of August, having returned from the obsequies of our departed Christian, while examining my conscience in the evening, I had several visions. I recall nothing of the first one. In the second, it was as though I saw a pavilion or a dome descend from heaven and rest on the grave of our Christian. Then it seemed to me that someone picked up the two ends of the pavilion, drawing it upwards, as if to take it to heaven. However, I did not discern how it was lifted nor the persons doing so. The vision continued a very long time. I felt, at the time, that God wished me to understand the state of the soul of that good Christian.[8]

[5] Ibid., 153.
[6] Ibid., XX, 81.
[7] Ibid., 79.
[8] Latourelle, *Etude sur . . . Brébeuf*, II, 228.

Within the next two or three weeks Father Brébeuf was granted three other heavenly visitations. In his private notes the mystic reported:

On August 12th or 13th, I seemed to perceive a high mountain peopled with women saints. Perhaps there were some men saints, also, but they seemed to me to be mostly women. They were arranged on the mountain as though in an amphitheatre, from the base to the summit in diminishing rows until they were reduced to a single one. She was our Lady seated at the crest of the mountain. The thought of our Joseph Chihwatenhwa came to mind, but I did not recognize him as among those on the mountain. I concluded that the vision demonstrated the excellence of the Blessed Virgin over all the saints.[9]

Two weeks later, on August 27, 1640, while attending the community's evening prayers, Brébeuf beheld

. . . a man suspended in the air. At first I did not recognize the man, but later I recognized him . . . he was covered with repulsive sores much like those inflicted by certain contagious diseases . . . even the air around him was infected. No doubt anyone near him would contract the disease. I reflected that the vision signified the unhappy state of that poor soul as well as the evil others contracted from associating with him.[10]

Who was that wretched man so in need of spiritual reformation? Father Brébeuf, of course, never revealed the man's name. We can but conjecture that if the person were available, Jean de Brébeuf would most certainly have striven mightily to rescue him from the clutches of sin.

On the last day of August Father Brébeuf was vouchsafed a vision which must have enhanced his unbounded love and devotion for the Blessed Virgin Mary. He saw, he said, a lady's cloak

. . . of ravishing beauty . . . decorated with gold embroidery and pearls. The cloak was draped over a lady who, I doubt not, was our Lady . . . Later, there appeared at her side a shape like a huge globe which was opening, revealing many objects of great beauty . . . the like of which I never saw nor even read about. Then I experienced profound admiration and love of God, but also some fear of being deceived.[11]

What the vision portended, perhaps only the future would reveal.

Jean de Brébeuf's exalted mystical experiences did not divorce him from the practical reality of missionary activity among the

[9] Ibid., 229.
[10] Ibid., 230.
[11] Ibid.

Hurons. During the summer of 1640 when the Hurons, as was their custom, were scattered broadcast, fishing, hunting, tilling the fields, or off on their lengthy trading expeditions, the Jesuits gathered at Sainte Marie to assess their situation. Since the summer of 1634, when Father Brébeuf returned to Huronia after his enforced exile in 1629, the number of missionaries had increased from three to thirteen and the lay helpers from two to fourteen. The initial, grueling spadework was fairly well accomplished. Thanks to Jean de Brébeuf's linguistic ability, many of the Jesuits conversed with satisfactory fluency in the Huron tongue. The indigenous culture was sufficiently understood to permit the missionaries to highlight the basic problems inhibiting the wholesale conversions of the people. Initial contacts had been made with every village and family in such manner that a Blackrobe, be he feared, hated, or respected, was no longer a stranger. Now it was time to consider expanding the effort to more distant nations. This was all the more essential since, without doubt, the Hurons were a declining people. Ravages of illness and continued hostile incursions of the Iroquois had reduced the Huron population perhaps even as much as one half since Samuel de Champlain first visited them in their homeland. If the Hurons were to be, as the Jesuits fondly hoped, the stepping-stone to the innumerable tribes dwelling south and west of them, this seemed to be the moment for initiating first contacts with them.

The nation in nearest proximity to the Hurons was a closely related folk whom the Hurons gave the unpronounceable name of Khionontaterons. Because they supplied great quantities of tobacco to the Hurons, the French called them the Petuns or the Tobacco Nation.[12] The Petuns lived just west of the Hurons proper in the Bruce Peninsula and east of the Blue Mountains. The Petuns, composed of two clans, the Wolf and the Deer, numbered some ten villages. Their total population might have been as high as twelve thousand. A sedentary people like the Hurons, they raised corn, hemp, beans, sunflowers, and large quantities of tobacco. Once, previous to the arrival of Europeans, the Petuns and the Hurons had been bitter enemies, waging cruel war against one another. A common enemy, the Iroquois, caused the

---

[12] The word *petun* was borrowed from the Portuguese word *petum.*

Petuns and the Hurons to effect an alliance which lasted down to the final destruction of the Huron nation.[13] By language and customs they were so similar to the Hurons that the Jesuits took it for granted that their conversion to Christianity would follow once the Hurons rejected paganism. However, the Hurons were loathe to allow the French, lay or missionary, to contact the Petuns lest the absolute monopoly of trade they exercised be disturbed. For the Jesuits, the Petuns were not a major concern. They looked farther to the south, to the Neutrals.

The Hurons called the Neutrals the Attiouandaronks which meant "The People who speak a slightly different tongue."[14] The boundaries of their country were, roughly, the Niagara River on the east, Lake Erie on the south, Lake St. Clair on the west and ". . . a hazy Huron-Neutral frontier on the north, about seventy-five miles from Huronia proper."[15] The name Neutral, which the French gave them, was something of a misnomer. Though the Neutrals sought to remain on good terms with both the Hurons and the Iroquois, actually they traded with the Hurons and, in times of trouble, such as famine, they threw themselves on the mercy of the Hurons.[16] Physically the Neutrals were considered to be ". . . taller, stronger and better proportioned . . ." than the Hurons.[17] Their national and local governmental institutions were almost an exact counterpart of their Huron neighbors. Their religious beliefs and practices differed hardly at all, except that they were addicted to a sort of lycanthropy. Many feigned insanity, induced, they maintained, by their individual demons. Under that influence the afflicted were permitted ". . . all possible extravagances and any liberties they choose . . . they take embers from the fire, and scatter them around; they break and shatter what they encounter, as if they were raving, though in reality, . . . they are as self-collected as those who do not play this character."[18]

[13] Tooker, *Ethnography of the Huron Indians*, 12.

[14] Jenness, *Indians of Canada*, 300.

[15] Hunt, *Wars of the Iroquois*, 50. See *Relations*, XXI, 207. In the *Relation* of 1640-1641, Lalemant said that the Neutral village nearest Sainte Marie was a distance of five days walking directly south from the mission of St. Joseph. This would locate that village in Halton county, Ontario, possibly at Lake Medad. For a scholarly discussion of the location, see *Relations*, XXI, 316-17.

[16] *Relations*, XX, 49.

[17] Ibid., XXI, 199.

[18] Ibid., 201.

The economic resources of the country of the Neutrals far surpassed their Huron neighbors. Fish and wild game still abounded and the supply of beavers had not, as yet, been exhausted. Hence, the Neutrals lacked neither meat or fish for food nor peltries for clothing. Agriculturally, the Neutrals produced quantities of tobacco, corn, and hemp.[19] They had not become effective traders, however, because they had no large quantities of birch trees from which to fashion canoes.[20] Long before Europeans made contact with either the Neutrals or the Hurons, the former had become economically dependent on the latter. This situation brought about a valuable trade monopoly for the Hurons who were willing to go to almost any lengths to protect it. No matter what the objective, trade or missionary activity, the Hurons were determined to prevent the French from invading the country of the Neutrals.

Contrary to the wishes of the Hurons, some French traders ". . . made journeys into this country of the Neutral Nation for the sake of reaping profits and advantage from furs . . ."[21] As noted earlier, in 1626 Father Joseph de la Roche Daillon, a Recollet, visited the Neutrals, staying with them through the winter of 1626-1627. Unable to converse in either Huron or the language of the Neutrals, he could communicate only by signs. He was so badly treated by both the Neutrals and the Hurons, ". . . who feared the removal of their trade, . . ."[22] that, at Father Brébeuf's urging, some French traders went to the Neutral country and escorted him back. From that really heroic missionary effort, brief and unsuccessful as it was, the French learned of the Neutral contacts with numerous as yet unknown nations to the west and south of their country.[23]

[19] Harold E. Driver, *Indians of North America*, 236.

[20] Hunt, *Wars of the Iroquois*, 51.

[21] *Relations*, XXI, 203.

[22] Ibid., 205.

[23] Ibid., 201. Regarding the knowledge the Neutrals had of western tribes, Lalemant remarked: "Some old men related to our Fathers that they had acquaintance with a certain Western Nation, against which they were going to make war, and which was not far removed from the sea . . . " It is to be hoped that he did not believe the fish story accompanying that geographic information. The old men told Lalemant that this western tribe successfully fished for *vignots* (our periwinkle, the edible snail, not the flower) which were so big that it was all they could do to stretch their arms around one of them.

For the Jesuits now seeking an opportunity for westward and southward expansion, the Neutral nation appeared to be a golden door. And, in Jerome Lalemant's opinion, the moment had come to pass through that door. In his *Relation* of 1640-1641 he wrote:

> . . . our orders were not to . . . devote ourselves to teaching more distant nations before laboring among those nearer. As this had been done in preceding years, we found ourselves, at the beginning of autumn [1640], ready and able to allot two workers to this mission [of the Neutral nation] without doing any harm to the former ones.[24]

Probably there was little question in Lalemant's mind as to whom he should assign this difficult and possibly dangerous task. Elaborating on his choice of Jean de Brébeuf, Lalemant explained: ". . . as God has given him for this purpose a special blessing, namely in the language, it seems that this ought to be to us a presumption of what his divine Majesty demanded on this occasion . . ."[25] Important as Brébeuf's phenomenal ability with native languages certainly must have been, probably far more important was his sympathetic understanding of the aboriginal mind, his perception of diplomatic nuances in their council meetings, and his sincere love of the people. The Indians, like little children everywhere, were quick to sense veiled disdain or intolerance of themselves and their customs. Of all the Jesuits in Huronia, Jean de Brébeuf was, undoubtedly, the only one who could possibly succeed. For a companion Lalemant gave Brébeuf that lovable, sometimes imprudent, but always devoted young Pierre Joseph Marie Chaumonot. One can be grateful for that choice. If Father Chaumonot had not accompanied Brébeuf, we would probably know very little about a bitterly trying period of his life.

On All Souls' day, November 2, 1640, with the land already blanketed deep in snow and the lakes and streams frozen solid, Jean de Brébeuf, with his vigorous young Jesuit companion and two of the laymen attached to Sainte Marie, trudged southward bound for the country of the Neutrals. The laymen accompanied the two missionaries ". . . as much to assist them in their journey as to make a show of trading with their help, and to pass as merchants in the country, in case that without this inducement the

[24] Ibid., 187.
[25] Ibid.

doors of the cabins should be shut against them . . ."[26] The minute apostolic band stopped first at Father Brébeuf's mission of St. Joseph at Teanaustayé where he expected to obtain provisions and guides, as had been previously agreed upon. But, when those who had given their word

. . . failed them, they could do nothing else than appeal to heaven. After offering a prayer, Father Brébeuf met a young man who had no thought of making this journey. I do not know [wrote Lalemant] by what impulse he addressed him; however, having said to him only these two words, "Quio ackwe," "Come, let us go away together," the young man, without opposition, immediately followed them, and remained their faithful companion.[27]

At St. Joseph's the Jesuits and their companions made up shoulder packs containing paper, ink, their breviaries, trinkets to use as gifts or as "coin" to be paid for purchasing food and lodging, two thousand porcelain beads as a gift to the national council of the Neutral nation, blankets for each, some spare clothing, and ". . . a supply of bread baked under the cinders after the manner of the country, and which they kept for thirty or forty days, that they might have it in case of necessity."[28]

Writing to one of his Jesuit friends, Father Philip Nappi, at Rome, Father Chaumonot described the outward journey.

. . . we were six days on the road, always in woods with no place to rest or find shelter. The paths traversing the woods are difficult, being very little used, cluttered with brush, cut by swamps, brooks, and rivers, without bridges other than a few trees broken across them by age or blown down by the wind. Winter is the best time for travel because the snow renders the paths more even. But it must be packed down . . . otherwise you sink in at every step. There is still another advantage in winter travel. The water courses are frozen so we were able to pull our baggage along on sleds. It is true that there is no shelter from the wind which was very violent and extremely cold. But . . . we proceeded bravely and joyfully, despite cold, fatigue, and countless falls on the ice, whereof my knees have retained a good reminder.[29]

---

[26] Ibid., 205.

[27] Ibid.

[28] Ibid., 223.

[29] Ibid., XVIII, 39. Chaumonot's complete letter to Nappi is not given in *Relations*, XVIII, but it is contained in its entirety in his autobiography, pp. 70-71. The complete title of Chaumonot's autobiography is: *Un missionnaire des Hurons: autobiographie du père Chaumonot de la compagnie de Jésus*, edited by Félix Martin.

After walking for five days and spending four nights in the open, Father Brébeuf and his small party reached ". . . the first village of the Neutral nation named Kandoucho, to which they gave the surname of All Saints . . ."[30] because they arrived on November 7, 1640, during the octave of the feast of All Saints.

Standing in the midst of that village, surrounded by a people to whom the very appearance of the two Jesuits was as exotic as visitors from Mars would be to us, the immediate problem was how to begin the apostolate. With a charming simplicity, Father Chaumonot explains that the two missionaries, in effect, performed what we would call a parlor trick. "We were received," he relates,

pleasantly, especially after we convinced them that by our writing skill we could tell them what had been said or done at a great distance. Here is the experiment we performed for them. Father Brébeuf left the cabin and walked away a good distance. Then one of the men told me a story, practically whispering it. This was his story: "I went hunting and found a deer. I took an arrow from my quiver, bent the bow and killed the deer with the first shot. I threw the carcass over my shoulder, brought it to my cabin and invited my friends to a feast." When I finished writing down his little story they called Father Brébeuf back. He took the piece of paper and repeated to them, word for word, everything that had been said. This feat astonished them. Then they took the piece of paper and turned it over and over, saying to one another: "Where is the figure representing the hunter; where is the picture of the deer; where is the caldron and the cabin for the feast?" We used the occasion to explain to them that just as Echon knew from the writing on the paper what they said to me, so from the writings of our ancestors, we learned the truths of the faith.[31]

Performing sleight-of-hand tricks, as it were, for a group of timorous, unsophisticated Neutrals in a small, unimportant village served to gain passage farther into the country. But if Father Brébeuf hoped to establish a permanent mission among the Neutrals, diplomatic protocol required much more. He must formally appear before an assembly of the captains and ancients of the Neutral nation to enlighten them as to his intentions.[32] In the case of the Neutrals, that step was vitally important because the Jesuits

[30] *Relations*, XXI, 207.
[31] Chaumonot, *Autobiographie*, 70-71.
[32] *Relations*, XXI, 207.

knew full well that Hurons, opposed to the missionaries, had saturated the minds of the Neutrals ". . . with all the ill-natured remarks that had been made concerning us in our quarters in the past years . . ."[33] He set out, therefore, for the village where Tsohahissen, the captain who managed public affairs for the Neutrals, resided. En route, Brébeuf and his companions passed through many small villages and hamlets ". . . on arriving at which the Fathers were much surprised to find that terror had gone before them and had caused the doors of the cabins everywhere to be closed."[34]

A series of fortuitous circumstances prevented Father Brébeuf from concluding formal agreement with the leaders of the Neutral nation, officially permitting him to openly evangelize the people. Reaching Tsohahissen's village, which was ". . . in the midst of the country . . . ," he learned that the important captain chanced to be away at war and would not return until spring. Appealing to those in charge of the nation's affairs in the captain's absence, Father Brébeuf explained his plan ". . . of publishing the Gospel throughout the extent of these territories, and of forming, by this means, a special alliance with them."[35] As a gift, binding the agreement, the missionary proffered a valuable collar of two thousand porcelain beads to the public treasury.

Tempting as the offer must have been, the council of captains, whom Brébeuf addressed, replied that, in the absence of the chief captain of the country, they could not accept the present since, according to custom, they would thereby be obliged to make gifts in return. And this they were not authorized to do. If, however, the missionaries were willing to await the captain's return, ". . . we could, in the meantime go freely into the country, in order to give therein such instructions as we pleased."[36] Interpreting that response as at least a sort of visitor's visa, the two missionaries dropped any pretense of being traders and openly declared their intention of seeking to Christianize the Neutrals. To clarify their position, as well as for the protection of their lay companions, the

[33] Ibid.
[34] Ibid.
[35] Ibid., 209. The Neutral village at which the meeting occurred was not named by Brébeuf. It is thought to have been on the right bank of the Grand River near Brantford, Ontario. See ibid., 317.
[36] Ibid., 209.

two Jesuits returned with their associates to Kandoucho, their point of entry in the country of the Neutrals. Directing the laymen to return to Sainte Marie, Brébeuf and Chaumonot launched their apostolate, trusting their lives to a people whom they clearly realized were anything but friendly.[37] Though the two Jesuits were, thenceforth, perfectly aware of the ever present danger of death, they calmly proceeded traveling through the country, visiting one small village after another, heralding the gospel to any who would listen. But, dogging their footsteps, were inimical Huron emissaries bent on thwarting the missionary efforts.

Hostile Hurons visiting the Neutral nation strove by every means to instill unreasoning fear of the two Jesuits. Particularly vicious were the calumnies spread by Awenhokwi, a nephew of one of the chief captains of the Hurons. Passing from one Neutral village to another, like a harbinger of doom, he solemnly warned the captains and elders of the little hamlets to ". . . beware of these Frenchmen unless they were willing to see the country ruined from their not having anticipated us. And . . . added that, in case they should refuse to carry out the scheme [of murdering the two missionaries], the Hurons had resolved to accomplish it immediately after the return of the Fathers . . ."[38] For the poor, gullible, superstitious Neutrals, so utterly dependent on the Hurons, mere urging might have been inducement enough to slaughter the strangers. But the Huron emissary offered an irresistible bribe, iron hatchets. For the Neutrals these hatchets were almost as important an advance to them as guns were for the Hurons. Father Chaumonot remarked: "This was an extremely valuable present to these people who still had nothing better with which to chop wood or cut things than a sharp stone bound to a handle with a thong."[39]

When that wily Huron ambassador, Awenhokwi, chanced to meet the two valiant missionaries in one of the villages of the Neutrals, he posed as the friend of the priests, almost forcing them to travel farther into the country of the Neutrals with him.

[37] Ibid.

[38] Ibid., 213.

[39] Chaumonot, *Autobiographie*, 70-71. Concerning these iron trade axes, see George I. Quimby, *Indian Culture and European Trade Goods*, 70-71. Hundreds of these have been unearthed. They appear to have been forged of strap iron over a wedge-shaped center piece.

Undeceived, Father Brébeuf prudently declined the invitation. Shortly afterwards, ". . . when they [Brébeuf and Chaumonot] had heard of the speeches and propositions of this fellow, they consulted with some Indians of the country concerning the designs this Awenhokwi could have had in urging them so strongly to make the journey with him, and they surmised nothing but evil therein."[40] Later another and even more vicious Huron visitor came among the Neutrals. This man, named Oëntara,

. . . entertained the country with all the evil speeches and calumnies . . . that we had bred the malady in our own house; that our writings were only sorceries; that we had caused everyone among the Hurons to die, under pretense of presents; that we were arranging to bring all the rest of the world to the grave, adding that they should everywhere close the doors of the cabins against us, unless they wished shortly to see desolation everywhere . . .[41]

With Father Brébeuf scouring the country, striving to attract the people to the feet of the gentle Christ, and his detractors in hot pursuit close behind him, spreading their vicious calumnies, it was not long before the Neutral nation was in a turmoil. Two months after entering the country Father Brébeuf was summoned to appear before the chief captains of the country. Now they ". . . declared that they had power to decide pressing affairs in the absence of Tsohahissen, that they began to think our undertaking was of this nature, and that, therefore, they would deliberate upon it immediately."[42] At the council's meeting both Oëntara and Jean de Brébeuf were given a hearing, each in the other's presence. Before that important gathering Father Brébeuf ". . . pertinently refuted all these evil persons, silencing each one and filling them with confusion . . ."[43] Refuting the detractors was not enough; the venom, once dropped into the hearts of the poor, superstitious Neutrals, was not so easily cast out. Rendering its judgment, the council decreed that, though there was nothing but good in what the missionaries taught, the Neutral nation refused the present of the rich porcelain collar and, thereby, declined to enter the alliance which Father Brébeuf wished to make with them. Pressed for a reason, the council first responded that their

[40] *Relations*, XXI, 213.
[41] Ibid., 213, 215.
[42] Ibid., 215.
[43] Ibid.

national ". . . treasury was poor, and that they had no means of making one in return."[44] To this the gentle Norman Jesuit replied that he would gladly contribute the collar to their treasury, asking nothing in return but that the Neutrals would regard the missionaries as brothers. Forced to it, the chief of the council finally admitted that the Neutrals believed Awenhokwi, remarking, to end the discussion: ". . . do you not know . . . the danger in which you are and in which you are putting the country?"[45]

During the fatal evening, while the council of the Neutral nation was debating the case of the two missionaries, Father Brébeuf calmly performed his nightly spiritual exercises. In the midst of them he was granted a vision which he related to Father Chaumonot. In his autobiography the latter recounted:

One evening, while the assembly was debating whether they should kill us, Father Brébeuf made his [customary] examination of conscience. During it he had a vision. An infuriated being, bearing three darts or javelins, threatened both of us as we were praying. After his threatening gestures he threw one of the javelins, but a hand appeared and adroitly diverted the dart in its flight. A second and third time the same thing happened. When he recounted the vision to me, I agreed with him that someone was plotting against us. Avoiding panic, we heard one another's confession and tranquilly went to sleep. Before the night was over our host returned from the council where two Hurons had offered hatchets for crushing our heads. He told us that on three different occasions we were on the point of being killed by young hotheads who offered to do the deed. But each time the elders restrained them. To us, that explained the significance of Father de Brébeuf's vision.[46]

Saved from a cruel death, apparently by divine intervention, Jean de Brébeuf and his companion were not spared from constant harassment by the Neutral populace almost everywhere. The missionaries promptly became aware that people shrank from even the sight of them. Everything about these strange Frenchmen engendered fear bordering on hysteria. Their dress, their personal belongings, their simplest gesture seemed to offer convincing proof that the missionaries were menacingly powerful sorcerers. The Neutrals soon believed that their strange visitors went about poisoning the country. If they rinsed their dishes in a

[44] Ibid., 217.
[45] Ibid.
[46] Chaumonot, *Autobiographie*, 72-73.

brook, they did so just to contaminate the stream. If they knelt in prayer, they were conjuring their powerful demons. It was accepted as a "well-known fact" that in whatever cabin the two Jesuits took shelter all the children, promptly sickening, died of a bloody discharge and all the women became barren. At some cabins they were gruffly refused shelter; at others they were treated as repulsive slaves. They were refused food unless exorbitant prices were paid. Everywhere people spoke openly of killing and eating Echon and his companion. Yet, while often threatened menacingly, the two Jesuits were never physically harmed, except, when on one rare occasion, a Neutral, feigning insanity, spat on Father Chaumonot, called him vile names, and tried to tear the cassock off his back.[47]

At the very depths of their misery, with nearly every Neutral hand raised against the two itinerant missionaries, Jean de Brébeuf was granted a most consoling vision. "On February 7 [1641]," he noted,

it seemed as though I saw two hands clasped in friendship. Also, I saw, as it were, the center portion of a globe. Again, on several days, as I believe, during evening prayers, I seemed to behold a multitude of crosses, which I fervently embraced. At prayers on the following evening I was striving to conform myself to the Divine Will, saying: "May Thy will be done, O Lord," I heard a voice saying to me: "Take up and read." In the morning when I picked up the small golden book, *The Imitation of Christ*, I chanced upon the chapter on the Royal Road of the Holy Cross. Whereupon my soul experienced a great peace and quiet about things that might chance to happen.[48]

One brief passage in the chapter read by Jean de Brébeuf must indeed have uplifted his spirit. "The higher a person is advanced in spirit, the heavier crosses shall he often meet with; because pain of his banishment increases in proportion to his love."[49] Like unto his Master, Christ our Lord, the Neutrals treated Jean de Brébeuf as though he were "a worm and no man."[50] And realizing this, he rejoiced therein.

---

[47] *Relations*, XXI, 235.

[48] Latourelle, *Etude sur . . . Brébeuf*, II, 232-33.

[49] Thomas A'Kempis, *The Imitation of Christ*, edited by J. M. Lelen, 129-30. There are, of course, innumerable editions of this once popular little book. The one used here was edited by J. M. Lelen at New York in 1941.

[50] The phrase is taken from Psalm 21:7.

After seemingly endless weeks of travel, wading through deep snow and crossing frozen lakes and rivers, and long, bitterly cold nights in the open with no shelter to protect them from the biting wind, the two intrepid missionaries visited eighteen Neutral villages, on each of which they conferred a saint's name. At ten of the small settlements they tarried, instructing anyone willing to listen. As a probing operation they had accomplished all that could be expected. Perhaps if they now returned to Kandoucho, the first Neutral village encountered, they might have some lasting success since there the two missionaries ". . . seemed to be the least unwelcome."[51] There Jean de Brébeuf planned to remain until spring when men would be sent from Sainte Marie to escort them home. On their way to Kandoucho they were snowbound at Teotongniaton, a village to which the two Jesuits had given the name of St. William.[52] "This misfortune," as Lalemant said in his *Relation* of 1640-1641, ". . . was the cause of the greatest good and the greatest comfort they had in their whole journey . . ."[53] Seeking shelter from the storm, the two weary Jesuits were graciously received by a remarkable Indian matron ". . . who endeavored to give them as much satisfaction as all the others in the past had given them occasion for sorrow."[54]

Like unto the valiant woman of the Old Testament, that generous lady ". . . opened her hand to the needy . . ."[55] even despite the fact that "In all the other cabins of the village they did not cease to cry after her that she must drive away the Fathers . . ."[56] Even when her neighbors threatened to kill her after the departure of the two missionaries, she preferred risking that danger ". . . to sending the Fathers away at a time when they might perish in the snow."[57] Noticing that the Jesuits ate no meat, because it was Lent, their gracious hostess ". . . took the trouble of making them a separate dish seasoned with fish, which was much better than

[51] *Relations*, XXI, 235.
[52] The location of the village of St. William may have been near the present city of Woodstock, Ontario.
[53] Ibid.
[54] Ibid., 225.
[55] Proverbs 31:20.
[56] *Relations*, XXI, 227.
[57] Ibid.

she would have made for herself."[58] Following their mother's example, her children often had quarrels with their playmates and
". . . even fought in defense of the Fathers."[59]

Jean de Brébeuf and Pierre Chaumonot were particularly
grateful to that kind lady for patiently

> . . . teaching them the language, dictating the words to them, syllable by
> syllable, as a teacher would do to a little pupil. Because of her extraordi-
> nary patient kindness they were able to harmonize the dictionary and syn-
> tax of the Huron language with those of these tribes, and accomplished a
> work which of itself would deserve that one make a stay of several years
> in the country . . .[60]

Bringing to fruition a major mental task of such proportions
would have been a gigantic contribution which, one would be
certain, could have been accomplished only in the peace and
quiet of Sainte Marie. But Brébeuf did so in an Indian cabin
where the din was often so great, even at night, that no one
could sleep.

Jean de Brébeuf fervently longed to garner the soul of his
generous hostess, but, for the moment, baptism could not be
conferred ". . . as her inclination to receive this was not yet sufficient."[61] However the whole lengthy and very hazardous excur-
sion was not lacking in some tangible results. Many of the dying,
both infants and adults, were baptized. Also, far to the southeast
in the neighborhood of the Niagara River, the two apostolic
vagabonds came upon the Awenrehrnon, a small tribe of mixed
Huron and Iroquois stock, who had fled to the Hurons in 1639,
seeking protection from the powerful Five Nations.[62] They joyfully welcomed Jean de Brébeuf who had nursed their sick when
they were among the Hurons in exile from their homeland. Father
Brébeuf considered them sufficiently instructed, but the time was
not propitious for baptizing them. Nonetheless he rejoiced at
finding them, for these Indians, already inclined toward Christianity, would, in future, provide a solid basis from which to
launch an effective crusade among the Neutrals when the mis-

---

[58] Ibid., 225.
[59] Ibid., 227, 229.
[60] Ibid., 231.
[61] Ibid., 229.
[62] Ibid., 253.

sionaries returned there, as Brébeuf was confident they would, and no later than the coming fall of 1641. Jean de Brébeuf would surely lead that crusade, at least so he thought.

But now with spring rapidly approaching the wandering missionaries decided it was time to return to Sainte Marie. Jerome Lalemant, their superior, was of the same mind, especially since he had heard no direct word from them since that day in November when the forests swallowed them up. Letters sent them in care of Huron travelers brought no replies probably, as Lalemant surmised, because the bearers either lost them or threw them away out of malice or fear. Wherefore, Robert Le Coq, that doughty, trustworthy lay assistant to the Fathers, was sent out with a few friendly Hurons and a couple of French laymen, also assistants of the Jesuits, to escort Jean de Brébeuf and Pierre Chaumonot back to Sainte Marie.

Robert Le Coq's arrival in the country of the Neutrals created great excitement among those who actually saw him. This was the Frenchman whom the Hurons told them had been deliberately done to death by the powerful sorcery of the Jesuits. Yet here he was, alive and well, though bearing the characteristic marks of a sufferer from smallpox. His deeply pitted face was proof incontrovertible, as the Indians themselves well knew. Those among the Neutrals who had survived the disease bore similar blemishes. Jerome Lalemant noted that when the Neutrals saw Le Coq they were ". . . disabused of the belief that . . . we were undying demons and masters of maladies . . . which we disposed at our good pleasure. Since so slight a thing was enough to begin the opening of their eyes, in time they may be entirely disabused and become thereby more fit for the enlightenment and visitations of heaven."[63]

A tiring journey on foot lay before Jean de Brébeuf on the return trip to Sainte Marie. In mid-March the snow still lay deep in the forests and most of the lakes and streams were still frozen solid. Crossing a large lake on the ice, Father Brébeuf fell heavily on his left shoulder, breaking his collarbone.[64] As best they could his worried companions strapped the useless left arm to his great body and tried to hurry on, hoping to secure better treatment for him at Sainte Marie. Days of excruciating pain and bitterly cold

[63] Ibid., 235.
[64] Latourelle, *Etude sur . . . Brébeuf*, II, 86.

nights in the open were passed uncomplainingly by the gentle giant. His companions begged him to let them make a rude sled of cedar bark so that they could pull him along and save him jolting the broken bone at each step. Jean de Brébeuf kindly declined their generous offer. It was bad enough for each one to slog his way through heavy snow without having to drag his great bulk behind them. He would walk; and where he was unable, he would crawl.

Jean de Brébeuf could make light of the accident if he chose, but Pierre Joseph Marie Chaumonot wanted the whole truth known. He wrote:

Crossing a frozen lake, a journey consuming two days, he [Brébeuf] was carrying the provisions on his back, since there were no inns. He fell on the ice with such force that it was a long time before he could even move. He was much weakened by the fall in which he broke one of his clavicles. But he said nothing about this to the doctor until two years later. His legs were so bruised that he was unable to lift his feet off the ground. For a dozen leagues he shuffled along avoiding any rise in the road. When he came to hills he crawled up them on all fours in the snow. Going down, he slid on the snow. Many times his companions wanted to help him, offering to pull him [by sled] the rest of the way, but he always declined.[65]

Toward noon on March 19, 1641, the feast of St. Joseph, patron of New France, the weary little party trudged into Sainte

[65] RAPQ, 1924-1925, 69. François Gendron is one of those romantic characters who appeared in New France. The son of a farmer, born near Chartres in 1618, he had five years of medical studies at Orléans and then came to New France to donate his services to the missionaries. Arriving in 1643, he spent a year at Sillery to familiarize himself with Indian life. He met Brébeuf there and treated him. Gendron then went to Huronia and remained until 1650. Then he returned to France and was ordained a priest in 1652. For a time he was called to the royal court to treat the queen. He was greatly sought after because he was believed to have found a cure for cancer while he was in New France. His "Erie Stones," a mixture of herbs compounded into a simple ointment made him a wealthy man. But he used his wealth to treat the poor and help them in their needs. He died at Orléans in 1688. He published one book about the Huron country, *Quelques particularitez du pays des Hurons en la Nouvelle-France*. This was published at Paris in 1660. François Gendron was not the only professional physician in New France at the time. Robert Giffard de Moncel, doctor in ordinary to the king, a title of honor only, had arrived at Quebec in 1634 with his wife, two children, and a group of colonists. He became the regular physician for the Hôtel-Dieu at Quebec. His daughter, Marie Françoise, who was born at Quebec, was the first girl of Canadian birth to enter a convent. She joined the community of hospital nuns in charge of the Hôtel-Dieu at Quebec.

Marie. After celebrating their Masses, the two returned wanderers must certainly have reported the results of their four-month sojourn to Jerome Lalemant, the superior. Then, of course, the other missionaries must have an account of what happened. And, finally, what was to be done about Father Brébeuf's broken bone? Gentle, retiring little Isaac Jogues, at the moment, was responsible for the care of the sick, but, of course, he knew nothing about how to set a bone. His ministrations would be of no help, much as he probably regretted it. A layman, Joseph Molère, was the community's official pharmacist, but no physician. The most they could do was to bind Father Brébeuf's left arm tightly to his body and hope for the best. Not until two years later, at Sillery in 1643, was any professional attention given to Father Brébeuf's broken collarbone.

But Jean de Brébeuf, neither at the time or afterwards, had anything to remark about his constant, nagging suffering. As to his four months in the country of the Neutrals, they should have been an extremely discouraging interlude in the life of a great and zealous apostle. Seeing himself daily held up as the one great national menace, the stumbling block to the conversion of a people, might well have taken the heart out of a lesser man, no matter how dedicated he might be. Yet in spite of the ever present threat of a horrible death at the hands of the Neutrals, Jean de Brébeuf was anxious to renew the effort in the fall of the year. Now he knew the language of the Neutrals. Also, he had met the captains and ancients of the country. He had taken their measure and gotten them to admit that what he taught was good in itself. All he need now do was to demonstrate to them that Christianity was not only good in itself, but good for them. But for Jean de Brébeuf working for the conversion of the Neutrals, or even the Hurons, was about to end for a long period of time.

Chapter IX

"Exiled" to Sillery

Listening to Jean de Brébeuf's account of his months among the Neutrals, Jerome Lalemant must have been pondering how he could, with the most consideration, inform this founder of the mission among the Hurons that he had become, like Christ, his Master, a stumbling block to the Hurons, the stone rejected by the builders. Huron enemies of the Jesuits had spread a vicious falsehood that, while Father Brébeuf was in the country of the Neutrals, he had traveled far to the east where he made contact with the Seneca clan of the Iroquois, bitter enemies of the Hurons. Treating secretly with them, the tale continued, Brébeuf had accepted a bribe to betray the Hurons. In due course, it was predicted, ". . . the disastrous effects of this treachery would be felt."[1] The story was so generally accepted that Brébeuf's life was in grave danger. To Lalemant, the only prudent course of action required Jean de Brébeuf's returning to Quebec for a time until the vicious gossip died away. Besides, the giant Norman had been seven years among the natives. It was time to give him some rest.

[1] *Relations*, XXIII, 35.

And, too, his broken bones really should receive attention even though Father Brébeuf made light of his condition.

Early in May 1641 Jean de Brébeuf left Sainte Marie in the company of Father François Du Peron. For their protection Father Lalemant sent along ". . . four Frenchmen and six Indians, both Christians and catechumens, who, being the first to go down the river, fortunately escaped three encounters with Iroquois bands, in which five canoes of Hurons, who followed a day or two after, were attacked."[2]

On reaching Three Rivers, very early in June, Father Brébeuf found the beleaguered little outpost in the throes of a serious crisis brought on by the Iroquois. Heretofore, while the Hurons and Iroquois were traditional enemies, constantly launching small raiding parties against one another, there had not been a concerted effort by the Iroquois to blockade the trade route used by the Hurons to reach the French trading center. Since 1624, when the Dutch established Fort Orange, the Iroquois had enjoyed easy access to European goods at that post by way of the Mohawk and the Hudson. But by 1640 Iroquois sources of peltries in their own country had dried up. Unlike the Hurons, the Five Nations enjoyed no ready approach to western sources of furs. In that year, 1640, the Iroquois, as a nation, seemed to have realized that if they were to continue procuring goods from the Dutch, particularly guns, it behooved them to make peace with the Hurons with the privilege of sharing their sources of furs. The only other alternative was annihilating the Hurons so that they could have a monopoly of trade with both the Dutch and the French. The Iroquois made overtures of peace in 1640 and the Hurons apparently agreed to parley. But, for some unknown reason, the meeting never took place.[3]

In the spring of 1641 the Iroquois launched their campaign designed to obtain complete monopoly of the trade with both the Dutch and the French. Their opening gambit was the mailed fist

[2] Ibid.

[3] Ibid., 263. In the summer of 1645, Governor Montmagny arranged an uneasy peace with the Mohawks who claimed, falsely, to have authority to speak for all five Iroquois cantons. In his address to the assembled French and their Indian allies at Three Rivers, Kiotseaeton, spokesman for the Mohawks, chided the Hurons for their failure to keep their word five years earlier, when the Iroquois offered to negotiate a peace.

in the velvet glove, an offer of peace with the French, excluding, however, any of the French native allies. At the end of April 1641, a band of five hundred Iroquois left their country, some bound for the Ottawa River trading route and others for Three Rivers. On June 5 a flotilla of twenty Iroquois canoes appeared before Three Rivers, ". . . all laden with well-armed men; others appeared in the middle of the river, equipped in like manner . . ."[4] François Marguérie, a Frenchman captured by the Iroquois near Three Rivers in February 1641 along with Thomas Godefroy, was sent ashore alone to explain the presence of the Iroquois. The released captive announced that the Iroquois, numbering three hundred fifty men and carrying thirty-six harquebuses among them, were seeking ". . . peace with the French but not with . . . Algonkins and Montagnais whom they hate unto death and wish to exterminate entirely."[5] Marguérie returned to the Iroquois bearing them news that the French were happy to parley, but the issues were of such import that the governor must be summoned to attend.

Arriving at Three Rivers on June 12, 1641, with a flotilla of shallops carrying seventy armed men, Governor Charles Huault de Montmagny met with the Iroquois. It soon became evident that these haughty Indians expected the French, in return for a promise of peace, to betray their own Indian allies, giving the Iroquois guns and allowing them to assume a monopoly of the whole fur trade. Soon sensing that the governor had no intention of accepting any of these conditions, the Iroquois faded away during the night, but not before a number of their young braves attacked an Algonkin fur flotilla in broad daylight during the very time their elders were parleying with the French. The governor pursued them, approaching close enough to engage in a brisk exchange of shots, but not with any effect. The net result of the meeting, as the French clearly understood, was that the Iroquois

---

[4] Ibid., XXI, 35.

[5] Ibid., 37. A harquebus was a heavy, portable firearm invented in the middle of the sixteenth century, originally requiring some solid support other than that supplied by the user. The weapon was gradually refined until it could be fired from the shoulder. Its effective range is said to have been about five hundred paces. Toward the end of the sixteenth century, the weapon was replaced by a true musket.

disdainfully flung down the gauntlet, declaring war on both the French and their Indian allies.

The desperate character of the situation was undeniable for the French in Canada as much as for their native allies. In 1641 the total French population was hardly more than three hundred including men, women, and children. Equally dangerous was the fact that the minute population lived so far apart from one another that what little fighting strength existed could not be quickly rallied. The small settlement of Beauport, five miles down the St. Lawrence from Quebec, had a population of about fifty. Beaupré, some fifteen miles farther down the river, boasted some forty residents. The population of the outpost at Three Rivers was no more than sixty. And Quebec itself boasted a little if it claimed one hundred fifty.[6] Unless the crown sent adequate military aid New France was ripe for the plucking by the hordes of braves the Iroquois could launch against it. To procure that assistance Montmagny sent Father Paul Le Jeune back to Paris ". . . to explain the importance of the aid which we need to resist the efforts of these barbarians."[7] With his arresting personality, as one of his biographers describes him, Le Jeune, through the good offices of Cardinal Richelieu's niece, the duchesse d'Aiguillon, procured from the cardinal a corporal's guard of thirty or forty soldiers and also sufficient funds to build fortifications ". . . on the roads by which the Iroquois come . . ."[8] to attack the French settlements.

[6] Lanctôt, *History of Canada*, I, 172.

[7] *Relations*, XXII, 31.

[8] Ibid., 34. Through the good offices of the duchesse d'Aiguillon, Richelieu's niece, funds were provided for erecting a fort at the mouth of "the River of the Iroquois." On modern maps the site of the fort is called Sorel and the river, the Richelieu. The fort was approximately seventy miles up the St. Lawrence from Three Rivers.

The duchesse d'Aiguillon was Marie Madeleine de Vignerot, daughter of Françoise Duplessis, Cardinal Richelieu's sister, and René de Vignerot, marquis du Pont de Courlai. In 1620, at the age of sixteen, she was married to Antoine de Beauvoir, marquis de Combalet. Her husband was killed in battle two years later. She never remarried, though her famous uncle wanted the young widow to marry the comte de Soissons, third in line for the French crown. From 1625 to 1630 she was at court as one of the ladies-in-waiting to the queen. In 1638, Richelieu had his niece made duchesse d'Aiguillon, a tiny little duchy located at the confluence of the Lot and the Garonne. A sincerely pious lady, she was greatly devoted to St. Vincent de Paul and helped him in his work. She was the generous foundress of the Hôtel-Dieu at Quebec, a hospital which is still very much of a going concern. This lovely lady died at the age of seventy-one in 1675.

Since Father Barthélemy Vimont,[9] superior of all the Jesuits in New France, came up to Three Rivers with Governor Montmagny, Jean de Brébeuf promptly learned the new tasks to which he would be assigned. During the previous season, 1640-1641, Father Paul Ragueneau had been detained at Quebec to act as agent for the Huron mission, gathering supplies and attending to the inevitable details of a quite large mission operation. Brébeuf's physical limitations would not prevent his assuming that responsibility, releasing Ragueneau for active mission work among the Hurons. Father Brébeuf would also be in charge of the mission center begun at Sillery in 1638.

The mission of St. Joseph at Sillery, a scant four miles up the St. Lawrence from Quebec, resulted from pious propaganda broadcast by Father Paul Le Jeune in his *Relation* of 1634. Therein he proposed that the nomadic tribes of New France would be more quickly converted if they could be gathered into villages and transformed into farmers, as the Jesuits had done so successfully at their Reductions in Paraguay.[10] If some pious Frenchman of means would provide craftsmen to clear land, build houses, and teach the Indians to till the soil, Le Jeune believed that the wandering Algonkins and others could be induced to settle, accept Christianity, and, quite quickly and easily, adopt European culture. In 1637 Noel Brûlart, chevalier de Sillery, commander of the Knights of Malta, deeply impressed by Le Jeune's proposal, made just such an offer. He donated an initial $12,000 to finance the project and promised an annual subsidy of $1,200 to support it.

[9] Barthélemy Vimont was born on January 17, 1594, at Lisieux in Normandy. He entered the Jesuit novitiate at Rouen on November 16, 1613. He did his philosophical studies at La Flèche, 1615-1618, while Father Massé was there. Vimont may have then conceived the desire of spending his life among the Indians of New France. In 1629 he sailed for Canada with Captain Charles Daniel. In 1630 he was recalled to France when New France was in the hands of the English. In 1639 he returned to Quebec where he landed on August 1. He was commissioned to assume the office of superior of all the Jesuits in Canada and continued in that position until 1645 when he was succeeded by Jerome Lalemant. His major apostolic work was confined to the French. It was he who baptized the infant Louis Jolliet on September 21, 1645. He returned to France in 1659 and died there, at Vannes, on July 13, 1667. He was greatly respected by Governor Montmagny. Before he left New France permanently, in 1659, he had made one journey to France, in 1645, on mission business.

[10] Ibid., VI, 45.

For the site of their "reduction," the Jesuits selected a small bay between "la pointe de Puiseaux et la pointe Saint Joseph," about thirty acres fronting on the St. Lawrence and a hundred acres in depth reaching to a high cliff at the rear. On the land they erected a stone house forty-seven feet long and twenty-six feet wide. On April 14, 1638, Father Paul Le Jeune and Father Jean de Quen settled at the new mission with two Christian Indian families. In time the mission had a chapel built of stone as well as the necessary barns. The mission compound was eventually surrounded by a stone wall, part of which remains today.[11]

Visiting Quebec after an absence of seven years, Jean de Brébeuf must have been delighted to perceive the many improvements introduced during his long absence. Governor Montmagny, aided by the engineer, Jean Bourdon, had established an urban plan for the lower town which was beginning to take on the characteristics of a typical Norman village.[12] On the promontory above there stood a proper brick fortress with a stone guardhouse where a sentry was always on duty. Across the *place d' armes* the parish church of Quebec, Notre Dame de Récouvrance, erected by Champlain in 1633 in fulfillment of a vow he had made in 1629, burned to the ground on June 14, 1640, together with the small Jesuit residence beside it.[13] The loss was particularly disastrous to the missionaries among the Hurons because all

[11] Noel Brûlart de Sillery was born at Paris on December 25, 1577, the scion of an ancient noble family. At eighteen, enrolling in the Knights of Malta, he began a distinguished military career, climaxed by his appointment as commander of his order's commandery at Troyes. That position awarded him an annual income of 40,000 *livres*, roughly about $30,000 in today's values. From 1614 forward, he entered his country's diplomatic service, holding the post of ambassador at Madrid and then at Rome. In 1625 he withdrew from court life entirely and devoted himself to prayer and good works. At the age of fifty-seven he was ordained a priest. That year, 1634, he developed an interest in the plight of the aborigines in New France through reading Le Jeune's *Relation*. His first inclination was to establish and endow a school for Indian girls, but, in 1637, he gave the necessary funds to found the mission at Sillery. He died on September 26, 1640. Other members of this family were equally pious and generous. Brûlart's brother François provided the funds requisite to establish the Jesuit college at Reims. Another brother, Jean Baptiste, became a Capuchin. His sister Catherine was abbess at Longchamps near Paris. Another sister established a religious congregation of nuns devoted to hospital work.

[12] Lanctôt, *History of Canada*, I, 159.

[13] *Relations*, XIX, 65.

the supplies they needed so badly went up in flames with the Jesuit residence where the supplies had been stored.[14]

For Jean de Brébeuf, as for practically everyone else, layman and cleric alike, the most encouraging innovation was the presence of two groups of nuns, both recruited in great measure by Father Paul Le Jeune. The Ursulines, led by the incomparable Mère Marie de l'Incarnation, came to instruct young girls, both French and Indian. Reaching Quebec on August 1, 1639, Mère Marie and her companions settled in a rude cabin erected on the spot where the Ursulines are still found in Quebec today, at the end of the little rue du Parloir.[15]

A more striking addition to the life of New France was the presence at Sillery of a hospital and three nursing nuns, members of the congregation of the Hospitalières de la Misericorde de Jésus de Dieppe. Reaching Quebec on August 1, 1639, Mère Marie Guenet de St. Ignace and her two companions were brought to the site of a still unfinished building being prepared for them. The nuns gently declined to settle because ". . . there was no water there. It is true that the river [the St. Charles] flows near it, but the cliff there is so steep that it would be very difficult to go up and down it. Since water is an absolutely essential commodity for a hospital, we decided to abandon the site . . ."[16]

On visiting Sillery, the hospital nuns decided to settle there until a building at Quebec could be prepared for them in a more suitable location. They occupied a small, substantial residence at Sillery which was owned by Pierre de Puisseau, sieur de Montrenault. During the last days of August 1640 the nursing nuns opened their doors and began caring for the sick, especially Indians. They remained at Sillery until May 29, 1644, when they returned permanently to Quebec because of the threat of an Iroquois raid.[17]

[14] Ibid., 67.

[15] The most scholarly study of Mère Marie de l'Incarnation is: Mother Denis Mahoney, O.S.U., *Marie of the Incarnation, Mystic and Missionary*.

[16] *Les annales de l'Hôtel-Dieu de Québec, 1637-1716*, compiled by Jeanne-Françoise Juchereau and Marie Andrée Duplessis, edited by Albert Jamet, 21.

[17] Ibid., 49. The problem of water was solved by digging a very deep well. The new site at Quebec where the hospital was built is very close to the same steep cliff.

At Quebec the hospital nuns built the Hôtel-Dieu on the site where it is found today. For many years a notice over the door of the hospital chapel asked all who entered to pray for the repose of the souls of the duchesse d'Aiguillon, the hospital's foundress, and her uncle, Armand Jean du Plessis, cardinal, duc de Richelieu. Though his niece might long since have gained heaven, her uncle must be grateful for any prayers. He had much to answer for when he met his God on that cold day at Paris, December 4, 1642. Of his death his latest biographer wrote: "He died with the same serene indifference to his own faults as he had exhibited towards the human misery of those he had sacrificed to the Moloch of the state . . ."[18]

One of the early events marking Father Brébeuf's labors at Sillery was an extremely consoling one, the solemn baptism of his cherished friend, Sondatsaa, a highly respected Huron chief from the village of Ossossané. That remarkable man accompanied Father Brébeuf when he came down from the Huron country in 1641. Sondatsaa declared his desire for baptism in an oblique manner, reminiscent of husbands everywhere and in all ages. If he returned unbaptized, he confessed, he would dread meeting his wife who would not fail to reproach him, saying "Perhaps the love of some other woman has hindered you from pursuing so great a good . . . This is the first salutation I expect from my wife on arriving home."[19] Though Father Brébeuf was hesitant, the governor himself pleaded the Huron chief's cause so successfully that Brébeuf acquiesced. When Sondatsaa was baptized on June 26, 1642, by Father Vimont, at that moment the ranking ecclesiastical authority in New France, the governor stood sponsor and gave the Indian his own name, Charles. At the conclusion of the ceremony Governor Montmagny astonished everyone by presenting the new Christian with a handsome harquebus, a priceless gift that made Sondatsaa the envy of every Indian present.[20]

Together with his apostolic responsibilities at Sillery, Jean de Brébeuf fell heir to the duties of procurator, or general finance and procurement officer, of the Huron mission. That office imposed the obligation of reporting conditions in the mission to the

---

[18] O'Connell, *Richelieu*, 243.
[19] *Relations*, XX, 217.
[20] Ibid., 219.

Jesuit general at Rome. Fulfilling his duty, Father Brébeuf wrote to the general, Mutius Vitelleschi, on August 20, 1641:

Very Reverend Father in Christ:

Since I exercised the office of consultor at the mission among the Hurons and now am procurator at Quebec for that mission, I think I am required to submit to your Paternity a report on the conditions of the mission.

First, as to our Jesuits working among the Hurons, the greatest peace and union flourishes among them. Religious discipline [among them] is observed as perfectly as it is in the large colleges [in France]. Exact observance of every regulation is augmented with each passing day. Everyone strives to advance in virtue, mortification and self-abnegation so well that I doubt whether such admirable virtue could be discovered anywhere in so small a group.

As for our lay assistants, each, according to his ability, strives to grow in perfection, especially those who have dedicated themselves to our Society. As to that group, . . . nothing, in my opinion, is done not in conformity with the Society's institute or to the wishes of your Paternity. If any practice to the contrary still persists, it will be discontinued. However, we do think that in this area that sort of person is not only useful but necessary. Nevertheless, we admit such men only under the conditions customary in our houses or colleges [in France]. We are sending your Paternity the form of civil contract we enter into with these men for approbation. If another is returned, we will observe it.[21]

Father Jerome Lalemant, superior of the Huron mission, gives the greatest satisfaction. The good order prevailing there is due, under God, to his virtue and prudence. In very truth zeal for God's house devours him, so desirous is he to promote religious observance. He is no less zealous for the conversion and salvation of the Indians. Due to his example and encouragement all our Fathers are equally as zealous. Among the Hurons there are about sixty whose virtue and fervor is a great consolation to us. The number increases slowly but we hope it will continue growing, if only we persevere. Besides, the opportunity to extend our zeal and industry to wider fields unfolds daily. This year we started two new missions. One is among the Algonkins whom we call Nipissings, a very primitive group. The other is for a people we call the Neutrals among whom the harvest promises to be abundant. That nation is composed of about forty well-populated villages. That mission was recently confided to Father Chaumonot and myself. We lived there for five months during which we suffered much. Some heard us willingly but many reviled us, heaping insults upon us. Yet when we left we were invited to return by the chiefs. I believe Father Chaumonot will accomplish great things for Christ in that area. He has already made great

---

[21] The laymen who had dedicated themselves to the Society of Jesus were known as *donnés*. The origin of this group, their relationship to the Jesuits, and their contribution to the mission effort will be discussed in a subsequent chapter.

strides in acquiring the language of those people whose tongue differs not greatly from Huron. He is surely a remarkable man.

As for the mission at Quebec, Christianity flourishes in a remarkable degree. Almost all the Indians at the mission of St. Joseph [at Sillery] are Christians. We hope that their faith and virtue will go far towards convert-ing the rest of the nations. At the residence of Conception [Three Rivers] there are also many Christians and their number increases daily.

The conversion and submission of the Indians is, in my opinion, in great measure due the zealous charity and industry of Father Barthélemy Vimont, the superior of these Canadian missions. Strangely, in this work he has many adversaries among our people who, unable to acquire facility in the languages, have not been assigned to instruct the natives. I cannot explain why these people resent our generosity to the Indians. Perhaps they believe that thereby they are themselves deprived to some degree. This situation often gives rise to sharp discussions here, much to the harm of this mission.

As I see it, there are two ways of remedying this situation. The first would be to decrease the number of those who, lacking facility in the languages, are not sufficiently occupied most of the time. They are discontented and they incur numerous expenses without fruit. They take the place of many young men who could learn the languages quickly and become excellent missionaries. There are far too few laborers here at Quebec. Among the Hurons there is a surplus of eminently virtuous and zealous missionaries as one could hope for the glory of God.

The second remedy would be increasing authority of the superior of the missions, allowing him to send back to France people who are useless or even dangerous. Letters from the provincial are delayed as long as a year and sometimes two. In the meantime, internal peace and concord suffer as well as dissatisfaction of the people. Your Paternity, yourself, or through the provincial could remedy this unhappy situation.

Presently Father Provincial is, himself, very well disposed towards the missions in New France. Nevertheless, I urge your Paternity to [further] stimulate that interest. I have nothing further to add. I write nothing concerning the nuns at Quebec. We do nothing for them which is contrary to our institute.[22] We could hardly do so since there is no one else to care for them. I add that through them we are able to gain many souls.

I take note of the letter your Paternity wrote last year to the whole Society on the occasion of the centenary of our establishment.[23] I sent it to our

---

[22] In his constitutions St. Ignatius Loyola declared: ". . . they [that is, Jesuits] ought not to take a curacy of souls, and still less . . . take charge of religious women or any women whatever to be their confessors regularly or to direct them. However, nothing prevents them in passing from hearing the confessions of a whole monastery for special reasons." See *The Constitutions of the Society of Jesus*, 262-63.

[23] The Society of Jesus was founded by St. Ignatius Loyola in 1540. In 1640 the Jesuits were celebrating the centenary of their foundation.

Fathers among the Hurons where, undoubtedly, it will be read with great fruit.

I beseech your Paternity to bestow your blessing on your sons living in this distant land and I pray the great and good God to preserve you in health for years to come.

<table>
<tr><td></td><td>Your very humble and obedient son</td></tr>
<tr><td>At Quebec in New France</td><td>and servant in Jesus Christ</td></tr>
<tr><td>August 20, 1641</td><td>Jean de Brébeuf.[24]</td></tr>
</table>

Lest it be thought that Jean de Brébeuf was, quite uncharacteristically, sharp in his criticism of some of his brethren, it should be pointed out that he was but confirming what his predecessor, Paul Ragueneau, had already written to Rome. On July 28, 1641, Ragueneau wrote to the Jesuit general: "No one should be sent here who is not of proven virtue and possesses a pliable nature and a head for learning languages with ease. Those who cannot acquire the languages will find no occupation here. They are not only useless, but they displace people who could become valuable laborers."[25] That the request of Ragueneau and Brébeuf was heeded by Vitelleschi is demonstrated by his letter to Vimont, dated at Rome, February 25, 1643: "I am writing to the provincial [instructing him] that not only should no one be sent unless there is hope of him being useful to you, but also that he is to recall those who are not of help."[26]

Sheer curiosity urges one to try to discover whom the "problem children" might have been. Of the Jesuits in New France in 1641, fourteen of those who were in the Huron country were excluded from criticism by Brébeuf. In the Quebec area Enemond Massé, sixty-six in 1641, was the revered patriarch of the missionary effort in New France. Father Anne de Noüe, aged fifty-four, distinguished for his saintly humility, never could learn an Indian language, but he was dearly loved for his willingness to take on any task, even farming or carpentering. Just five years later he

[24] ARSJ, Gal. 109, II, ff. 365, 365v, 366, 366v, 367, 368v. The original of the letter, which Brébeuf wrote in Latin, is in very poor condition. Theodore Besterman, in his edition of Brébeuf's writings has an English translation of this and other letters of the martyr. See *The Travels and Sufferings of Father Jean de Brébeuf . . . as Described by Himself*, 183-85. The translation given here is not Besterman's. A very incomplete version of the letter is contained in *Relations*, XX, 103, 105.

[25] Rochemonteix, I, 433.

[26] Ibid., 433-34.

died a martyr of charity. Vimont, the superior, evidently had Brébeuf's respect. Ambroise Davost, then fifty-seven, after two years,
1634-1636, among the Hurons, was sent back to Quebec with Father Daniel to launch a school for Huron boys. Perhaps his Huron
ability was not too great, but, if he was appointed to handle those
children, he must have learned enough of their language to be
understood. When the project failed Davost continued the school,
instructing French children, though most of the time he was ill,
suffering from scurvy. In 1643 he was sent back to France because of his health which was so bad that he died aboard ship.
Charles du Marché, thirty-nine, first labored at Miscou where he
contracted scurvy. He was brought back to Quebec until he recovered sufficiently to help out at Three Rivers. He returned to
France in 1647 and died there in 1661. Jean de Quen, aged thirty-
eight in 1641, though not a particularly forceful character, was a
very active missionary. Appointed superior of the whole mission
in 1656, he was hardly a successful administrator, being replaced
in 1659, the year in which he died at Quebec. Claude Quentin,
aged forty-four, had no head for native languages. He ministered
for a while to the French at Miscou, but a serious attack of scurvy
required his recall to Quebec. After twelve years he was sent back
to France where he died in 1676 at La Flèche.

Possibly poor Father Nicolas Adam was one of those against
whom Brébeuf's criticism was leveled. Reaching Quebec on June
12, 1636, Father Adam promptly fell sick from scurvy which so
afflicted him that he was confined to his bed for three months.[27]
He firmly believed that he was cured miraculously on September
8, the feast of the Nativity of the Blessed Virgin Mary. His health
recovered, Father Adam's intellectual troubles began. Since he
seemed incapable of learning an Indian language, he was appointed to teach the French children attending the sketchy school
opened at Notre Dame des Anges. Subsequently, the only information surviving about Nicolas Adam occurs in a letter sent by
Vitelleschi to the superior of the mission in New France. On December 20, 1640, the general wrote: "At my order, the provincial
will promptly recall Father Adam. Certainly, I did not send him
to Canada nor did I approve of his going."[28] When Father Paul

[27] *Relations*, XII, 191.
[28] Rochemonteix, I, 433.

Le Jeune went back to France in the late summer of 1641, Father Adam accompanied him. In France, Adam spent the remaining days of his life teaching in various Jesuit colleges. He died in 1651.

Two other missionaries were thus singled out by the Jesuit general. Georges d'Eudemare was forty-seven when he reached New France in 1636. In 1643, Vitelleschi wrote to Canada: "Regarding Father d'Eudemare, I am writing to the provincial to recall him and any others who are not useful there."[29] For reasons no longer known, that peremptory order was not obeyed. In spite of his inability to learn a native language, D'Eudemare served as chaplain at Fort Richelieu, becoming, apparently, so knowledgeable about Iroquois affairs that he was consulted about that hostile people when an important crisis arose concerning them in 1648. Father d'Eudemare died at Montreal, probably in 1649.

Father Claude Quentin also made no progress overcoming the language barrier. Landing in New France in 1635, at the age of thirty-eight, he spent three years at Three Rivers striving vainly to acquire Algonkin. Then he was sent off to Miscou to minister to the French fishermen who gathered there, fishing for cod off the Grand Banks. He too contracted scurvy, so seriously that he was brought back to Quebec in 1641. There he remained, managing the mission's business affairs until October 21, 1647, when he went back to France. He died at La Flèche on October 31, 1676, three and a half months short of his eighty-first birthday.

It is significant that each of the three Jesuits recalled to France suffered severely from scurvy. All had been stationed at Miscou caring for the sailors of the fishing fleets from France. Crews from fishing vessels brought their catch ashore to dry the fish and salt them down in barrels with much less salt than was required if the catch was packed "wet," aboard ship.[30] While ashore the sailors were given spiritual ministration by the Jesuit assigned to them. As everyone knows, scurvy is a disease arising from a deficiency of vitamin C. Even very severe cases can be cured by the ingestion of any fruit or vegetable containing that vitamin. The medical profession points out that victims of serious

29 Ibid.
30 Andrew Hill Clark, *Acadia: The Geography of Early Nova Scotia to 1760*, 75.

attacks of scurvy suffer from profound mental depression, lassitude, and general lack of energy together with loss of hair and teeth, severe hemorrhages, disorders of vision, and cruel muscular pains. Perhaps purely physical debility explains much of the discontent Brébeuf encountered among some of his brethren at Quebec. Whatever the reason, Jean de Brébeuf considered that lack of unity existed and should be corrected. Mystic he might be, but heavenly visitations did not cloud his practical judgment nor prevent him from speaking out forcefully when occasion demanded it.

The mission at Sillery, during the fall of 1641 until the spring of 1642, was the scene of unusual activity. In September Paul de Chomeday de Maisonneuve, the indomitable Jeanne Mance, and a company of some fifty men settled at Sillery to wait out the winter before migrating to their destination, the island of Montreal. All the experienced Quebec residents decried the venture as patently foolhardy, warning that a settlement on that great island would be attacked by the Iroquois within a few days of the arrival of the people. Everyone at Quebec urged Maisonneuve to settle his colonists on the island of Orléans where the two settlements, thus not far separated, could assist one another in case of attack. Believing firmly in the divine origin of the inspiration prompting a settlement at Montreal, the sieur Maisonneuve responded to all arguments: ". . . if all the trees on the Island of Montreal were to turn into Iroquois warriors, my duty and honor require that I establish a colony there."[31]

The presence of half a hundred sincerely devout Frenchmen at Sillery through the winter of 1641-1642 proved a great blessing. With the example of so many pious Europeans before them, the Christian Indians all the more easily adapted themselves to a sedentary culture and Christian morals. On May 17, 1642, Maisonneuve and his party took possession of their island in the presence of Governor Montmagny. Father Vimont celebrated Mass for them and preached, predicting that, like the biblical grain of mustard seed, Montreal would grow and prosper.

The devout sincerity of the Indians inhabiting the little sedentary village at Sillery quickened the hearts of their missionaries, especially that of Jean de Brébeuf. Here was incontrovertible

---

[31] Lanctôt, *History of Canada*, I, 176.

proof that savages, imbued with the grace of God, could, indeed, abandon their superstitions and practice the Christian virtues. In fact, the Fathers found it necessary to restrain the zeal of their neophytes. During the winter of 1641-1642, the Indians at Sillery, unknown to their missionaries, met secretly together to determine ". . . means of keeping themselves in the faith."[32] Observing that the French imprisoned malefactors, the Indians decided that those who fell into any error should be ". . . put into prison and made to fast four days without eating or drinking."[33] Though Father Brébeuf insisted that the Indians were proceeding with too much severity, the zealous Christians ". . . did not cease to pursue their point and to say resolutely that they had formed a plan among themselves that the first of their number who should commit any fault, however inconsiderable, should suffer imprisonment and fasting."[34]

The first to request the severe punishment was one of the chiefs. He struck his wife in anger because she failed to accompany him to Mass on a weekday morning. Father Brébeuf pleaded the cause, pointing out that the wife regretted disobeying, that she loved her husband and a similar thing would not happen again. But the chief, rigorously righteous, insisted that he deserved punishment, ". . . for I have let myself be carried away by my indignation; give me a note, so that I may do penance for my sins."[35] The crisis was allayed by persuading husband and wife to approach the confessional.

A really serious fault came to everyone's attention when a young pagan brave became inebriated. His Christian relatives marched him off to Quebec and asked the governor to put him in the dungeon. Governor Montmagny acquiesced, but the next day, Christmas, the kindly governor released the culprit with a warning of future severe punishment if the youth failed to stay sober.[36] On his release the young brave was advised by the Christians that he must eschew his paganism or be excluded from the village. Instead of resenting the treatment, the released prisoner replied:

[32] *Relations*, XX, 143.

[33] Ibid., 143, 145.

[34] Ibid., 145.

[35] Ibid., 149. The note requested by the chief would have been addressed to the governor, petitioning him to put the chief in the dungeon.

[36] Ibid., 149, 151.

"You have done me a kindness . . . as for my sorcery, it is a thing that I have already abandoned and which I shall never take up again."[37] With such encouragement many pagan Indians stopping at Sillery were drawn to ask for baptism.

Among these were two Hurons, Atondo and Okhukwandoron, men of importance in their home village of Ossossané.[38] Having come down to Three Rivers in the fall of 1641, they made such a late start on their homeward voyage that they turned back, fearing that they would die of cold before they could reach home. Father Brébeuf, receiving them at Sillery, employed the long winter days instructing them. In their own country, even in their own cabins, both had been offered instructions by Father Charles Garnier. But, related Atondo: "Their discourse did not please me; I sent them my nephews and nieces to occupy them. As for me, I rejected the matter, thinking that its consideration should be deferred to some other time."[39] When properly instructed, these two erstwhile orphans of the storm were solemnly baptized in the presence of the governor, Maisonneuve, Jeanne Mance, and an impressive gathering of Frenchmen.[40] At Easter the two new Christians, now named Paul (Atondo) and Jean Baptiste, received holy communion kneeling beside the governor.[41] The two conversions were particularly gratifying to Father Brébeuf, who had already baptized Atondo's son, because he was aware that the new converts would urge all their ". . . countrymen to be baptized."[42]

The spring of 1642 found Jean de Brébeuf almost entirely occupied with mundane matters. As agent for the Huron mission he was obliged to gather a vast mountain of supplies, everything that fourteen Jesuits and their nineteen lay aids might need for a whole year. Should any item be forgotten, the missionaries would be forced to make do for a complete year. Brébeuf gathered what he could at Quebec, but his best source was the holds of supply ships arriving from France. There was a heart-sinking rumor, in the spring of 1642, that the whole supply fleet had been attacked

[37] Ibid., XXI, 153, 155.
[38] Ibid., XXII, 135.
[39] Ibid., 151.
[40] Ibid., 139.
[41] Ibid.
[42] Ibid., 153.

by the English off Dunkirk. For once the rumor was false and the great supply fleet arrived safely.[43] From the crates and bales delivered to the Jesuits, Father Brébeuf extracted the innumerable items needed in the Huron country: bolts of black serge for cassocks, leather to make or mend shoes, paper and ink, soap, candles, medicines, carpenter's tools, altar wine, seeds for planting, pictures for the rude little chapels, porcelain beads to pay for services rendered by Indians, cheap rings, yards of gaudy ribbon, religious medals, strap iron for the blacksmith's forge, lead for bullets, gunpowder, pious books, and little holy pictures to be used as gifts to the Indian children. Most important of all were the packets of letters from Europe to the Jesuits in Huronia. Family news, notices about Jesuit activities in France and around the world, communications from the provincial in France and the general in Rome, these were all anxiously awaited at Sainte Marie among the Hurons.

All of these and a hundred items more must be freighted to Three Rivers and made up into bundles which could be packed into the fragile canoes. If all went well, about two months and many portages later the Jesuits at Sainte Marie would receive their supplies.

As spring stretched into the summer of 1642 the missionaries and the French colonists waited anxiously for the arrival of the annual Huron fur brigade on which the economic life of New France, in large measure, depended. Would the Huron successfully evade Iroquois ambushes or would this be another disastrous season with no furs brought down to Three Rivers? Finally, on July 17, 1642, four Huron canoes, carrying twenty-five Hurons and Frenchmen, put in at Three Rivers. Among the latter were Father Isaac Jogues and Father Charles Raymbault.[44] Jogues, the

[43] Ibid., 39.

[44] Charles Raymbault was born on April 6, 1602, at Senlis, France. He entered the Jesuit novitiate at Rouen on August 24, 1621. He studied philosophy at La Flèche, a kind of pious hotbed of interest in the missions of New France. He was ordained at Bourges, where he studied theology and then went back to Rouen as treasurer of the novitiate and agent for the Canadian mission, a post he held until 1637. Reaching Quebec in the summer of 1637, he went immediately to Three Rivers to learn Algonkin. In 1640 he planned on laboring among the Indians of the Lake Nipissing region, but those natives had retired to the Huron nation because of hunger. Raymbault, and his companion, Claude Pijart, wintered at Sainte Marie, laboring with the Nipissings. The following summer, 1641,

executive officer of Lalemant, the superior, was the Jesuit best informed about practical needs at Sainte Marie. Raymbault, broken in health, the victim of an advanced case of tuberculosis, was coming back to Quebec to die. Their news from Huronia was a mixed bag. Conversions had noticeably increased, but the Iroquois were waxing bolder, even daring to employ small bands in night attacks on Huron villages.[45]

Isaac Jogues and his Jesuit companion brought news of an important discovery. In September 1641 they had accompanied a nation, hitherto uncontacted, to their homeland. This folk, calling itself the Ojibwa, had invited the two missionaries to attend the tribe's Feast of the Dead in their own country. They dwelt on the banks of a treacherous river filled with boiling rapids which connected Lake Huron with a vast body of water above, or superior to, the Lake of the Hurons. On that upper lake, the two missionaries learned, dwelt numerous nations, the Illinois, the Sioux, the Cree, all of whom, the Ojibwa maintained, were anxious to meet the French.[46] And how many nations lay beyond that, who knew?

With the arrival of the annual supply fleet from France, there was reason to hope that the Iroquois threat might be lessened. Father Le Jeune's visit to France, pleading for adequate military aid, had not been entirely in vain. Forty soldiers disembarked, paraded up the rue de la Montmagne and reported to Governor Montmagny for duty. For the first time since its erection Fort St. Louis finally seemed something like a true garrison, resounding to the sound of marching feet and military commands shouted somewhat boastfully to a small company of real soldiers. Shortly, Governor Montmagny took his troops up to the mouth of the River of the Iroquois and set them to building Fort Richelieu on the right bank of the river which came to bear the great cardinal's

Raymbault attended the Nipissing Feast of the Dead. There he met the Ojibwa who invited him to visit their homeland. This he did with Father Isaac Jogues. From that visit, the French learned of the existence of Lake Superior and at least the names of some of the Indian nations dwelling on its shores or near it. Though a tall, robust man, Raymbault's health rapidly declined after his return from the Ojibwa visit. He was, apparently, suffering from an advanced case of tuberculosis. He came down from Huronia with Father Isaac Jogues in the fall of 1641 and was taken to Quebec where he died on October 22, 1642. He was the first Jesuit to die at Quebec. The governor, Montmagny, had him buried beside Champlain.

[45] Ibid., 305.
[46] Ibid., XXIII, 225.

name. Just a week after the work began, on August 20, 1642, three hundred Iroquois roared out of the woods attempting to destroy the place. To the credit of the soldiers, entirely unprepared for the type of attack screaming Indians launched, they beat off the Iroquois with the loss of only one Frenchman.[47]

That summer of 1642 Jean de Brébeuf must surely have hoped that he would be allowed to return to Huronia. The very presence of Jogues and Raymbault at Quebec would seem to enhance his chances. Since, clearly, Father Raymbault was in no condition to return, Sainte Marie among the Hurons would be shorthanded without a replacement. Isaac Jogues was the logical Jesuit to retain at Quebec for he knew more about the mission's needs than anyone else. Besides, the only new recruit the Jesuits received that summer was Father Francesco Giuseppe Bressani, by birth a Roman, who certainly ought to be kept at Sillery for a year or more learning at least the rudiments of Huron to say nothing of acquiring more facility in French.[48]

Things were not quite that simple, however, and to some extent Jean de Brébeuf, himself, was unwittingly responsible. His success with the two young pagan Hurons during the previous winter engendered an elaborate plan in Father Vimont's mind. If a school were opened at Sillery for such young men, wouldn't that be a marvelous way of creating a corps of zealous lay apostles? Determining to implement the plan, Barthélemy Vimont an-

[47] Lanctôt, *History of Canada*, I, 178.

[48] Francesco Giuseppe Bressani was born at Rome on May 6, 1612. He entered the Jesuit novitiate there on August 15, 1626, at the early age of fourteen. He did some of his ecclesiastical studies at the Jesuit college in Paris, which, perhaps, explains his interest in the missions of New France. He arrived at Quebec in the summer of 1642 and spent the remainder of that year in the Quebec area, chiefly at Sillery with Father Brébeuf. Then he was sent to Three Rivers. Thence he set out, on April 27, 1644, for the Huron country. Three days later he was captured by the Iroquois, dragged off to their country and cruelly tortured. Given to an old Indian woman, she sold him to the Dutch at Fort Orange because he was useless, even as a drudge. The Dutch arranged his return to France. Landing at La Rochelle, on November 15, 1644, he again sailed for Canada and was at Three Rivers in July 1645 when the Iroquois came to parley for peace. That summer he returned to the Huron country and remained there until 1648 when he was briefly sent to Quebec to seek added missionary assistance. The following year, 1649, when the Huron mission was destroyed Bressani was again sent to Quebec seeking help. In 1650, when he started back to Huronia, he met the Hurons and their missionaries fleeing to Quebec. He was then returned to Europe and spent the rest of his life in Italy. He died at Florence on September 9, 1672.

nounced in his *Relation* of 1642-1643: "It was for this reason that
I again detained Father Jean de Brébeuf, who had wintered here
last year and has not yet gone up again, in order to instruct and
take charge of these Hurons."[49] Alas for his hopes! Jean de Brébeuf was doomed to at least another year's separation from his
Hurons while he watched Isaac Jogues set off gaily for the land
so dear to Echon.

Before dawn on August 1, 1642, Father Isaac Jogues left Three
Rivers in the company of thirty-seven Hurons and three Frenchmen, two of whom were René Goupil and Guillaume Coûture.
The flotilla of twelve canoes spent that night peacefully at a spot
about forty miles upstream. The next morning they set out, hug-
ging the north bank of the St. Lawrence where tall water reeds
would, they hoped, screen their passing from any lurking Iroquois.
At full light the Hurons spotted signs of a small Iroquois party.
Judging that the skulking group consisted of no more than four
warriors, the Hurons continued, confident that they could drive
off such a small force. But these few were evidently a scouting
party for in a moment a howling mob of seventy Mohawks surrounded the Huron flotilla. The Hurons, abandoning the canoes,
fled to the woods on shore, only to be pursued and captured along
with Isaac Jogues, René Goupil, and Guillaume Coûture who surrendered voluntarily rather than abandon the Jesuit.[50] Those
whom the Mohawks did not slaughter immediately were forced,
after preliminary torture, to march to the Mohawk capital, Ossernenon.[51] After a year's captivity, during which René Goupil was
brutally murdered, Jogues was rescued by the Dutch who arranged his passage back to France. Reaching France on Christmas day, 1643, Jogues returned to Quebec in early July 1644.[52]

The capture of Isaac Jogues and his party by the Mohawks inflicted a crushing blow on the Huron mission. The loss of so

[49] *Relations*, XXIV, 105.
[50] Lucien Campeau, "Un site historique retrouvé," *Lettres du Bas-Canada*
VI (1952), 35. Campeau places the capture of Jogues on the north bank of the
St. Lawrence, a mile downstream from the present town of Lanoraie.
[51] Ossernenon is unquestionably the present Auriesville, New York. This is
roughly two hundred miles from the place where Jogues was captured. Presently,
the Jesuits operate an elaborate shrine on the site of the Mohawk capital.
[52] *Relations*, XXXIX, 175-225. Jogues' own account of his capture, torture,
and rescue by the Dutch in a letter he wrote to his provincial, Jean Filleau.

capable a missionary, one so well versed in the Huron tongue, saddened everyone, especially since it was expected that the saintly thirty-five-year-old missionary would surely be tortured to death. In addition some of the leading Christian Hurons were of the captured party. The loss of these pillars of the Huron church would be sorely felt. Again, all the supplies for the coming year were lost to the enemy with no hope of replacing them that season. In his *Relation* of 1642, dated October 4, Father Vimont added a further homely little touch: "The poor Fathers will chiefly regret the loss of the letters written to them by several persons of merit. The Iroquois have scattered them about here and there on the banks of the river, and the waters have carried them away . . . The highway robbers have taken this consolation away from them."[53]

Not the least disastrous result of the capture was its effect on the Indian nations that were friendly to the French. Just how powerful as allies against the Iroquois were these Frenchmen? At Three Rivers an Algonkin chief stated the case succinctly to Father Jacques Buteux:

This time we will see whether the Iroquois fear you . . . As soon as your brother [Jogues] reaches their country the captains will assemble, and, if the French name frightens them, . . . they will bring back your brother and the two Frenchmen . . . If . . . they despise you, . . . they will make them suffer a thousand tortures . . . A captain will . . . incite the young men to go and hunt Frenchmen . . .[54]

Thence forward the very existence of the Huron mission depended on French conquest of the Iroquois. And other Indian nations stood by awaiting the outcome.

The report of the capture and almost certain forthcoming martyrdom of Isaac Jogues must have brought profound sorrow to Jean de Brébeuf. It was he who had warmly greeted that twenty-nine-year-old recruit when he reached Huronia on September 11, 1636,[55] nursed him through a serious illness,[56] taught him the Huron language, and guided his early apostolic efforts with the Indians. Given Brébeuf's own burning desire for martyrdom, he

[53] Ibid., XXII, 271, 273.
[54] Ibid., 283, 285.
[55] Ibid., XIII, 87.
[56] Ibid., 93, 95.

must have begrudged Jogues his opportunity. But now Brébeuf
was doomed to another winter at Sillery. And, on October 1, 1642,
in compliance with his obligation, he again wrote to the Jesuit
general at Rome reporting on the state of the mission.

Having assured the general of the profound peace and exemplary mutual charity evident among the Jesuits in New France,
Father Brébeuf earnestly besought his major superior to use his
influence to obtain military aid against the Iroquois. He wrote:

It is greatly to be feared that, unless a prompt remedy is found, all trade as
well as the church in Canada will be entirely destroyed. Assuredly, our most
Christian king and our most eminent cardinal seemed greatly disposed to
help us when Father Le Jeune left France. Now, however, no one with influence is urging the matter and we hesitate to impose the task on anyone
else. We are, however, writing to France conjointly with our governor, a
most capable man who has accomplished much for New France, explaining
the precarious nature of our situation unless we are given help. Urging from
your Paternity might significantly influence those assigned to obtaining aid.
Here is the basis of the problem. The Dutch, who supply guns to our enemies,[57] ought to be entirely driven out of these territories. Because they are
heretics, they continually obstruct the conversion of large numbers of Indians. Or, at least the Iroquois themselves ought to be crushed by force of
arms. May God grant his favor to the afflicted Hurons before your Paternity
leaves us for heaven.[58]

Coming from the gentle, considerate Jean de Brébeuf, the
statements smack of a vindictiveness one would hardly expect
from such a saintly man. It must be remembered, one supposes,
that Brébeuf was a child of his times. To him the heretical Dutch
were men of bad faith who refused to accept the completely
obvious truth that Catholicism was the one, true religion. Those
religiously erroneous Europeans were deliberately thwarting missionary efforts to convert the Indians, Hurons and Iroquois alike.
As Richelieu had solved the Huguenot problem in France, the
only effective means of treating the Dutch was to drive them off
the continent by force of arms. Had the crown of France been
sufficiently powerful, Brébeuf's suggestion, already offered by

---

[57] Hunt, *Wars of the Iroquois*, 165-75, devotes a whole chapter to the question of the Dutch trade in firearms with the Iroquois. He concludes that, while
the Iroquois obtained more guns from the Dutch than the Hurons did from the
French, on balance, both Dutch and French were equally guilty of arming the
aborigines.

[58] Latourelle, *Etude sur . . . Brébeuf*, II, 107-14.

others, might have been followed. But France had her hands full at the moment supporting the Lutheran, Gustavus Adolphus, in his conflict against the Holy Roman Empire. Far be it from Richelieu to be so lacking in perceptivity as to offend the Dutch and possibly cause a rupture between France and Gustavus Adolphus. It might be further indicated that in October 1642 Father Brébeuf knew nothing of the kindness the Dutch were later to manifest to Isaac Jogues and Francesco Bressani.

Though he assuredly longed to return to the Huron nation after the news of Isaac Jogues' capture reached Sillery, for Jean de Brébeuf the winter of 1642-1643 was a period of true consolation. Established almost by accident, the school for young men at Sillery produced remarkable fruit. Armand Andewaraken, who, in 1636, had spent some time at the short-lived seminary for Huron boys at Quebec, came down to Sillery, in the fall of 1642, to ". . . forsake the world and enter into religion."[59] With him came Ignace Saokaretchi, a young pagan Huron ". . . of an excellent disposition, gentle, peaceable, obedient, industrious, and endowed with a good mind . . ."[60] On Christmas eve Ignace was solemnly baptized in the chapel of the Ursuline convent.[61] In mid-January Pierre, a Huron from the village of Aronté, came to Sillery from Fort Richelieu, ". . . expressly to be instructed in the faith."[62] Working in the hospital for his keep, Pierre was baptized by Father Brébeuf on March 8, 1643.[63] A month after Pierre's arrival two friends from his village came in from Fort Richelieu ". . . in order to come in quest of Father de Brébeuf, so as to be instructed by him."[64] These two were baptized at Quebec on March 25, 1643. All these fervent neophytes begged to remain permanently at Sillery where, as they said ". . . it is hardly possible to offend God . . ."[65] But the Jesuits encouraged them to return to the Huron country and become lay apostles to their own

[59] *Relations*, XXIV, 107. By "entering into religion," Armand meant becoming a Jesuit.

[60] Ibid., 111.

[61] Ibid.

[62] Ibid., 113. Jones, 134, locates this village at lot 18 or 19, concession XIII, Tiny township, Simcoe county, Ontario, about two miles south of the present town of La Fontaine.

[63] *Relations*, XXIV, 115.

[64] Ibid.

[65] Ibid., 119.

people. Toward the middle of June they went back in the company of some hundred Hurons who had come down for the trading. The whole experiment was so successful that the Jesuits hoped to continue it. Father Vimont warned, however, ". . . I know not whether the rage of the Iroquois will not deprive us of this consolation; and them, of so great a good fortune."[66]

Indeed Vimont's fears were amply justified, for the summer of 1643 was one of constant alarm. The Iroquois separated into small raiding bands strategically stationed at all the likely places of ambush along the St. Lawrence from Montreal to Three Rivers.[67] On June 9, 1643, one group, hiding on the island of Montreal, successfully plundered a Huron fur flotilla of thirteen canoes carrying sixty men. The Iroquois captured twenty-three Hurons as well as their peltries and, sad to relate, Father Jerome Lalemant's *Relation* of 1642-1643 together with all the letters sent down by the missionaries.[68] Then, adding insult to injury, the Iroquois captured five Frenchmen at Montreal. On June 12, 1643, a raiding party of Iroquois, including two Hurons captured with Father Jogues, camped only twelve miles above Three Rivers. The Hurons, escaping, brought Brébeuf the news that Jogues still lived, but René Goupil had died a martyr's death.[69]

Determined to drive off the Iroquois, Governor Montmagny armed four shallops and came up to Three Rivers. Patrolling the river from there to Fort Richelieu, the governor discovered to his chagrin that the Iroquois had cut a road through the forest above Fort Richelieu, thus circumventing the fort and permitting them to reach the St. Lawrence unmolested. Father Barthélemy Vimont noted, with thinly veiled disgust, that if the French crown had seen fit to send

. . . the soldiers for whom he [the governor] was hoping, . . . he would no doubt have proceeded even into the country of the Iroquois with two hundred or three hundred Algonkins and Montagnais who offered themselves to keep him company; and I believe . . . that he would have constrained those proud barbarians to an honest place, or have entirely subdued them.[70]

[66] Ibid., 121.
[67] Ibid., 273.
[68] Ibid., 275. A copy of that *Relation* was sent down to Quebec and forwarded to France. This was included in the *Relation* of 1644.
[69] Ibid., 281.
[70] Ibid., 289.

Military aid would arrive a year later and then not in sufficient strength.

Ambushes and even open attacks in strength continued throughout the summer. On August 15, 1643, a contingent of Iroquois appeared before Fort Richelieu, sending a renegade Huron alone in a canoe to parley with the French. Questioned about Father Jogues, the Huron produced a letter from the poor captive addressed to the governor.[71] In it the future martyr warned: "The design of the Iroquois is, as far as I can see, to take if they can, all the Hurons; and, having put to death the most considerable ones and a good part of the others, to make them both but one people and only one land."[72] Answering the letter, Montmagny hastily sent Father Brébeuf to Fort Richelieu, hoping that he might find means of forwarding it to Jogues. But the renegade Huron messenger refused to return to the Iroquois, ". . . fearing lest the Iroquois . . . should take him for a spy . . . and there was no way of persuading him to do anything else."[73]

Summoned upriver by Governor Montmagny in mid-August, Jean de Brébeuf continued on at Three Rivers until late October of 1643. It was from there he wrote his report for that year to the Jesuit general. He said in part:

As I write these lines a messenger reports that nine Hurons have been killed, a great number wounded and all the supplies we were sending have been lost. The shipment was quite large and absolutely essential to our people living among the Hurons. From this, one can perceive the desperate condition of affairs in Canada. Yet, the more profound the wretchedness, the richer these shores are in celestial blessings. Wickedness has no place here, but virtue and piety abound . . . among our people who prove themselves true, legitimate sons of the Society . . .[74]

When the fleet left for France in mid-September 1643, an air of foreboding settled on the colony of New France. Threats of Iroquois incursions at almost any point along the St. Lawrence drove the Indians to advance their annual winter hunt a good three months. The south shore of the great river, the best area for capturing large game, was closed because the Iroquois patrolled

[71] Ibid., 293.
[72] Ibid., 297.
[73] Ibid., 307.
[74] Latourelle, *Etude sur . . . Brébeuf,* II, 116-18.

it so effectively.[75] The Algonkins and some few Hurons, settled near Quebec or Three Rivers, anticipated a lean winter in which many would die from bitter cold and gaunt hunger. Father Vimont lamented: "Disease, war, and famine are the three scourges with which God has been pleased to smite our neophytes since they commenced to adore him and submit to his laws."[76] In spite of these afflictions, they remained loyal to the French. And those who embraced Christianity held firmly, for the most part, to their newfound religion. Even more, young Huron braves in greater number came down seeking instructions from the great Echon.

That season Jean de Brébeuf was detained at Three Rivers, the most exposed French village, where his very presence was a steadying influence on both French and aborigines. Risking torture and death, four young men made the hazardous journey from Huronia to Three Rivers to be instructed. Two other Huron braves, just escaped from the Iroquois band which attacked Montreal, also reached the precarious haven at Three Rivers, all six meeting there at the beginning of November 1643. Under Brébeuf's inspiration they applied themselves so diligently that within two months they were baptized.[77]

The spiritual consolation these six youths afforded Father Brébeuf was sadly counterbalanced by the apostasy of one of his important converts. Etienne Pigarouich, once the most famous sorcerer among the Algonkins, settled at Sillery after his conversion. There he proved himself most zealous in urging others to prayer and in punishing the wicked.[78] In the fall of 1643 he went up to Three Rivers where he fell in with a group of his pagan countrymen, all extremely indolent, arrogant, full of superstition, and very profligate. Etienne's Christian fervor vanished as quickly as light snow under a brilliant sun. Abandoning his lawful wife, he took a concubine and assumed all his former vices. On Christmas day, Father Brébeuf strove diligently to bring Etienne to his senses, but to no avail. The next day, the feast of St. Stephen,

---

[75] *Relations*, XXV, 107.
[76] Ibid., 105.
[77] Ibid., XXVI, 25.
[78] Ibid., XXV, 249.

Etienne's patron saint, the prodigal repented of his own accord and, on December 28, publicly confessed.[79]

Soon after the beginning of 1644, when Father Brébeuf had returned to Sillery, Etienne and a group of his pagan friends followed the great missionary, hoping to be fed and sheltered through the winter. During the journey Etienne, completely ignoring his promises to reform, lapsed into his sinful ways. Instead of the charitable welcome he expected, the Jesuits at Sillery, the nuns at the hospital, and the governor coldly rejected his every advance. Toward spring the chastened Etienne returned to Father Brébeuf begging absolution. But Echon, usually so understanding, coldly dismissed the profligate without granting his request. Only when Etienne joined a war party were steps taken. Father Brébeuf gave the prodigal a letter to Father Jacques Buteux, chaplain at Montreal, advising Etienne's rehabilitation, provided he manifested sincere and permanent repentance. And, indeed, Etienne again repented, begging to be publicly flogged. Buteux remarked, however: "Even after all this he may relapse. He fears this and has begged me to manage so that he may not be where that wretched woman is who has been his rock of scandal."[80] Despite his defections Etienne's repentance influenced others beneficially for: "Following his example, a great sorcerer and some others became converted . . ."[81]

The spring of 1644 brought with it a grave crisis. Wholesale attack on the colony by the Iroquois was more than a possibility. Even the Indian allies of the French expected the worst with such certainty that Noel Tekwerimath, captain of the Indians at Sillery, went up to Three Rivers and begged Father Brébeuf to write to the hospital nuns, urging ". . . that as soon as the crops were sown, they were to withdraw to Quebec . . ."[82] The same advice was offered by the Jesuits at Quebec as well as the governor. Thus importuned, the nuns yielded and moved to Quebec, occupying a new building being prepared for them, though as yet it had no roof.[83]

[79] Ibid., 255.
[80] Ibid., 281.
[81] Ibid.
[82] Ibid., 195.
[83] Ibid., 193.

As for the missionaries among the Hurons, since no supplies had reached them for three years, somehow, this year, essential merchandise must be gotten through. Also, official communications from the Jesuit general must reach them since the time had come to change both the superior of all the Jesuits in New France as well as the superior of the Huron mission. Further, new missionary recruits were awaiting transportation to Huronia. And Jean de Brébeuf still yearned to return.

Since there appeared no hope of the Hurons risking the Iroquois ambuscades on the long journey from Huronia, the Jesuits at Quebec planned a rescue mission of their own, employing the six zealous young Huron braves who had wintered with Father Brébeuf. On April 27, 1644, with the mighty St. Lawrence barely free of ice, the six daring young Christians loaded three small canoes with essential supplies and set out, hoping so early in the season to escape the Iroquois. With them went Father Bressani and a young French boy. The little flotilla advanced up the St. Lawrence only fifteen miles when a carelessly discharged musket revealed its presence to a group of Iroquois. These swooped down and easily captured all eight of the people bound for Huronia. Fifteen days later Henry Stotrats, one of the captives, a pathetic caricature of himself, stumbled into Three Rivers and reported the disaster.[84]

Just when the future of the Huron mission was thus so hopeless, a happy event quickened the hearts of everyone. In early July 1644 a leaky old tub of a sailing ship limped into Quebec bearing Father Isaac Jogues and, wonder to behold, twenty-two soldiers sent by the queen of France, Anne of Austria. The troops had orders to go up to the Huron country for the protection of the mission.[85] Shortly one small flotilla of Huron canoes reached Three Rivers, bearing among the passengers Father Pierre Pijart. Four such flotillas left the Huron country, but only this one escaped the Iroquois.

Here was Jean de Brébeuf's long-awaited opportunity. It could not be denied that Pierre Pijart was much better informed than Brébeuf regarding the conditions and needs of the Jesuits among the Hurons. Besides, with an escort of twenty-two soldiers and

[84] Ibid., XXVI, 35.
[85] Lanctôt, *History of Canada*, I, 181.

some three score Huron braves, what better opportunity could be had for reaching Huronia safely? At last, release came. With Father Vimont's consent, Jean de Brébeuf was free to go. Accompanying him were two new missionaries, Noel Chabanel and Leonard Garreau.[86]

Finally, on a hot day in early August 1644, the twenty-two boisterous soldiers were dispersed among twenty heavily laden canoes manned by sixty Hurons who were on their way home. Father Brébeuf quite probably feared what the example of those near barbaric French soldiers might have on the Hurons. But at least during the long, tedious journey to Sainte Marie, skulking Iroquois would, he hoped, hesitate to launch an attack on a flotilla protected by so many well-armed men. Anyway, for Jean de Brébeuf, Huronia was the threshold of heaven which he earnestly hoped to enter through the bloody door of martyrdom.

[86] Noel Chabanel was born on February 2, 1613, at Saugues (Haute-Loire). He entered the Jesuit novitiate at Toulouse on February 9, 1630. Most of his life as a Jesuit in France was spent at Toulouse. He reached Quebec on August 15, 1643, and went to the Huron country the following summer. Though a brilliant man, he simply could not learn the Huron language, possibly because everything about the Indians repelled him. Though superiors offered to return him to Quebec, he refused to "break away from the cross God had given him." He was killed by an apostate Huron on December 8, 1649.

Leonard Garreau, son of a noble family, was born at Aridieux (Saint-Yrieix) near Limoges in 1609 or 1610. He entered the Jesuit novitiate at Bordeaux on September 27, 1629. He came to New France with Father Chabanel and spent a year at Sillery before being sent to Huronia. Most of his apostolic effort was expended on the Tobacco Nation. When the Huron mission was closed, Father Garreau cared for them on the Ile d'Orléan until 1654 when he was sent to Three Rivers. He was then directed to establish a mission among the Ottawa. On August 30, 1656, he and the Ottawa were attacked by Mohawks who mortally wounded the Jesuit. He died at Montreal on September 2, 1656.

Chapter X

Release from Exile

The first blush of autumn color tinged the hardwoods, as though welcoming the great Echon, when on September 7, 1644,[1] his bark canoe swung off Georgian Bay into the quiet waters of the narrow, sluggish Wye River. Advancing slowly upstream, Jean de Brébeuf began to perceive buildings reminiscent of the Norman villages he had known in his youth. Through the trees he caught sight of a high narrow steeple crowned with a weather vane in the form of a rooster, just as were most of the steeples of the village churches in his Norman homeland.[2] Drawing closer, Brébeuf

---

[1] *Relations*, XXVI, 71. In his *Relation* of 1643-1644, Vimont says that Brébeuf went back to the Huron country in 1644. In 1645 the Jesuits at Quebec began keeping a house diary called *Le Journal des Jésuites*. An entry in it for 1645 reads: "Twenty-two soldiers sent to the Hurons . . . lodged with us [there] and took their meals at our table, returned a year to the day later. They reached the Hurons on September 7 and arrived [back] at Montreal on September 7, a year later." *Journal des Jésuites*, 9. Since the convoy bearing the militia was the only one to reach Huronia in 1644, Brébeuf arrived there on the same day as the soldiers.

[2] Older Norman churches in France are all found having their steeples surmounted by a weather vane formed like a rooster. Later, more modern churches have steeples surmounted by a cross. Perhaps originally the rooster was used to remind the faithful of St. Peter's triple denial of Christ and the crowing of the cock after the third denial.

discovered a high wooden palisade running parallel to the right bank of the Wye, walling in the western side of the mission of Sainte Marie. About halfway along the lengthy palisade he found a water gate, hinged in the middle, which opened to allow entrance for his canoe. Passing through it, Father Brébeuf discovered he had emerged into a water lock some ten feet square. While delighted Jesuits and laymen called greetings the lock slowly filled, lifting the canoe to a second and third lock where he was able to leap ashore.[3]

Trooping to the chapel, the Jesuits with Father Brébeuf and their two new recruits, Noel Chabanel and Leonard Garreau, knelt to thank God for their safe arrival and the successful shipment of vital supplies brought with the convoy. Kneeling on the chapel's plank floor, Brébeuf saw a room, some forty by thirty feet. Above him sturdy hewn rafters supported a planked, steeply pitched roof. To one side was a great limestone fireplace and before him an altar of dressed wood on which rested the tabernacle embellished with the pictures of seven angels which Father Brébeuf remembered so well. There was a lovely painting depicting the Mother of God and another portraying our Lord agonizing on his cross. It is no wonder that Jerome Lalemant wrote home that the Indians considered the chapel ". . . one of the wonders of the world."[4]

Leaving the chapel, Brébeuf was taken to the Jesuit residence, forming the west wing of the chapel complex. Here on the ground floor were the refectory, kitchen, and community room, all heated by two massive fireplaces and furnished with sturdy, rough-hewn tables and chairs. On the second floor was a dormitory with ten or twelve cubicles separated from one another by partitions some eight feet high, but not reaching the ceiling. Each contained a low bed, a stool, and a small chest. Thus, each missionary enjoyed some privacy.

---

[3] Wilfrid Jury and Elsie McLeod Jury, *Sainte-Marie among the Hurons*, 65-71. The water to fill the locks was procured from springs at the north end of the mission complex. It was carried to the locks by a canal. This stretched, north to south, about one hundred twenty feet. Then, making a right turn, it ran for another seventy-five feet and emptied into the highest lock. The total drop over the length of the canal is approximately five inches.

[4] *Relations*, XXIII, 23.

In the east wing of the chapel complex were a cobbler shop, a carpenter shop, and a blacksmith shop. Under portions of the area were cellars, some as large as fourteen feet long, five feet wide, and six feet deep. Only one of these subterranean rooms could be entered by a stairway. All the others had openings only through trapdoors in the floor above them.[5]

Adjacent to the chapel building were several other structures, all made of logs laid horizontally. Some were storage barns, animal stables, and the like. Others were dwellings for the lay assistants. All of these very substantial structures were surrounded by a stout palisade, except on the east where the palisade was interrupted by a high limestone wall plus two large stone bastions which protected that approach to the mission.[6] Over all, the area for the exclusive use of the Europeans measured about three hundred sixty by two hundred thirty feet, but wider at the north than at the south.

South of the court for the Europeans, but separated by a high, staunchly built palisade, was a large area devoted to the use of those Christian Hurons who came to the mission, staying for various lengths of time. Here was built a quite large chapel, much more spacious than that reserved for the Jesuits and the French laymen. Though its floor was only of pounded dirt, it, too, had a soaring steeple, but surmounted by a cross. Immediately south of the Indian chapel was a cemetery where Christian Indians found their last resting place. Before Sainte Marie's sad demise twenty-one graves had been opened, only one of which contained the remains of a Frenchman, young Jacques Douart[7] who was treacherously murdered by a pagan Huron.

[5] Jury, Sainte-Marie, 41.

[6] Ibid., 81. The nearest source of limestone is three miles from the site of the mission. There is a limestone quarry near the present Port McNicoll which is still being quarried. Geologists report that the limestone used at Sainte Marie came from that source.

[7] Jacques Douart came up to the mission in 1642 at the age of sixteen. Toward sunset on April 28, 1648, while strolling a short distance from the mission, he was killed by a blow from a hatchet wielded by one of two Huron brothers, both pagans, who had been hired by some Huron captains, enemies of the Jesuits. Douart was merely a chance victim. The brothers determined to kill the first Frenchman they encountered and Douart happened to be the one they met. Of course, Douart was very much alive when Brébeuf returned in 1644.

Within the double palisaded Indian compound, measuring four hundred five by one hundred seventy-five feet, were some Huron long houses, an Algonkin dwelling, and a rather large hospital in which the sick, both men and women, were nursed by the mission's infirmarian. At the southern apex of the mission was a pentagonally shaped building of two levels, a watchtower from which guards could survey the south whence raiding Iroquois could be expected to approach. Overall, the whole mission of Sainte Marie measured about seven hundred sixty-five feet, north to south.

An important factor in establishing a permanent, central mission was the hope that the Jesuits and their assistants might succeed in farming operations of sufficient magnitude to eliminate the necessity of buying food locally from the Hurons or depending almost entirely on shipments from Quebec. Soon fields were cleared on the left bank of the Wye where, even today, ". . . the most productive soil of the surrounding district is found."[8] Crops of corn, squash, beans, peas, sunflowers for their seeds, wheat, and other edibles were grown. Since the French at Quebec were already growing beets, radishes, lettuce, purslane, parsley, cucumbers, and melons, it can be taken for granted that seeds of these were brought up and grown successfully. What true Frenchman could be content without a kitchen garden? The need for altar wine, and perhaps even a small supply of table wine, was supplied from wild grapes found in the Huron country. But the French must have brought along cuttings from vineyards in France for grapevines on the hillside just north of the mission site are not native to the area.[9]

No farm is worthy of the name without the sounds of cackling hens, crowing roosters, grunting pigs, and the lowing of cattle. Transporting chickens and suckling pigs by canoe presented no major problem to men who managed to bring up a forge, an anvil, scrap iron, and even a small cannon. As early as 1637 chickens scratched in the dirt around mission cabins, though preventing packs of dogs and bands of young children from causing their untimely death was a constant problem.[10] By 1648 Father Paul

[8] Ibid., 34.
[9] Ibid., 31.
[10] *Relations*, XIII, 93.

Ragueneau informed the Jesuit general that pork was available at Sainte Marie, indicating, undoubtedly, that the swine population had increased and prospered.[11]

Freighting cattle some eight hundred miles over half a hundred portages would seem to most people an insurmountable undertaking. Yet in the summer of 1646 Jean Caron, a lay volunteer, brought up a young calf and during the fall of that same year Eustache Lambert managed to bring two others.[12] To anyone at all familiar with the habits of these capricious young animals, the unending patience it must have required to keep them reasonably quiet in a balky canoe during the long paddling day will understand what a job it was. The calves had to be at least weaned since there was no source of milk for them above Three Rivers. And a weaned calf is not a small animal, nor would it be a comfortable companion in a birchbark canoe. Many a night Caron and Lambert must have worked at repairing their canoes to make them watertight for the following day's travel. In due time the miniscule herd prospered so well that Father Ragueneau reported to the Jesuit general, on March 1, 1649: " . . . we have not merely fish and eggs, but also pork and milk products, and even cattle . . ."[13]

Viewing the meticulously accurate reconstruction of Sainte Marie, as it stands today, we cannot help wondering who could possibly have accomplished such a gigantic feat in a raw wilderness hundreds of miles from Quebec, which was, itself, hardly even a true village with few craftsmen, no horses, and almost no labor force.[14] Aware of the marvelous accomplishments of Jesuit brothers in Europe, it would be supposed that these valiant and talented men were at Sainte Marie in large numbers. Actually, during the whole seventeen years of Jesuit missionary activity in Huronia only five brothers labored on the Huron mission. These were, in the chronological order of their arrival at Sainte Marie, Dominique Scot, Louis Gaubert, Ambroise Brouet, Pierre Masson,

[11] Ibid., XXXIII, 255.

[12] *Journal des Jésuites*, 44, 64. Caron and Lambert were both laymen.

[13] *Relations*, XXXIII, 255.

[14] The first horse imported to Quebec arrived on June 25, 1647, and was presented to the governor. That poor animal lived out his life without ever again seeing any of his kind. Twelve horses were brought over in 1665 and by 1668 horses were said to be abundant. See ibid., XXX, 183; XLIX, 161; LI, 173.

and Nicolas Noirclair.[15] Only one of them, Louis Gaubert, possessed any noteworthy skill as a craftsmen. He was an excellent
blacksmith, ". . . a master craftsman, probably more artist than
tradesman."[16] On the whole very few brothers came to New
France chiefly because the number available in France was inade-
quate to the needs at home. And also, as Nicolas Perrot pointed
out in his *Mémoire*, "The few European lay Brothers the Jesuits
had were as unaccustomed to aboriginal ways as the missionaries themselves."[17]

As substitutes for Jesuit brothers, when Father Brébeuf and
his two missionary companions permanently established the Huron mission in 1634, he took along ". . . three hardy young men
and two little boys . . ."[18] Of these young men François Petit-Pré
was a hunter whose skill was most valuable during periods of near

[15] Desjardins, "Le frère Dominique Scot," 208-31. He discusses the biography of Dominique Scot at some length. Father Desjardins, a recognized historian of stature, holds that Dominique, the son of Abraham Martin, *dit Ecossois*,
was born at Calais on September 19, 1619, and brought to New France in 1620.
Dominique and his brother Eustache, aged fifteen and thirteen respectively, seem
to have been the two young boys sent to the Huron country in 1634. In the fall
of 1638 Dominique came back to Quebec and returned to France where he entered the Jesuit novitiate at Paris on December 1, 1638. Completing his novitiate
training, Brother Scot returned to Huronia, arriving in late September or early
October 1640. Until the spring of 1645, Brother Scot served the mission as tailor,
launderer, and infirmarian. Never robust, Scot was sent down to Quebec in the
summer of 1645 to consult the physician about his declining health. On October
24, 1645, he was sent back to France because of a serious pulmonary condition.
In France Scot worked at various colleges until his death which probably occurred in 1659.

Of the other four brothers practically no biographical details are known.
Brother Louis Gaubert reached Canada in 1636, served on the Huron mission and
died at Quebec on July 20, 1679. Brother Ambroise Brouet came to Canada in
1641. He arrived at Sainte Marie in 1645. He returned to France, probably after
Sainte Marie's demise, and died sometime after 1676. Brother Pierre Masson was
born in 1609. He came to New France in 1646, arriving on September 20. He
went directly to Sainte Marie, apparently to replace Brother Scot for Masson was
a tailor and a gardener. Brother Nicolas Noirclair was born at Nancy in 1599. He
entered the Jesuit novitiate on December 24, 1625. He reached New France before 1647 and came up to Huronia in 1648. After the destruction of Sainte Marie
he went back to France, sailing on September 21, 1650.

[16] Jury, *Sainte-Marie*, 53.

[17] Nicolas Perrot, *Mémoire sur les moeurs, coustumes et religion des sauvages
de l'Amérique Septentrionale*, edited by J. Tailhan, 258.

[18] *Relations*, VI, 41. Paul Le Jeune to the provincial of the Province of
France, 1634.

famine. Simon Baron enjoyed some small reputation as a surgeon, which might have meant that he was a barber by trade. Robert Le Coq soon became the mission's business agent traveling almost yearly between Quebec and Huronia. At least one of the two boys, Dominique Scot, performed domestic chores and possibly accompanied the missionaries as they journeyed about the Huron country. By the next year, 1635, another layman, Mathurin, arrived.[19] All of these except, perhaps, Dominique, were salaried workers. These few men constituted the whole labor force available to the missionaries. What little building took place during the first five years was of Huron construction and accomplished by the Indians themselves, with, probably, some help from the French laymen. Not until Father Jerome Lalemant reached Huronia in 1639, with grandiose plans already formed in his mind, that an architect, carpenters, blacksmiths, tailors, cobblers, vinterers, and other skilled craftsmen were sought for erecting Lalemant's stupendous Sainte Marie. He would duplicate among the Hurons the Reductions so successfully established by Jesuit missionaries in South America thirty years before.

Though Jerome Lalemant never laid eyes on an Indian before he reached Canada, nor had he conferred with any Jesuit who knew the Hurons as they existed in their homeland, Lalemant formulated detailed plans for the proper method of administering the Huron mission before he sailed for New France. Just as his fellow Jesuits had done in Paraguay, he would establish a town on the banks of a river. Surrounding it with a strong palisade, he would build a church, a rectory, a school, a hospital, and establish a Christian cemetery, properly fenced and pleasantly shaded by the spreading branches of mighty trees. In time the Indians would settle about the "reduction" and form themselves into a Christian republic with similar satellite "reductions" scattered throughout Huronia.[20]

Quite well aware that his projected program would involve funds far beyond the meager stipend a parsimonious crown granted each missionary annually, Lalemant, it would seem, launched a fund-raising campaign among friends of the missions

[19] Jones, 31.
[20] Rochemonteix, I, 286.

in old France as well as among government officials. One of Lalemant's benefactors was Cardinal Richelieu himself. Writing to thank that eminent statesman, Lalemant remarked how profoundly grateful he was

. . . that it has pleased Your Eminence to extend your zeal and your charity even to this end of the world where we are, assigning a fund for the maintenance of some of our Society who work here for the conversion of the barbarians. It must be confessed, Monseigneur, that it is one of the touching consolations that we have received, to see ourselves remembered by a personage whom glorious deeds have rendered deserving of praise from all posterity . . .[21]

Richelieu's motives might well not have been quite as pure as Lalemant pretended that they were. Actually, the great cardinal ". . . perceived in the plan, a jumping off place, an advanced post destined to insure for France domination of the west."[22]

Since Lalemant could not hope to obtain the proper craftsmen from the ranks of the Jesuit brothers in France, he adopted an institution then prevalent in France itself. In various Jesuit colleges with a paucity of brothers, superiors instituted a system of engaging pious laymen of proven stability with whom they entered into a lifetime contract. On their part the Jesuits obliged themselves to provide all of the material and spiritual needs of these men for their whole lives. The men, themselves, agreed to serve the Jesuits for life, binding the agreement by pronouncing private vows of poverty, chastity, and obedience, which were renewed semiannually at the request of each man.[23] These men

---

[21] *Relations*, XVII, 219. Jerome Lalemant to Richelieu, March 28, 1640. Toward the end of the letter Lalemant urged the cardinal to expel the British and the Dutch by force of arms, remarking: "I regard it as certain that not for a hundred years hence, and perhaps never, shall we see ourselves rid of these . . . enemies of God and of the state, if Your Eminence does not put your hand to this work."

[22] Rochemonteix, I, 387.

[23] The term "private vows" arises from an ecclesiastical definition in Catholic canon law. As to their validity and efficacy, private and public vows are resultantly the same. However, he who pronounces public vows is considered to have been accepted by some religious order or congregation which thereby binds itself to that person. Such is not the case with those who pronounce private vows. For a quite complete explanation of the institution of the *donnés*, see Jean Côté, "Domestique séculier d'habit, mais religieux de coeur," *Lettres du Bas-Canada* IX (1955), 69-75.

were not Jesuits, not even a species of "third order" for such a grade had long since been expressly prohibited by St. Ignatius himself. They came to be called *donnés* because they gave themselves unrestrictedly to the service of the Jesuits in whatever capacity the local Jesuit superior asked them to serve.

With the consent of the provincial of the Province of France, Etienne Binet, Jerome Lalemant introduced the *donnés* at Sainte Marie with outstanding success. During the ten years the mission flourished thirty dedicated men became *donnés*. Among them were some highly skilled craftsmen, perhaps the most valuable of whom was Charles Boivin, a competent carpenter who probably should be considered an architect. If any one single individual should be credited with instrumenting Jerome Lalemant's dream, that man must surely have been Charles Boivin. From 1640 forward Boivin is listed among the personnel of the mission as the manager in charge of construction. He remained at the mission of Sainte Marie through the whole of its ten-year existence and returned to Quebec in 1650, where he was frequently engaged to erect various buildings including the Ursuline convent, destroyed by fire in 1650, a chapel for the Jesuit college, and various other structures.[24]

[24] Concerning Charles Boivin and his two brothers, François and Guillaume, see Paul Desjardins, "Apôtres laïques des missions de la Nouvelle-France. II: Les donnés Charles et Guillaume Boivin," *Lettres du Bas-Canada* IX (1955), 220-30.

It should be noted that the institution of the *donnés* was not introduced without some discussion with the Jesuit general. As originally proposed by Lalemant, the *donnés* would take vows, wear a distinctive habit, and the whole Society of Jesus would accept responsibility for their support. That proposition was vetoed at Rome because a similar institution in India had given rise to endless financial trouble. Also, as proposed, the institution seemed to be a "third order," an organization already forbidden by St. Ignatius. Besides, as suggested, the *donnés* might well be considered a religious congregation and, as such, would be forbidden to bear arms, though Lalemant conceived of the *donnés* as a fighting force in case of need. See Rochemonteix, I, 301. Vitelleschi's letter to Lalemant, January 25, 1643. A modification of the plan, excluding the objectionable features was proposed and approved by the Jesuit general in a letter to Lalemant, dated December 25, 1644. See ibid.

Considering the nature of the *donnés*, one wonders how these pious men were recruited. In his article on the *donnés*, noted above, Côté seems to indicate that some were recruited in France. Perhaps Charles Boivin and his brothers were some of these. Others, such as the famous Pierre Boucher, went up to Huronia as young boys and simply stayed on as *donnés*, at least for a time.

Assisted by salaried French workmen[25] and, undoubtedly, a great deal of help from the Hurons, Sainte Marie arose on the broad plain beside the gently flowing Wye on the exact spot where its fantastically accurate reproduction stands today. The mission was probably not as complete on Brébeuf's arrival in 1644 as it has been here described. No contemporary documentation gives us exact dates as to when any given portion of the complex was completed. However it is certain that the whole was certainly finished before the Jesuits themselves condemned it to the flames on May 15, 1649.[26]

Returning to the events attending Jean de Brébeuf's arrival at Sainte Marie, he and Jerome Lalemant soon retired to the superior's small room where Brébeuf presented the letters appointing Father Paul Ragueneau superior of the Huron mission and, at the same time, commissioning Father Lalemant to succeed Father Vimont as superior of all the Jesuits in New France.[27] With the official business completed Father Brébeuf anxiously inquired as to how the mission was progressing. Well, perhaps it must be admitted that Lalemant's great plan of one central headquarters, whence missionaries sallied forth to various individual Indian villages on brief excursions, had not been too practical. Experience taught that living more or less permanently in the Indian villages, the system Brébeuf originally introduced, was much more practical and fruitful. Hence, seven centers had been designated, six of them ". . . with pastoral residences . . . with quite substantial

---

[25] The number of salaried workmen at Sainte Marie was never large. The largest number present at any one time was seven, in 1647 and 1648. See Jones, 365, 378. Among the workmen were some justly famous names in the subsequent history of New France, for example, Charles Le Moyne, father of the properly famous Le Moyne brothers, and Médard Chouart des Groseilliers.

[26] By far the most scholarly study of the physical features of Sainte Marie is Paul Desjardins' *La résidence de Sainte-Marie aux Hurons.*

[27] No document specifically says that Brébeuf brought these letters. But, from a lengthy letter of Lalemant's to his provincial, dated May 15, 1645, it is clear that he knew of his appointment to the new post. See *Relations*, XXVIII, 39-101. Since Brébeuf was the only Jesuit arriving in 1644, he must have brought the documents. Since Lalemant could not leave Huronia until the spring of 1645, Father Paul Ragueneau, very considerately, stayed at Ossossané until Lalemant left Sainte Marie.

chapels, each with a bell.[28] Missionaries assigned to each center lived there most of the year, returning to Sainte Marie for only short periods of rest or to make a retreat. Though the number of conversions had increased and Christians were less subject to ridicule, still Iroquois raids and seasons of famine kept the number of Christians at a rather low level in spite of the heroic zeal of dedicated missionaries.

By far the greatest obstacle to the Christianization of the Hurons was ". . . the fury of the Iroquois enemy . . ." These demons closed the route to Quebec, destroying trade and regularly slaughtering the poor Hurons even in their villages. If France did not ". . . soon make an extraordinary effort to overthrow this enemy . . . ," the Huron nation would inevitably be destroyed.[29]

And what would become Jean de Brébeuf's particular arena of apostolic labor now that he was at last free to be an active missionary again? He would replace Father Pierre Pijart who, until his departure during the summer of 1644, had been the apostle of the five Huron villages in the vicinity of Sainte Marie. The Ataronchronons, residents of these villages, comprised the least numerous of the four Huron clans.[30] St. François Xavier, lying about five miles almost due south of Sainte Marie, was on a bend of the Wye River and easily reached by water. Ste. Anne, some two miles southeast of Sainte Marie, could be reached only by walking over the rolling hills. Three miles southeast of Ste. Anne was the village of St. Denis. About four miles further eastward and a little north one came to the village of St. Jean. Trudging overland

[28] Ibid., XXIX, 257, 259. The "churches" were: La Conception at Ossossané, St. Joseph at Teanaustayé, St. Michel at Scanonaenrot, St. Ignace at Tahententaron, St. Jean Baptiste at Cahiagué, and St. Esprit among the Nipissings which had no permanent location for those natives were still nomads. The seventh center was, of course, Sainte Marie itself.

[29] Ibid., XXVIII, 59.

[30] See Jones, 447, who points out that the Ataronchronons were really not a distinct Huron clan but ". . . a congeries of other Huron clans, who, in the latter years of Huronia's existence, had, in small detachments, moved nearer to Fort Ste. Marie on the Wye, and had occupied the country mainly north of Mud Lake, whence they derived their name of People who dwelt beyond the fens."

from St. Denis to St. Jean,[31] Father Brébeuf may have often crossed the site of his martyrdom. As yet no Huron village existed there.

At last, after his years of absence, Jean de Brébeuf resumed his missionary labors among the Hurons. His soul was again visited by mystical experiences. In his private spiritual notes he recorded:

October 8, 1644. In the chapel of the Blessed Virgin Mary among the Hurons, in the evening, during prayers before supper, I seemed to behold spots of red or purple blood staining the cassocks of each of our men as well as myself. No one was exempted. While admiring the sight, it crossed my mind that all of us were covered with justice as though by a blood-stained cloth.[32]

Making the rounds of the villages under his charge, Jean de Brébeuf sensed a vastly different spirit among the Hurons than that which existed when he had gone down to Sillery in 1641. The Christians, now solidly grounded in their religion, practiced their faith openly, boldly condemning practices contrary to Christian morality. Pagans still outnumbered the Christians, but they were less hostile to the missionaries. Many, however, still firmly believed that the numerous misfortunes that were afflicting the Huron nation had their origins in the powerful sorceries conjured by the Blackrobes.

Numerous Huron infidels insisted that Christianity sowed the seeds of the eventual total destruction of the nation. Since the arrival of the missionaries hundreds of people had fallen victim to diseases previously never known. And, sad but true, Christian families were more cruelly afflicted than the infidels.[33] Many times since the Jesuits arrived famine stalked the land once so fertile.[34] These misfortunes so depleted the military strength of the Hurons that there was serious doubt whether an invasion in

[31] Jones locates these five villages as follows: St. François Xavier, lot 93, concession II, Tiny township, Simcoe county, Ontario; Ste. Anne, lot 9, concession III, Tay township; St. Denis, lot 3, concession V, Tay township; St. Jean, lot 6, concession X, Tay township; St. Louis, lot 11, concession VI, Tay township. See his tabulated list of Huron sites, 262-64.

[32] Latourelle, Etude sur . . . Brébeuf, II, 233. Father Brébeuf must have used the word "justice" here in the technically theological sense of sanctitas et justitia, that is, those whose souls are imbued with sanctifying grace whereby they became "sons of God and heirs of heaven."

[33] Relations, XXVIII, 41.

[34] Ibid., XXVII, 65.

strength by the Iroquois could be repelled. Besides, in various skirmishes with the dread foe units of Christian Hurons seemed to be consistently defeated.[35] Furthermore, many Huron captains complained bitterly that the French refused to furnish them harquebuses while the Dutch and English supplied the Iroquois with those powerful weapons in increasing numbers.[36] Given such obvious uneven odds in firepower and military strength, unless the French arranged some sort of lasting peace soon, the Hurons would be defeated so completely that they would simply cease to exist as a separate nation.

During the late summer of 1645 the Hurons began to hope that the French actually would take positive steps to repel the Iroquois or at least contain them within their own country, opening the trade route to Three Rivers for the Hurons. Early in August 1645, the military detachment sent to Sainte Marie the previous year started back to Three Rivers in a flotilla of sixty canoes ". . . laden with French, with Indians and with furs."[37] Reaching Three Rivers, the Hurons discovered a peace parley in progress involving Governor Montmagny, the Mohawks, and the Algonkins. The timely arrival of the Hurons completed the council brought about by the diplomacy of the governor. In the summer of 1644 when a band of Hurons, with a few Algonkins, captured three Iroquois on the shores of the St. Lawrence, one was given to the Algonkins while two others were awarded to the Hurons who took them to Three Rivers with every intention of torturing them to death. Hastily summoned from Quebec, the governor with great difficulty persuaded the Algonkins and Hurons to surrender the prisoners through whom he hoped to arrange a peace parley.[38] Shortly after May 18, 1645, the governor sent one Iroquois, laden with presents, back to the Five Nations with orders to inform his people that the other captives would be freed ". . . to smooth the earth and to bring about universal peace among all nations . . ."[39] That considerate treatment bore fruit. On

[35] Ibid., XXVIII, 43.
[36] Ibid., XXVII, 71.
[37] Ibid., 277. Among the French were Father Jerome Lalemant, bound for Quebec and his new responsibility, and Brother Dominique Scot who came down for reasons of health.
[38] Ibid., XXVI, 57-61.
[39] Ibid., XXVII, 245.

July 5, 1645, the erstwhile Iroquois prisoner ". . . made his appearance at Three Rivers, accompanied by two men of note among those people . . ."[40]

Peace negotiations began at Three Rivers on July 5, 1645, in the presence of Governor Montmagny, Father Barthélemy Vimont, and Father Paul Le Jeune as well as a concourse of Algonkins, Montagnais, Attikamegues from the upper St. Maurice River valley, a few Hurons, and a number of French, including among them interpreters versed in the languages of these tribes.[41] In the strikingly picturesque language employed by all Indians on such formal occasions, each group offered presents, expressing their grievances and stating the conditions required before they would negotiate a peace. The council had been in session for two months when the Huron flotilla arrived on September 10, 1645.[42] On September 23, at a final dramatic meeting, peace seemed assured when the leader of the Iroquois delegation thus addressed the governor: "Onontio, you have dispersed the clouds; the air is serene, the sky shows clearly; the sun is bright. I see no more trouble; peace has made everything calm; my heart is at rest; I go away happy."[43]

The flowery speeches, the feasting, and all the outward signs of a stable peace were in evidence at the end of the meeting, but how much of all of it was honest diplomacy and how much the most devious chicanery? When the leader of the Iroquois delegates addressed the assembly he had asserted: "I am the mouth of the whole of my country; you are listening to all of the Iroquois, in hearing my voice."[44] Well, perhaps, but, if so, why were there no representatives from the four other cantons, the Oneida, the Onondaga, the Cayuga, and the Seneca? Did these few Mohawks really have authority to speak for the Five Nations as a whole? And was it not strange that the Iroquois canton farthest removed from the Huron country was the only Iroquois clan to send representatives? Be that as it may, some hope of peace was better than nothing. Hence, hostages were at least exchanged and

[40] Ibid., 247. The leader of the delegates was named Le Corchet, the Hook, by the French.

[41] Ibid., 251, 253.

[42] Ibid., 279.

[43] Ibid., 303.

[44] Ibid., 253.

the ambassadors from each of the nations present went off home to arrange, hopefully, tribal agreement to the terms of peace agreed upon at Three Rivers.

Unknown to the French allies, a private agreement with the Iroquois ambassadors, one smacking of treachery, sowed the seeds of profound discontent before the meeting had dispersed. At a secret meeting between the governor and the Mohawks, the leader of that delegation frankly declared that the price of peace for the French and the Hurons was their abandonment of the Algonkins to the good pleasure of the Iroquois. Since the Algonkins controlled the Ottawa River their destruction at the hands of the Iroquois clearly meant their eventual monopoly of the Huron trade. At first the governor declined, but, when he understood that this concession was the price of peace, even a temporary one, he consulted with Vimont and Le Jeune, seeking advice. Apparently the three Frenchmen proposed a compromise. Distinguishing between Christian and pagan Algonkins, the governor informed the Iroquois that the French would agree to no peace which did not include all Christians. But, ". . . as for the latter, [that is, the pagans,] they themselves are the masters of their own actions, nor are they united with us like the others."[45] Even if the Iroquois would agree to such a fantastic declaration, how were they to distinguish Christians from pagans? Differentiating a Huron from an Algonkin was simple enough. But how distinguish a Christian Algonkin from a pagan?

A secret of such moment could hardly be kept for long; nor was it. A Huron named Tandihetsi, leaving the council meeting with the three Mohawk ambassadors, went with them as far as Fort Richelieu. On the way the Mohawks

. . . told him the secret of their country, to wit, that no peace was desired with the Algonkins, but it was desired with the Hurons and the French; that

[45] Ibid., XXVIII, 151. The objective truth of this incident cannot be questioned. It was reported by Father Jerome Lalemant who, though present at Three Rivers during the last days of the peace negotiations, was unaware of what had been done until January of 1646. He immediately asked Governor Montmagny whether the story was true. Then Montmagny, in the presence of Father Jean de Quen, revealed the whole matter. Profoundly shocked, Lalemant recorded the exact details of the affair in the house diary, writing it in Latin. He closed his account of the affair by saying: "What was surprising therein was that our Fathers sent us no word of all that." *Journal des Jésuites*, 27-28.

the French had consented thereto, and that consequently nothing but the opportunity was now awaited for exterminating the Algonkins, and that three hundred Mohawks could certainly come by the middle of February for the execution of this plan.[46]

Tandihetsi parted company with the Mohawks at Fort Richelieu and went on to Montreal where he reported his news to the Algonkins. Then, and rather belatedly, Jacques Leneuf de la Potherie, governor of Three Rivers, summoned the Algonkins to a council at which he ". . . declared to them the whole matter, to the end that they should look to their affairs."[47] No more short-sighted concession could have been granted. The Ottawa, who controlled the river highway to Huronia, were of Algonkin stock. Now, by agreement with the French, the Mohawks were at liberty to attack them and infest the route the French Jesuits must take to reach Sainte Marie.

As far as the Hurons in their homeland were concerned the peace treaty had little effect. The fur flotilla of 1645 returned safely bringing French wares ". . . of which . . . they had seen themselves robbed, during five or six years past, by hostile Iroquois, who were rendering that commerce impossible, or, at least, so perilous that it cost life and martyrdoms of fire [to] most of those who fell into their hands."[48] Nor did the four Iroquois cantons nearest the Hurons end their incursions since, as Father Paul Ragueneau reported on May 1, 1646, ". . . it is only the fifth [Iroquois canton], the most distant from here, which has entered into the treaty of peace that began last year."[49]

While the governor held council at Three Rivers, Jean de Brébeuf was quietly engaged in making his annual retreat at Sainte Marie. On Friday, August 18, 1645, with the consent of his superior, Father Paul Ragueneau, Brébeuf pronounced privately the following vow:

During the Exercises of the year 1645, August 18. Every day from now on at the time of communion, with the consent of the superior, I will vow that I will do whatever I shall know to be for the greater glory of God and for His greater service. The conditions of this vow are twofold: 1) I, myself,

[46] *Relations*, XXVIII, 149.
[47] Ibid.
[48] Ibid., XXIX, 247.
[49] Ibid., 249.

when the matter appears properly, clearly and without doubt, will judge a thing to be for the greater glory of God; 2) if there appears some doubt, I shall consult the superior or the spiritual father.

As to the declaration of this vow, note the following: 1) I vow that whatever is of precept, so that it would be a mortal sin according to the precept, may be also a sacrilege, by force of the vow; however, should it be a venial sin according to precept, let it remain a venial sin according to the vow. 2) In a matter that is only of counsel and not of precept, yet very important, and which might work exceedingly to the glory of God, I shall be held to accomplish this matter under the penalty of mortal sin; but in a matter not too important, I shall not be held, except under venial sin. 3) So that I may be held under venial sin by force of my vow in a matter not notably important, it must be clearly and certainly evident to me, and with no doubt, that that matter may be to the greater glory of God, whether I myself judge it to be so from the divine law, from the "election" in the Spiritual Exercises, from the dictates of reason, from the grace of God, or whether the superior or spiritual father judge the matter to be such.[50]

Jean de Brébeuf's purpose seems clear enough. Obliging himself, in every thought and action, to seek always the greater glory of God was a means of increasing to the ultimate his union with God. How he observed the vow in practice, as certainly he did, remains a matter between himself and God. We are dealing here with a "country" which most poor mortals will never explore this side of heaven. Thomas Merton, in his foreword to William Johnston's commentary on *The Mysticism of the Cloud of Unknowing*, remarks:

One of the chief problems of mystical theology is to account for a loving, unitive and supernatural love of God that is beyond concepts, and to do so in language that does not in one way or another become completely misleading. The mystical theologian faces the problem of saying what cannot really be said . . . Mystical theology is negative in the sense that every positive statement is immediately qualified with: "but that is not it."[51]

[50] Latourelle, *Etude sur . . . Brébeuf*, II, 217-19. It should, perhaps, be explained that in using the word "precept," Father Brébeuf refers to the Ten Commandments. By the word "counsel," he refers to the practice of virtue, such, for example, as found expressed in the beatitudes. Employing the term "sacrilege," Brébeuf meant profanation of a sacred person, himself. Commenting on Father Brébeuf's pronouncing the vow, Latourelle remarks: "This vow, binding one to perform always and in every action that which is most pleasing to God is not uncommon among those called to the level of mysticism. Several others in New France are known to have similarly bound themselves, e.g. Father Chaumonot, Mother Catherine of St. Augustine, and Mère Marie de l'Incarnation." Ibid., 218.

[51] William Johnston, *The Mysticism of the Cloud of Unknowing*, x-xi.

The casual observer may, perhaps, question the prudence of such a vow, or how, practically, one might observe it. It can, however, hardly be doubted that Jean de Brébeuf sought, by means of the vow, so to strengthen his intimate union with God that he could say, as St. Paul said to the Galatians 2:20: "And I live, now not I; but Christ liveth in me."

Completing his retreat, Father Brébeuf was again assigned to minister to the Huron villages in the neighborhood of Sainte Marie. In the early fall of 1645, when the Hurons came back from Three Rivers, all the Jesuits at Sainte Marie were astonished at finding Father Bressani among those returning, and with him Father Antoine Poncet de La Rivière back from Quebec after an absence of five years.[52] Undaunted by the horrible tortures inflicted upon him by the Iroquois in the summer of 1644 Father Bressani came up, determined to dedicate himself to the conversion of the Hurons. Though unable, as yet, to speak the Huron language fluently, his very presence was of inestimable value. His mangled hands and scarred features trumpeted his heroic adherence to the faith he wished to impart to the Hurons. As Father Paul Ragueneau wrote in the *Relation* of 1645-1646, "The cruelties which some Hurons who escaped saw him suffer among the Iroquois, and his mutilated hands, the fingers having been cut off, have rendered him a better preacher than we, since the time of his arrival and have served more than all our tongues to give a better conception than ever to our Huron Christians of the truths of our faith."[53]

And with what holy envy Jean de Brébeuf must have beheld that scarred victim! The great, gaunt Echon had longed for martyrdom since his first day in New France, now twenty years behind him. And here before him was Francesco Bressani, two decades his junior who had as yet to spend even a year as a missionary. Still he bore the marks of trial by soul-rending suffering which Brébeuf prayed might be his own glorious prize. Well, let him be patient; his time was coming, and not too long hence for the Iroquois were becoming bolder every day.

In the spring of 1646 a band of Iroquois raided a frontier Huron village at dawn and captured a company of women just going

[52] *Relations,* XXX, 69.
[53] Ibid.

off to work in their fields. The enemy accomplished his work so quickly that ". . . two hundred men in arms who ran up at their first cries, could not arrive soon enough to save one of them . . ."[54] Toward the end of the summer, when a Huron army encountered a strong Iroquois force, the latter asked for a parley. One of the Iroquois, a former Huron captive, convinced a portion of the Hurons that treachery had been done to them and their Algonkin friends at Three Rivers in the fall of 1645. Whereupon, portions of the Huron force retreated while the rest were defeated. "Some were massacred on the spot, and others dragged into captivity, most having found their safety only in flight."[55] In daring retaliation a Huron force undertook a twenty-day march to the country of the Seneca where in dead of night they successfully attacked a village, killing many, put the place to the torch, and struck terror into the hearts of the remainder.[56] Thenceforth, none put any faith in the treaty made at Three Rivers in 1645.

As the danger to the nation from the Iroquois grew, the pagan Hurons increased their opposition to the missionaries. Instead of reiterating the accusation of sorcery, the pagans employed a new tactic, purportedly refuting the principles taught by Christianity. A rumor was circulated maintaining that what the Jesuits taught about heaven and hell was pure fiction. An Algonkin, the story went, revealed that he personally knew that souls were immortal, indeed, but that after death they received new, vigorous bodies and dwelt in a most blissful country.[57] A tale was circulated of the apparition of a phantom of prodigious size. He scoffed at the Christian doctrine concerning life after death, assuring his hearers that the place of torture, taught by the missionaries, was a cruel device employed to frighten the Indians.[58] An even more effective falsehood was circulated by the pagans. They claimed that a Christian woman, buried by the Jesuits in their cemetery, had risen from the dead purposely to refute the teachings of the missionaries. Heaven, she claimed, was a place where the French

[54] Ibid., XXIX, 249.
[55] Ibid., 251.
[56] The Seneca dwelt along the western shore of Seneca Lake in what is now upstate New York. The journey of twenty days made by the Hurons meant a walk of well over four hundred miles.
[57] Ibid., XXX, 27.
[58] Ibid.

welcome Indian Christians with cruelties but the Indians who reject Christianity go ". . . after this life into a place of delights where everything good abounds and whence all evil is banished."[59]

Nonetheless, the missionaries enjoyed great consolations, even from unexpected sources. Late in the fall of 1645 Jean de Brébeuf was dispatched northward to seek out a small band of Hurons settled in a ". . . retired country, surrounded on all sides by lakes, ponds and rivers which made this place inaccessible to the enemy."[60] That small handful of Hurons had fled their homeland, taking refuge among the Algonkins, hoping to escape the incursions of the Iroquois. Somehow, a lone Christian family among these refugees sought the ministrations of a missionary. Accompanied by a young Frenchman, Brébeuf paddled northward for five or six days ". . . to a place named Tangouen . . ."[61] bringing the consolations of religion to that devout family. The head of the family could not moderate his joy beholding his poor cabin become the house of God. So grateful were these simple people that they piously importuned Father Brébeuf continuously, hardly allowing him any repose. The great Echon spent several days with that devoted little group, hidden away in their fastness, departing only when the threat of heavy ice forming on the waterways ". . . placed him in danger of dying from both hunger and cold, and of perishing in the lakes and rivers which they had to cross."[62]

Returned to his pastoral work in the villages near Sainte Marie, Brébeuf sensed a widespread apprehension among the Hurons. Within the nation converts to Christianity were becoming so numerous that the pagans feared they would soon be obliged to give up public practice of their time-honored sorceries wherein, they felt, lay safety for the country. When the pagan captains in the village most addicted to the ancient practices of sorcery failed to attract many participants, they offered a compromise. "They

[59] Ibid., 29.

[60] Ibid., 87.

[61] Ibid.

[62] Ibid., 89. Jones, 166, thinks that the probable location of this group of Hurons was in the vicinity of Wanapitei Lake, roughly forty miles north of Sudbury, Ontario. To reach the area by canoe, it would be necessary to paddle up Georgian Bay to the French River and breast the current of the French to the mouth of the Wanapitei River which flows out of the lake of the same name. By water, the voyage would be in the neighborhood of two hundred miles.

traversed the streets, shouting in loud voices that pity be taken
on a country which is going to ruin because old customs are neglected; that the faith is too rigorous, in never granting dispensa-
tions from its laws; and that at least people may cease for one
night and one day to perform Christian services."[63] One zealous
Christian launched a counter crusade. Following the captains
from cabin to cabin he loudly announced

. . . the threats of God against sinners and their crimes with an eloquence
and force of argument so urgent that all the Christians remained in their
duty; and even several infidels did so, admiring so holy a freedom in a private individual, who had, of himself, no authority except that which his love
for the faith and his zeal caused him to assume.[64]

Some of the pagans attacked the rising Christian tide with devious threats. A captain with exalted standing among the sorcerers attempted to force Christian women to participate in lewd
dances held to be a particularly effective protection for the country. Approaching a newly converted woman, previously a star
performer, he warned that unless she returned to her former practices she would be secretly killed and her death attributed to Iroquois raiders.[65] Her demise, thus falsely reported, might well set
off a conflagration bringing a disastrous end to the whole nation.
"They will oblige me," the woman replied, "by making me die for
so good a cause [that is, avoiding offending God]; and you oblige
me by warning me of it as a friend; for now I shall think, with
more truth than ever, that I am dead to the world and that I must
live to God alone."[66]

The Christians, too, planned for the future of the nation. Understanding that the infidel captains were as much concerned
about maintaining their positions of authority as they were in
"saving the nation," the Christians at the mission of St. Ignace
suggested a compromise of their own. If the captains would cease
harassing the Christians, especially those not yet having ". . .
sufficient firmness in it . . . ,"[67] the Christians would provide the
captains with rich presents. But the missionaries wisely vetoed

[63] *Relations*, XXIX, 273.
[64] Ibid., 275.
[65] Ibid., XXX, 23.
[66] Ibid., 23, 25.
[67] Ibid., XXIX, 271.

the proposal, pointing out that ". . . the infidels may thence take occasion to annoy the Christians in the hope of drawing from them similar presents."[68]

During the early months of 1646 the pagans were aroused to a new intensity of hatred for the Christians. Suddenly the people were afflicted with an epidemic of severe dysentery. Nor were the missionaries spared. Father Leonard Garreau, off evangelizing the Nipissings, fell victim, and so seriously that Father Claude Pijart rushed him back home to Sainte Marie. There, poor Garreau was so prostrated that his death was momentarily expected. In fact, they had already made his coffin. But ". . . it pleased our Lord to restore him to us, as if brought again to life . . ."[69]

Thoroughly frightened at the prospect of another decimating epidemic, such as had been suffered some years before, the pagan Hurons at the mission of St. Joseph performed a solemnity known as "universal madness," hoping to ward off the threatening calamity. Custom permitted everyone to act in any manner he chose, the madder the better. While this bedlam progressed, a pagan attacked Father Charles Garnier with a hatchet, intent on killing him. The blow was deflected in time by a courageous Christian who was wounded, but not seriously.[70]

Unrest within the Huron nation was compounded by the continued belligerence by various war parties of the Iroquois with whom the Hurons believed they had arranged a permanent peace at Three Rivers during the last days of September 1645. In fact, however, only the Mohawks sought peace; nor could they persuade the four other members of the Iroquois confederacy to join them in their quest for peace. Even for the Mohawks the peace proposal implied conditions far different than either the French or the Hurons or any of their Indian allies understood. The Mohawks sought to inject themselves as middlemen between the French and all other Indian nations. This point had been made clear by the Mohawk spokesman at the parley at Three Rivers in the summer of 1645, when he urged the Hurons ". . . to make haste to speak, not to be bashful, like women; and after taking the resolution to go to the Iroquois country, to pass by that of the

---

[68] Ibid.
[69] Ibid., XXX, 125.
[70] Ibid., 101.

Algonkins and the French."[71] The Mohawk spokesman also encouraged the Algonkins to hunt diligently so that the Iroquois would benefit by their skill in collecting beaver pelts. The primary objective of the parley of 1645, as far as the Mohawks were concerned, had been to arrange a commercial treaty. And it was this they believed themselves to have consummated. If diplomacy failed, the only alternative would be complete annihilation of the Hurons in order to gain control of the trade in peltries with the western nations whence the Hurons were already obtaining their supply of furs.

But the bartering season of 1646 dashed Iroquois hopes of gaining control of the trade by treaty. That summer a flotilla of eighty Huron canoes reached Montreal unmolested.[72] The number of peltries offered for trade was so great that all the available European goods were sold and the Indians took back a dozen bales of skins because the French had nothing more to offer in exchange for them.[73] Of that richest fur flotilla the Iroquois procured not even one single pelt. In their opinion, then, the Hurons had flagrantly violated the terms of the treaty of 1645.[74] Thenceforth, the die was cast. The Iroquois determined that the Huron nation must die and with it the French missionaries because they were destroying the most sacred traditions of Indian culture, their precious religious practices. To the Iroquois ". . . there is nothing . . . so repulsive at the beginning as our doctrine, which seems to exterminate everything that men hold most dear . . ."[75]

The Hurons, however, were serenely unaware that their very economic success in the summer of 1646 had sealed their fate. The news they brought home seemed to confirm the belief that the Iroquois sincerely intended to respect the peace. They reported that the incredibly courageous Father Isaac Jogues, already a victim of Iroquois cruelty, had gone back to the country of the Five Nations in the early summer of 1646 to arrange final confirmation of the peace negotiations begun the year before.

[71] Ibid., XXVII, 263.
[72] Ibid., XXVIII, 141.
[73] Ibid., 231. The total value of this one shipment of furs was 320,000 *livres*. In New France a *livre* was worth twenty *sous* or about the present value of the French *franc*. See Lanctôt, *History of Canada*, I, 322.
[74] Hunt, *Wars of the Iroquois*, 84.
[75] *Relations*, XXIX, 47-49.

After a seven-day parley, June 10 to 16, 1646, the captains of the Mohawks sealed the peace with presents and accepted gifts from Jogues and his companion, Jean Bourdon, acting governor of Three Rivers.[76] By June 27, 1646, Isaac Jogues was back, reporting complete success as well as the fact that the Iroquois had invited him to open a mission among them. Even as the Hurons paddled away from Montreal bound for home Isaac Jogues was about to depart on his return journey to the Five Nations, delighted to have been selected to be the first apostle among those people. Joining a group of Iroquois, Jogues, and his lay companion, Jean de La Lande,[77] left Three Rivers on September 24, 1646, half suspecting the fate awaiting them.

The last news the French received from Isaac Jogues bode no good for him and Jean de La Lande. At the site of Fort Richelieu the Iroquois traveling with the two Frenchmen abandoned them. Undaunted, Jogues and his companion pushed on until about the middle of October they reached Ossernenon, on a high bluff overlooking the Mohawk River. Instead of a gracious reception the Indians promptly made captives of the two Frenchmen, stripped them naked, and beat them unmercifully, screaming at them: "You will die tomorrow; be not astonished. But we will not burn you; have courage; we will strike you with the hatchet and will set your heads on palings . . . so that when we capture your brothers they may still see you."[78] On the evening of October 18, 1646, as he left a cabin, Isaac Jogues sank under the blow of a hatchet which an Indian buried in his head. Early the next morning Jean de La Lande suffered the same fate. The heads of the victims were severed from the bodies and impaled on the town's ramparts.[79] Their bodies were hurled into the quietly flowing waters of the Mohawk River.

---

[76] Ibid., 47-61.

[77] Jean de La Lande was born in France, probably at Dieppe, but the date of his birth is not certainly known. He assuredly was in New France by 1642. That year on December 14 when the effects of Jean Nicolet were up for auction, La Lande purchased two books. When he became a *donné* does not appear, but such was his status when he went to the Iroquois country with Isaac Jogues. He was martyred there on October 18 or 19, 1646.

[78] Ibid., XXXI, 117.

[79] Ibid.

It was not until June 4, 1647, that the French knew the fate of Isaac Jogues. Then they learned it from a young Huron captive of the Iroquois who escaped and brought the sad tidings to Father Jacques Buteux at Three Rivers. All through the spring of 1647 constant reports of Iroquois raids along the St. Lawrence had filtered in to the French settlements. But when the martyrdom of Father Isaac Jogues was known for certain, the French knew that the Iroquois had dug up the hatchet. The illusory peace was at an end. War to the death against the Hurons began with the martyrdom of Isaac Jogues.

At the return of the highly successful fur flotilla of 1646, the Huron nation settled back into its normal fall activities, harvesting the corn, fishing, hunting, and preparing for the coming winter. Father Brébeuf began his fourth year of caring for the villages near Sainte Marie, visiting each ". . . continually with great fatigue."[80] Beginning his fifty-fourth year, Jean de Brébeuf was feeling his age and the effects of the rugged, abstemious life he had led. But, at last, after so many seemingly fruitless years, the Hurons were showing clear indications of accepting Christianity in increasingly larger numbers. He was deeply consoled witnessing the ". . . fervor of these good neophytes, and a spirit of faith in them that savors naught of barbarism, and causes us to bless God's mercies which spread so abundantly from day to day, to the outer confines of the new world."[81] Indeed the Hurons and the missionaries stood in grave need of the mercy of God for they were all about to be tried by fire and sword.

In the dead of winter at the beginning of 1647 Onondaga braves, appearing on the Huron frontier, ". . . were pursued by a troop of Huron warriors, who were victorious; the chief of the enemies was killed on the spot, others were taken prisoners, and the remainder put to flight."[82] Most of the captives died under torture, but Annenraes, a renowned chief of the Onondaga, was spared and allowed to return home loaded with presents in the hope that ". . . this man, who had great authority among the Onondaga . . ."[83] might arrange peace between his people and

[80] Ibid., XXXIII, 143.
[81] Ibid., 69.
[82] Ibid., 117.
[83] Ibid., 119.

the Hurons. Perhaps adroit diplomacy could divide the strength of the united Five Nations, aiding the Hurons to avert war. Throughout the spring and summer of 1647 the Hurons and Onondaga exchanged ambassadors with apparent friendship.[84] In the meantime the Hurons added one more string to their bow.

The Susquehannah, long-time allies of the Hurons, might be induced to lend military aid to embattled Huronia.[85] An embassy headed by Charles Ondaaiondiont, an exemplary Christian, was dispatched to these friends of the Hurons beseeching help against the terrible Iroquois. The Susquehannah agreed to send representatives to the Iroquois, begging them to lay down their arms and think of lasting peace, ". . . which would not hinder the trade of all these countries with one another."[86]

True to their promise, the Susquehannah sent an embassy to the Onondaga to whom they gave presents, seeking to arrange a peace. If that diplomatic maneuver succeeded, the Mohawks, most warlike of the Five Nations, would be encircled and greatly weakened. To destroy that possibility, the Mohawks, in January 1648, treacherously fell upon the Huron embassy to Onondaga and slaughtered it.[87] Simultaneously the Mohawks induced the Seneca, their faithful allies, to concentrate a large force in the country of the Neutrals. Not only did the treacherous murder of the Huron ambassadors change the whole situation, but the deployment of troops arranged by the Mohawks cut off any opportunity for the Susquehannah warriors to contribute military forces to the now truly beleaguered Hurons.[88]

During their desperate diplomatic maneuvering, nature itself had been unkind to the Hurons. Crop failures for two successive years brought back the specter of famine, as it did not too many years before. Sick and hungry, hundreds of Hurons flocked to Sainte Marie begging aid in their desperate need. Then it was

[84] Ibid., 119, 121.

[85] Ibid., 129-33. Ragueneau noted that the Susquehannah ". . . speak the Huron language and have always been friends of our Hurons." This tribe is thought to have been of kindred blood with the Hurons. They inhabited the headwaters of the Chesapeake Bay, and they would, if hostile, threaten the rear of the Five Nations.

[86] Ibid., 131.

[87] Ibid., 125, 127. That treachery so shamed the Onondaga hostage, Scandacuati, that he killed himself.

[88] Hunt, *Wars of the Iroquois*, 90.

that the agricultural activity of the lay assistants of the Jesuits proved its value. In his *Relation* of 1647-1648 Father Paul Ragueneau wrote:

> This house is a resort for the whole country . ; . During the past year we have reckoned over three thousand persons to whom we have given shelter . . . and, as a rule, three meals to each one . . . in a strange country, we feed those who themselves should supply us with the necessities of life.[89]

But practicing the corporal works of mercy, even on so massive a scale, failed to win over a hard core of pagans.

Fairly widespread illness in the nation, scarcity of food, and constant threats of a massive Iroquois invasion, all conspired to arouse the wrath of pagan Hurons against the missionaries. During April 1648, six Huron captains, all pagans, met at a village five leagues from Sainte Marie. The country, they undoubtedly agreed, was in the gravest danger and all because the ancient practices propitiating the nation's guiding spirits were not only ignored by so many Christians but positively denounced by the French missionaries. The anger of these offended spirits must be soothed, and in what better manner than to kill a Frenchman as a sign that the pagans were attacking ". . . Jesus Christ in the person of those who adore him."[90] Two despicable brothers agreed to take on the task; they would prowl about Sainte Marie and kill the first Frenchman whom they might meet unattended. On the evening of April 28, 1648, when the day's work was done, Jacques Douart, a young *donné* of twenty-two, was sauntering along a short distance from the palisades when the two villains buried a hatchet in his head killing him instantly.[91] The following day Christians from the neighboring villages flocked to Sainte Marie protesting the outrage. "This murder," they told the missionaries, "teaches us that there is a conspiracy against you."[92] Who could guess what the enraged pagans might do next?

The dastardly murder violently shook the whole Huron nation as much by its malice as because the deed might seriously endanger relations with the French at the very moment when the Hurons could ill afford to lose the friendship of their strongest

[89] *Relations*, XXXIII, 77.
[90] Ibid., 231.
[91] Ibid., 229.
[92] Ibid., 231.

ally. Wherefore, ". . . the most notable persons . . . were summoned to a meeting on the matter."[93] Those who instigated the crime ". . . showed themselves in their true colors as enemies of the Faith, saying that the doors of their villages should be closed to us [the Jesuits], and that we should be driven from the country. Some even added that all the Christians should be banished from it, and their number be prevented from increasing."[94]

The Christians declared that the instigators of the murder were the ones ". . . who desire to ruin the country; doubtless they receive some secret reward from our enemies for betraying us."[95]

After three days of endless oratory the assembly offered presents, customary on such occasions, to the "family" of the murdered man. Addressing Father Ragueneau on behalf of the whole nation, a universally respected elder statesman averred:

My brother, . . . here are all the nations assembled . . . We are now but a handful of people; you alone support this country, and bear it in your hand . . . Have pity on us . . . We come here to weep for our loss, as much as for yours . . . The blow that has fallen on your nephew has cut the bond [holding the nation together]. My brother, have pity on this country. You alone can restore life to it . . . Against him who struck this blow shall our indignation be turned, for you we shall never have aught but love.[96]

In the end the violent death of Jacques Douart brought the missionaries and the whole Huron nation closer together than they had ever been. Closing his account of the incident, Father Ragueneau concluded: ". . . in it we observed God's loving providence for us, and for our Church, such a fatherly protection and such powerful guidance that we see very well how true is the saying of the Scriptures: *Dicite justo quoniam bene.*"[97]

Despite internal dissension and constant rumors of hostile war parties on their frontiers, the Hurons mustered a trading flotilla for departure in the early days of June 1648. Father Francesco Bressani accompanied the fleet, carrying with him two hundred fifty Huron braves. Among the letters he brought down to Quebec was Father Jean de Brébeuf's official report to the Jesuit

[93] Ibid.
[94] Ibid.
[95] Ibid., 233.
[96] Ibid., 235-39.
[97] Ibid., 249. The scriptural quotation is taken from Isaias 3:10. In English it reads: "Say to the just man that it is well."

general concerning the state of the Huron mission. This last communication from the martyr's hands reads:

I consider it wholly superfluous for me to write to your Paternity regarding the state of the Huron mission since I am sure that the Reverend Paul Ragueneau, our superior, will have written about it at great length. The dispositions of our people in the house could hardly be better. Profound peace, unity, and gentleness abound among them and our lay associates. This may be attributed to the effort of each one striving for piety, virtue, and perfection. Also, Christianity happily advances. Our Christians grow daily not only in numbers but also in virtue.

So many opportunities arise for promulgating the Gospel to more distant peoples that soon the faith would spread if it were not that our lack of workers restrains our desires. Wherefore, our first and most pressing petition to Reverend Father Provincial is that he send more workers to this vineyard which, more than ever before, is ready for the harvest.

The temporal status here is prosperous as the spiritual. Though last year we received no supplies at all from France, we have abundance, even superabundance. From this it can be concluded that, thanks be to God, all is well with us.

As for other matters, numerous and very grave difficulties so inhibit our labors that they seem to menace the very existence of this mission. Some of these difficulties are shared by both us and the Hurons. These are the enemies whom we call the Iroquois. They interrupt communications, paralyze commerce and devastate the country by frequent bloody raids. Other difficulties are ours alone. They arise from the animosity of certain Huron pagans. Their hatred has grown to a point where they slaughtered one of our lay helpers. They plan a similar fate for us if occasion offers. Fortunately, God has turned this last disaster to our advantage. The Huron nation made ample reparation for the murder. Thus, the faith, far from suffering any lessening, has been greatly strengthened, so true is it that to those who love God everything works together unto good. As to other difficulties, we are confident of the future for if God is for us who can be against us?

Only one thing is of prime concern to me. It is a point which the Reverend Paul Ragueneau would not wish to mention, I am sure. His modesty would prevent it and, perhaps, he should not indicate it. I fear that the papal bull, published when your Paternity was elected general, limiting superiors to a term of three years, may oblige us to change superiors. Given our situation, that would be a serious inconvenience to the mission.

In truth, the present superior, Father Paul Ragueneau, is a remarkable man in every way. There is no one here equal to him and I do not think one will arise in the future. The mission is greatly in his debt for the prudence, energy, and sweetness with which he governs. In this unique situation I consider him the only man capable of governing in the circumstances existing here. It is true that we have among us many excellent religious endowed with innumerable talents of nature and grace, but all, in my opinion, are his inferior in everything, but particularly as to the ability to govern. Besides, no one here has ever had experience as a superior.

If we must be given another superior, he should be someone already here, not someone with no experience of the country. This is why I wrote last year to Rev. Father Provincial that if it were at all possible Father Ragueneau's continuing his present office was most important to the mission. Now I suppose the die is cast and we expect letters this year announcing a change or that Father Ragueneau may continue. If the matter is still undecided, I beg your Paternity to prolong his term of office. Conditions are not always the same nor are needs the same. At the end of another three years someone else might succeed him, not perhaps so fruitfully, but certainly with less risk than now. This is the only thing I beg from your Paternity, disposed, though I am, to accept whatever happens if it be different than what I ask. The little I beseech I wish only in so far as it redounds to the greater glory of God. It is for me to propose, but God disposes. As to the rest, I ask for your Paternity's blessing.

> Jean de Brébeuf
> The Residence of Ste. M. of the Hurons
> in New France
> June 2, 1648.[98]

Jean de Brébeuf was not to receive an answer to his official report before he reaped the martyr's crown a little over ten months after he had sent his letter off to Rome. Paul Ragueneau would, indeed, stay on as superior of the Huron mission. But for only two more years. Even then Ragueneau was not removed from office, the office was removed from him. In 1650 the Huron mission and its great central house of Sainte Marie was no more.

---

[98] Latourelle, *Etude sur . . . Brébeuf*, II, 129-30. The Jesuit general to whom Brébeuf addressed his letter was Vincent Caraffa, who succeeded to the office in 1646 on the death of Mutius Vitelleschi. Brébeuf's plan for Ragueneau's continuance in office after three years stemmed from a papal brief, *Prospero felicique statui*, issued by Innocent X just previous to Caraffa's election in 1646. The brief directed that no superior should hold office more than three years. Father Ragueneau became superior of the Huron mission in 1645 and would, in obedience to Innocent X's brief, relinquish office in 1648. See Harney, *Jesuits in History*, 259.

Chapter XI

The Sounds
and Portents of Death

Jean de Brébeuf recorded the literal truth when he reported to
the Jesuit general, Vincent Caraffa, that the Iroquois were devastating the country by their frequent and bloody raids which ter-
rorized everyone. Alas, Isaac Jogues' prophecy, enunciated five
years ago in his letter to Governor Montmagny, was about to
come true.[1] Admirable strategists, the Iroquois began systematic
attacks on the Huron frontier while, at approximately the same
time, viciously attacked the Neutrals, frightening them into abject submission.

The first major attack of the Iroquois campaign fell on the
mission of St. Jean Baptiste at Cahiagué,[2] the principal town of
the Rock clan. The "old China hands" among the missionaries
felt a particular predilection for the Rock clan and their principal

[1] *Relations*, XXIV, 297. Jogues to Montmagny, June 30, 1643.

[2] Jones, 262, believes that Cahiagué was at lot 20, concession X, Oro township, Simcoe county, Ontario. This would place it almost exactly at the junction of
Highways 11 and 20 and about a mile almost due west of the town of Hawke-
stone. In his biography of Champlain, Bishop, *Champlain*, 196, holds that the village was at the present site of the town of Warminster. If Jones is correct, the
Indian village was about a mile and a half from the shores of Lake Simcoe.

town, Cahiagué. The great Samuel de Champlain had come there on August 17, 1615, with twelve armed Frenchmen to accompany the Hurons on a punitive expedition against the Iroquois. Departing thence on September 8 with five hundred Hurons he attacked, on October 10, an Onondaga town which was so well fortified that he was unable to subdue it.[3] In 1639 the Jesuits established the mission of St. Jean Baptiste at Cahiagué toward whose people they felt a special obligation because, even after twenty-two years, the Rock clan still held Champlain in admiration for his ". . . many excellent virtues . . . and in particular his chastity and continence with respect to women."[4]

During the eight years of its existence the mission of St. Jean Baptiste had but one pastor, the incomparable Father Antoine Daniel. At last, during 1647, the Rock clan, on Huronia's eastern frontier, ". . . met with so many defeats in the past years that they were compelled to leave their country, which was too much exposed to the enemy, and to withdraw into other and more populous villages, which are also more easily defended."[5] Probably it was a sad day for Antoine Daniel when he watched his rude little mission chapel dismembered at Cahiagué not far from the delightful little lake which the Hurons called Ouentaroni and we know as Lake Simcoe.[6] Perhaps more distressing to the members of the Rock clan was the inevitable fact that being assimilated into villages of other groups probably meant losing their identification as a recognizably distinct clan. As for Father Daniel, he was sent to the mission of St. Joseph at Teanaustayé, a village whose people justly deserved to be called, in the biblical meaning, a stiff-necked generation.

Probably delighted with their success, the Iroquois promptly turned on the Neutrals, a retiring people who for generations had striven to get along with everybody. During the summer of 1648 the whole of Huronia was ". . . threatened by a hostile army, . . ."[7]

---

[3] Champlain, III, 74. Bishop, *Champlain*, 203, places the village Champlain attacked ". . . within the present city of Syracuse [New York], where sluggish Onondaga Creek flows into Onondaga Lake."

[4] *Relations*, XX, 19.

[5] Ibid., XXXIII, 81.

[6] Jones, 203. He tells us that in English the Huron word "Ouentaroni" means Fish-Spearing Lake.

[7] *Relations*, XXXIII, 81.

of Iroquois numbering about three hundred warriors which, for once, was driven off by the Hurons. As they retreated the Iroquois braves poured into the country of the Neutrals, who had no quarrel with them and courteously offered hospitality. Treacherously, the Iroquois warriors divided themselves strategically among the Neutral cabins and ". . . massacred or seized all who might have resisted before the latter could perceive their evil design, because they all commenced the massacre at the same moment."[8] Those dastardly warriors killed a great many Neutrals and ". . . took away all the captives they could."[9]

In Huronia both the French and the Hurons expected that such base treachery would assuredly result in the Neutrals promptly attacking the Iroquois. But that crafty nation knew its adversary far better. In his *Relation* of 1648-1649 Father Ragueneau noted: ". . . there seems to be no stir in that direction, and they continue their neutrality. Some say that it cannot be for a long time, and that the intention of the Neutral Nation is to get back their captives peacefully and amicably, and then to seize their opportunity to avenge, in their turn, their losses."[10] If such was their plan, the Neutrals were never to have their opportunity. The rumored patience of the Neutrals would never be rewarded. Before any opportunity for revenge came their way, the Iroquois swept through the country of the Neutrals with fire and sword scattering them to the four winds.

Through the trading season of 1647 the Huron braves had stayed at home to ". . . defend their threatened country."[11] By the following season ". . . the necessity of obtaining hatchets and other French trade goods compelled them to expose themselves . . ."[12] to the danger of ambush on the route to Three Rivers as well as to the possibility of the Iroquois invading their country in their absence. Two hundred fifty Hurons ". . . led by five brave captains resolved to die or to pass through in spite of all the enemy's resistance."[13] Toward the end of June 1648, the fur flotilla set out from Huronia, having among its people a few Frenchmen and Father Francesco Bressani, sent down again to transact the mission's business. For that missionary the expedition must

[8] Ibid., 83.
[9] Ibid., 81.
[10] Ibid., 83.

[11] Ibid., 69.
[12] Ibid., XXXII, 179.
[13] Ibid.

have been a consoling one for a good half of the Hurons were ". . . Christians and Catechumens."[14] Surely to the surprise of the Hurons their large flotilla with its valuable cargo of furs encountered no opposition in the more than two-hundred-league journey until the fort at Three Rivers was almost in sight. And then the scene changed.

As was their custom, the Hurons ". . . pushed their canoes in among the rushes to put themselves in proper attire previous to showing themselves before the French, that is, they painted their faces in various colors; they greased their hair; in a word they wished to appear in orderly condition."[15] Finished with their primping, they pushed on totally unaware that all the while an Iroquois force was observing them from an ambuscade. When the Iroquois attacked the Hurons met the assault with intrepid courage. Father Bressani ". . . ran about everywhere, inspiring the Hurons with courage and watching carefully to see if anyone needed his assistance . . ."[16] Two French laymen bravely joined the melee, but ". . . stopped short, not knowing whom to strike for they could not distinguish the Iroquois from the Hurons."[17] One of them even slapped an Iroquois on the back, calling ". . . Courage, my brother! Let us fight bravely."[18] The French at the fort heard the firing of guns and rushed to help, but before they could join the fray the Iroquois fled. It was a proud Huron company which beached the canoes and paraded the Iroquois they had taken captive.

Informed of the arrival of the Hurons, Governor Montmagny hastened to Three Rivers to greet them formally and receive their "word." The first "word," accompanied by suitable presents, was a salute of honor offered the governor and all of the French; the second was a petition that the warehouse be opened for trading; and the third was a request that prices for goods be reduced.

The fourth and fifth were in thanksgiving for the trouble taken in going to teach them in their country amid so many dangers, and through so many enemies who threatened but fire and flames. They gave two presents for

[14] Ibid.
[15] Ibid.
[16] Ibid., 183.
[17] Ibid.
[18] Ibid.

that purpose because, they said, that was of much greater importance than anything else on earth. They begged us to persevere constantly, stating that the country had a great affection for a doctrine that promised a life as sweet in its delights as it was long in duration.[19]

At that moment the French, especially Father Bressani and the Jesuits present, must have been certain that the day when every Huron would be a baptized Christian was not far off.

From Three Rivers, Father Bressani went down to Quebec, reporting to the superior of all the Jesuits in New France, Jerome Lalemant. After a couple of months sojourning at Quebec, Bressani started back for Sainte Marie among the Hurons. On the homeward journey he must have sung with delight for he was bringing with him some gallant new recruits. These were: Father Jacques Bonin, Father Adrien Grélon, Father Adrien d'Aran, Father Gabriel Lalemant, and Brother Nicolas Noirclair. Jerome Lalemant remarked, as he watched these missionaries depart: "It is a great blessing to see the courage and zeal of these good Fathers . . . so great joy showed itself on their countenances that one would have said that they were all about to take possession of a crown and an empire."[20] And, in a sense, they were; at least one of them was.

[19] Ibid., 187. This was Montmagny's last official contact with the Hurons. On August 20, 1648, he was succeeded by Louis d'Ailleboust de Coulonge et d'Argentenay who had come to New France in 1643 to join Maisonneuve's colony at Montreal.

[20] Ibid. Adrien Grélon, born at Périgueux in 1617, entered the Jesuit novitiate at Bordeaux on November 5, 1637. He arrived in New France in 1647 and spent a year in the Quebec area before being sent to Huronia in 1648. He labored among the Tobacco people until 1650 and then returned to Quebec. Lack of funds obliged the Jesuits to reduce their staff by sending several missionaries back to France. Grélon was among those ordered home in the autumn of 1650. He died in France in 1697.

Jacques Bonin was born at Ploermel on September 1, 1617. At the age of sixteen he entered the Jesuit novitiate at Paris. He came to Canada in 1647 and went to Sainte Marie in 1648. He was also sent back to France in 1650. From France he was sent to the mission on Martinique where he died on November 4, 1659.

Adrien d'Aran, a native of Rouen, was born on September 9, 1615. He became a Jesuit on September 7, 1635, at Paris. Arriving at Quebec in 1646, he went to the Huron mission in 1648. When that mission was destroyed in 1650, he returned to France and spent the rest of his life at Vannes where he died on May 24, 1670.

Gabriel Lalemant was the least likely volunteer who offered himself for the mission of New France. A slight little man, plagued constantly with poor health, Gabriel was not blessed with the rugged physique of his uncle, Charles, nor the incisiveness of his uncle, Jerome, to say nothing of the endurance of his cousin, Father Antoine Poncet de La Rivière. The youngest child of Jacques Lalemant, a Parisian lawyer, Gabriel was born at Paris on October 10, 1610. Ten days after Gabriel's birth his uncle Jerome entered the Jesuit novitiate at Paris. Three years previously, his uncle Charles had entered the order's novitiate at Rouen. It was practically foreordained that Gabriel would receive his education in the Jesuit college of Clermont at Paris where, despite chronic ill health, he did so brilliantly that his family had high hopes for his future. His oldest brother, Bruno, entered the Carthusians and all of his three sisters became Carmelites at the Paris convent of that contemplative order. Gabriel entered the Jesuit novitiate at Paris on March 24, 1630, just when his uncle Charles, driven out of New France by the English, was at Paris recruiting prayers petitioning God to allow the Jesuits to return to their lost mission. When Gabriel pronounced his first vows, perhaps on March 25, 1632, the feast of the Annunciation and Jean de Brébeuf's thirty-ninth birthday, he was allowed to add a vow to devote himself to the foreign missions, which, to him, must surely have meant New France.

When Gabriel Lalemant completed his ecclesiastical studies in 1639 instead of gaining his heart's desire, he spent the next seven years doing academic work in the Jesuit colleges of France, including two years at Bourges where he held the office of prefect of studies, the equivalent of the dean of a liberal arts college, an obviously important post since he was completely responsible for the curriculum of a large academic institution. Capable he might be in the academic world, but that, to Gabriel Lalemant, was not his true vocation. Annually he renewed his vow to go on the foreign missions and, also annually, he petitioned leave to go. But with equal regularity superiors refused permission, pointing to his obvious lack of physical stamina, his recurrent ill health, and his unquestioned value as an academician. Finally in 1646 the provincial, Etienne Charlet, gave in. Perhaps the young Father Lalemant would not be able to stand the missionary life, but his uncle,

Jerome, was superior of the mission of New France at the moment and he could be trusted to ship his nephew back home if life in a raw country was too much for his delicate health.[21]

Sailing from La Rochelle on June 13 with Father Claude Quentin, Father Amable du Frétat, and Brother Pierre Masson, Gabriel Lalemant reached Quebec on September 20, 1646.[22] His uncle, Jerome, kept him two years in the Sillery area serving a sort of apprenticeship, introducing him to the Indian manner of life, and allowing him to learn something of the native languages. At last, early in August 1648, when Father Bressani left for Sainte Marie, Gabriel was allowed to go along. The voyage to Sainte Marie, trying enough for the most robust, must have been almost more than Gabriel could bear. Never having enjoyed good health, at thirty-nine the new missionary was hardly the best candidate for the sort of journey required to reach Huronia. On their arrival the newcomer and his fellow travelers were greeted with crushing news. The first Jesuit among the missionaries in Huronia had shed his blood at the hands of the Iroquois.

No Jesuit missionary among the Hurons, not even Jean de Brébeuf, had borne the heat and labors of the day as had Antoine

---

[21] Rochemonteix, II, 85-87. There is no satisfactory, complete biography of Gabriel Lalemant. Rochemonteix tells us that Gabriel was the youngest of six children, three boys and three girls. Only one, the second son, married. When Gabriel was leaving for New France, he paid a visit to his three Carmelite sisters who gave him, as a parting gift, the relics of some martyrs. After Gabriel's martyrdom, his mother, who had been widowed quite young, entered the convent and died as a nun.

[22] Amable du Frétat was born at Clermont-Ferrand in 1614. He entered the Jesuit order on August 24, 1632. He landed at Quebec on September 20, 1646. He remained in New France until October 21, 1647, when he returned to France.

Brother Pierre Masson was born in 1609. He came to New France with Gabriel Lalemant. He was a tailor by trade. Nine days after reaching Quebec he set out for Sainte Marie among the Hurons with Jean Caron, a salaried employee of the mission, and Joseph Boursier *dit* Desforges, a *donné*. After Sainte Marie was destroyed, Brother Masson returned to Quebec and labored in New France until his death at Quebec on October 18, 1695.

Joseph Boursier *dit* Desforges was born in France in 1625. When he came to Canada is unknown, but he became a *donné* in 1646 at the age of twenty-one. That year he went up to Huronia and remained there until the mission was closed. When he came back to Quebec he went to France and entered the Society of Jesus as a brother. He returned to New France in 1654 and is thought to have remained there, working as a brother, until his death in 1688.

Daniel. Save for his two-year absence, 1636 to 1638, while conducting the ill-fated seminary for little Huron boys at Quebec, Daniel had labored unceasingly with the Rock clan at Cahiagué and the neighboring villages on Huronia's southern frontier, the area most exposed to the incursions of the Iroquois. His fellow Jesuits spoke of him as the one among them who ". . . always bore his soul in his hands . . . awaiting with hope and love the blessing of the death which fell to his portion."[23] From the day the mission of St. Jean Baptiste at Cahiagué was opened in 1639 until the Rock clan abandoned the village in 1647, Antoine Daniel had devoted himself exclusively to that mission. Except for two years, 1640 and 1641, when he was aided first by Pierre Chaumonot and then by Simon Le Moyne, he ministered to the Rock clan all alone.

Considering Antoine Daniel's temperament, everyone agreed that he was surely the proper missionary for the Rock clan. He was blessed with ". . . an indefatigable care, a generous courage in enterprises, an insurmountable patience, an unalterable meekness; and with a charity which knew how to excuse everything, bear everything, and love everyone."[24]

At the closing of the mission of St. Jean Baptiste, Daniel was assigned to assume the apostolate at Teanaustayé, the mission of St. Joseph, which had been served since 1640 by Charles Garnier. The Cords who dwelt there were no strangers to Antoine Daniel. He could well remember when the Hurons at Teanaustayé heaped abuse on the missionaries, encouraging even the children to throw stones and all sorts of rubbish at them.[25] But what an astonishing change had been brought about in just a few short years. By the summer of 1648 ". . . the Faith had long sustained itself with lustre . . . the Christians were increasing in number, and still more in holiness, through the indefatigable labors of Father Antoine Daniel."[26] But then the blow fell.

The spring and early summer of 1648, the Hurons felt, introduced an era of true peace. Onondaga envoys were in Huronia; a Huron delegation was off arranging a stronger alliance with the

23 *Relations*, XXXIV, 93, 95.
24 Ibid., 93.
25 Ibid., XVII, 117.
26 Ibid., XXXIV, 87.

Susquehannah; and so far the peace treaty with the Iroquois arranged at Three Rivers in 1645 seemed to be respected. Contingents of Huron traders set off for Three Rivers while great numbers of Huron braves launched an expedition, bent on prowling the Iroquois country in a show of strength. But how incorrectly they understood their cunning foe!

Late in June 1648, Antoine Daniel returned to Sainte Marie to make his annual retreat, completing the exercises on the morning of July 2. His brethren urged him to enjoy a few days respite from his exacting labors at Teanaustayé, but he ". . . would not take even a day of rest, feeling himself called by God to the labors of his mission."[27] Blithely, that Thursday morning, July 2, Antoine Daniel shouldered his pack of supplies and set off on foot across the rolling hills for St. Joseph's mission, a baker's dozen miles to the south. Fording the sluggish Hog Creek and the more pretentious Sturgeon River, he reached his mission set on the brow of a high hill overlooking the marshland drained by the Coldwater River. Probably the late afternoon and evening were spent listening to his Christians recount the news of events during his absence. The next morning, July 3, a Friday, Father Antoine heard the confessions of a large number of his people and at Mass preached with great unction to his flock, ". . . telling them that they should prepare themselves for death."[28] Perhaps Daniel had no premonition of an impending calamity; perhaps the subject of his homily arose naturally. But the fact is that for nine years he had been ". . . awaiting with hope and love the blessing of the death which fell to his portion."[29]

At dawn on Saturday, July 4, Father Daniel had barely finished celebrating Mass when lookouts shouted that Iroquois in great numbers were attacking the village. The few braves left at home rushed to combat, their pastor encouraging them to fight bravely. Pagans in such great numbers clamored for baptism that Father Antoine resorted to administering the sacrament by aspersion.[30] Very quickly the howling enemy breached the palisades and put the torch to the village. The Christians gathered in their

[27] Ibid., 95.
[28] Ibid.
[29] Ibid.
[30] Ibid., 89.

rude little chapel begged Father Daniel to flee while there was still time. But he replied: "I must face death here, as long as I see here any soul to be gained for heaven."[31] And he might even help to save the lives of at least some of his flock. As the screaming enemy swept toward the chapel Father Daniel suddenly and dramatically appeared at the entrance, hoping that the surprise would delay the Iroquois long enough for his people to flee.

For a moment the Iroquois were taken aback ". . . to see one man alone come to meet them . . ."[32] But it was only for a moment. Quickly recovering, the Iroquois rained arrows on his exposed body and ". . . inflicted upon him a mortal wound from an arquebus shot, which pierced him through and through in the middle of his breast . . ."[33] "Pronouncing the name of Jesus, he blessedly yielded up his soul to God, truly a good pastor, who exposes both his soul and his life for the salvation of his flock."[34] Then the Iroquois rushed upon his lifeless body as if he alone was the object of their rage. They stripped him naked and exercised a thousand indignities. When the flames consuming the village swept over the chapel they cast Daniel's body into the inferno, making of it a truly whole-burnt offering.

Antoine Daniel's effort to buy time for his beleaguered flock succeeded in part. Many escaped, hiding themselves in the depths of the surrounding forests. But their presence was revealed by the cries of thoroughly frightened children whose mothers sought in vain to stifle their sobs. Others fled to Sainte Marie, taking refuge behind the stout walls of that religious fortress in the wilderness. But the Iroquois succeeded in slaughtering or capturing some seven hundred ". . . souls, mostly women and children, though the number escaping was much greater."[35] Father Paul Ragueneau wrote in his *Relation*: "We tried to assist them out of our poverty, to clothe the naked, and to feed those poor people, who were dying of hunger; to mourn with the afflicted, and to console them with the hope of Paradise."[36] As for Father Antoine Daniel, Paul Ragueneau recorded as his epitaph: ". . . he has left behind him with us the example of all his virtues; and with all the Indians, even the infidels, so tender an affection for his memory,

31 Ibid., 91.   34 Ibid.
32 Ibid.   35 Ibid., 99.
33 Ibid.   36 Ibid.

that I may say in truth that he has ravished the hearts of all those who have ever known him."[37]

After the Iroquois army had withdrawn from Teanaustayé, driving their captives before them, Jesuits from Sainte Marie, accompanied by lay helpers, visited the ruins of that village hoping to collect the body of their blessed martyr in order to give it Christian burial. But the heat of the burning chapel had been so intense that everything, including the dead bodies cast into it, had been reduced to ashes.[38] Sometime after Father Daniel's death he appeared to Father Pierre Joseph Marie Chaumonot, often his co-worker and a dear friend. No whit surprised at the apparition, the lovable, impetuous Chaumonot boldly asked why

. . . the divine goodness had permitted the body of his servant to be so unworthily treated after his death, and so reduced to powder that we had not even had the happiness of being able to gather up its ashes. "Truly God is great and adorable forever [Daniel answered] he has regarded the reproaches cast on this his servant, and in order to recompense them . . . he has given me many souls who were in Purgatory, who have accompanied my entrance into heaven and my triumph there."[39]

If, as has been so frequently remarked, the blood of martyrs is the seed of Christians, then Antoine Daniel's blood was not shed in vain. Subsequent to his martyrdom, missionaries in Huronia experienced a profound interest in Christianity throughout all the Huron clans. In his *Breve relatione*, Francesco Bressani remarked:

The faith had . . . taken possession of almost all the country; public profession of it was made everywhere; and not only private persons, but the chiefs themselves, were at once its sons and protectors. The superstitious rites which were formerly of more than daily occurrence, so began to lose credit that an infidel who asked for one of them by way of remedy for an ailment of his, in the village of la Conception [Ossossané], could never, prominent though he was, obtain his end. Persecutions against us . . . ceased; cursings against the faith . . . changed into blessings; I could almost say that the people were already ripe for heaven . . .[40]

[37] Ibid.

[38] Ibid., 97. See Jones, 21. On the site of the chapel has been found the fused base of a brass crucifix. The chapel must have been a quite substantial structure to have generated heat intense enough to melt brass. Even in our day it is unusual for a human body to be utterly reduced to ashes in a fire.

[39] Chaumonot, *Autobiographie*, 91. Chaumonot says that Father Daniel appeared ". . . in the state of glory, having the aspect of a man of about thirty, though he died at the age of forty-eight."

[40] *Relations*, XXXIX, 245.

Father Paul Ragueneau, superior of the Huron mission, re-corded elatedly in his *Relation* of 1648-1649:

Since our last *Relation* [of 1647], we have baptized nearly thirteen hundred persons; but what consoles us the most is to see the fervor of these good neophytes, and a spirit of faith in them that savors naught of barbarism, and causes us to bless God's mercies which spread so abundantly from day to day to the outer confines of this new world.[41]

Recalling that Ragueneau was writing his *Relation* for propa-ganda purposes, one could be tempted to wonder if he might not have been inclined to exaggerate somewhat. However, it happens that less than a year after he finished his *Relation* Father Ragueneau composed the official report on the Huron mission which he submitted to Vincent Caraffa, general of the Jesuits. In that quite jejune, factual communication, Ragueneau said:

Christianity has certainly made progress here in many ways beyond our expectation. We baptized, the past year, about one thousand seven hundred . . . Nor are these, albeit barbarians, such Christians as one might be inclined to suppose, ignorant of things divine and not sufficiently qualified for our mysteries. Many indeed understand religion, and that profoundly; and there are some whose virtue, piety, and remarkable holiness even the most holy Religious might envy without sin.[42]

A frightening crisis in the early summer of 1648 seemed to confirm the Jesuits in their belief that Huronia was well on the way to becoming a totally Christian nation. Before its destruction, July 4, Teanaustayé was the scene of terror

. . . inspired by a hostile army, that was reported to be but a half a league from the village . . . the women thought only of flight and the men of resist-ing the attack; fear and dread reigned everywhere. Amid all those alarms the Christians, the catechumens, and even many infidels, hastened to the church, some to receive absolution, others to hasten their baptism; all feared hell more than death. The Father [probably Daniel] knew not whom to hear, for while he wished to satisfy some, the others pressed him and cried to him for pity. It was a combat of the Faith, which lived in their hearts and gave them a legitimate right to what they desired. Thus the Father found himself, fortunately, compelled to grant their requests. Many were armed from head to foot and received baptism in that state. After all, it turned out to be a false alarm; but the Faith and the holy promises of

41 Ibid., XXXIII, 69.
42 Ibid., 257. Ragueneau's *Relation* was dated April 16, 1648. His letter to Caraffa bears the date March 1, 1649.

those persons who were baptized in haste, were, nevertheless, earnest. The Holy Spirit is an excellent teacher; and, when he calls anyone to the Faith, he abundantly supplies whatever may be deficient in our instructions.[43]

In the midst of these unsettling conditions, the Jesuits assembled at Sainte Marie, after the arrival of their new recruits, to parcel out the missionary work for the coming year.[44] All of the new recruits would, of course, remain at Sainte Marie studying the Huron language and assisting the veteran missionaries until such time as they acquired sufficient fluency to be sent out to some more distant location. As for Father Jean de Brébeuf, he would reside at Sainte Marie, but each Monday morning, with a pack on his back, he would set out to make the rounds of the villages near Sainte Marie, St. Xavier, St. Anne, St. Denis, St. Louis, St. Jean, and even St. Ignace which was a good eight miles southeast of Sainte Marie.[45] The physical effort involved in that assignment was no small burden for Brébeuf, now an aging fifty-five and honed down by his long years among the Hurons.

During the progress of the meeting, suddenly all of the missionaries sensed the presence of Father Antoine Daniel. Only Father Chaumonot seems to have actually seen his martyred friend, but everyone felt his presence. Father Ragueneau reported the experience in his *Relation* of 1649: "Another time he was seen to be present at an assembly that we held in regard to means for advancing the Faith in these countries, when he appeared, strengthening us with his courage, and filling us with his light, and with the spirit of God with which he was completely invested."[46] That consoling grace and strengthening of their courage was soon to be needed by every Jesuit among the Hurons for the deluge of horrible war was but a few months away.

---

[43] Ibid., 99. For a description of Huron armor, see Tooker, *Ethnography of the Huron Indians*, 30. Body armor was made from thin branches of trees tightly sewn together and interlaced with cords. Shields were also used, some large enough to cover the whole body. Sometimes a small shield made of boiled hide was carried. The armor was effective against arrows tipped with stone, but not against those with iron points.

[44] *Relations*, XXXIV, 97.

[45] This was the distance between St. Ignace I and Sainte Marie. Jones, 263, locates St. Ignace I at the east half of lot 22, concession VIII, Medonte township, Simcoe county, Ontario.

[46] *Relations*, XXXIV, 97.

On his rounds of the villages Father Brébeuf must certainly have stopped by at the new village which the people of Tahententaron were erecting. Jean de Brébeuf must have nurtured a particular predilection for the inhabitants of that village. It was he who first preached the gospel to them ten years ago, only to be rejected by them in a most peremptory manner. Perhaps it was through Brébeuf's influence that those people were never once neglected. The mission of St. Ignace was established there and slowly the attitude of the people softened. By 1648 Father Ragueneau could declare that the people at St. Ignace manifested ". . . a fervor and an innocence that astonish the infidels, and which we would never have expected to see in so short a time . . ."[47] It was fortunate for the Hurons at St. Ignace that their faith was so strong and their fervor great for during the winter and early spring of 1647-1648 they were sorely afflicted.

During the winter some three hundred people from St. Ignace went off a distance of two days' journey in the direction of the Iroquois to hunt, expecting to bag big game. When most of that large party was scattered through the woods, a band of Seneca attacked some of them, killing seven and capturing twenty-four, both men and women. Sadly, most of those killed or captured were exemplary Christians who had ". . . encamped together the better to say their prayers, night and morning; and in truth they lived there in innocence, and spread everywhere a fragrant odor of Christianity."[48] Just a few days later, when the Hurons returned to the scene of the disaster to collect the bodies of their slaughtered comrades, they were ". . . surprised by about a hundred Mohawk Iroquois, at a distance of four or five leagues from the village [of Tahententaron]; about forty of our people were killed or taken captive. This has since compelled those who dwelt at St. Ignace to come nearer to us, and to shelter themselves better against the incursions of the enemy."[49]

---

[47] Ibid., XXXIII, 141. The Jesuits who labored at St. Ignace I and II were: 1639, Brébeuf and Chastellain; 1640, Daniel and Le Moyne; 1641-1643, Garnier and Le Moyne; 1644, Garnier and Ménard; 1645, Garnier and Du Peron; 1646, Ménard and Chaumonot; 1647, Brébeuf and Chaumonot; 1648-1649, Brébeuf, Chabanel, and after about February 1649, Gabriel Lalemant. See Jones, 310-80.

[48] *Relations*, XXXIII, 85.

[49] Ibid., 89.

The solidity of their faith was never more magnificently manifested than by those poor captives snatched from their homes and families. The most notable among them, a captain named Nicolas Annenharisonk, gathered the Christian captives around him exhorting them thus:

"This is the moment when we must be Christians . . . let us be careful not to forget our hopes in heaven at a time when there is nothing more to be hoped for in this world. God will be with us in the midst of our misfortunes . . . Now, my brothers, let us say our prayers." He began and all followed him with greater peace and fervor than they had ever felt. The enemy gazed on so novel a proceeding with astonishment, but I have no doubt that the angels looked upon it with loving eyes.[50]

The missionaries learned of this edifying conduct from a Huron woman who fortunately escaped and returned to her village. Her captor was an Onondaga Iroquois, a hostage left with the Hurons whose representatives were just then in the Onondaga homeland attempting to negotiate a peace. That hostage not only freed his captive but insisted on returning to the Hurons, telling the Mohawks that he would rather suffer torture and death at their hands than to behave as an enemy of the Hurons while among them as a hostage for a peace mission. So the Mohawks allowed him to return to the Hurons and take his captive, the Christian woman, with him.[51]

After those two disastrous attacks the Hurons at St. Ignace determined that they must abandon their village and remove closer to the sheltering walls of Sainte Marie. Scouring the country north of their village they came upon an ideal location on the east side of a horseshoe bend of the Sturgeon River about three miles north and a little west of their original village. Sainte Marie lay about six miles almost due west of the location they chose. The site was the absolutely ideal one for an Indian village. A level plateau of about fifteen acres was surrounded on three sides by a ditch some fifty feet deep which ended on the shore of the Sturgeon River.[52] Only on the fourth side, facing toward the east,

---

[50] Ibid., 165.

[51] Ibid., 167.

[52] Wilfrid Jury, "St. Ignace II," *The Canadian Catholic Historical Association Report*, 1946-1947, 15. Jury's archaeological investigation ended forever the discussion of the location of St. Ignace II. It was on the west half of lot 5, concession IX, Tay township.

was there no natural protection. At no point within several miles of the chosen site did nature provide a stronger defense. Probably working against time, the people surrounded the whole plateau with a palisade of high poles set a foot apart and interwoven with brush and bark. Within their palisaded compound the Indians erected nearly thirty buildings. All of the structures, save one, were typical Huron long houses. In the center of the village was a chapel, including a residence for the Jesuits, which measured ninety-nine by sixty feet.[53] When the new village was ready for occupancy the Indians of St. Ignace must certainly have felt that within the walls of their staunch palisades on the high bank above the Sturgeon River they could withstand the most powerful attack the Iroquois could muster.

The *Relation* of 1648-1649 gives us details of one charming little incident related to the removal of the Hurons of St. Ignace to their new village. Pierre Joseph Marie Chaumonot, who had worked with these poor, suffering people for two years, regretted seeing the crude little chapel at St. Ignace I dismantled. He had said Mass there innumerable times and had, certainly, baptized many Hurons in it. Going there to pay a final visit, Father Chaumonot remained a long time on his knees, his face mirroring the regret within his soul. A staunch Christian, Ignace Onakonchiaronk, noticing the priest's distress, addressed him thus:

Aronhiatiri, my mind is quite cast down, not for my affliction, but for yours. You seem to be forgetting the word of God which you preach to us every day. I imagine that the sorrow that appears on your face is caused by our afflictions, because this church that was so flourishing is about to be dispersed. This chapel is about to be taken down; many of our Christian brothers are dead or captive; those who remain are about to scatter in every direction, and to run the risk of losing the Faith. Is it not that which is troubling you? Alas, my brother, is it for us to seek to fathom God's designs, and can we really understand them? What are we? Nothing. He knows well what should be done, and sees more clearly than we do. Do you know what he will do? Those Christians who are about to disperse will carry their Faith with them, and their example will make other Christians where there are none as yet. Let us remember that we are nothing, that we cannot see anything; and that he alone knows what is good for us. It is sufficient, I assure

---

[53] Ibid., 22.

you, to comfort me in my adversity, when I see how miserable I am in every respect, to think that God provides for everything, that he loves us and knows very well what we need.[54]

That simple Indian, Ignace, was a prophet, indeed. The destruction of St. Ignace II and the scattering of the Hurons to the four winds would carry the faith to the Sioux and the Cree in the west and to all the nations along the Mississippi Valley. Claude Allouez would find them at Green Bay and along the Fox River in Wisconsin. Jacques Marquette would baptize Hurons at Chequamegon Bay on Lake Superior who had been instructed by Jesuit martyrs in Huronia. Thirty years after the dispersal of the Hurons, Christians among them would go far, by their example, toward converting the very enemies who brought about the downfall of their once great nation.

And what of Jean de Brébeuf in all of these stirring events? In his biography of Brébeuf, Father Félix Martin unhesitatingly asserts: "On the advice of Father Brébeuf, the people at St. Ignace decided to emigrate, but not to separate . . . He was asked to choose a site [of the new village]."[55] Martin also infers that Father Brébeuf was responsible for the manner of erecting the new palisades and the internal arrangement of the village. That opinion is most certainly based on the fact that Brébeuf, many years before, had suggested to the Indians that they erect their palisades in rectangular shapes so that men in bastions could better protect a village. Certainly, Father Brébeuf must have encouraged the people to evacuate their village which was so exposed to the Iroquois, once the mission of St. Joseph at Teanaustayé had been destroyed in July 1648. As for selecting a site for the new village, well as Father Brébeuf might have known the area, the Indians themselves certainly knew it better. They would also be intimately aware what areas they could consider without encroaching on the geographical rights of other villages.

As for the construction of the palisades and the buildings at St. Ignace II, Father Bressani tells us: "The place was impregnable to the barbarians, both from its position and because of the fortifications which we had made there."[56] With the complex at

[54] *Relations*, XXXIII, 169.
[55] Martin, *Hurons et Iroquois*, 246.
[56] *Relations*, XXXIX, 247.

Sainte Marie so far advanced, the French could well afford to lend the Indians a hand in constructing their new village and helping them fortify it. Surely, at least the largest building within the compound could not have been erected by the Indians themselves. They could not have roofed a building sixty feet wide nor have archaeologists found any Huron cabin showing evidence of partitions within it, as was the case with the largest structure at St. Ignace II.[57]

In his most enlightening report on the evacuation of St. Ignace II, Wilfrid Jury informs us that many post molds, especially pertaining to the largest structure within the compound at St. Ignace II, showed clear evidence of supporting columns made of split logs, an operation which the Indians could not have accomplished with the tools available to them. We must, then, reasonably assume that skilled craftsmen from Sainte Marie greatly assisted the Indians in constructing their new village. Yet, however impregnable it was thought to be, it was actually an altar prepared for the sacrificial victims, Jean de Brébeuf and Gabriel Lalemant together with their many neophytes who died with them.

---

[57] Jury, "St. Ignace II."

Chapter XII

Martyrdom

Through the fall and winter of 1648 and 1649 everything, nature as well as man, conspired to effect the downfall of the Huron nation. During the summer of 1648 a devastating drought had parched the whole of Huronia, withering the corn. There would be no harvest from the Huron fields and little opportunity of trading to supply the deficiency. In the late fall and early winter, when the Indians always hoped to bag large game, the hunters returned empty-handed. Even the fishing was poor. When hard winter set in conditions were so desperate for the Hurons that Father Paul Ragueneau said, in his *Relation* of 1648-1649: "What increases the public misery is that famine has been prevalent this year in all these regions, more than it has been in fifty years, most of the people not having wherewith to live, and being constrained either to eat acorns, or else to go and seek in the woods some wild roots. With these they sustain a wretched life, . . ."[1] From their own meager stores, the missionaries did their best to alleviate the misery surrounding them on every side. Over six thousand poor

[1] *Relations*, XXXIV, 197.

refugees swarmed around Sainte Marie seeking not only protection from the dread Iroquois but scanty rations of food to retain the breath of life within them.[2]

But famine, that ruthless killer of the weak, the elderly, and the children, was not the worst nor the most destructive enemy of the Hurons. Unknown to them, the Iroquois, in the autumn of 1648, as Hitler was to do with the Jews, had determined that the "final solution of the Huron problem" was the utter extermination of that nation. Perhaps the very success of the Huron fur flotilla of 1648 brought the Iroquois to their drastic decision. The Five Nations could, obviously, blockade the trade route to Quebec. They were able, as they proved conclusively at St. Joseph, to capture any Huron frontier town, slaughtering, leading people off as prisoners for torture, death, or adoption into their own clans. Iroquois incursions had already been so successful that ". . . fifteen villages have been abandoned, the people of each scattering where they could, . . ."[3] Iroquois raids had been so successful that Ragueneau reported: ". . . whatever place we go, we see there nothing but crosses, present miseries, and fear of greater evil, death being for most, the least evil that can befall them."[4]

Cruel and inhuman the Iroquois tactics might be, but they were not enough to unerringly divert the Huron trade monopoly with the northern and western tribes to themselves. So long as the Hurons controlled the Lake Simcoe-Georgian Bay area, they could control the flow of furs from their economically dependent neighbors. And, alas for the Hurons, those neighbors were the only sources from which furs could be obtained in quantity by either the Hurons or the Iroquois. For the Iroquois there was, therefore, only one possible solution. The Huron nation must be utterly destroyed and their land laid waste. And, in the process, the Blackrobes, who defied the ancient gods and decried the native Iroquois culture, must be forever eliminated.[5] The only question for the Iroquois, and the more observant of the Hurons as well as for the missionaries, was not whether the Hurons should

[2] Ibid., 199.
[3] Ibid., 197.
[4] Ibid., 199.
[5] Hunt, *Wars of the Iroquois*, 91.

be attacked in force, but where and when the decisive blow would fall.

In his *Relation* of 1648-1649, Father Ragueneau recounted the opening of the final Iroquois campaign against the Hurons thus:

The Iroquois, enemies of the Hurons, to the number of about a thousand men well furnished with weapons and mostly with firearms, which they obtained from the Dutch, their allies, arrived by night at the frontier of this country, without our having any knowledge of their approach; although they had started from their country in the autumn, hunting in the forests throughout the winter, and had made over the snow nearly two hundred leagues of a very difficult road, in order to come and surprise us.[6]

While the Iroquois army was slowly and stealthily working its way toward Huronia, Jean de Brébeuf spent the fall and winter season of 1648-1649 caring for the villages committed to his charge. At the beginning of the season Brébeuf's companion was a fellow martyr, Noel Chabanel.[7] A true saint, even if he had not been a martyr, Chabanel could not have been more than company for Jean de Brébeuf. For, try as he might, Noel Chabanel simply could not master a native language. At the beginning of the new year, 1649, Father Ragueneau recalled Chabanel, assigning him to labor with Father Charles Garnier among the Petuns because, as Chabanel wrote to his brother Pierre, also a Jesuit, ". . . I, as being more robust of body, was sent upon a mission

---

[6] A large portion of the journey made by the Iroquois to the Huron country was probably made by canoe. The Mohawks could ascend the Mohawk River to Lake Wood Creek whence they could portage to the Oswego River and reach Lake Ontario. Skirting the eastern end of that lake, they could travel by water to Lake Simcoe, though they would be obliged to make several portages. The Seneca, the most western clan of the Iroquois, could march around the western end of Lake Ontario.

[7] Noel Chabanel was born at Saugues (Haute-Loire) on February 2, 1613. On February 9, 1630, he entered the Jesuit novitiate at Toulouse. He spent all of his life as a Jesuit in France at that city, except for one year at Rodez where, after his ordination, he taught rhetoric. He arrived at Quebec on August 15, 1643, and spent the rest of that year, probably at Sillery, studying Algonkin, having been assigned as missionary to Indians who spoke that language. He reached Huronia on September 7, 1644, in company with Jean de Brébeuf, who, that year, returned to the Huron mission after an absence of almost four years. Though he was an excellent academic scholar in France, he simply could not master an Indian language. When superiors suggested he return to France where he would be eminently useful, he refused, declining to desert the cause to which he dedicated himself. He was killed on December 8, 1649, by an apostate Huron who later confessed his crime.

more remote and more laborious, but not so fruitful in palms and crowns as that of which my cowardice has, in the sight of God, rendered me unworthy."[8] Now Gabriel Lalemant, having been in Huronia nearly six months, was ready to try his wings. In contrast to Noel Chabanel, Gabriel Lalemant, like his mentor, Brébeuf, had a positive gift for learning the native languages. Pierre Joseph Marie Chaumonot, Gabriel's tutor in the Huron tongue, wrote to Father Jerome Lalemant after Gabriel's martyrdom: "I had the honor to be, for about three weeks, instructor in the Huron language to your good nephew . . . The pains he took in learning the Huron language, and the progress he made in it, were almost incredible; some of our Fathers have thought that God has rewarded this great diligence by that blessed death."[9]

Surely, Jean de Brébeuf and Gabriel Lalemant were the long and the short of it as they journeyed from village to village instructing the Indians. The broad-shouldered Echon strode along, his long legs eating up the miles, while his diminutive companion scrambled after, striving to keep up with his giant fellow Jesuit. The grizzled old campaigner must have treated his mere tyro of a helper with the greatest consideration. To Brébeuf, Gabriel Lalemant probably seemed the merest boy, so young, so untried, so burning with apostolic zeal, with so much to learn before he could possibly be an effective missionary among these natives who were just beginning to grasp the true meaning of Christianity. But to Brébeuf, the young Lalemant was the *spes gregis*, the hope of Huronia's future, even though ". . . he was of an extremely frail constitution, and almost without other strength than what his zeal and fervor supplied him."[10] Besides, Brébeuf and Gabriel Lalemant were, spiritually, kindred souls. Both yearned to sacrifice their lives for the salvation of the Huron nation. Committing his most intimate thoughts to paper sometime before his arrival in New France, Lalemant wrote, addressing Christ himself: ". . . it is necessary that your blood, shed no less for these barbarians than for us, be efficaciously applied to them; I wish to cooperate therein with your grace, and to sacrifice myself for them . . . your kingdom should be extended to all nations; I desire

---

[8] *Relations*, XXXV, 161.
[9] Ibid., XXXIV, 221.
[10] Ibid., XXXIX, 255.

to spend my blood and my life in order to extend it to these."[11]
Aware, as he must have been, of Jean de Brébeuf's deserved reputation for sanctity, Gabriel Lalemant could hardly have refrained from confiding in his companion who shared his ambition.

Making their rounds together through the bitter winter of
1648-1649, the two missionaries often stopped at St. Ignace II, in-
specting the progress of the construction and urging the men
there to hasten. Jean de Brébeuf must have been only too well
aware that the new St. Ignace was, for practical purposes, the last
bastion of Huron defense against the Iroquois. So many frontier
villages had been destroyed by the enemy or abandoned by their
Huron inhabitants that, should the Iroquois attack in force, they
must be met and defeated at St. Ignace or the whole Huron nation would fall before them. The practically impregnable fortress
of Sainte Marie ought to withstand any force the Iroquois could
mount against it. But, suppose those wily tacticians simply by-
passed it, sweeping northward to destroy the populous towns of
the Bear clan which could hardly be expected to defend themselves successfully? At all cost St. Ignace must be the final, defini-
tive battleground, if the Hurons hoped to survive. And, let it not
be thought that the Iroquois were unaware of the strategic importance as was Jean de Brébeuf and, perhaps too, the captains
at St. Ignace.

Week by cold, weary week, Jean de Brébeuf and Gabriel
Lalemant made their rounds to St. Anne, St. Denis, St. Louis, St.
Jean, and St. Ignace, baptizing, instructing, shriving, and encouraging their neophytes. The winter season, despite the bitter cold,
had certain advantages for the dedicated missionaries. Paths were
well marked in the deep snow and rivers were frozen solid. Besides, cold weather drove the none too warmly clad Hurons in-
doors, huddled around their fire pits. Scarcity of food that winter,
even small game, was, in itself, incentive enough to encourage the
people to husband their energies. They were, quite likely, willing
to welcome the visiting missionaries and listen to their instructions. And, it could be presumed, that the kindly Echon always
brought small gifts for the children and whatever food he and

[11] Mère Marie de l'Incarnation Guyart, *Ecrits spirituels et historiques*, edited
by Albert Jamet, IV, 223.

Lalemant could collect to augment the scant diet the hungry villagers had to offer.

For Jean de Brébeuf and Gabriel Lalemant, the week of March 7-13, 1649, was no different than the eight or ten weeks before it which the two missionaries had spent together. On Saturday, March 6, they had come back to Sainte Marie to help out with the hordes of Hurons milling around the great mission center. The place was normally crowded with the usual complement of weekend visitors come to be shriven and attend Sunday Mass at Sainte Marie. Now hundreds of refugees, many of them infidels, but numerous Christians too, were camped within the Indian compound and outside the palisaded walls to the east of the stout stockade protecting Sainte Marie. Besides lending a hand exercising the spiritual and corporal works of mercy, Brébeuf and Lalemant refreshed themselves, spiritually and physically, enjoying the restful peace pervading the community's residence. When the press of work abated, on Sunday, March 7, Echon and his companion replenished their supplies, preparing for another week of tramping over hill and dale ministering to their own suffering people. On Saturday, March 13, the two were back again, tired, indeed, but probably consoled. In the villages under their charge, Brébeuf and Lalemant were able to report a growing fervor among the people, a new willingness on the part of the infidels to accept baptism and reject their pagan practices. But, somehow, there was a tension in the air, a kind of frightening expectancy, as though any moment a terrible catastrophe was about to engulf the whole nation.

During Saturday, March 13, the members of the Jesuit community noticed that the normally cheerful, agreeable Jean de Brébeuf seemed to emit an inexplicable glow of internal joy so strikingly that few failed to notice his radiant countenance. Presently, all the Jesuits at Sainte Marie became aware that his impending martyrdom had been revealed to Jean de Brébeuf by some sort of divine revelation. Our Lord, they knew, made known to Father Brébeuf not only the time and place of his painful death but also the tortures he must endure. Strangely, his hands, so often raised in administration of the sacraments, were not to be mutilated. Not one of the Jesuits doubted the truth of what they learned. That Jean de Brébeuf was a mystic, often favored with supernatural visitations, must have long been common knowledge among his fellow Jesuits laboring so closely with him among the Hurons. Accepting the fact that they must suffer the loss of the greatest among them, their concern centered on how they could preserve something of him. Would this great, hulking body be consumed to ashes as that of their precious Antoine Daniel? Hoping to preserve some part of him, someone suggested that the surgeon, François Gendron, open one of Brébeuf's veins and draw some of his blood so that they might have a relic to revere. Ghoulish as the proceedings might seem to the twentieth-century mind, Jean de Brébeuf submitted to the business, probably in deference to the wishes of his brethren.

Very early on Monday morning, March 15, 1649, Jean de Bré-beuf and Gabriel Lalemant left Sainte Marie, beginning their normal weekly rounds of the villages under their care as though nothing catastrophic awaited them. One cannot help but wonder what their fellow Jesuits thought, especially the superior, Paul Ragueneau, as the line of trees hid those two mismatched figures from their view. When next would the community see these two warriors of Christ and what would their condition be? Jean de Brébeuf, so tall and gaunt as if made of whang leather, might endure torture. But what of that poor, sickly mite of a Gabriel Lalemant? His delicately nurtured body, so frail, really only a fragile vessel containing the burning flame of his indomitable will to serve God to the last gasp, how could he endure? There was nothing for it but to commend their two valiant companions to the hands of God. None, least of all Paul Ragueneau, would think of detaining them for that would be, they ardently believed, to thwart the will of God.

During that cold, blustery Monday, Jean de Brébeuf and Gabriel Lalemant must have called at one or other mission center, possibly St. Anne and St. Denis, before reaching St. Louis[12] where the two missionaries planned to spend the night, as indeed they did. That was the fateful night on March 15-16.

[12] No evidence supports the statement that Brébeuf and Lalemant first visited other villages before stopping for the night at St. Louis. Only the distances involved lead to the conclusion. St. Louis was only three miles from Sainte Marie. Well-trodden paths must long since have been worn between St. Louis and Sainte Marie. Hence, it could hardly have taken the two Jesuits all of a day to reach St. Louis.

Four miles to the east and slightly south of St. Louis, the new St. Ignace II stood foursquare in the path of any marauding Iroquois force daring to attack it. The new palisades of stripped pine, rearing fifteen feet above ground, glistened in the pale light of that cold March night. Confident of the impregnable character of their new fortress, most of the able-bodied men were off hunting or scouting, on the search for a large Iroquois force rumored to be in the country.[13] Within the village the elderly, the sick, the women, and children plus a corporal's guard of braves left to guard the place slept peacefully, believing themselves doubly secure. What foolhardy band of Iroquois braves would be so imprudent as to attempt scaling a fifty-foot ditch as well as a stout fifteen-foot palisade, expecting to take the village by surprise? But the Sturgeon River at the base of the ditch was frozen solid and the high embankment, rock hard from penetrating frost, gave excellent footing. Underbrush and scrub timber, instead of pulling away from loose soil, were held fast by the very frost permeating the soil in which they grew. Stealthily, and indeed easily, the Iroquois warriors scaled the high bank, skirted the palisades until they reached the narrow eastern entrance to the village. This confined space, not more than a hundred feet wide, had not been finished because all the building material, long logs, great strips of bark, and the rest, had yet, in part, to be brought through it.[14]

It was at that point that the enemy made a breach at daybreak [March 16, 1649], but so secretly and promptly that he was master of the place before people had put themselves on the defensive, all being then in a deep sleep, and not having leisure to reconnoiter their situation. Thus this village was taken, almost without striking a blow, there having been only ten Iroquois killed. Part of the Hurons, men, women, and children, were massacred then and there; the others were made captives, and reserved for cruelties more

---

[13] *Relations*, XXXIX, 247.

[14] Ibid., XXXIV, 125. See Jury, "St. Ignace II," 19. The evacuation of that portion of the palisades shows gaps of four to eight feet. Jury suggests "The apparent carelessness of the builders, in leaving this side thus exposed, in spite of their obvious plans to doubly fortify it, can be explained only if at the time of its destruction the village was still under construction and material for building was being carried through these gaps from the level lands to the east rather than up the high banks that surrounded the other three sides."

terrible than death.[15] Three persons alone escaped, half naked, in order to give warning thereof to the neighboring village, called Saint Louis, not more than three miles distant.[16]

At the news of the capture of St. Ignace none of the Huron leaders at St. Louis, certainly not Jean de Brébeuf, thought for a moment that the Iroquois army would retreat, satisfied with their single conquest. Huron captains at St. Louis understood quite well the meaning of the fall of St. Ignace. This was their strongest defense, built specifically, with the physical help and sound strategic advice of the French, for the very purpose of thwarting the enemy's intent of overrunning the whole country. The fall of St. Ignace sounded the death knell of the Huron nation. And well the Huron captains at St. Louis knew it. Within a short time the Iroquois forces would come screaming upon St. Louis. Hurriedly, the captains made what preparations they could to withstand the assault which would roll over them before the sun tinged with pink the cold snows covering the ground around the village. The women and children were hurried off into the adjacent forest. Then the leaders

. . . exhorted our Fathers to do the same, as it was not their office to handle javelin and musket. But Father Brébeuf gave them to understand that there was at that time something still more necessary than arms, which was recourse to God and the sacraments, which others than they could not administer. He therefore resolved, with Father Gabriel Lalemant, his companion, not to forsake them, even unto death; . . .[17]

At first light a strong detachment of the Iroquois army, boiling out of the woods, stormed the none too strong palisades of St. Louis. Within, besides the aged and sick, a small force of about eighty men

. . . resolved to defend themselves well, repulse[d] with courage the first and second assault, having killed among the enemy some thirty of their most venturesome men, besides many wounded. But, finally, number had the advantage, the Iroquois having undermined with blows of their hatchets

[15] *Relations*, XXXIV, 125. In his *Relation* of 1648-1649, Ragueneau informs us that St. Ignace II ". . . had been abandoned by most of its people at the beginning of the winter, the most apprehensive and the most clear-sighted having withdrawn from it, foreboding danger; thus the loss of it was not so considerable, and amounted only to about four hundred souls."

[16] Ibid., XXXIX, 247.

[17] Ibid., 249.

the palisade of stakes, and having made a passage for themselves through considerable breaches.[18] Then, all the men being taken prisoners, they put everything to fire and flame, with which . . . [were] consumed, in their own country and in their own cabins, all the feeble and sick old men who had not been able to escape by flight.[19]

Then it was that the extent of the Iroquois campaign became all too evident. Leaving contingents of warriors at St. Louis and St. Ignace, to guard prisoners and prepare for their subsequent torture, the main force of the enemy hastened northward ". . . in order to inspire terror on all sides before the country can come together to resist him, he hastens hither and thither wounds, kills, and sets fire to the villages which are already abandoned; and, by means of the incursions which he makes, persuades the inhabitants that he has a whole army for the final ruin of all those regions."[20] Even those so fortunate as to escape the incensed Iroquois warriors helped spread despair. "The women, the children, and many centenarian old men passed all night on the ice [of the Sturgeon River], in order to flee to the Tobacco nation, more than forty miles distant; and they terrified it by exaggerating the number and forces of the enemy . . ."[21]

The stark drama within the confines of the village of St. Louis was played out to its bitter end with Jean de Brébeuf and Gabriel Lalemant on center stage. At the first shout of alarm, some five hundred villagers fled, begging the two missionaries to come with them.[22] Though at the beginning of the attack there was ample time for the two Jesuits to escape,

> . . . their zeal could not permit them, and the salvation of their flock was dearer to them than love of their own lives.[23] They employed all the moments of that time, as the most precious they ever had in the world; and, during the heat of the combat, their hearts were only fire for the salvation of souls. One was at the breach, baptizing the catechumens; the other, giving absolution to the neophytes, both animating the Christians to die in the sentiments of piety, with which they consoled them in their miseries. Accordingly, never was their faith, or the love which they had for their good Fathers and pastors more lively.[24]

---

18 Ibid., XXXIV, 127.
19 Ibid., XXXIX, 249.
20 Ibid., 251.
21 Ibid.

22 Ibid., XXXIV, 127.
23 Ibid., 127, 129.
24 Ibid., 129.

At the lull in the battle, following the first assault of the Iroquois, an infidel, clearly comprehending the hopelessness of their plight, urged the Hurons to flee while some faint hope of escape remained. To this suggestion a valiant Christian named Etienne Annaotaha replied scornfully: "What, could we ever abandon these good Fathers who have exposed their lives for us? The love which they have for our salvation will be the cause of their death; there is no longer time for them to flee across the snows. Let us then die with them, and we shall go in company to heaven."[25] And, under the second assault of the Iroquois, the village of St. Louis was taken and all the Hurons within it, mostly Christians, became captives of the enemy, among them ". . . our two Fathers, the pastors of that church."[26]

If the Iroquois warriors were unaware of the great prize falling into their hands by the capture of the mighty Echon, the renegade Hurons among them were quick to inform them. Here was the most powerful of all the French sorcerers, the most hated of all the Blackrobes. At all costs this pale giant of a man must be saved for the most exquisite torture ever devised. As for that wisp of a companion, he was worth torturing, of course, and unto death, but he would hardly furnish them much sport. So the haughty conquerors, after killing out of hand the old, the sick, and the squalling children, set fire to the village and marshaled their captives into line for the march back to St. Ignace where the Iroquois had ". . . left a good garrison, that it might be for them a sure retreat in case of misfortune, and that the victuals which they had found there might serve them as refreshments and provisions for their return."[27]

As though the Iroquois could not wait to reach their appointed scene for torture of their two Blackrobe victims, those fiends in human form promptly stripped the missionaries naked and tormented them by chewing on their fingers and tearing out some of their fingernails. Together with the Huron captives, Brébeuf and Lalemant were forced to run across the snow-covered

[25] Ibid.

[26] Ibid., 131.

[27] Ibid. See also ibid., 137. There Ragueneau explains that the Jesuits learned these details from an old woman who escaped and bore the news to the mission of St. Michel whence it reached Sainte Marie.

countryside to St. Ignace II, about three miles to the east. Chilled to the bone by the harsh March wind, aching from the pain in their hands, the poor, saintly victims watched many a weakened, stumbling Huron felled by a howling Iroquois burying an iron hatchet in his head. Reaching the still intact palisades of St. Ignace, the missionaries were greeted by two long lines of Iroquois warriors intent on forcing their prize victims to run the gauntlet. A ". . . hailstorm of blows with sticks [fell] on their shoulders, their loins, their legs, their breasts, their bellies, and their faces, there being no part of their bodies which did not then endure its torment."[28]

While the Iroquois victors busied themselves preparing gibbets for the torture victims, Jean de Brébeuf, surrounded by the Christian Hurons, his fellow captives, encouraged them, crying

My children, let us lift our eyes to heaven at the height of our afflictions; let us remember that God is the witness of our suffering, and will soon be our exceeding great reward. Let us die in this Faith; and let us hope from his goodness the fulfillment of his promises. I have more pity for you than for myself; but sustain with courage the few remaining torments. They will end with our lives; the glory which follows them will never have an end.[29]

Buoyed up by Father Brébeuf's encouragement, his suffering neophytes besought him to ask God to strengthen their faith so that they might die loyal to his teachings.

Incensed by that demonstration of courage, the Iroquois dragged Jean de Brébeuf and Father Lalemant to the posts tied to which they would endure the most painful torments their conquerors could conjure. When the two missionaries were ". . . fastened to the post where they suffered . . . and where they were to die, they knelt down, embraced it with joy, and kissed it piously as the object of their desires and their love, and as a sure and final pledge of their salvation." Because the two martyrs spent more time in prayer than pleased their captors, ". . . Some Huron infidels, former captives of the Iroquois, naturalized among them, and former enemies of the Faith, were irritated . . . because our Fathers, in . . . captivity had not their tongues captive."[30] Maddened beyond restraint, those traitors to their own

28 Ibid., 141.
29 Ibid.
30 Ibid.

Huron people flung themselves on the two Jesuits, wounded Gabriel Lalemant's hands and pierced Brébeuf's body repeatedly with sharp awls and iron points. For the Iroquois that treatment was only child's play, hardly worthy of the refinements any one of the Five Nations could bring to the torturing of a powerful sorceror and a cordially feared and hated foe whose religious faith they abhored.

The Iroquois braves gathered a couple of dozen iron trade hatchets which they placed in fires until they were white-hot. Then, stringing them on green withes, the fiendish savages draped them over Father Brébeuf's shoulders. If he leaned forward the hatchets rested on his back, searing the flesh to the bone. If he leaned backward the hot iron hatchets ate into the flesh and muscles of his bare chest. If he stood upright, absolutely still, ". . . these glowing hatchets, touching . . . alike on all sides, were a double torture . . ."[31] Refining that cruel technique, the Iroquois pressed red-hot hatchets under Brébeuf's arms, on his loins, and branded him with them in the most sensitive parts of his body.

But the Iroquois could elicit no moan of pain from Jean de Brébeuf, who ". . . suffered like a rock, insensible to the fires and the flames, without uttering any cry, and keeping a profound silence, which astonished his executioners themselves; no doubt his heart was then reposing in his God."[32] Irritated to howling frenzy, the great Echon's tormentors wrapped Brébeuf's body, from the waist to the shoulders, in resinous bark and set that afire so that their victim's torso was one vast blister, the cooked flesh sloughing off as loose pieces of the bark fell from him. Surely Jean de Brébeuf could then be said, like unto his divine Master, to have become a worm and no man. To reason that by divine intervention Jean de Brébeuf experienced none of the excruciating pain which such inhuman treatment inflicted is to detract from the glory of his martyrdom. While it is possible, of course, for God to have spared his servant, there is no reason to conclude that this was the case. As the missionary most respected as well as most feared,

[31] Ibid., 143. See also ibid., 29. Christophe Regnault's description of how the Indians did this.
[32] Ibid., 143.

it behooved the mighty Echon to outdo the Indians in every respect. Great warriors among the natives chanted war songs under
torture, boasted of their personal bravery, and hurled defiance at
their enemies unto their last breath. Echon, the chief of all
Christ's warriors among the Indians, must not only do the same,
but must far outstrip the performance of the bravest Indian warrior. Reacting to torture so heroically as to strike awe and wonder
in the hearts of his enemies, he thus won admiration not only
for himself but also for the doctrines and manner of life which
he preached.[33]

Commonly, captive Indian warriors boasted of their deeds of
bravery, especially if such actions had been vented on that nation
into whose hands they fell captive. Jean de Brébeuf, on the contrary ". . . preached to those infidels, and still more to many good
Christian captives, who had compassion for him." Jean de Brébeuf's incredible courage under torture and his inspired exhor-
tation to the infidel enemy as well as his precious Christian
neophytes threw the Iroquois braves into a wild passion of anger.
"Those butchers, indignant at his zeal, in order to hinder him
from further speaking of God, gagged his mouth, cut off his nose,
and tore off his lips; but his blood spoke much more loudly than
his lips had done; and, his heart, not being yet torn out, his tongue
did not fail to render him service until the last sigh, blessing God
for these torments and animating the Christians more vigorously
than he had ever done."[34]

Suddenly, a new form of torture occurred to the infidel Hurons. Knowing the importance of baptism, these vile traitors decided to baptize Father Brébeuf with great kettles of boiling
water, not once but several times. As they poured the scalding
water over Jean de Brébeuf's poor wounded body, they shouted
derisively: " 'We baptize you to the end that you may be blessed
in heaven; for without proper baptism one cannot be saved.' Others added mockingly, 'We treat you as a friend, since we will be
the cause of your greatest happiness in heaven; thank us for so
many good offices, for the more you suffer, the more your God
will reward you.' "[35] Even though shouted in derision, and by Hu-

[33] Ibid.
[34] Ibid., 143, 145.
[35] Ibid., 145.

rons who had rejected Christianity, the very remark demonstrated how effective Jean de Brébeuf's teaching of the Hurons had been.

Toward mid-afternoon the Iroquois began to tire of their sport. It was hardly much fun to batter away at that tall, gaunt body when they could not elicit any response save involuntary movements. Burning his body, searing it, wounding it with sharp awls, none of these painful tortures evinced the screams of pain or terror which the Iroquois expected to enjoy hearing Jean de Brébeuf emit. Whatever they did, the great Norman merely gazed on them pityingly while within he must have begged God to forgive them for his tormentors knew not what they did. Toward four in the afternoon the Iroquois gave up. Preparing for his end, the Indians scalped Father Brébeuf, cut off his feet, stripped flesh in great strips from his thighs, seared it and ate it with gusto. This, his tormentors readily admitted, was an exceptionally brave man. Eating his flesh and drinking his blood, they hoped, would bring to the grizzly participants a part of his indomitable spirit.

Finally, at about four in the afternoon, one of the Iroquois warriors buried a hatchet into Father Brébeuf's jaw, severing that bone on one side of his face. Then a whole horde of Iroquois fell on his body, ripping a gaping hole in his chest from which one of them wrenched out the great heart of Jean de Brébeuf. So he died, as he ardently wished, a martyr, having suffered as Paul Ragueneau reported in his *Relation* of 1649, ". . . as many cruelties as ever the rage of tyrants obliged the martyrs to endure . . ."[36] Father Paul Ragueneau, Jean de Brébeuf's first biographer, closed his lengthy account of his saintly friend thus: "His death has crowned his life and perseverance has been the seal of his holiness . . . He died while preaching and exercising truly apostolic offices, and by a death which the first apostle to the Hurons merited. His martyrdom took place on the 16th day of March in the current year, 1649."[37]

From the primary accounts of the martyrdom of Jean de Brébeuf and Gabriel Lalemant, it is not immediately evident whether Father Lalemant was forced to stand by, bound and helpless, while he watched the horrible torments afflicted upon his revered

[36] Ibid., XXXIX, 139.
[37] Ibid., XXXIV, 195.

companion. It is, however, quite clear that the delicate Lalemant bore the same character of tortures and with equal fortitude. "At the height of these torments," wrote Paul Ragueneau, "Father Gabriel Lalemant lifted his eyes to heaven, clasping his hands from time to time, and uttering sighs to God whom he invoked to his aid."[38] During his torture Father Lalemant's hands were cut off, his eyes gouged out, and glowing coals thrust into the empty sockets. In spite of his obvious frailty, Gabriel Lalemant endured horrible tortures from six in the evening until nine the next morning, March 17, 1649. As if in exasperation, the Iroquois finally struck him a blow with a hatchet behind the left ear with such force that the soft gray tissue of his brain lay exposed to view. There was no part of his body, ". . . from the feet even to the head, which had not been broiled, and in which he had not been burned alive, even the eyes into which those impious ones had thrust burning coals."[39] Finally, the Iroquois, ". . . weary of seeing him languish so long in the atrocious torments of a day and a whole night . . ." killed him ". . . with a hatchet blow and an arquebus shot, which an enemy himself, out of pity, fired at him . . ."[40] Penning a brief but touching eulogy of Father Lalemant, Francesco Bressani recorded: "Father Gabriel Lalemant had come last to this war, and gained the victory among the first. He had asked God for this grace during many years; and, having obtained it from him, it could not be denied him . . ."[41] Gabriel Lalemant expired at about nine o'clock on the morning of March 17, 1649.

Since no European was present to witness the suffering of these two valiant soldiers of Christ, how did his companions learn the details of their martyrdom? In his *Relation* of 1649, Father Paul Ragueneau testified: "I have learned all this from persons worthy of credence, who have seen it and reported it to me personally, and who were then captives with them, but who, having been reserved to be put to death at another time, found means to

[38] Ibid., 143.
[39] Ibid., 147, 149.
[40] Ibid., XXXIX, 253.
[41] Ibid., 255.

escape."[42] Paul Ragueneau's testimony harks back hauntingly to the ending of St. John's gospel: "This is that disciple who giveth testimony of these things, and hath written these things; and we know that his testimony is true."[43]

At nine in the morning on March 16, 1649, the Jesuits at Sainte Marie, noticing off to the east great columns of black smoke smearing the cold blue sky, knew with dread certainty that the mission of St. Louis had fallen to the Iroquois. Aware that Jean de Brébeuf and Gabriel Lalemant were there or at St. Ignace, the missionaries sorrowfully concluded that in either case their two valued companions were probably already captives of those fiends in human form. Shortly, two Christian Hurons ran pantingly into Sainte Marie announcing that the Jesuits' worst fears were only too well realized. Promptly, the whole lay personnel of the mission stood to arms, believing that before the day was over Sainte Marie itself would be under siege. Each of these ". . . resolved to sell his life very dearly and to die in a cause which, being for the interests of the Faith and the maintenance of Christianity in these countries, was more the cause of God than ours; moreover, our greatest confidence was in him."[44] Lookouts posted in the two stone towers guarding the mission's main entrance and sentinels pacing the eastern palisades throughout the

[42] Ibid., XXXIV, 149. In our current era, people are inclined to believe that such barbaric treatment as was suffered by Jean de Brébeuf and Gabriel Lalemant could not possibly have happened anywhere but in a raw, new world at the hands of an uncivilized tribe of aborigines. Let it be recalled, however, that just eight years later, in May 1657, St. Andrew Bobola, also a Jesuit, was killed by a group of anti-Catholic Cossacks in almost the identical manner. Captured at Janow in Poland, he was dragged behind a running horse several miles to Pinsk. Stripped naked there, he was burned all over his body as though he were a dead pig. His nose and lips were cut off. His tongue was pulled out by the roots through an opening in the back of his neck. He was scalped and the skin of his back peeled off. He was "baptized" with scalding water and one of his hands was all but severed from his arm. Finally, he was decapitated and his body thrown into a pool of excrement. In 1730, seventy-three years after his martyrdom, Father Bobola's incorrupt body was examined by physicians who testified as to the truth of the manner of his death. In 1922 Bobola's body was brought to Rome where it rests in the Jesuit church of the Gesu. Father Bobola was canonized in 1938. See Philip Monaci, *The Life and Martyrdom of Blessed Andrew Bobóla of the Society of Jesus.*

[43] John 21:24.
[44] *Relations*, XXXIV, 131.

day and far into the evening saw no signs of an approaching enemy force or even of skulking spies.

At nightfall the Iroquois sent scouts to reconnoiter the condition of Sainte Marie. ". . . their report having been made in [the Iroquois] council of war, the decision was adopted to come and attack us the next morning, promising themselves a victory which would be more glorious to them than all the successes of their arms in the past."[45] But the Huron Bear clan determined to have something to say about that. At Ossossané, where the fiery Pierre Joseph Marie Chaumonot was pastor, the braves, hastily arming themselves, prepared to do battle with the foe. ". . . the next morning, the seventeenth of March, about three hundred warriors, who, while awaiting more powerful help, secreted themselves in the ways of approach, intending to surprise some portion of the enemy."[46] They had not long to wait for about two hundred Iroquois, the advance guard on its way to open the attack on Sainte Marie, encountered the Huron troops. Most of the Hurons promptly fled ". . . after some skirmishing, and were eagerly pursued until within sight of our fort, many having been killed while they were in disorder in the midst of the snows."[47]

However the Iroquois were far from having it all their own way. The more courageous of the Hurons, standing their ground, drove the enemy force back to St. Louis where the Iroquois took refuge behind that village's palisades which had not been destroyed when the place was put to the torch. When Iroquois runners reported their repulse, the main body of their army rushed into the battle. A furious conflict ensued, lasting far into the night before the Iroquois finally defeated that valiant band of Hurons who lost all but about twenty men and all of those were badly wounded. Now nothing but a mere corporal's guard of Frenchmen was left to defend Sainte Marie and all its inhabitants.

All through the night of March 17-18, 1649, ". . . our Frenchmen were in arms, waiting to see at our gates this victorious

---

[45] Ibid. This was true because thus far the Iroquois had never even attempted to storm such a well-defended European emplacement. Had they been able to take Sainte Marie, they could well have been bold enough to attack Three Rivers, for example.

[46] Ibid., 133.

[47] Ibid.

enemy."[48] Expecting to die the following day, they had recourse to heaven.

We redoubled our devotions, in which were our strongest hopes, since our help could come only from heaven. Seeing ourselves on the eve of the feast of the glorious Saint Joseph, the patron of this country, we felt ourselves constrained to have recourse to a protector so powerful. We made a vow to say, every month, each a Mass in his honor during the space of a whole year, for those who should be priests. And all, as many as there were people here, joined to this by vow, sundry penances, to the end of preparing us more holily for the accomplishment of the will of God concerning us, whether for life or for death; for we all regarded ourselves as so many victims consecrated to our Lord, who must await from his hand the hour when they should be sacrificed for his glory, without undertaking to delay or wish to hasten the moments thereof.[49]

Surprisingly, after their victory on March 17, the Iroquois failed to follow up their obvious advantage by attacking Sainte Marie in force. On the following day, March 19, the feast of St. Joseph,

. . . a sudden panic fell upon the hostile camp, some withdrawing in disorder, and others thinking only of flight. Their captains were constrained to yield to the terror which had seized them; they precipitated their retreat, driving forth in haste a part of their captives, who were burdened above their strength, like packhorses, with the spoils which the victorious were carrying off, their captors reserving for some other occasion the matter of their death. As for the other captives who were left to them, destined to die on the spot, they attached them to stakes fastened in the earth, which they had arranged in various cabins. To these, on leaving the village, they set fire on all sides, taking pleasure at their departure in feasting upon the frightful cries which these poor victims uttered in the midst of those flames, where children were broiling beside their mothers; where a husband saw his wife roasting near him; where cruelty itself would have had compassion at a spectacle which had nothing human about it, except the innocence of those who were in torture, most of whom were Christians.[50]

[48] Ibid., 135.
[49] Ibid.
[50] Ibid., 137. The fact that the Iroquois had fled was learned from an old Indian woman left to die by fire at St. Ignace among those tied to stakes in the cabins there. She escaped and fled to St. Michel, a mission located about seven miles almost directly south of St. Ignace. Seven hundred men there took to the warpath against them. When that Huron force had not overtaken the Iroquois after a two days' march, it turned back, partly for want of provisions and ". . . partly the dread of combating without advantage an enemy encouraged by his victories, and one who had mostly firearms, of which our Hurons have very few, all these things obliged them to retrace their steps . . ." Ibid.

On Saturday morning, March 20, when there was assurance of the departure of the Iroquois, Father Ragueneau sent Father Jacques Bonin with Christophe Regnault, François Malherbe, and five other Frenchmen to search for the bodies of the martyred Jesuits at the place of their torture. Christophe Regnault, then a *donné* and later a Jesuit brother, described what they discovered:

We found them both, but a little apart from each other. They were brought to our house and laid uncovered on strips of bark, where I examined them at leisure for more than two hours to see if what the Indians had told us of their martyrdom and death was true. I examined first the body of Father de Brébeuf, which was pitiful to see, as well as that of Father Lalemant. Father de Brébeuf had his legs, thighs, and arms stripped of flesh to the very bone; I saw and touched a number of great blisters, which he had on several places on his body, from the boiling water which these barbarians had poured over him in mockery of holy baptism. I saw and touched the wound from a belt of bark, full of pitch and resin, which roasted his whole body. I saw and touched his two lips, which they had cut off because he constantly spoke of God while they made him suffer. I saw and touched all parts of his body, which had received more than two hundred blows from a bludgeon. I saw and touched the top of his scalped head; I saw and touched the opening which these barbarians had made to tear out his heart. In fine, I saw and touched all the wounds of his body, as the Indians had told and declared to us.[51]

The grieving French community of Jesuits and laymen mourned their dead through all of Saturday, keeping vigil through the night until Sunday, March 21. On that morning Father Ragueneau relates:

We buried these precious relics on Sunday, the 21st day of March, with so much consolation and such tender feelings of devotion in all those who were present at their obsequies, that I know none who did not desire a similar death, rather than fear it; and who did not regard himself as blest to stand in a place where it might be, two days thence, God would accord him the grace of shedding both his blood and his life on a like occasion. No one of us could prevail upon himself to pray to God for them, as if they had any need of it; but our spirits were at once directed toward heaven, where we doubt not their souls were. Be this as it may, I entreat God that he fulfill in us his will, even to death, as he has done in their persons.[52]

After the solemn obsequies held on that sad Sunday, they buried the pitifully mutilated remains of Jean de Brébeuf and

[51] Ibid., 35.
[52] Ibid., 149, 151.

Gabriel Lalemant just inside the south door of the chapel reserved for the use of the Huron Christians. It was only fitting that
the great Echon should find, as it was supposed, his last resting
place among his beloved Hurons to whose conversion he had
dedicated almost the whole of his priestly life. Beside him they
buried Gabriel Lalemant, that frail, gentle Parisian who should
never have been allowed to come to Huronia. Gabriel and God
knew his true destiny. To accomplish it Gabriel's divine Master
brought him to the country of the Hurons so that he might go
thence to heaven as a martyr.

The withdrawal of the Iroquois army, instead of encouraging
the Hurons, unaccountably acted as a signal for precipitate flight.
Within two weeks of the martyrdom of Jean de Brébeuf fifteen
Huron villages were abandoned, ". . . the people of each scattering where they could, in the woods and forests, on lakes and rivers, and among the islands most unknown to the enemy."[53] It was
as though the Huron nation took abject flight from a horde of demons in human form.

Yet the Hurons could have defeated the Iroquois if they had
only stood together. Arms, even guns, and man power were not
lacking to the Hurons. Rather it was cohesive leadership and an
indomitable will to defend the homeland. Famine and recurring
epidemics as well as frequent defeats in local skirmishes finally,
perhaps, drained away the Huron will to resist. Never had the
Iroquois attacked in such force and assuredly not in winter when
deep snow should have prevented an enemy from invading Huronia. The Iroquois were, therefore, devils and not men who
needed nothing and were hard to kill. When that attitude came
to be shared commonly, the familiar world of Huronia ". . .
seemed suddenly [to be] melting down and running from under
their feet, and, with no thought beyond the immediate future,
they [the Hurons] incontinently fled in all directions."[54] Only

[53] Ibid., 197.

[54] Hunt, *Wars of the Iroquois*, 93. The Hurons could have mustered an army
nearly twice the size of that which invaded their country. In the fighting at St.
Louis and St. Ignace, the Hurons lost about one hundred seventy-five men while
the Iroquois lost two hundred.

Sainte Marie remained, a beacon in a wilderness, attracting hundreds of Christian Hurons who huddled around it, confused, frightened, and starving, hoping the missionaries could save them.

Desperate as the situation was, at least Sainte Marie remained unharmed. Since the Iroquois, at the height of their success, dared not attack it, the French could reasonably expect that their mission fortress would not fall under siege in the near future, if ever. Most of the Huron villages north of Sainte Marie were still intact, though in nearly every cabin widows mourned the loss of a husband fallen or captured by the dread enemy. Missions in those villages must be attended at all cost for the people in them needed most of all the encouragement the missionaries could give them. Besides, spring was on the way and perhaps the drought would end. By summer and fall, perhaps, new crops would be available to feed the people. In the meantime, the Jesuits would beggar themselves to feed the pitiable crowds who came hungry to their door. Father Paul Ragueneau and his companions must, somehow, breathe hope into the Hurons.

Chapter XIII

The End of the Dream

Though Father Paul Ragueneau and his missionary companions
strove diligently to instill hope for the future into the discouraged
Hurons, their efforts were all but fruitless. Within two weeks of
the destruction of St. Ignace II, the site of Jean de Brébeuf's
agonizing martyrdom, the massive mission center of Sainte Marie
saw itself ". . . stripped bare [of Huron villages] on every side,
[itself] . . . the only one which remained standing in these places
of terror . . ."[1] Literally all the Huron villages were burned and
abandoned ". . . lest they should serve as retreat and fortresses
for the Iroquois."[2] Becoming nomads again, hordes of surviving
Hurons fled to the depths of forests or island fastnesses far removed from the terrible Iroquois. There they eked out a bare living, feeding on acorns and wild roots or from fishing when they
dared. Only a few hundred remained around Sainte Marie, buried
in shocked despair, waiting for the missionaries to do something
for them. For a limited period the missionaries could feed the

[1] *Relations*, XXXIV, 197.
[2] Ibid.

starving, frightened refugees. But when their stores were depleted what would become not only of the Hurons but also of the French residing at Sainte Marie?[3] Besides, with the whole of Huronia swept bare of its people, ". . . it would be but rashness in us," Ragueneau wrote, "to dwell in a forsaken place whence the Hurons have retired, and where the Algonkins were unable to have further trade; not one would come to see us there except the enemies, who would discharge on us alone the whole weight of their hostility."[4] The only sensible plan was to flee with the fleeing since, as Father Ragueneau correctly declared, ". . . we do not live here for ourselves, but for the salvation of souls, and for the conversion of these peoples."[5] The only question was, where could the Hurons be gathered together again. Wherever that might be, there the Jesuits would follow, continuing their apostolic work.

Because many Hurons fled to the Petuns, situated west of Huronia, some consideration was given to removing mission headquarters there. The Jesuits had already established three missions among the Petuns at which Fathers Charles Garnier, Noel Chabanel, and a recent recruit, Leonard Garreau, were already laboring. Father Garnier made some attempt to collect the Hurons among the Petuns, writing to his brother, Father Henri de St. Joseph, a Carmelite in France, that he was setting out on April 26, 1649, in quest of the scattered Hurons.[6] However the Hurons, cowering under the walls of Sainte Marie, feared settling among the Petuns because the country of that nation was just as vulnerable to attack as was their own. If the Iroquois could lay waste Huronia, what prevented them from invading the Petuns? Certainly no natural barrier stood in their way.

Those Hurons who sought asylum in the shadow of Sainte Marie's palisades strongly favored fleeing to an island in Lake Huron. In theory, at least, their reasoning was sound. Provided an island home could furnish a living, an attack by the Iroquois

---

[3] Jones, 392. In 1649, after the martyrdom of Father Brébeuf, there were fifteen Jesuits at Sainte Marie as well as twenty-six laymen. Three Jesuits were with the Tobacco Nation. Father Chaumonot was on Christian Island with the Hurons from Ossossané and Father Poncet de La Rivière was at Manitoulin Island.

[4] *Relations*, XXXIV, 203.

[5] Ibid.

[6] Jones, 387. Garnier's letter was dated April 25, 1649.

would, possibly, be repelled more readily if the Hurons could perceive the approach of enemy war canoes. One such possible place was an island the Hurons called Ahouêndoë, known in our day as Christian Island.[7] After the disastrous defeat the Hurons of Ossossané suffered on March 17, 1649, they fled first to the Neutrals and then to the island of Ahouêndoë. Their peppery little pastor, Pierre Joseph Marie Chaumonot, followed them, arriving on May 1, 1649.[8] For Chaumonot's parishioners, whom he said were called the people of the "believing village,"[9] the island was an unfortunate choice. Though only a little more than a mile of open water separates the southern tip of it from the nearest mainland, the then heavily wooded island afforded little open space for planting corn without expending tremendous amounts of physical effort. In their half-starved condition preparing new fields was almost beyond the strength of those refugees.[10]

Since the Hurons were no longer safe in their homeland, the Jesuits gave serious consideration to finding a safe refuge for at least those immediately encamped around Sainte Marie. A possibly excellent location seemed to be at the mission of St. Pierre on a very large island situated somewhat over a hundred miles north and west of Huronia. The Indians called the place Ehaentoton, a Huron word which, rather fittingly, meant "the island of castaways."[11] The island, which we call Manitoulin, was the hunting ground of Algonkin nomads whom Father Claude Pijart and Father Poncet de La Rivière, Gabriel Lalemant's cousin, had been evangelizing since the fall of 1648.[12] The Jesuits had reason to believe that the Algonkins would receive the Hurons kindly because the latter had often allowed them to winter in Huronia.[13] The

[7] Ibid., 172. In English, the Huron word "Ahouêndoë" means an island in the lake.

[8] Chaumonot, *Autobiographie*, 96. Christian Island is now an Indian reservation. The few Indians living there are cared for, spiritually, by the pastor of St. John's Church, Waubaushene. Fittingly, the pastor is a Jesuit. The island has about two thousand acres of land which, for the most part, is very sandy.

[9] *Relations*, XXXIV, 217.

[10] Ibid., 215. The major mass of the island is about eight miles west of the mainland. A narrow, southern hook of the island is about a mile offshore.

[11] Jones, 200.

[12] *Relations*, XXXIV, 203.

[13] Ibid., XXXIII, 153. These Algonkins spent the winter of 1647-1648 with the Hurons. Father Poncet de La Rivière spent the winter of 1648-1649 with the Algonkins on Manitoulin Island. See ibid., XXXIV, 203.

island, much larger than Huronia, is seventy-five miles long and twenty-five miles wide as compared to Huronia's width of forty miles and length of hardly thirty miles. Describing what he hoped would be the new homeland of the Hurons, Paul Ragueneau said enthusiastically:

This island, it has seemed to us, must be a more suitable abode, for our purpose, because in that place we shall be better able than in any other to occupy ourselves with the conversion of the Hurons and of the Algonkins; for we shall approach the Eskiaeronnon, Aoechisaeronon, and Aoeatsioaenronnon, Algonkins and countless other allied peoples, continually proceeding westward, and removing ourselves from the Iroquois, our enemies.[14]

But Father Ragueneau's decision found no favor with the Hurons. How could they possibly make the long canoe voyage to that distant island? Undernourished as they were, how would they muster the strength to accomplish such a trying trip hampered by the sick, the elderly, and all the women and children? Even if they escaped the Iroquois bands lurking about Huronia, how did they know that the Algonkins, or even some unknown nation, might not drive them off? Ehaentoton was the mysterious unknown while Ahouêndoë was at the very door of their homeland. Besides, since many exiled Hurons had already taken refuge there, they would be among relatives, friends, and neighbors.

Finally, twelve of the most important captains of the Hurons came to Father Ragueneau, entreating him ". . . in the name of all this desolate people . . ."[15] to accompany them to Christian Island. For three whole hours the captains pleaded their cause. Stripping the women of their porcelain necklaces, the captains offered these as presents from their women and children. "They added that we knew well enough in what esteem they [the women] held these necklaces, which are their ornaments and all their beauty."[16] All this, the women would gladly surrender because they ". . . wished us to know that the Faith would be more precious to them than all their goods; and that our instructions would be held dearer than all the riches which the earth could furnish them."[17] The

---

[14] Ibid., XXXIV, 205. Each of the groups mentioned were divisions of the Algonkins. The last named were the Nipissings.

[15] Ibid., 209.

[16] Ibid.

[17] Ibid.

most telling argument introduced by the grave captains was saved for last.

They said that they made these presents in order to revive in our persons the zeal and the name of Father Echon . . . ; that he had been the first apostle to the country; that he had died to assist them even to his last sigh; that they hoped his example would touch us, and that our hearts could not refuse to die with them, since they wished to live as Christians.[18]

After three whole days of pleading, the Huron captains finally persuaded Father Ragueneau. The Jesuits would accompany the Hurons to Ahouêndoë which, henceforth, was called the Island of St. Joseph. One senses that Ragueneau was not well pleased with the decision. Perhaps Father Chaumonot warned him that the island offered very little fertile land, no wild game, and hardly any ready shelter. Some have criticized Paul Ragueneau for not insisting on the Hurons moving to Manitoulin Island, a fertile land far removed from the Iroquois. Let it be recalled, however, that his was not the choice. The Hurons were determined to migrate to that ill-fated Christian Island and, like Ruth in the Old Testament, whither the Hurons went there also the missionaries would follow. Making the best of a bad choice, Ragueneau wrote:

We could not doubt that God had chosen to speak to us by their [the Hurons] lips; and, although . . . we all had entertained another design, we all found ourselves changed before their departure, and with a common consent we believed that it was necessary to follow God in the direction whither he chose to call us, whatever peril there might be in it for our lives, and in whatever depths of darkness we may continue, for the remaining future, which is not in our power.[19]

Once the decision was made, on each of the Jesuits lay the

. . . necessity of bidding farewell to that old home of Sainte Marie, to its structures, which, though plain, seemed, to the eyes of our poor Indians, master-works of art; and to cultivated lands, which were promising us an abundant harvest. That spot must be forsaken, which I may call our second fatherland, our home of innocent delights, since it has been the cradle of this Christian church; since it was the temple of God, and the home of the servants of Jesus Christ.[20]

Much as they cherished Sainte Marie, the Jesuits could not abandon it, leaving it standing, ". . . for fear that our enemies, only too

---

[18] Ibid.
[19] Ibid., 211.
[20] Ibid., XXXV, 81, 83.

wicked, should profane the sacred place, and derive from it an advantage . . ."[21] Therefore, it must be dismantled, taking what could be transported, and the whole complex, at last, given over to the flames.

The most precious relics to be removed were the remains of Jean de Brébeuf and his fellow martyr, Gabriel Lalemant, which had lain in their graves within the Indian chapel for some seven weeks. Father Ragueneau determined to take them away with him, firmly believing that those two heroic apostles would some day be raised to the altars. Then their relics would be sought as treasures beyond price. Hence, Ragueneau directed Christophe Regnault, a *donné*, the mission's cobbler, to exhume the bodies and prepare the remains for transportation. Describing his task, Regnault wrote:

When we left the country of the Hurons, we raised both bodies out of the ground and set them to boil in strong lye. All the bones were well scraped, and the care of drying them was given to me. I put them every day into a little oven which we had, made of clay, after having heated it slightly; and, when in a state to be packed, they were enveloped separately in some silk. Then they were put into two small chests, and we brought them to Quebec where they are held in great veneration.[22]

When they deposited Jean de Brébeuf's body in the grave, they placed a small lead plate in the coffin on which they had inscribed: "Father Jean de Brébeuf, burned by the Iroquois, 16, 17, March, 1649." By accident, or perhaps design, the small plate was left in the grave to be found three hundred five years later by a fellow Jesuit, Father Denis Hegarty.[23]

[21] Ibid., 83.

[22] Ibid., XXXIV, 35.

[23] Horatio P. Phelan and Léon Pouliot, "Notes sur les reliques de Saint Jean de Brébeuf a l'occasion d'une récente découverte," *Lettres du Bas-Canada* VIII (1954), 137-46. From its destruction in 1649 until 1789 nothing is known about the area. In that year, British superintendent of Indian affairs, William Claus, concluded a treaty with five Ojibwa chiefs, purchasing from them much of the northern portion of Simcoe county for £101. One of the geographic landmarks used in the treaty, signed at York on May 22, 1789, was ". . . certain French ruins . . ." Kenneth E. Kidd, *The Evacuation of Sainte Marie I*, 14. The first white man to acquire title to the land on which the mission stood was Samuel Richardson, a Welshman, who was granted title in 1829. But he seems to have done nothing about his claim. In 1837 a crown patent bestowed part of the land on Pierre Thibeau. Through the following seventy-five years the land passed through various

In preparation for their exodus the French laymen built a small ship and a large log raft fifty or sixty feet long.[24] Then they methodically stripped Sainte Marie's buildings of everything portable, hinges, bellows for forges, strap iron, anvils, tools, every scrap of food available, as well as all the sacred vessels and cherished ornaments of the two chapels. Finally, came the saddest moment for everyone. At dusk on Saturday, May 15, 1649, the *donnés* and the salaried workmen set the torch to Sainte Marie among the Hurons.[25] From their vantage point on the Wye River,

hands until it finally was purchased by James Playfair, a local sportsman, who, fortunately, left the ruins untouched, but built a hunting lodge within the Indian compound. At his death the property was purchased by the Wye River Hunting Club and then by A. W. Taylor. In 1940 the Jesuits purchased the property. Professional evacuation of the site was begun in 1941 under the direction of the Royal Ontario Museum, Toronto. For two years, 1941-1943, Kidd, a competent archaeologist, directed the work. World War II suspended operations. In 1947 work began again under the direction of the Museum, but the archaeologist in charge was Wilfred Jury, who continued the work until its completion. In 1954 a careful, respectful evacuation of the Indian cemetery was completed, except for one spot, the place where the outside cloaca for the hunting lodge had stood. Though everyone else shied away from evacuating that most repelling site, Father Denis Hegarty, S.J., himself a trained archaeologist, assumed the none-too-attractive task. On Tuesday, August 17, 1954, Father Hegarty unearthed Brébeuf's original grave which measured seventy-nine inches by thirty-three, but tapering to thirty inches at the feet. At the spot where the left shoulder would have been, Father Hegarty found a lead plate measuring three inches by an inch and a half on which was inscribed, in French, "Father Jean de Brébeuf, burned by the Iroquois, 16, 17, March, 1649." The subsequent history of the relics is interesting. Lalemant's skull was sent to his sisters in France where it was preserved at Sens until rioters, during the French Revolution, destroyed it. Brébeuf's nephews sent a silver bust mounted on ebony as a reliquary for their uncle's bones. The last Jesuit of the old Society in Canada, Father Joseph Cazot, gave it, together with relics of Lalemant and Garnier, to the nuns of the Hôtel-Dieu at Quebec where they remained until 1925, the year these martyrs were beatified. Then Brébeuf's skull was divided, front to back, by Dr. Charles Vezina. The right half remains at the Hôtel-Dieu and the left half was given to the Jesuits.

[24] *Relations*, XXXV, 83.

[25] Ibid., XXXIV, 225. There Ragueneau says that they burned the mission and left it on May 15. See ibid., XXXV, 83, where he says "It was between five and six o'clock, on the evening of the fourteenth of June that part of our number embarked in a small vessel we had built. I, in company with most of the others, trusted myself to some logs, fifty or sixty feet in length . . ." Perhaps the mission was actually burned on May 15 and the sad departure was delayed until June 14. However, it would seem illogical for the French to have destroyed their greatest protection against the Iroquois and then to have delayed their departure for a whole month. Perhaps the explanation lies in a simple error on the part of the people in France who edited the account of the departure.

aboard the small boat and the clumsy raft, every Frenchman watched with sinking heart while the flames from the great burning complex lighted up the countryside and stained the sluggish Wye bloodred. How could they help reflecting on the decade of endless, weary toil expended erecting that great mission center which ". . . though plain, seemed, to the eyes of our poor Indians, master-works of art . . ."[26] That evening ten years of grueling labor was consumed in a fiery holocaust. They could not know that three hundred years later Sainte Marie among the Hurons would rise from the ashes, so accurately reconstructed that if Paul Ragueneau walked through the mission's east gate today he would be perfectly at home.

The sorry little flotilla of one small ship, a long unwieldy raft, and, surely, a fleet of Huron canoes crept timorously out of the mouth of the Wye River, making its way toward the island of Ahouêndoë, a good thirty miles by water from Sainte Marie. Mounting a careful watch, the ill-assorted flotilla crept slowly around Midland Point, across the mouth of outer Penetang Harbor, up the wide channel between the mainland and Beausoleil Island, and, keeping Giant's Tomb and Beckwith Islands well off to the right, the whole flotilla ". . . landed without mishap after a few days, . . . where the Hurons were awaiting us, and which was the spot we had fixed upon for a general reunion, that we might make of it a Christian island."[27] Of that precarious immigration Paul Ragueneau wrote:

God doubtless led us on this journey; for, even while we coasted along those deserted lands, the enemy was in the field, and on the following day he delivered his blow upon some Christian families whom he surprised, during their sleep, along the road which we had followed; some were massacred upon the spot, others led away captive.[28]

It behooved the French to set to work promptly, erecting a staunch mission center for themselves and a palisaded village for the Hurons before winter when the lake waters might freeze, affording the Iroquois a natural bridge over which an attack could

[26] Ibid., XXXV, 81.
[27] Ibid., 83. Probably the flotilla landed about a mile or so from the present village of Christian Island. It is there, not more than fifty yards from shore, that the ruins of Sainte Marie II are found.
[28] Ibid.

be launched. At once the forests rang with the sounds of axes felling trees for the structure the French planned. Unlike mainland Huronia, on the island stones were so plentiful that laborers had no difficulty erecting stone walls. "In consequence, thank God," reported Ragueneau, "we found ourselves well protected, having built a small fort according to military rules, which, therefore, could be easily defended, and would fear neither the fire, the undermining, nor the escalade of the Iroquois."[29]

Feeding the large, destitute population quickly became a serious problem. The Hurons from Ossossané, arriving first, planted corn in late May or early June. But, ". . . summer droughts had been so excessive that they lost hope of their harvest, unless heaven should afford them some favoring showers."[30] Even though rain fell the very day Father Ragueneau's contingent arrived, the harvest was far from adequate for the great numbers to be fed. The land was fertile enough, but most of the poor refugees were already so debilitated from previous seasons of drought that ". . . hardly one family in ten . . . had been able to apply itself to the labor needed to cultivate a field of Indian corn in a place which, when they came to it, was but a thick forest, unprepared in any way for tillage."[31] Throughout the summer and autumn, the people lived on wild fruits, acorns, bitter roots dug in the forests or small fish, all of which ". . . aided rather in postponing for a little time their death than in satisfying the needs of life."[32]

[29] Ibid., 85. See also Jones, 6-8. Ragueneau informed us that the fort's walls were fourteen feet high and made of stone and mortar. In shape, the building was square, about seventy-five feet to a side, with bastions at each of the four corners. In the approximate center of the fort there was a cistern, nine feet square, in solid masonry. Long before the present writer examined it, the fort showed some signs of having been surrounded by a moat. The walls of the fort are now, on the average, less than four feet high, but still quite discernible. One peculiarity of both Sainte Marie I and II is the cement employed. Ragueneau distinctly says that the ingredients for the cement used at Sainte Marie II were found on the island. See *Relations*, XXXV, 85. Engineers who studied the remains of the fort report that the foundations of the building were laid in hydraulic cement. In quality, the cement was much like the *Vicat*, a standard article manufactured and much used in France. Certainly, it would have been difficult to have obtained that article in any quantity at Christian Island in 1649. Strangely, the secret of how the cement was manufactured on the island seems to have been lost. See a discussion of this point in ibid., XIX, 270.

[30] Ibid., XXXV, 85.

[31] Ibid., 87.

[32] Ibid., 89.

When winter howled down the great sweep of Georgian Bay, enveloping the unprotected island in several feet of snow, raw starvation stalked through every cabin. And it was a very severe winter, ". . . covering the ground with three or four feet of snow, and freezing all the lakes and rivers."[33] Then the people became

. . . dying skeletons, eking out a miserable life, feeding even on the excrements and refuse of nature . . . Even carrion dug up, the remains of foxes and dogs, excited no horror; and they even devoured one another, but this in secret; . . . Mothers fed upon their children; brothers on their brothers; while children recognized no longer, in a corpse, him whom, while he lived, they had called their father.[34]

Many of the poor beleaguered people fled over the ice to the mainland even though they were well aware that they would almost certainly fall into the hands of the Iroquois. But, ". . . poverty compelled numbers of families to go thither, to seek death as much as life, in the open country given over to the fury of the enemy."[35] Even for those who stayed on the island the whole winter was long horror, ". . . passed in constant fear and expectation of a hostile party of Iroquois . . ."[36] coming to exterminate everyone.

From the food store the missionaries brought with them the Jesuits gave alms, exceeding, ". . . perhaps, what prudence asked of us . . ."[37] Their very generosity brought heartache to the devoted Jesuits. As their supplies diminished it became necessary to choose which of the needy most required alms. Going from cabin to cabin, each missionary gave out little copper tags to those in the most dire need. These poor wretches dragged themselves, at midday, to the door of the mission where their small tags were presented. "To some was given a certain quantity of acorns, which they cooked, first boiling them in a lye made from ashes . . . We distributed to others a small portion of smoked fish . . . The more favored among them received a little Indian meal, boiled in water."[38] Yet, what a cruel and bitter experience it must have been for the missionaries to help some and deny others, knowing full

33 Ibid.
34 Ibid.
35 Ibid., 91.
36 Ibid.
37 Ibid., 89.
38 Ibid., 99.

well that refusal quite likely condemned some to death from starvation!

As though their sorrow was not enough, surrounded by their starving Christians, another blow fell on the grieving Jesuits. Toward the end of November 1649, two Christian Hurons, escaping from a band of three hundred Iroquois, reached the new Sainte Marie. They informed everyone that the Iroquois were even then debating whether to cross the water and attack the Hurons on their island retreat or vent their wrath on the Petuns.[39] Even in their weakened condition, a host of Huron braves planned taking to the field. But, prudently, Father Ragueneau, dissuading the Hurons, sent messengers to inform the Petuns of the imminent threat to their nation. Certainly, he also sent warning to the four Jesuits laboring among the Tobacco and the Hurons who had taken refuge with them. These missionaries were: Charles Garnier and Noel Chabanel at the mission of St. Jean; Adrien Grélon and Leonard Garreau at the mission of St. Mathias.[40] Father Ragueneau recalled Noel Chabanel, ". . . having thought it wiser not to keep two missionaries exposed to danger; considering besides that the famine, in that quarter, was so severe that sufficient food for both could not be obtained."[41]

Apparently the war captains of the Petun village of Etharita, where the mission of St. Jean lay, learned nothing of the tactics employed by the Iroquois, especially at St. Louis among the Hurons. Etharita, a village with a population of ". . . five or six hundred families . . ."[42] surely could have gathered a military force of at least one warrior for each family. The Iroquois force marching against them was known to be composed of about three hundred braves. Not content to await an attack behind what little protection their village offered, the Petun braves boiled out of their palisaded village on December 5, 1649, going in search of the foe, ". . . fearing lest the Iroquois should escape them and desiring to surprise the latter while they were still on the road."[43] But the clever Iroquois, approaching by a roundabout route, captured a

[39] Ibid., 107.
[40] Jones, 359.
[41] *Relations*, XXXV, 147.
[42] Ibid., 107.
[43] Ibid., 109.

man and a woman just emerging from the Petun village. Learning from those two unfortunates the undefended condition of the village, the Iroquois promptly attacked it like ravenous wolves.

On December 7, 1649, at about three in the afternoon, the Iroquois swarmed into the helpless village, ". . . spreading immediate dismay, and striking terror into all those poor people, bereft of their strength, and finding themselves vanquished when they thought to be themselves the conquerors."[44] Scenes of incredible cruelty occurred similar to those at St. Louis and St. Ignace II. Infants, snatched from their mothers, were heartlessly thrown into burning cabins. Children witnessed the horrible deaths of their mothers. The able-bodied were marshaled into long lines to be driven into captivity while the sick, the aged, and the helpless were ruthlessly slaughtered.

Father Charles Garnier, the only missionary then at the village, was in an Indian cabin instructing its inmates when the Iroquois burst into the village. Hastening immediately to his rude chapel, where he found some Christians assembled, he cried to them: "We are dead men, my brothers. Pray to God and flee by whatever way you may be able to escape. Bear about with you your faith through what of life remains; and may death find you with God in mind."[45] The Christians begged their missionary to flee with them, but, ". . . unmindful of himself, he thought only of his neighbor."[46] As he scurried about the village, absolving the Christians or baptizing those who requested that sacrament, he met his own death.

A bullet from a musket struck him, penetrating a little below the breast; another, from the same volley, tore open his stomach, lodging in the thigh and bringing him to the ground. His courage, however, was unabated. The barbarian who had fired the shot stripped him of his cassock, and left him weltering in his blood, to pursue the other fugitives.[47]

Even after receiving so horrible a wound, the zealous Garnier struggled to his feet, taking a few steps, attempting to reach a dying Indian to comfort him. Shortly, his body drained of its life's blood, Charles Garnier collapsed and died. A Christian woman,

[44] Ibid.
[45] Ibid., 111.
[46] Ibid., 113.
[47] Ibid.

who witnessed the Jesuit's death, escaped her captors and related the details of the martyrdom of Charles Garnier to his superior, Paul Ragueneau.[48]

During that same sad period, the night of December 7-8, 1649, Noel Chabanel, a martyr to duty long before, suffered a martyr's death at the hands of a Huron renegade. Recalled to the island headquarters, Father Chabanel set out from St. Jean on December 5 with seven or eight Christian Hurons, stopping briefly at the mission of St. Mathias.[49] On the morning of December 7, he started off again, traveling that day ". . . six long leagues over a most difficult road . . ."[50] At nightfall Chabanel and his Huron companions stopped to rest. While the Indians slept Father Chabanel

. . . was watching and in prayer. Towards midnight he heard a noise, accompanied with cries, partly of a victorious hostile force who occupied that road; partly, also, of captives, taken that very day in the village of Saint Jean . . . On hearing the noise, the Father awoke his men, who fled at once into the forest, and eventually saved themselves . . .[51]

Fleeing back to St. Mathias, the Hurons told their missionaries that Father Chabanel, after accompanying them a little way, had fallen on his knees, saying to them, "It matters not that I die; this life is a very small consideration; of the blessedness of paradise, the Iroquois can never rob me."[52]

At daybreak, December 8, 1649, Noel Chabanel continued walking toward the island whither he had been summoned. Reaching the Nottawasaga River, he encountered Louis Honareennhak, a Huron who happened along in his canoe. Though once baptized, Louis had apostatized and was a violent opponent of the missionaries.[53] His story was that he helped Father Chabanel by taking, with the missionary's consent, the Jesuit's

[48] RAPQ, 1924-1925, 78. A day or two after Garnier's martyrdom, Father Leonard Garreau and his companion went to St. Jean in search of Father Garnier's body. ". . . it was hardly recognizable, covered with blood and ashes from the fire . . . they buried it there where the chapel had been, of which no sign remained." Sometime before the Jesuits all left Huronia Garnier's body was brought to the outpost on Christian Island and his relics were taken to Quebec.

[49] Jones, 397.

[50] *Relations*, XXXV, 147.

[51] Ibid., 149.

[52] Ibid.

[53] Ibid., 151.

hat, a bag containing his writings and a blanket ". . . which our missionaries used as a robe and cloak, as mattress and cushion, for a bed, and for every other convenience, even for a dwelling-place, when in the open country, and when they have, for the time, no other shelter."[54] It was not long before the Jesuits knew for certain that the vicious apostate had robbed Father Chabanel, killed him, and thrown his body into the Nottawasaga River. Noel Chabanel's body was never recovered. At last, however, he had fulfilled his vow, made two years before, to remain on the Huron mission until death despite his utter revulsion for everything about the Indians.[55]

On their island refuge the devastating winter of 1649-1650 continued taking its inexorable toll of the Hurons. Illness, starvation, and discontent played havoc, especially with the pagans. On the mainland some infidel captains of the Petuns, exasperated with the progress of Christianity, accused the two remaining missionaries of directly causing the country's calamities. A decision was taken to kill the two missionaries and the ringleader of the movement was Father Chabanel's murderer. That fact was learned from ". . . a trustworthy person [who] told us [the Jesuits] that he had heard from the man's own lips, his boast that he was the murderer; that he had rid the world of that common carrion of a Frenchman and had thrown his body into the river, after braining him at his feet."[56]

At the beginning of March 1650, the famished Hurons risked a trip to the mainland in search of acorns or to fish in the coves where the ice had broken up. Some, crossing the ice on foot, fell through into the frigid waters of the lake and were quickly drowned. Others were promptly attacked by Iroquois warriors. In less than two days, beginning on March 25, 1650, one hundred fifty families were slaughtered. Only one man escaped to bring back to the island the disastrous news.[57] After two such calamitous attempts, two sage old captains came to consult privately with Father Ragueneau. Drastic action was required, and promptly, if the poor remnant of the Hurons was to survive.

[54] Ibid., 149.
[55] Ibid., 157.
[56] Ibid., 169.
[57] Ibid., 187, 189.

"My brother," they said to Paul Ragueneau,

take courage. You alone can bestow life on us, if you will strike a daring blow. Choose a place where you may be able to reassemble us, and prevent this dispersion. Cast your eyes toward Quebec, and transport thither the remnants of this ruined nation. Do not wait until famine and war have slain the last of us. You carry us in your hands and your heart. More than ten thousand have been snatched away by death. If you delay longer, not one will remain and then you would know the regret of not having saved those whom you could have withdrawn from danger, and who disclosed to you the means. If you listen to our wishes, we will build a church under the shelter of the fort at Quebec. There, our faith will not die out; and the examples of the Algonkins and the French will hold us to our duty. Their charity will alleviate, in part, our miseries; and, at the least, we shall sometimes find there a morsel of bread for our little ones, who, to sustain life, have for so long lived on acorns and bitter roots. After all, if we must die with them, death there would be far easier than in the midst of the forests, where no one would assist us to die well; and where, we fear, our faith would in time become enfeebled, whatever resolution we had to prize it more than our lives.[58]

If the Hurons would not take refuge on Manitoulin Island, then the only sensible solution was that for which the two captains pleaded so strongly. Famine and war were certainly exterminating the Christian Hurons who clung so desperately to their missionaries. Therefore it was decided to risk the hazardous journey to Quebec with the three hundred people who remained on the island. "It was not without tears," wrote Father Ragueneau,

that we left a country which possessed our hearts and engaged our hopes; and which, reddened with the glorious blood of our brethren, promised us a like happiness, and opened to us the way to heaven and the gates of paradise. But yet, self must be forgotten and God left for God's sake, I mean that he is worthy of being served for himself alone, without regard to our interests, were they the most holy that we could have in the world.[59]

On Friday, June 10, 1650, when all was in readiness, the long convoy of canoes carrying all of the Jesuits, all of their French assistants, and the whole three hundred Hurons, pushed off from Sainte Marie II and Huronia was abandoned forever.[60] Passing along the country he knew so well, Father Ragueneau saw nothing but traces of Iroquois cruelty and signs of their treachery. In

[58] Ibid., 195.
[59] Ibid., 197.
[60] Ibid., 75.

the land where thousands had once dwelt, no sign of a permanent Huron dwelling remained. With the relics of his martyred friends, Brébeuf, Lalemant, and Garnier, in the canoe with him Ragueneau could see nothing but signs of true genocide. As though the country itself was a new messenger to a latter-day Job, Father Ragueneau could say only: "The Lord giveth; the Lord taketh away; blessed be the name of the Lord."

Midway during their fifty-day retreat from Huronia, the sorry convoy encountered a band of forty Frenchmen, including Father Bressani, and a few Hurons sent out from Quebec to rescue the Huron missionaries from starvation. Joining the descending fleet, all continued their desolate way, reaching Quebec on July 28, 1650.[61] As a final plea for charity toward his bitterly afflicted Hurons, Father Ragueneau wrote in his *Relation* of 1650:

I pray our Lord to grant genuine feelings of a truly Christian charity to all those who have so rich an opportunity for putting it into practice. Until more can be done, we, as their fathers, shall endeavor, at whatever cost, to provide for their necessities. On their journey down we had fed them; in their own country, God had given us the means of alleviating, in part, their miseries. For them we shed our blood, and spent our lives; could we after that, refuse them, so far as might be in our power, that which was extraneous to us? They come every day to our house for the allowance that is served out to them; they themselves have built their own cabins, and they will try by their labor to provide for themselves a part of their support. If, after having exhausted our resources, we find ourselves powerless to continue our charities, and behold them dying here of famine, close to our Frenchmen, there remains to us at least this consolation, that they will die Christians.[62]

True to Father Ragueneau's promise, the Jesuits never abandoned the Hurons. At first they camped outside the fort at Quebec and were fed by the nuns from the hospital, the Ursulines, the French, and even by some of the Algonkins. On March 26, 1651, the Jesuits settled the Hurons on property they owned on Isle d'Orléans, building them a strongly palisaded village. But when the vicious Iroquois continued harassing them there, some Hurons simply gave up, throwing themselves into the arms of their terrible enemy. About two hundred Hurons remained in the Quebec area. These were settled at Notre Dame de Lorette, nine

[61] Ibid., 207.
[62] Ibid., 211.

miles northwest of Quebec, on land owned by the Jesuits. At that
site the greatest living friend of the Hurons, Pierre Joseph Marie
Chaumonot, was their pastor and continued to care for them until
1691 when old age forced his retirement.

In the three centuries and more since the destruction of Sainte
Marie the Hurons have ceased to exist as a distinct people. Inter-
marriage with the French and absorption by other Indian nations
as well as migration westward has effectively eliminated any tribal identity of the Hurons. As with the nation, so with the Huron
language, that tongue is lost forever. The last Huron who could
speak his native tongue died nearly a century ago. But the memory of Jean de Brébeuf will never die so long as the Catholic
Church raises an altar to her martyrs, far from the least of whom
was Echon, Jean de Brébeuf.

Chapter XIV

Canonization

François de Harlay, archbishop of Rouen, who claimed ecclesiastical jurisdiction over New France, read Father Paul Ragueneau's
Relation of 1649 with consuming interest.[1] That exalted prelate

[1] François de Harlay was born at Paris in 1585 and died on March 22, 1653.
He was of a noble family related to many of Europe's princely houses. In 1616 he
was appointed archbishop of Rouen and primate of Normandy. Unlike far too
many of his contemporary prelates, De Harlay was an apostolic man who strove
to raise the religious level of his diocese. He was a man of great erudition, so
much so that even his critics declared his mind to be a library in itself. For all
that, he lacked, it would appear, sufficient knowledge of canon law to understand
that he could not, on his own authority, extend the boundaries of his diocese. He
simply asserted ecclesiastical authority over New France without any reference to
the papacy. He might possibly have done so because the few diocesan priests who
migrated to the New World asked him for ecclesiastical faculties either because
they were from his diocese or they sailed from ports within it. The Jesuits, however, obtained their churchly authority from Rome. The question of episcopal
jurisdiction in New France did not emerge as a serious problem until 1657 when
the Abbé Gabriel de Queylus, a Sulpician, arrived to assume spiritual care of
Montreal. Queylus announced that he was vicar-general of the archbishop of
Rouen, who by then was François de Harlay-Chanvallon, his predecessor's
nephew. Asserting that he had supreme ecclesiastic jurisdiction in New France,
Queylus proceeded to exercise it, ignoring the authority of the superior of all the
Jesuits, even over his own subjects. A troubled period followed which was solved,
in 1658, when François de Laval was appointed to be the first episcopal authority
in New France.

must have been deeply impressed with the Jesuit's remarks in the fourth chapter of his little work. "I would gladly," he asserted concerning his martyred brethren,

call them by that glorious name [of martyrs] not only for the love of God and for the salvation of their neighbor, they exposed themselves to death, and to a cruel death, if ever there was one in the world, for they could easily and without sin have put their lives in safety, if they had not been filled with love for God rather than themselves. But much rather would I thus call them, because, in addition to the charitable dispositions which they have manifested on their side, hatred for the faith and contempt for the name of God have been among the most powerful incentives which have influenced the mind of the barbarians to practice upon them as many cruelties as ever the rage of tyrants obliged the martyrs to endure who, at the climax of their tortures, have triumphed over both life and death.[2]

If Ragueneau's statements were true, the Jesuits killed by the Indians had certainly fulfilled the conditions requisite for the Church to call them true martyrs. They had been killed out of hatred for the faith and they had all died willingly. If the Church declared them martyrs, they would add luster to the archdiocese of Rouen.

Though Father Ragueneau's position offered him no official opportunity to instigate proceedings which might lead to the Church's declaration of heroic sanctity regarding his dear companions, Archbishop de Harlay could and did. Promptly, he wrote to New France, ordering sworn testimony gathered from all who could testify to the truth of the heroically virtuous lives and deaths of the slain Jesuits. With such a document available it was De Harlay's evident intention, as it was, ecclesiastically, his prerogative, to institute the long, involved process leading to the canonization of Isaac Jogues, René Goupil, Jean de La Lande, Jean de Brébeuf, Gabriel Lalemant, Charles Garnier, Noel Chabanel, and Antoine Daniel.

In 1650, after reaching Quebec from the Huron country, Father Paul Ragueneau composed a very lengthy document called in English: *Memoirs Concerning the Life and Virtues of Fathers Isaac Jogues, Anne de Nouë, Antoine Daniel, Jean de Brébeuf, Gabriel Lalemant, Charles Garnier, Noel Chabanel and . . . René*

[2] *Relations*, XXXIV, 139, 141.

Goupil.[3] The document, which in print fills ninety pages, was formally sworn to by eyewitnesses of the contents or by those who had learned the details of the martyrdom from trustworthy witnesses. The whole bulky manuscript was forwarded to the archbishop who, considerately, sent a copy of it back to the Jesuits in New France. There, Father Ragueneau read it carefully and, again under oath, declared that everything contained in the document was true.

Though authorities in France seem to have taken no further steps to forward the cause of the martyrs toward canonization, a cult in their honor developed in New France. Soon people were reporting miracles which, they claimed, were due to the intercession of the martyrs. Two such instances might be mentioned. In the Hôtel-Dieu at Quebec a very sick Protestant soldier vehemently declared to the nuns, anxious to convert him, that he would die rather than abandon the faith of his fathers. His pious nurse clandestinely dipped a relic of Jean de Brébeuf into the sufferer's medicine, praying that the martyr would cure the soldier both in body and mind. Though the soldier's health did not improve, he spontaneously asked to receive instructions and became a Catholic.[4]

A second instance was considered much more striking than the first. In 1663 the venerable relics of Father Brébeuf were considered to be directly instrumental in curing a woman of demoniacal possession. Charles de Lauson de Charny, Bishop Laval's vicar-general, testified that on August 9, 1663, a woman, suffering for two years from possession by a demon, was instantly cured when she touched some relics of Father Brébeuf.[5]

---

[3] RAPQ, 1924-1925, 3-93. Father Anne de Nouë's name was included probably because the Jesuits in New France considered him a martyr of charity. During the winter of 1646 he set out from Three Rivers to administer the sacraments to soldiers stationed at the present Sorel, a distance of about fifty miles. Caught in a blizzard, he froze to death on February 1 or 2, 1646. He had advanced upstream only six miles.

[4] Martin, *Hurons et Iroquois*, 289.

[5] Ibid. Were it not for the man who attested to the incident, it probably would deserve little credence. Charles de Lauson de Charny was no impressionable ecclesiastic. Born at Paris in about 1629, he was one of the three sons of Jean de Lauson, governor of New France from 1651 to 1656. Charles reached Quebec on July 1, 1652, at the age of twenty-three. Six weeks later he married Louise Giffard, a child of thirteen. In 1656 when his father, wearied of the posi-

In the years immediately following the martyrdom of Jean de Brébeuf, cures of both body and mind, attributed to his intercession, were, apparently, granted chiefly to those among whom he lived and labored. Undoubtedly, the most striking such blessing was received by the Iroquois who was considered to have been the martyr's executioner. He was an Oneida whom the French called *Cendre-Chaude*, a name which might be rendered in English as "Hot Cinder." He not only became a Christian, but an enthusiastic apostle. Through his life Hot Cinder manifested the greatest devotion and reverence for his heroic victim, Jean de Brébeuf. Hot Cinder's greatest boast was that it fell to him to have dealt the deathblow to Father Brébeuf.[6]

Perhaps the most accurately attested case of Jean de Brébeuf's celestial intervention concerned Mère Marie de Saint Augustin, an Augustinian nun at the Hôtel-Dieu at Quebec. Born Marie-Catherine de Simon de Longpré at Saint-Sauveur-de-Vicomte, Lower Normandy, in 1632, she joined a convent of nursing nuns at Bayeux where her older sister had preceded her. She was then only twelve years old. Her mistress of novices, considering her a rather frivolous child, thought of dismissing her, but Marie-Catherine refused to leave, saying that she would depart from Bayeux only for New France. She came to Quebec in 1648 when she was only sixteen. Despite frequent bouts of serious illness, Mère Marie was treasured at the hospital because she was a very competent nurse, a good businesswoman, and, above all, because she was a true mystic. Though she never saw Father Brébeuf in the flesh, she very seriously considered him her sole spiritual director who had been assigned her by God himself. Mère Marie

---

tion of governor, returned to France, Charles administered the colony for a year. In October 1656 his wife, aged seventeen, died, after presenting him with a daughter. Charles returned to France, leaving his infant daughter at Quebec. In France he became a priest and, in 1659, promptly returned to New France where he became Bishop Laval's vicar-general. Given his background and experience, it would seem highly unlikely that he would be unduly impressed by just any hysterical lady. It seems, therefore, that the woman really well could have been afflicted in the manner described.

[6] Ibid., 290. Objectively, it would seem that Hot Cinder was piously exaggerating. Considering the innumerable wounds inflicted on Father Brébeuf during his martyrdom, who could say which one caused his death or by whom that one was inflicted.

frequently saw Father Brébeuf who always carried a palm, indicating that he was a martyr. When the nun died in 1668, Bishop Laval, himself a very holy man, asked Father Ragueneau to write her biography. Ragueneau published his *La Vie de Mère Catherine de Saint-Augustin* at Paris in 1671. The book, replete with references to Father Brébeuf, gave further impetus to his cult both in Canada and France.

Just as there are fashions in dress, so there are fashions in pious devotions. With the passing years the Jesuit martyrs of North America became a legend. They well might have so remained except for the consuming interest of one nineteenth-century Jesuit, Father Félix Martin. Born October 14, 1804, at Auray in Brittany, Martin entered the Jesuit novitiate on September 27, 1823. In 1842 he and four Jesuit companions were sent to Montreal to open a college. Two years later, in 1844, while visiting Quebec, the nuns at the Hôtel-Dieu gave him a great mass of original manuscripts pertaining to the Jesuits in New France.[7] Spurred on by such an inestimably precious discovery, Father Martin's major interest became, thenceforth, the history of the Jesuits in New France. Visiting the Huron country in 1855, he made a rough map of the ground plan of Sainte Marie and identified several outlying mission sites.[8] In 1858 he was the general editor for the Canadian government's excellent three-volume edition of the *Jesuit Relations*.

Father Martin's most cherished hope was to see the canonization of the North American martyrs. On visits to Europe, especially Rome, he managed to collect at the Collège Sainte-Marie an impressive archive of primary material on the subject. At Rome particularly he made every possible effort to interest the central administration of the Society of Jesus and the Vatican in introducing the cause of the martyrs for canonization. His first hopeful sign occurred in 1859 when the diocese of Quebec established a commission to investigate the facts concerning the lives

[7] Georges-Emile Giguère, "Histoire du culte: le père Felix Martin, promoteur de la cause des martyrs canadiens," *Lettres du Bas-Canada* III (1949), 39. These manuscripts had been given to the nuns by Father Cazot before his death in 1800. The nuns not only gave Martin all the manuscripts, but swore under oath that they were the ones given them and that, while in their care, they had not been tampered with in any way.

[8] Jones, 7.

and deaths of the martyrs with a view to moving for their eleva-
tion to the Church's altars. Father Martin was appointed president of the commission.

Félix Martin did not live to see anything like the realization of
his dream, dying at Paris on November 25, 1886. Yet his crusad-
ing pen gave initial impetus to the movement, especially his biog-
raphies of Jogues, Brébeuf, and Chaumonot. Through his efforts
the memory of the martyrs was freshened.

Just two years before Martin's demise the first formal step toward canonization of the martyrs was taken. In 1884 the American bishops, at the Plenary Council, held at Baltimore, petitioned
the Holy See for the beatification of Isaac Jogues, René Goupil,
and the Iroquois maiden, Kateri Tegawitha.[9] Also, that very year
the American Jesuits opened the shrine on the site of Jogues' martyrdom at Auriesville, New York, honoring the martyrs. Two
years later, in 1886, the Canadian bishops at their Plenary Council held at Quebec forwarded to Rome a petition requesting the
Holy See to institute the process leading to the canonization of
the martyrs. The wording of that petition indicated that devotion to the martyrs was still deeply rooted in the hearts of the
Canadian faithful. The bishops wrote: "Four Jesuits, immolated
within a period of eighteen months, are venerated as true martyrs
not only because of the circumstances of their deaths, but also for
the miracles attributed to them and the memory of them which
is preserved."[10]

Though no positive action resulted from the effort of the
American and Canadian bishops, Félix Martin's crusade found a
new and valuable leader in Father Arthur Edward Jones, a Jesuit

[9] Kateri Tegawitha, whose Indian name is variously spelled, was a young
Mohawk girl baptized in 1675 in her home village of Gandaouagué. As a child
she had been badly burned and had been terribly marked from smallpox. An unattractive cripple, she was a village drudge most of her life. In 1677, together
with a rather large group of Iroquois, she migrated to a mission village on the
St. Lawrence opposite Montreal which was and is called Caughnawaga. She died
there in the odor of sanctity on April 17, 1680. Her cause has been introduced
and advanced toward canonization. Her relics are preserved in the church of
St. Francis Xavier at Caughnawaga, the original mission's name, which is still in
charge of the Jesuits. The custodian of Kateri's relics and the *postulator* of her
cause, is Father Henri Béchard, a native-born American who has spent his life
in Canada.

[10] Giguère, "Histoire du culte," 70-71.

and one of Martin's old students.[11] Stationed all of his priestly
life, except for one year, at the Collège Sainte-Marie, Father
Jones continued enriching the institution's archives and publishing studies concerning the seventeenth-century Jesuits in Huronia. Not only did he become the recognized authority on that
area, he was also acknowledged as the most informed scholar concerning its historical geography. Rounding out his erudition, Father Jones made himself perhaps the last scholar commanding a
thorough knowledge of the Huron language. His monumental
tome, *8endake Ehen; or Old Huronia*, is the most scholarly work
concerning the area which has ever been produced.

The process of moving one of God's elect from a local reputation for sanctity to a formal declaration of sainthood is a most involved operation. A mere description of the process occupies
thirty pages of Woywod's *Critical Commentary on the Code of
Canon Law.* In essence, the process comes down to a true ecclesiastical trial in which a *postulator*, in effect a defense lawyer,
presents any writings of the subject, eyewitness testimony concerning his life, and the like. He is opposed by an official, collo-
quially known as the devil's advocate, who honestly strives to
disprove the subject's qualifications for the honor of sainthood.
Once the evidence is gathered it is submitted to three separate
committees, each of whom must, independently, hand down a
favorable judgment regarding the heroic virtue of the subject as
well as the authenticity of the miracles said to have been performed through the intercession of the subject. After all of this
minute investigation, the Holy Father issues a decree declaring
that the subject may be called blessed and devotion in his honor
may be practiced publicly.

The preliminary process for the beatification of the North
American martyrs may be said to have begun in 1892 when the

[11] Arthur Edward Jones was born at Brockville, Ontario, on November 17,
1838, of English parents. He was educated at Collège Sainte-Marie in Montreal
while Father Martin was there. After his ordination, July 2, 1873, he spent his
whole life, except for one year at Guelph, 1881-1882, at his alma mater chiefly
as pastor of the church of the Gesu which stood beside the college building. Very
recently the college building was torn down. From 1882 until his death, Father
Jones was archivist at Sainte-Marie. He died on January 19, 1918. Before his
death he knew that the cause for the beatification of his beloved martyrs had
finally been officially introduced.

postulator of the cause appointed Father Jones vice-postulator for Canada. It was not, however, until 1904 that the case was actually officially instituted and not until 1917 that it was formally presented to the Sacred Congregation of Rites for examination. Eight long years later, on June 2, 1925, the Jesuit martyrs were finally beatified by Pius XI.[12]

The beatified are not automatically raised to the altars as saints, though, presuming sufficient interest, the final step is, at last, possible. The procedure for canonization is, in effect, a complete repetition of the whole process gone through for beatification. There is, however, one unique exception. The cause for canonization of the beatified may not be introduced without proof that new miracles have occurred through the intercession of the beatified. Even if that condition is met, the case may not be introduced without the express consent of the Holy Father. At long last, five years after their beatification, the North American martyrs were canonized by Pius XI on June 29, 1930.

Natural curiosity induces one to wonder what were the miracles accepted and to whom did they occur. In his decree, *Militantem ecclesiam,* declaring the canonization of Jean de Brébeuf and his companions, Pius XI recounted the essential details of two. Marie Robichaud, born in 1898 at Shippengan, New Brunswick, entered a congregation of nursing sisters in 1920. Five years later, in 1925, she was gravely afflicted with fibrocaseous tubercular peritonitis. Attending physicians finally declared that further treatment was useless. The afflicted nun, and her community, sought the miraculous intercession of the North American martyrs. On June 9, 1925, she was instantly and permanently cured. Alexandrina Ruel, a healthy young lady until 1907, was stricken with severe pains in her stomach. When an operation was performed for the removal of her appendix, the organ was declared to be tubercular. Her constant state of poor health became critical in 1918 when a second operation revealed tubercular peritonitis affecting the whole abdomen. When the medical profession gave up on the case, she had recourse to the intercession of the North American martyrs. She was cured, instantly and permanently, as her physicians attested under oath.

[12] *Acta Apostolicae Sedis,* XVII (1925), 314-18.

On June 29, 1930, the Vatican Basilica was magnificently decorated in preparation for the solemn canonization of the North American martyrs. When the diocesan and regular clergy were gathered, together with the prefects and officials of the Roman Curia, as well as cardinals, patriarchs, archbishops, bishops, and abbots, Pius XI made his dramatic entry with the impressive splendor which only St. Peter's and the vicar of Christ can muster. After delivering his long, eloquent exposition of the heroic lives and valiant deaths of the North American martyrs, Pius XI solemnly pronounced the age-old formula:

In honor of the Holy and Undivided Trinity, for the exaltation of the Catholic Faith, and the increase of the Christian Religion, by the authority of our Lord Jesus Christ, the Blessed Apostles Peter and Paul, and Ourselves, after mature deliberation, and having many times implored the divine aid, by the counsel of our venerable brothers, Cardinals of the Holy Roman Church, and of the Patriarchs, Archbishops, and Bishops met together in the City, we have decided and defined the Blessed Jean de Brébeuf and his companions Martyrs, Gabriel Lalemant, Antoine Daniel, Charles Garnier, Noel Chabanel, Isaac Jogues, René Goupil [and] Jean de La Lande . . . to be Saints, and have inscribed them in the catalogue of Saints, ordering that their memory shall be cherished and honored with pious devotion by the Universal Church . . .[13]

Then it was that, for the very first time, and by Pius XI, himself, was heard intoned: *"Sancte Joanne et Socii, orate pro nobis!"*

And so, also, we end this review of the life of Jean de Brébeuf: "Saint Jean de Brébeuf, pray for us, for all of us can use your prayers!"

---

[13] Ibid., XXII (1930), 507.

BIBLIOGRAPHY

MANUSCRIPT SOURCES

France

Chantilly, Archives de la Province de Paris de la Compagnie de Jésus
    Fonds Brotier: Carton Anciennes Missions
Paris, Archives Nationales
    Série F⁵ A. Missions, Canada

Canada

St. Jérôme (Terrebonne) P.Q., Archives of the Gallo-Canadian Province of
the Society of Jesus
    Mémories de 1652. Until recently these archives were housed at Col-
    lège Sainte-Marie and were referred to as ACSM. The archives are now
    kept at Notre-Dame de Montserrat, 175 boul. des Hauteurs, C.P. 130,
    St. Jérôme (Terrebonne), P.Q., Canada.

Italy

Rome, General Archives of the Society of Jesus
    Francia 5, I, II, Epist. Gener., 1628-1638
    Francia 6, I, II, Epist. Gener., 1636-
    Francia 11, Catologi Trienniales, 1615-1633
    Francia 22, Catologi, 1558-1639
    Gal. 39, Extra Gal., 1609-1663
    Gal. 109, I, II

PRINTED PRIMARY SOURCES

Acta Apostolicae Sedis XVII (1925), 314-18. *Canadensis regionis.* Official decree of the Holy See, June 2, 1925, beatifying the North American martyrs

Acta Apostolicae Sedis XXII (1930), 497-507. *Militantem Ecclesiam.* Official decree of the Holy See, June 29, 1930, canonizing the North American martyrs

Les annales de l'Hôtel-Dieu de Québec, 1637-1716, compiled by Jeanne-Françoise Juchereau and Marie Andrée Duplessis, edited by Albert Jamet. Québec: Hôtel-Dieu de Québec, 1939

Biard, Pierre. *Relation de la Nouvelle-France, de ses terres naturel, du pais et des habitans* ... Lyons: Muguet, 1616

Boucher, Pierre. *Histoire veritable et naturelle des moeurs et productions du pays de la Nouvelle-France vulgairement dit le Canada.* Paris: Lambert, 1664

Brébeuf, Jean de. *Doctrine chrétienne du R.P. Ledesme de la Compagnie de Jésus. Traduicte en langage Canadois autre que celuy des Montagnars pour la conversion des habitants dudit pays.* Rouen: L'Allemant, 1630

———— *The Travels and Sufferings of Father Jean de Brébeuf among the Hurons of Canada as Described by Himself,* edited and translated by Theodore Besterman. London: Golden Cockerel, 1938

Bressani, Francesco Giuseppe. *Breve relatione d'alcune missioni de' PP. della Compagnia di Giesù nella Nuova Francia.* Macerata, Italy: Grisei, 1653

Campeau, Lucien, editor. *Monumenta Novae Franciae: La Première Mission d'Acadie (1602-1616).* Quebec: Presses de l'Universite Laval, 1967

Champlain, Samuel de. *The Works of Samuel de Champlain,* edited by H. P. Biggar. 6 vols. Toronto: Champlain Society, 1922-1936

Charlevoix, Pierre François Xavier de. *The History and General Description of New France,* translated and edited by John Gilmary Shea. 6 vols. New York: John Gilmary Shea, 1870

Chronique de l'Ordre des Carmélites de la Réforme de Sainte-Thérèse. Troyes: Anner-André, 1861

Collection de manuscrits contenant lettres, mémoires et autres documents historiques relatifs à l'histoire de la nouvelle-France. 4 vols. Quebec, 1883-1885

Daniel, Charles. *Voyages à la Nouvelle-France du Captaine Daniel de Dieppe, 1629,* edited by J. Felix. Rouen, 1881

"Documents Relating to Negotiations with England, 1629-1633," *Canadian Archives for 1912,* 18-53. Ottawa: Parmelee, 1913

Du Creux, François. *History of Canada and New France,* edited by J. B. Conacher. 2 vols. Toronto: Champlain Society, 1951-1952

Gendron, François. *Quelques particularitez du pays des Hurons en la Nouvelle-France, remarquées par le Sieur Gendron, docteur en médecine, qui a demeuré dans ce pays-là fort long-temps.* Paris: Louis Bilaine, 1660

Guyart, Mère Marie de l'Incarnation. *Ecrits spirituels et historiques,* edited by Albert Jamet. 4 vols. Quebec: Action Sociale, 1929-1939

Jouve, Odoric-Marie. "Une page inédite d'histoire Canadienne; relation du Recollet Denis Jamet, 15 juillet, 1615," *Nouvelle-France* XIII (1914), 433-44

Le Ber, Joseph, editor. "Documents inédits sur la prise de Québec par les Anglais, 1629," *Revue d'Histoire de l'Amerique Française* III (1949-1950), 587-94

Le Clercq, Christian. *First Establishment of the Faith in New France.* 2 vols. New York: Shea, 1881

Loyola, St. Ignatius. *The Constitutions of the Society of Jesus,* translated and edited by George E. Ganss. St. Louis: Institute of Jesuit Sources, 1970

Martin, Félix, editor. *Un missionnaire des Hurons: Autobiographie du Père Chaumonot de la Compagnie de Jésus.* Paris: Oudin, 1885

"Mémoires touchant la mort et les vertus des pères Isaac Jogues, Anne de Nouë, Antoine Daniel, Jean de Brébeuf, Gabriel Lallement, Charles Garnier, Noël Chabanel & un seculier René Goupil, 1652," *Rapport de l'Archiviste de la Province de Québec, 1924-1925,* 3-93

Perrot, Nicolas. *Mémoire sur les moeurs, coustumes et religion des sauvages de l'Amérique Septentrionale,* edited by J. Tailhan. Leipzig: A. Franck, 1864

Ragueneau, Paul. *La Vie de Mère Catherine de Saint-Augustin.* Paris, 1671

Roy, Pierre-Georges, editor. "Lettres de Saint Charles Garnier," *Rapport de l'Archiviste de la Province de Québec, 1929-1930,* 1-44

Sagard, Gabriel-Theodat. *Histoire du Canada et voyages que les frères mineurs Recollets y ont faicts pour la conversion des infidèles depuis l'an 1615.* 4 vols. Paris: Tross, 1866

———— *The Long Journey to the Country of the Huron,* edited by George M. Wrong. Toronto: Champlain Society, 1939

Thwaites, Reuben Gold, editor. *The Jesuit Relations and Allied Documents: Travels and Explorations of the Jesuit Missionaries in New France, 1610-1791.* 73 vols. Cleveland: Burrows Brothers, 1896-1901

Les veritables motifs de messieurs et dames de la Societé de Notre-Dame de Montréal pour la conversion des sauvages de la Nouvelle-France. Montréal: Sociéte Historique de Montréal, 1880

SECONDARY SOURCES

A'Kempis, Thomas. *The Imitation of Christ,* edited by J. M. Lelen. New York: Catholic Book Publishing Company, 1941

Batiffol, Louis. *The Century of the Renaissance.* New York: Putnam, 1916

Benôit, Pierre. *Maisonneuve.* Tours: Mame, 1960

Biggar, Henry P. *The Early Trading Companies of New France*. New York: Argonaut Press, 1965

Birch, Walter. *Domesday Book: A Popular Account of the Exchequer Manuscript*. New York: Young, 1887

Bishop, Morris. *Champlain: The Life of Fortitude*. Toronto: McClelland and Stewart, 1963

Blond, Louis. *La maison professe des Jésuites de la rue Saint-Antoine a Paris*. Paris: Editions Franciscaines, 1956

Bréard, Charles. *Histoire du Collège d'Eu*. Eu: d'Hocqulus, 1879

Brodrick, James. *Saint Francis Xavier (1506-1552)*. New York: Wicklow Press, 1952

Bushnell, David I., Jr. *The Tribal Migrations East of the Mississippi River*. Washington, D.C.: Bureau of American Ethnology, 1919

Carinci, Alfonsi, editor. *Acta canonizationis quibus Sanctissimus Dominus Noster Pius Papa XI . . . die 29 Junii A.D. 1930 beatis Joanni de Brébeuf, Isaac Jogues et Soc., M.M. . . . sanctorum caelitum honores decrevit*. Rome: Insulae Liri, 1932

Clark, Andrew Hill. *Acadia: The Geography of Early Nova Scotia to 1760*. Madison: University of Wisconsin Press, 1968

Clarke, Peter D. *Origin and Traditional History of the Wyandots*. Toronto: Hunter, Ross, 1870

Conibear, Frank, and J. L. Blundell. *The Wise One*. New York: William Sloane Associates, 1949

Coudy, Julien, editor. *The Huguenot Wars*. Philadelphia: Chilton, 1969

Coyne, James H. *The Country of the Neutrals*. St. Thomas, Ontario, 1895

Cranston, J. Herbert. *Huronia, Cradle of Ontario's History*. Minesing, Ontario: Huronia Historic Sites Association, 1959

Delattre, Pierre, editor. *Les établissements des Jésuites en France depuis quatre siècles*. 6 vols. Enghien: Institut supérieur de théologie, 1955

Desjardins, Paul. *La résidence de Sainte-Marie aux Hurons*. Sudbury, Ontario: La Sociéte Historique du Nouvel-Ontario, 1966

Devine, E. J. *Anthony Daniel, Victim of the Iroquois*. Montreal: Canadian Messenger, 1916

————— *Charles Garnier, Victim of the Iroquois*. Montreal: Canadian Messenger, 1916

————— *Jean de Brébeuf, Apostle of the Hurons, 1593-1649*. Montreal: Canadian Messenger, 1915

————— *Noël Chabanel, Missionary in Huronia, 1613-1649*. Montreal: Canadian Messenger, 1916

Dominian, Helen G. *Apostle of Brazil*. New York: Exposition Press, 1958

Donnelly, Joseph P. *Jacques Marquette, 1637-1675*. Chicago: Loyola University Press, 1968

————— *Thwaites' Jesuit Relations: Errata and Addenda*. Chicago: Loyola University Press, 1967

Douglas, David C. *William the Conqueror*. Berkeley: University of California Press, 1964

Driver, Harold E. *Indians of North America*. Chicago: University of Chicago Press, 1964

Eccles, William J. *The Canadian Frontier, 1534-1760*. New York: Holt, 1969

Faillon, Etiénne M. *Histoire de la colonie Française en Canada*. 3 vols. Villemarie: Bibliothèque Paroissiale, 1865

Fouqueray, Henri. *Histoire de la Compagnie de Jésus en France des origines à la suppression (1528-1762)*. 5 vols. Paris: Etudes, 1910-1925

────── *Martyrs du Canada*. Paris: Tequi, 1930

Fox, William S. *St. Ignace, Canadian Altar of Martyrdom*. Toronto: McClelland and Stewart, 1949

Gautier, Alexandre. *Le Collège de Rouen*. Paris, 1876

Glanville, L. de. *Histoire du prieuré de Saint-Lô*. 2 vols. Rouen, 1890, 1891

Hamy, Alfred. *Les Jésuites de Caen*. Paris: Champion, 1899

Harmand, R. *Essai sur la vie et les oeuvres de Georges de Brébeuf*. Paris: Société française d'imprimerie, 1897

Harney, Martin P. *The Jesuits in History*. New York: America Press, 1941

Huddleston, Sisley. *Normandy*. Garden City, New York: Doubleday, 1929

Hunt, George T. *The Wars of the Iroquois, a Study in Intertribal Trade Relations*. Madison: University of Wisconsin Press, 1960

Jenness, Diamond. *The Indians of Canada*. Ottawa: National Museum of Canada, 1958

Johnston, William. *The Mysticism of the Cloud of Unknowing*. New York: Desclee, 1967

Jones, Arthur E. *8endake Ehen; or Old Huronia*. Toronto: Cameron, 1909

Jouve, Odoric-Marie. *Les Franciscains et le Canada: l'établissement de la foi, 1615-1629*. Québec: Couvent des SS. Stigmates, 1915

Jury, Wilfrid. *Saint Louis: Huron Indian Village and Jesuit Mission Site*. London, Ontario: University of Western Ontario Press, 1955

────── and Elsie McLeod Jury. *Sainte-Marie among the Hurons*. Toronto: Oxford University Press, 1954

Kidd, Kenneth E. *The Evacuation of Sainte Marie I*. Toronto: University of Toronto Press, 1949

Kinietz, W. Vernon. *The Indians of the Western Great Lakes, 1615-1760*. Ann Arbor: University of Michigan Press, 1965

Knowles, David. *The Nature of Mysticism*. New York: Hawthorn Books, 1966

Lamontagne, P. A. *L'Histoire de Sillery*. Sillery: The author, 1952

Lanchantin, René. *Condé-sur-Vire*. Saint Lô: The author, 1960

Lanctôt, Gustave. *A History of Canada*. 3 vols. Cambridge: Harvard University Press, 1963

Latourelle, René. *Etude sur les écrits de Saint Jean de Brébeuf*. 2 vols. Montréal: Imaculée Conception, 1952-1953

Le Hardy, Gaston. *Histoire du protestantisme en Normandie depuis son origine jusqu'à la publication de l'Edit de Nantes.* Caen: Le Gost-Clérisse, 1869

Lingard, John. *The History of England.* 10 vols. Boston: Estes and Lauriat, 1883

Lunt, William E. *History of England.* New York: Harper, 1956

MacLennan, Hugh. *Seven Rivers of Canada.* Toronto: Macmillan, 1961

Mahoney, Mother Denis, O.S.U. *Marie of the Incarnation, Mystic and Missionary.* Garden City, New York: Doubleday, 1964

Marcham, Frederick G. *A History of England.* New York: Macmillan, 1937

Marie, Charles. *Notice sur les trois Brébeufs, le poète, le prieur-curé de Venoix et leur oncle le missionnaire martyr.* Paris, 1875

Martin, Félix. *Hurons et Iroquois: le P. Jean de Brébeuf: sa vie, ses travaux, son martyre.* Paris: Tequi, 1877

———— *The Life of Father Isaac Jogues,* translated by J. G. Shea. New York: Benziger, 1885

Matthew, D. J. A. *The Norman Conquest.* New York: Schocken Books, 1966

Middleton, J. E. *The First Canadian Christmas Carol, Jesous Ahatonhia, Huron Indian Carol, Circa 1641, by Father Jean de Brébeuf.* Toronto: Harris, 1927

Mollat, Michel. *Le commerce maritime Normand à la fin du moyen âge.* Paris, 1952

Monaci, Philip. *The Life and Martyrdom of Blessed Andrew Bobóla of the Society of Jesus.* London: Richardson, 1855

Morgan, Lewis H. *League of the Ho-dé-no-sau-nee or Iroquois.* New York, 1904

Morison, Samuel E. *Samuel de Champlain, Father of New France.* Boston: Little, Brown, 1972

Morse, Eric W. *Canoe Routes of the Voyageurs.* St. Paul: Minnesota Historical Society, 1962

O'Connell, Daniel Patrick. *Richelieu.* New York: World Publishing, 1968

Page, William, editor. *The Victoria History of the County of Kent.* 3 vols. London: St. Catherine Press, 1932

Piron, Paul. *Jean de Brébeuf, l'apôtre géant des Hurons.* Namur, 1943

Pouliot, Léon. *Etude sur les Relations des Jésuites de la Nouvelle-France (1632-1672).* Montréal: Messager, 1940

———— *Les saintes martyrs canadiens.* Montréal: Bellarmin, 1949

Prat, Jean Marie. *Recherches historiques et critiques sur la Compagnie de Jésus en France du temps du P. Coton, 1564-1626.* 5 vols. Lyons, 1876-1878

Puiseux, Léon. *Les Jésuites de Caen.* Caen: Hardel, 1846

Quimby, George I. *Indian Culture and European Trade Goods.* Madison: University of Wisconsin Press, 1966

———— *Indian Life in the Upper Great Lakes: 11,000 B.C. to A.D. 1800.* Chicago: University of Chicago Press, 1960

Raymond, Alfred. *Saint Noël Chabanel, Martyr du Canada.* Montréal: Fides, 1946

Robinne, Joseph. *L'Apôtre au coeur mangé.* Paris: Saint-Paul, 1949

Rochmonteix, Camille de. *Les Jésuites et la Nouvelle-France au XVIIe siècle.* 3 vols. Paris: Letouzey et Ané, 1895

Roelker, Nancy L. *Queen of Navarre, Jeanne d'Albret.* Cambridge: Harvard University Press, 1968

Rouvier, Frédéric. *Les Bienheureux martyrs de la Compagnie de Jésus au Canada.* Montréal: Messager, 1925

Roy, Joseph E. *Guillaume Couture, premier colon de la Pointe-Lévy.* Levis: Mercier, 1884

Saintonge, Frédéric. *Martyr dans l'ombre: Saint Noël Chabanel.* Montréal: Bellarmin, 1958

Salmon, J. H. M., editor. *The French Wars of Religion.* Boston: Heath, 1967

Talbot, Francis X. *Saint among Savages.* New York: Harper, 1935

———— *Saint among the Hurons.* New York: Harper, 1949

Thompson, James W. *The Wars of Religion in France, 1559-1576.* Chicago: University of Chicago Press, 1909

Tooker, Elisabeth. *An Ethnography of the Huron Indians, 1615-1649.* Washington, D.C.: Smithsonian Institution, 1964

Trelease, Allen W. *Indian Affairs in Colonial New York: The Seventeenth Century.* Ithaca: Cornell University Press, 1960

PERIODICAL LITERATURE

Barbeau, C. M. "Huron and Wyandot Mythology," Department of Mines, Geological Survey, *Memoir* 80, Anthropological Series No. 11, Ottawa, 1915

Barkley, Henry J. "An Episode of North American History: The Conquest of Canada by the Kirke Brothers," *Journal of American History* XIV (1920), 133-61

Beaurepaire, Charles de. "Notice sur le noviciat de Rouen," *Bulletin de la Commission de Antiquités de la Seine-Inferieure* VIII (1888), 58 sq.

Bégin, Joseph-Octave. "Le Père Jérôme Lalemant (1593-1673)," *Lettres du Bas-Canada* X (1956), 69-79

Bruce, G. W. "The Petuns," *Papers and Records of the Ontario Historical Society* VIII (1915), 34-39

Campeau, Lucien. "Notre-Dame-des-Anges," *Lettres du Bas-Canada* VIII (1954), 77-107

———— "Portrait de Saint Isaac Jogues," *Lettres du Bas-Canada* VI (1952), 133-40

———— "Protomartyr de la Huronie," *Lettres du Bas-Canada* II (1948), 161-73

———— "Un site historique retrouvé," *Lettres du Bas-Canada* VI (1952), 25-36

Campeau, Lucien. "Voyageurs et Martyrs," *Lettres du Bas-Canada* II (1948), 11-23

Champault, Philippe. "Les Gendrons médecins des rois et des pauvrés," Royal Society of Canada, *Proceedings and Transactions*, 2nd Series VI (1912), sect. 1, 35-120

Chapman, L. J. "The Physiography of South-Central Ontario," *Scientific Agriculture* XVIII (1937), 161-97

Chaussé, Gilles. "Le Père Paul Le Jeune, missionnaire-colonisateur," *Lettres du Bas-Canada* XII (1958), 5-17, 69-91, 133-63, 201-23

Côté, Jean. "Domestique séculier d'habit, mais religieux de coeur," *Lettres du Bas-Canada* IX (1955), 69-75

Couture, Théotime. "Manitouline (1600-1800)," *Lettres du Bas-Canada* III (1949), 175-85

Desjardins, Paul. "Apôtres laïques des missions de la Nouvelle-France. II: Les donnés Charles et Guillaume Boivin," *Lettres du Bas-Canada* IX (1955), 220-30

———— "Apôtres laïques des missions de la Nouvelle-France au XVIIe siècle. I: Saint Jean La Lande," *Lettres du Bas-Canada* IX (1955), 158-67

———— "Auxiliaires laïques dans les missions de la Nouvelle-France. III: Christophe Regnault," *Lettres du Bas-Canada* X (1956), 5-12

———— "Auxiliaires laïques des missions de la Nouvelle-France au XVIIe siècle. Le donné Robert Le Coq," *Lettres du Bas-Canada* XI (1957), 69-89

———— "Joseph Boursier *dit* Desforges, donné et Frère coadjuteur," *Lettres du Bas-Canada* X (1956), 154-59

———— "La résidence Sainte-Marie-des-Hurons: les auxiliaires laïques," *Lettres du Bas-Canada* XIX (1965), 2-16, 24-35

———— "Le donné Jean Guérin," *Lettres du Bas-Canada* X (1956), 80-99

———— "Le frère coajuteur Dominique Scot et Eustache Martin," *Lettres du Bas-Canada* X (1956), 208-31

Douglas, David. "Companions of the Conqueror," *History* XXVIII (1943), 129-47

Gervais, Euclide. "Le Père Anne de Nouë (1587-1646)," *Lettres du Bas-Canada* XVII (1963), 23-32

———— "Le Père François Bressany, S.J. (1612-1672)," *Lettres du Bas-Canada* XVI (1962), 220-25

———— "Le Père Philibert Noyrot," *Lettres du Bas-Canada* XIII (1959), 33-39

Giguère, Georges-Emile. "Histoire du culte: le père Felix Martin, promoteur de la cause des martyrs canadiens," *Lettres du Bas-Canada* III (1949), 34-71

———— "Le Noël Huron de Brébeuf," *Lettres du Bas-Canada* V (1951), 252-56

———— "Le P. Pierre Chastellain (1606-1684)," *Lettres du Bas-Canada* XVII (1963), 87-95

———— "Saint-Ignace-des-Martyrs," *Lettres du Bas-Canada* II (1948), 145-58

Harvey, Julien. "Nouveau reliquaire des Saints Martyrs Canadiens," *Lettres du Bas-Canada* IV (1950), 170-71

Hourigan, Denis J. "Dix ans d'excavation au fort Sainte-Marie," *Lettres du Bas-Canada* V (1951), 146-65

James, Charles C. "The Downfall of the Huron Nation," Royal Society of Canada, *Proceedings and Transactions*, 2nd Series XII (1906), sect. 2, 311-46

Jury, Wilfrid. "Flanagan Prehistoric Huron Village Site," University of Western Ontario, *Bulletin of the Museum* VI (1948), 1-9

———— "St. Ignace II," *The Canadian Catholic Historical Association Report*, 1946-1947, 15-27

Kidd, Kenneth E. "The Evacuation and Historical Identification of a Huron Ossuary," *American Antiquity* XVIII (1953), 359-79

Knowles, Nathaniel. "The Torture of Captives by the Indians of Eastern North America," American Philosophical Society, *Proceedings* LXXXII (1940), sect. 2, 151-225

Larivière, Florian. "Charles Garnier et la Crise de 1637 en Huronie," *Lettres du Bas-Canada* III (1949), 161-74

———— "Les écrits de St. Charles Garnier," *Lettres du Bas-Canada* III (1949), 21-33

Latourelle, René. "Le Journal Spirituel de Saint Jean de Brébeuf," *Lettres du Bas-Canada* III (1949), 5-20

Lusignan, Lucien. "Essai sur les écrits de deux martyrs canadiens," *Bulletin des Recherches Historiques* L (1944), 174-92

Macdougall, Angus J. "Joseph Antoine Poncet (1610-1675)," *Martyrs' Shrine Message* XXXVI (1972), 6-14

Neill, Edward D. "History of the Ojibways," *Minnesota Historical Collection* V (1885), 397-510

O'Brien, E. J. "Les Foulles au Fort Sainte-Marie," *Lettres du Bas-Canada* I (1947), 164-66

Orr, Rowland. "The Attwandarons or the Nation of the Neutrals," Ontario Province Museum, *Archaeological Report* (1913), 7-20

Phelan, Horatio P. and Léon Pouliot. "Notes sur les reliques de Saint Jean de Brébeuf a l'occasion d'une récente découverte," *Lettres du Bas-Canada* VIII (1954), 137-46

Potvin, Fernand. "L'itinéraire spirituel de Saint Antoine Daniel," *Lettres du Bas-Canada* IX (1955), 5-24

———— "Saint Antoine Daniel, martyr canadien," *Revue d'Histoire de l'Amerique Française* VIII (1954-1955), 395-414, 556-64; IX (1955-1956), 77-92, 236-49, 392-409, 562-70; X (1956-1957), 77-92, 252-56

Pouliot, Adrien. "La plus vieille maison du Canada," *Lettres du Bas-Canada* IV (1950), 25-39

Pouliot, Adrien. "Saint Joseph, patron des Hurons," *Lettres du Bas-Canada* X (1956), 13-19

Pouliot, Léon. "Le P. Claude Pijart (1600-1683)," *Lettres du Bas-Canada* XVIII (1964), 151-61

———— "Le P. Paul Ragueneau (1608-1680)," *Lettres du Bas-Canada* XVII (1963), 143-54

Roy, Pierre-Georges. "Jean Amyot," *Bulletin des Recherches Historiques* XI (1905), 217-19

———— "Le frères Boivin," *Bulletin des Recherches Historiques* XLVII (1941), 309

Speck, Frank G. "Notes on the Material Culture of the Hurons," *American Anthropologist* XIII (1911), 208-28

Trigger, Bruce G. "The Destruction of Huronia: A Study in Economics and Cultural Change, 1609-1650," Royal Canadian Institute, *Transactions* XXXIII (1959), 14-45

———— "The French Presence in Huronia: Structure of Franco-Huron Relations in the First Half of the Seventeenth Century," *Canadian Historical Review* XLIX (1968), 107-41

INDEX

About this book

Jean de Brébeuf, 1593-1649 was set in the composing room of Loyola University Press. The text is 11/13 Caledonia, the reduced matter 9/11, the footnotes 8/10. The display type is 24 Bulmer.

It was printed and bound by Banta Division, George Banta Company, Inc., using the Banta Book System on Whitman's 55-pound white paper and bound in Carolina coated cover.